Wielding the Ax

Ohio University Press Series in Ecology and History

James L. A. Webb, Jr., Series Editor

Wielding the Ax

State Forestry and Social Conflict in Tanzania,
1820-2000

Thaddeus Sunseri

OHIO UNIVERSITY PRESS

ATHENS

Ohio University Press, Athens, Ohio 45701
www.ohioswallow.com
© 2009 by Ohio University Press

Printed in the United States of America
Ohio University Press books are printed on acid-free paper ∞ ™

16 15 14 13 12 11 10 09   5 4 3 2 1

Library of Congress Cataloging-in-Publication Data
Sunseri, Thaddeus Raymond.
 Wielding the ax : state forestry and social conflict in Tanzania, 1820-2000 / Thaddeus Sunseri.
    p. cm.—(Ohio University Press series in ecology and history)
 Includes bibliographical references and index.
 ISBN 978-0-8214-1864-2 (cloth : alk. paper)—ISBN 978-0-8214-1865-9 (pbk. : alk. paper)
 1. Forests and forestry—Tanzania—History. 2. Forest policy—Social aspects—Tanzania—
History. 3. Forest policy—Political aspects—Tanzania—History. I. Title.
 SD242.T35S86 2009
 333.7509678—dc22

2008050356

Contents

Illustrations

Preface

During the summer of 2004 forests were in the headlines in Tanzania as a timber scandal captured the attention of the public. The Tanzanian independent daily the *Guardian* reported widespread illegal harvesting of timber for export throughout Rufiji District.[1] Businessmen bypassed village environmental committees to cut indigenous hardwood trees, obtaining licenses illegally from district-level forest officials or failing to obtain licenses altogether. In so doing they violated recent changes in Tanzanian forest law that empowered local communities to guard forests from overexploitation and degradation while garnering some timber profits. While the *Guardian* kept the scandal on the front pages daily, the minister of natural resources and tourism banned all logging and timber sales as the extent of illegal harvesting was being investigated. Furniture workshops and lumber cooperatives were suddenly short of timber, as police seized lumber suspected of being contraband.[2] Loggers avoided scrutiny by transporting their cargoes to the ports of Dar es Salaam and Kilwa Masoko under cover of night, until media exposure stopped the practice. Trucks loaded with hardwood logs lined the road south of Dar es Salaam awaiting inspection. Customs officials inspected log containers queued at Dar es Salaam harbor, most destined for India and China. Few exporters showed up for the inspections, and many containers that were forced open held contraband protected hardwoods such as *mninga-maji, mpingo,* and *pangapanga.*[3] Subsequent investigations determined that Tanzanian officials, in concert with local and foreign corporations, sanctioned much of the illegal timber harvesting.[4] Not long ago the characteristics of these trees were virtually unknown. In an age where so-called conflict timber fuels wars in some parts of Africa and the world, once marginal timbers have acquired great value, averaging about $300 per cubic meter at export, and as much as $1,500 per cubic meter once processed overseas.

As the logging scandal was revealed, tensions simmered between villagers west of Dar es Salaam and officials of the Ministry of Natural Resources and Tourism and their allies among conservationist non-governmental organizations (NGOs). For over a decade state officials and NGOs, led by the politically connected Wildlife Conservation Society of Tanzania (WCST), have accused villagers of entering government forest reserves to farm or cut down trees to produce charcoal for the Dar es Salaam market.[5] The charcoal trade is the most visible link between the Tanzanian countryside and its urban centers, accounting for as much as 80 percent of urban domestic fuel use and offering a vital means for rural communities to earn cash.[6] Bicycles and trucks stacked with twenty-eight-kilogram bags of charcoal ply the roads around Dar es Salaam from as far away as two hundred kilometers. Natural resources officials frequently confiscate the bicycles of illegal charcoal burners in forest raids.[7] In recent years plastic bags of charcoal, enough for a day's cooking, have appeared at Dar es Salaam street kiosks. Hardware stores and the main market at Kariakoo sell charcoal-heated irons, which in the West would be considered relics of an earlier age. At night tea vendors with charcoal braziers ply the streets serving their regular clientele, which include many storefront guards, while food vendors near bus stations grill chicken and fry potatoes and eggs in woks heated over charcoal fires.

Charcoal production is just one issue that pits villagers and urban consumers against state officials and conservationist NGOs in Tanzania. In recent years the minister of natural resources has evicted villagers from forest reserves, claiming that they are recent squatters who endanger forest biodiversity and water catchments needed for future generations. Kazimzumbwi Forest Reserve, just west of Dar es Salaam, has become the test case for the state to demonstrate its will to protect the forests. In 1998 government officials ordered police to destroy the huts and property of peasants living adjacent to Kazimzumbwi, claiming they had encroached into the forest reserve. Conservationists had urged the government to take action against forest encroachers for years, and the WCST even financed the policing of the forest for a decade.[8] This conflict coincided with a recasting of Tanzanian forest policy to include the private sector and international and local conservationist NGOs in forest management alongside the state and village councils. The importance of forestry for the Tanzanian state is seen in the promotion in 2006 of the minister of natural resources to head the Ministry of Finance, placing an ally of international conservationism and advocate of timber privatization at the center of the state power structure.[9] Recent changes in Tanzanian forest law aim to increase the extent of forest reserves by expanding them onto public lands that have never before been afforded state protection. Although conservationists and the state claim that peasants and pastoralists encroach into forest reserves, the National Forest Program for the first decade of the millennium does the opposite, pushing forest reserves onto village lands under the rubric of biodiversity preservation. This is the most revolutionary shift in Tanzanian forest policy since the 1950s, the fruition of patterns of state forestry that began with the German colonization of East Africa in the late nineteenth century.

This book is about the genesis of forest conflicts in Tanzania, which is also a story of changing relations of power over the forests and how the state wielded forestry as a tool for social control. From the nineteenth century to the present, forests have been at the fault lines of contact between rural societies and state forces that connected East Africa to an international commercial economy. Power over the forests was first invested in local chiefship. Among the Zaramo of the coastal hinterland, for example, chiefs were known as *mapazi,* wielders of ceremonial axes that symbolized authority over the forests.[10] The ritual authority of chiefs as ax wielders derived from the labor power of peasant men and women, who used "ax and fire" to open up forest lands for cultivation.[11] Chiefs displayed power over the forests by wearing an ax over their left shoulder in imitation of the most common method of carrying a work ax. In the mid-nineteenth century this local authority over forests was confronted with a trade frontier for forest products that put the East African mainland in the sites of the Zanzibar commercial state and Western merchants. American cloth and firearms merchants from Salem spearheaded trade connections to East Africa in the early nineteenth century, seeking copal, the prime ingredient in carriage varnishes. The Western exploration and mapping of East Africa was driven by the trade in products of the forests and woodlands, especially ivory, copal, and rubber, but also some hardwoods in international demand, particularly *mpingo* blackwood and various mangroves. Trade centered at Zanzibar enabled mapazi and other chiefs who controlled forests to solidify their power by distributing imported prestige goods and attracting followers, which in turn enabled them to defend their lands from outsiders. The capacity of the sultan of Zanzibar to enforce export tolls on some forest products by midcentury signaled the growing intrusion of quasi-state forces. By the 1880s German interlopers co-opted Zanzibar's mainland trade network, bringing an ideology of state control over land and forests. German colonial rule began in 1890 with the usurpation of "all ownerless wilderness, forest, cultivated land, and steppe," setting in motion ongoing conflicts over forests and their resources.[12]

Germans immediately introduced state forestry in Tanzania, drawing on models of scientific forest management that originated in eighteenth-century Europe and that were further developed in colonial Asia. German scientific forestry was predicated on separating people from forests in order to manage them as state reserves in order to ensure long-term sustainable production of fuel and timber for industry, domestic consumption, and export. Such plantation forestry assumed a permanent state bureaucracy to manage forests indefinitely. German forest management provided a blueprint for the British colonizers who replaced them after World War I, as well as for the independent government of Tanzania after 1961. Yet to a large degree scientific forestry was the road not taken under colonial rule owing to relative weakness of the colonial state, unfamiliarity with African timber characteristics, resistance from Africans, and half-hearted commitment to forest conservation in a colonial periphery. Nevertheless, scientific forestry cast the state as the proper steward of natural resources, while it viewed peasants and pastoralists as dire threats. Forestry empowered colonial and postcolonial rulers alike to engineer the rural population for development goals that often had little to do with forest management itself and was often destructive of forests.

Because the state forest economy depended on the labor power of peasant men and women to work the forests, it gave them important leverage in wresting concessions from the state or subverting the aims of forestry altogether. State control over forests sparked ongoing peasant resistance that included everyday acts of avoidance and obvious "weapons of the weak," such as arson and refusal to work, but also violent confrontations—such as the Bushiri and Maji Maji uprisings—and large-scale political mobilization, including the nationalist movement that led Tanzania to independence.[13] Peasants creatively undermined state forestry. When colonial foresters prioritized the *mvule* tree for commercial cutting, owing to its high export demand after World War II, some peasants insisted that these were "spirit trees" that demanded special protection, or at least compensation.[14] Peasants manipulated the borders of forest reserves by moving boundary markers, which won them access to farm land that helped to ensure survival.[15] So too did colonial officials learn to co-opt the ancestral value of forest shrines to bolster the power of their allies among African elites.[16] These cases remind us that the projection of authority over forests was not a linear story of progressive state control, but was negotiated constantly according to shifting constellations of power that were sometimes shaped by global events. The Great Depression of the 1930s, the world wars, the Cold War, early independence, and *ujamaa* socialism of the 1970s were all moments when peasants subverted the agenda of state forestry and returned to the forests, sometimes, and paradoxically, with state encouragement. Although scientific forestry in Tanzania has not always followed a uniform trajectory, the long-term trend has been for successive Tanzanian governments and their backers among international conservationists to force peasants out of the forests.

The Geographical Focus

Most attention to the history of people and their forests in Tanzania has been directed at the northeastern highlands, which includes a fringe of the Eastern Arc Mountains and Mt. Meru and Mt. Kilimanjaro.[17] There is good reason for this attention, since this region contains a large percentage of Tanzania's closed canopy forests and rain forests. Africans migrated to the region owing to soil fertility, abundance of rainfall, and scarcity of disease, while European settlers intruded by the late nineteenth century because of its temperate climate and suitability for sisal and coffee. It was also the earliest area of concerted German forest exploitation because of its concentration of readily marketable tree species (including most of Tanzania's conifers and softwoods), especially pencil cedar (*Juniperus procera*), *Podocarpus* spp., and camphor.[18]

In contrast, the coastal hinterland, which is the focus of this book, is a region where forests were not as dramatic, but which nonetheless had a complex history that is more typical of Tanzania as a whole, as well as much of eastern and southern Africa. The coastal hinterland runs from the Pangani River in northern Tanzania to the Rovuma River on Tanzania's southern border, and is sandwiched between the Eastern Arc range to the west and the Indian Ocean littoral on the east. Ecologically the region extends from Somalia, in the north, well south into Mozambique, which is the range of dry lowland coastal forests. Arriving from the Indian Ocean, the most obvious forest landscape of the coastal hinterland are the mangroves that punctuate river and creek outlets, lagoons, and wave-sheltered shores. That mangroves make up only 0.14 percent of modern Tanzania belies their historical and biological importance. Mangroves sustain the coastal food chain, which includes microbes, crabs, and fish, and shelter birds and mammals. In the largest river deltas, especially the Rufiji, mangroves snake up river arms for thirty kilometers. In tidal flats people wade out into the mangroves at low tide to fish or obtain firewood or building poles. For centuries traders from tree-scarce regions that fringed the Indian Ocean arrived to collect mangroves for construction poles and firewood. The mangroves sheltered people in times of conflict, offered farm land on delta islands, and provided an environment rich in fish.

Moving inland from the coast, the most dramatic feature of the coastal hinterland are its coastal forests, known locally as *vichaka* or *misitu*.[19] The coastal forests are dry lowland and mountain canopy forests that survive as island fragments from Somalia to Mozambique, rarely extending further than 150 kilometers inland. Although they are dots on a forest map of Tanzania, from the ground they are dense stretches that dominate the landscape. In the Matumbi and Kichi hills, south of the Rufiji, the coastal forests form a labyrinth of foliage that rise to an altitude of about five hundred meters on the hills that checker the region. Farther north, the coastal forests dominate the Pugu hills, about twenty kilometers inland from Dar es Salaam, and continue inland for about sixty kilometers. Nineteenth-century European travelers and Swahili caravan leaders readily described these forests as dense jungles that they traversed with care, fearful of being waylaid by local polities seeking a share of caravan wealth. This density in an otherwise open landscape attracted Africans seeking refuge in times of violence. The vichaka forests furthermore offered fertile lands for farming, secluded places for initiation rites, famine foods such as roots and wild fruit, and poles and firewood for building, cooking, or iron forging. Coastal forests also sheltered animal predators, such as leopards, elephants, and wild pigs that endangered crops and people, thus demanded constant vigilance and frequent hunting parties.

Surrounding the coastal forests are *miombo* woodlands and grasslands. Miombo is a landscape that encompasses a broad belt of south-central Africa, including about 40 percent of modern Tanzania. It is named for the dominant tree genus, *Brachystegia*.[20] Miombo lands have a single rainy season, shallow soils, and a ground cover that ranges from woody thickets to semicanopy forests. In the dry season woodlands become leafless and subject to grass fires, to which they have adapted. In the rainy season the foliage blossoms, making woodlands cool, shady refuges from the sun. Because woodlands harbor tsetse flies, the vector of sleeping sickness that prevents a cattle economy and threaten humans, colonial officials viewed miombo as an environment that was best transformed into grasslands or farm land by eliminating the trees and thicket altogether. Not until the late 1930s did colonial foresters target the woodlands for state forestry. Thereafter the woodlands became an obsession, a late-colonial problem that was the subject of international conferences.[21] Before then the woodlands entered into colonial planning as sites of agricultural expansion or sleeping sickness evacuations or as wildlife reserves.

This description of the coastal hinterland requires a consideration of the agricultural frontier that interacted with the forested environment historically. During the nineteenth century in particular a Swahili and Arab plantation economy pushed inland from the coastal littoral, cutting swaths of trees to open up the land for coconuts, sugarcane, sesame, and grain crops to feed the slave and commodity caravan traffic to and from Zanzibar.[22] The agricultural frontier pushed coastward as well, as villagers came to inhabit the islands of the Rufiji Delta and other coastal enclaves to carve out farms of rice, millet, bananas, and mangoes, in conjunction with mangrove exploitation and fishing. Farmers penetrated into the coastal forests in the face of violence and insecurity marked by the slave trade but expanded to adjacent woodlands and grasslands when security returned. Africans of the coastal hinterland colonized these forests by planting fruit trees, burying ancestors, and building fortified villages.

Forest history provides a lens to reassess key events in Tanzanian history, including trade expansion, rebellion, colonialism, and nationalism. Each of the coastal hinterland forest landscapes—mangroves, vichaka forests, and miombo woodlands—were sites of conflict that involved state foresters, African chiefs, and peasant communities. In many respects they form a chronology of colonialism itself. Mangroves attracted professional foresters from the beginning of colonial rule owing to their commercial value and their proximity to the main loci of colonial power along the coast. As colonial authority spread inland, the state saw coastal forests as sources of trade products, especially rubber, as watersheds needed for colonial agriculture, and as havens for anticolonial insurgents, particularly during the Maji Maji War (1905–7). Under British rule following World War I colonial officials targeted miombo woodlands and their communities for intense social engineering, reflecting a new phase of colonial rule, the "rule of the experts," when scientists and technocrats believed that they could transform the landscape through ambitious developmentalist enterprises.[23] More recently, the inclusion of the coastal forests, alongside the Eastern Arc forests, as biodiversity hotspots and "global property" has made them into sites of conflict between peasants and international conservationists acting in concert with the Tanzanian state and external donors, representing a form of neocolonialism.

Theoretical Approaches to Forest History

In an elegant overview of South Asian forest history, K. Sivaramakrishnan explains how this subfield has evolved over the past two decades in a way that follows the South Asian landscape itself.[24] Early South Asian forest history had a nationalist agenda, viewing the colonial period as rupturing a once harmonious relationship between people and the environment. Modern environmental degradation, according to this narrative, had its roots in the colonial usurpation of forests from local communities. Early Indian forest history therefore focused on social movements that were directed against the British colonial state in the face of loss of forest access. This metanarrative had a geographical profile. It began with studies that focused on the western Himalayas, where evergreen softwoods and subsistence farmers and pastoralists dominated, and moved down into the Indo-Gangetic Plain, home of past empires and worked landscapes of intensive farming with fragmented deciduous forests. The abrupt nineteenth-century British intrusion into the mountain forests evoked an "ecological landscape of resistance"[25] that contrasted with a centuries-old European trade presence in South India, where the panoply of emergent Western science was brought to bear. As Indian environmental scholarship moved down the mountains to the plains, it became more complex and contradictory and concerned with themes that moved beyond protonationalism in the forests to studies of wildlife, science, water, and continuities between precolonial, colonial, and postcolonial periods. Yet a common theme was "the steady expansion of land under the plow, at the expense of forest and grassland."[26]

A contrasting, but no less well-developed approach to forest history has been that of the United States. Here the dominant narrative is "one of the greatest episodes of global deforestation ever to be enacted," as immigration, population growth, westward expansion, industrialization, and railway construction progressively denuded the forest landscape.[27] A prominent agent of change in this narrative was the single-family homesteader and his ax, who made a clearing in the forest on land that he owned, often selling it and moving on to clear another parcel. While "improving the land" in this way was part of the story of American progress, nascent conservationists came to see the homesteader in a decidedly negative light, as backwoodsmen who misused a natural resource, threatening the nation with ecological collapse that would see it go the way of great empires of the past.[28] The American pattern of deforestation, Michael Williams writes, "can stand as a microcosm of forest life almost anywhere in the temperate world, at almost any time during the last 300 years."[29] Commercial logging on a grand scale followed homesteading in the nineteenth century as a devourer of forests, providing fuelwood to households, foundries, steamships, railways, and mines. In the twentieth century the threat of a timber famine was arrested by the creation of the U.S. Forest Service and national forest legislation that initiated federal acquisition and protection of forest lands.[30]

In contrast to these well-developed historiographies, forests have been missing as a subject of African historiography until recently.[31] It is an irony that a field dominated by materialist historians not so long ago neglected to consider African landscapes as more than just land to be farmed, grazed, mined, or owned. Ramachandra Guha writes, "a truly materialist approach would begin not with the economic landscape but with the natural setting in which the economy is embedded."[32] Because forests were considered to be outside the arena of production as the locales of preagrarian foragers, earlier studies focused on developed landscapes, if they considered landscape distinctions at all. Early studies of African trade never located forest products—such as ivory, rubber, copal, wax, and gums—in specific ecosystems, rather they were simply assumed to be coming from somewhere in Africa. Furthermore, trade studies assumed that the frontier of extraction simply petered out with the onset of colonialism, to be replaced by productive economies. As my study shows, the forest economy of extraction lasted well into the twentieth century and had several moments of revival during the period of mature colonialism.

The neglect of forests by historians has meant that studies of the African environment have until recently been left to conservationists, foresters, and policymakers, who saw African farmers and pastoralists in a decidedly negative light, as progressively desiccating the continent.[33] Famine, aridity, erosion, floods, and species extinction are among the consequences of the perceived African threat to the environment. Proponents of this view see the state, whether colonial or postcolonial, in alliance with metropolitan or international conservationists, as the best agent to protect tropical forests from human destruction. A recent study of early German environmentalism, for example, concludes that the colonies "provided unique opportunities for setting up forward-looking environmental programs."[34] The most cited modern overview of German forest policies in colonial Tanzania, written by a forester once active in Tanzania, concludes that Germany's emphasis on environmental management (*Landeskultur*) "was truly visionary and undoubtedly deserves to be considered the single most important legacy of German forestry involvement in East Africa."[35] Such environmental management included introducing new tree species, cataloguing indigenous trees, and reserving forests—policies that the British colonial state continued after World War I. The result, in this view, is that "the people of Tanzania now or in the future may benefit from the existence of forest reserves forced on them by colonial masters."[36] A similar assertion is that imperial forestry "gave birth to an environmental revolution still in process of saving humans from themselves."[37] For all its evils, in these views colonialism nevertheless ushered in an era of positive forest management that continues today in the form of international environmentalism.

These positive depictions of colonial forestry suffer from many problems, not the least of which is their ahistoricism, which posits a modern environmental consciousness on colonial administrators and foresters. They selectively choose their evidence in time and place, avoiding in-depth analyses that tell a more contradictory story. For example, while early colonial forestry protected forests that enclosed watersheds, it also allowed German settlers to denude tens of thousands of hectares of indigenous trees to make way for coffee and sisal plantations. While these studies commonly attribute deforestation to peasant and pastoral communities alone, they ignore or downplay large-scale state exploitation of timber, often with little or no effort to reforest. Most important, these studies do not adequately consider how state usurpation of forests deprived rural communities of important power bases, subsistence resources, and spiritual foundations, setting in motion struggles for economic and cultural survival that continue today.

This study argues that successive states in Tanzania have used forest policy as a means both to control a resource needed for economic development *and* to control rural populations in order to further that development agenda. The regulation of forests was therefore a tool for social mapping and engineering, which were higher state priorities than timber harvesting or protecting water catchments. This argument is informed by a framework of political ecology, which draws attention to the "political interests and actions of the various actors that participate in political-ecological conflict."[38] Political ecology calls attention to the destructive effects on the environment of capitalist-oriented natural resource extraction acting in concert with the state. It sees supposedly natural landscapes as resulting "from a spatial order that reflects the power relations of local and state institutions," highlighting the unequal power relations between local communities on one side and the state, development organizations, lending institutions, and international conservationists on the other. [39] In so doing, political ecology underscores that struggles over the environment and its resources emanate from the larger political economy. This framework reminds us that colonial environmental initiatives emerged in a context where colonies existed primarily to be of economic and strategic value to the metropole. It views environmental degradation as not simply an outcome of peasant backwardness, population pressure, or land misuse. Political ecology pays attention to how the colonial and postcolonial goals of transforming nature was embedded in labor processes; thus it is interested in who actually does the work of forest protection or exploitation, how labor is mustered, or how resistance to forest work shaped conservation patterns.[40] Moreover, political ecology reminds us that the outcome of imperial conservationism is locally specific and does not lead inevitably to deforestation, globalization of forests, or expropriation of forests from local communities, even though these have been the long-term trends.

Because African forests were highly gendered spaces, this study is attentive to how transformations in land use, perceptions of the environment, and demands for forest products ushered in changes at the household level that affected marriage obligations, labor allocations, ecological knowledge, and resource control.[41] In Tanzania male and female initiation rituals took place in the forests, and specific trees had important gendered meanings.[42] Forest resource extraction was also gendered, with women expected to obtain medicines, subsistence foods, and fuelwood in the forests, while men were more likely to hunt, cut down trees, and place beehives in the forests. In some regions ownership of specific trees was a male prerogative that bestowed de facto clan rights to land. Yet strict gender dichotomies with respect to forest use, such as that which Aylward Shorter notes in his study of Ukimbu, in western Tanzania, where women were confined to open, cultivated land while men monopolized forest activities, were often an outcome of colonial development planning and not necessarily an age-old pattern.[43] On the other hand, in some forests of Tanzania the colonial state introduced a system of licensed peasant cultivation called *taungya,* which appears to have feminized forest labor. With men absent as colonial wage laborers on plantations and in towns, women bore the burden of opening up land for colonial tree planting, which sometimes upset established gender boundaries. Women sometimes saw taungya as a burden, while chiefs perceived women's forest activities as undermining their authority. As a consequence of warfare or labor migration, as well, women often assumed control over ancestral trees and land, which opened up struggles within the household. Women often acted out these struggles in rain ceremonies, such as the Zaramo *kitala cha kutagusa,* performed before a large tree. Wearing men's clothes, brandishing men's weapons and tools, including the ax, and speaking in men's voices, women temporarily inverted the social order as a means of healing the land.[44] Such rites might be invoked as a consequence of forest innovations introduced before colonial rule, such as copal digging or rubber tapping, or colonial innovations, like taungya, which burdened women unduly. In modern Tanzania community forest programs mediated by conservationist NGOs often have differential effects on men and women, rich and poor, which exacerbate rural and gender inequality. Every stage of forest colonization, from the nineteenth century to the present, has entailed gendered struggles over labor and resources.

This book draws on a well-established literature on peasant studies and moral economies. Peasant studies drew our attention to peasant agency, rural differentiation and unequal access to resources, the centrality of the household to the labor process, the capacity of peasantries for collective protest, and the role of culture in shaping peasant attitudes to land.[45] Yet peasant studies as a field failed to look beyond the borders of the cultivated landscape to examine how peasants interacted with diverse environments.[46] In contrast, studies influenced by E. P. Thompson's concept of moral economy made clear how closely connected peasant economies and cultures were to forests and other natural resources and how severing peasants from these resources elicited social protest in defense of established rights.[47] The moral-economy approach offered "a vision of nature 'from the bottom up,'" and recreated the peasant moral universe, often cast as a defense of subsistence rights against market forces, most often seen as a right to the commons.[48] Moral-economy approaches highlight popular opposition to state forest reserves and restrictions on wood collection, grazing, and hunting. Such opposition included refusing to cooperate with forest demarcations, arson, attacks on forest guards, and organized protests that sometimes failed or sometimes fed nationalist movements.[49] These histories remind us of how deeply embedded the forests were in the economic and cultural landscapes of peasant and pastoralist communities.

The history of colonial scientific forestry is the history of the colonial state itself. James Scott points out that states create metaphorical (and actual) maps of their domains with the goal of "rationalizing and standardizing what was a social hieroglyph into a legible and administratively more convenient format."[50] Attempts to "make a society legible" include moving people to state-sanctioned villages, counting them and their huts, assessing their property, taxing them, studying their norms and beliefs, determining what they trade and consume, and conscripting them for work. In Scott's analysis, social engineers of various political stripes, backed by authoritarian states and a faith in science and technical progress, often applied scientific principles uncritically, creating schemes that went awry. This study touches on several of Scott's examples of state intervention, including transforming natural forests into monocrop tree plantations, attempts to sedentarize peasant shifting cultivators, and massive efforts to relocate rural people into centralized villages. The latter included both British colonial anti–sleeping sickness campaigns, which intersected with forest and wildlife policy, and Tanzania's ujamaa villagization of the 1970s, when 70 percent of the rural population was relocated into planned villages in just three years. Case studies of state forestry here also demonstrate the limits of high modernism and the failure of expert planning. For example, foresters who had learned to order the European landscape into monocrop pine plantations were challenged by unfamiliar colonial landscapes such as mangroves and miombo woodlands under conditions of labor shortage. Colonial foresters' attempts to reforest indigenous trees were frustrated by unfamiliar African growing patterns and soil properties. British attempts to create model villages called closer settlements were often undermined by the inability to protect them from crop predators that proliferated in part because of schemes to protect fauna in wildlife reserves. The anti–sleeping sickness campaigns of the interwar years that relocated tens of thousands of peasants from woodlands into planned villages unleashed a culture of peasant resistance that thwarted evictions from forest reserves after World War II.

Scientific forestry was in the end an assertion of state power over forests, usurping the authority of mapazi ax wielders, who had once mediated forest access with people in their domains. Yet, until recently, scientific forestry depended on the original ax wielders, the peasant men and women who worked in the forests. As long as forestry needed labor to cut forest borders, fell and transport trees, tend tree seedlings on forest plantations, and extract forest produce that had a market value, peasants were empowered to negotiate forest use under difficult circumstances. That use helped to ensure survival by giving them access to food and land in the forests or products with which to earn cash to pay taxes or buy household goods. The loss of labor leverage in the current era of biodiversity preservation, which values forests not as worked landscapes but as nature museums for Western tourists, is therefore a dramatic moment of peasant disempowerment in modern Tanzania.

The starting point of this book is the nineteenth century, when rural communities moved deeper into the forests of the coastal hinterland because of circumstances of insecurity and to take advantage of an emergent world demand for Tanzanian forest products. Chapter 1 shows that mainlanders colonized the coastal forests early in the century, although this was by no means the first time. As African communities under the leadership of immigrant chiefs occupied the forests, they gained power over them by incorporating them into their culture through religion and ritual. Desire for products of the forest—ivory, copal, and rubber—attracted Americans and other traders to Zanzibar and eventually drew them onto the mainland. There the sultan of Zanzibar established a network of trade stations that launched an external claim on the forests themselves, and paved the way for German colonialism in the 1880s. The Bushiri uprising of 1888–90 was in part an attempt by mainland societies to maintain control over their forests and resources against the advance of colonialism. The forest economy that was built on copal and rubber extraction was in a state of crisis as Germans assumed control over the mainland after 1890. Chapter 2 examines how the German colonial government built the foundations of a new forest order by introducing scientific forestry as a mechanism to assert authority over forests and their resources. This affected communities living in and around the coastal mangroves most directly owing to the long-standing economic importance of rafters for the export trade and to the proximity of mangrove ecosystems to centers of colonial control. The mangrove economy tested the limits of scientific forestry, particularly as peasant labor resistance undermined a mechanized timber industry and mangrove reforestation.

A perceived crisis of forest degradation in 1904 led colonial officials to launch forest reservation in virtually all coastal forests. This followed state efforts to curb peasant shifting agriculture and control local wood markets, paralleling colonial hunting and wildlife controls. These intrusions undermined the authority of chiefs and threatened the subsistence of coastal forest communities, leading many to participate in the Maji Maji uprising of 1905–7. Chapter 3 demonstrates the rebellion's connections to state forestry and how foresters used sites of conflict as a template for postwar forest reservation. During this period forestry was driven by the needs of railway construction, agricultural development, and social control. Despite forestry's impact, German rule ended with a minimal colonial knowledge of Tanzanian forests and tree species, and few timber trade connections to the metropole.

Chapters 4 through 6 examine state forestry under British rule in Tanganyika. These chapters demonstrate that British forest policy was driven largely by the goals of social engineering, including transforming Africans into colonial subjects, relocating scattered rural populations into concentrated villages, fostering agricultural development, and providing revenues for the colonial state. Chapter 4 highlights the role of African pitsawyers, part forest workers and part forest entrepreneurs, in opening up otherwise inaccessible and unprofitable miombo woodlands for timber exploitation. The interwar years saw a revival of forest extractive industries, as peasants survived the Depression by tapping copal and rubber, often with state encouragement. Tanzanian hardwood timbers like mvule and mninga finally entered world markets on a significant level. Despite encouraging peasants to work in the forests, the colonial state was obsessed with population relocations. Chapter 5 argues that the colonial administration used forestry as a tool to concentrate peasants into planned villages under the guise of controls for sleeping sickness and wildlife. Although these removals were a dress rehearsal for a dramatic expansion of forest reserves onto woodlands in the aftermath of World War II, they also fed popular opposition that would intersect with the nationalist movement. Chapter 6 discusses how a fourteenfold expansion of the forest estate in just fifteen years following World War II marked a rebirth of colonial scientific forestry. While the postwar development agenda evicted tens of thousands of rural dwellers from forests and woodlands, it also drew them into the forests as taungya licensed forest cultivators, as charcoal burners, as pitsawyers, and as sawmill workers.

The last two chapters examine Tanzanian forest policy since independence. Chapter 7 shows that the independent state saw forest exploitation as a positive good, a sign of economic maturity, and a means to create modern Tanzanian consumers of timber and fuel. This period saw the growing Tanzanian dependence on external aid and thus witnessed the arrival of new actors, including multilateral and bilateral donors, who promoted forestry as a means of revenue generation and agricultural development. During this period the charcoal economy that preoccupies modern environmentalist critiques had its real takeoff, both to fuel urbanization, and as a state-fostered export commodity to the Persian Gulf. The period ended with ujamaa socialism, when most rural dwellers were relocated into planned settlements, which itself had contradictory effects on Tanzania's forest cover.

A revolutionary paradigm shift began in the 1980s with a turn to biodiversity preservation as the leading framework for forestry policy. Chapter 8 examines how this shift empowered international conservationists to influence forestry at a time when a transition from socialism to market liberalization made the Tanzanian state beholden to international aid that often was linked to forest conservation. International and local conservationists in effect have emerged as the new colonizers of the Tanzanian forests, the new ax wielders, armed with a new discourse on forest use and access. Peasant communities whom the state had not long before urged to exploit the forests for development were now castigated as endangering a global asset, reversing patterns of forest use that go back over a century. At the same time, market liberalization has enhanced the export value of Tanzanian hardwood timbers, increasing pressure on coastal forests and woodlands.

Sources

This book is based on archival research conducted in Tanzania, Germany, and the United Kingdom, supplemented with oral interviews in the Tanzanian coastal hinterland. The archival sources overwhelmingly reflect the colonial interests and agendas that came to dominate Tanzanian peasants and their forests. Nevertheless, these sources elicit evidence of peasant agency in shaping the outcome of state forestry. The major source is the Tanzania National Archives in Dar es Salaam, which houses Forest Department files from German colonial rule to about 1980. The German records include files on scores of forest reserves demarcated before 1914, most of which still exist. Many of these files offer an exceptional local view of the impact of colonial forestry on villagers. Descriptions and maps of forests, their borders, and their relations to the surrounding countryside give us a picture of peasant settlement patterns in coastal forests and mangroves that later colonial and postcolonial maps have erased and denied.

British-era forest records are not as complete as those of the Germans for specific reserves, reflecting a neglect of forestry in the interwar years. Because British policy focused on resettlement of dispersed villagers, forest policy must often be culled from discussions of sleeping sickness campaigns and agricultural development. A sense of African discontent with forest laws can be teased from criminal records, which catalogue infractions such as poaching, illicit wood use, arson, and illegal settlement in forest reserves. Records improved as the Forest Department became better financed following World War II, when the importance of forest exploitation to the colonial economy increased. By the 1970s, as British oversight of Tanzanian forestry ended and Tanzanian foresters assumed control, official correspondence was increasingly in Swahili. Tanzanian archival sources are supplemented with those of the German Federal Archives in Berlin, the British National Archives, and the Plant Sciences Library of the Oxford Forestry Institute, which house the invaluable *Annual Reports of the Forest Department* (1923–78). German journals such as *Berichte über Land- und Forstwirtschaft* and *Deutsches Kolonial-Blatt* discuss forest policy from a colonywide perspective. The *Indian Forester, Empire Forestry Review,* and *East African Agricultural and Forestry Journal* are important sources for British forest policy. After independence, the increasing role of international financial institutions, development organizations, and NGOs emerges in reports commissioned by the World Bank, the FAO, national development agencies, and conservationist reports.

This study has benefited from interviews and conversations with villagers living adjacent to, and sometimes in, forests of the coastal hinterland conducted in 2001 and 2004. During this period forestry has become a highly politicized subject in Tanzania, as underscored by ongoing logging scandals, the eviction of peasants from forest reserves, the confiscation of bicycles of charcoal burners, and in some cases state violence directed at peasants and pastoralists. A new forest law in 2002 has empowered conservationist NGOs to take an active role in local forest policy. Despite this tense atmosphere, I found villagers willing to talk about forest history and the ongoing importance of forests for their community identity and economic survival.

Over the last one hundred and fifty years villages and populations surrounding forest reserves have not remained static—indeed, population relocation and sedentarization were major goals of colonial and postcolonial policies. Transformations in the economy have led men to migrate for work, often settling in regions other than their places of birth. Moreover, scientific forestry created and re-created forest boundaries, relocated people, forced others to migrate, and brought in outsiders as forest workers. The ujamaa period was massively disruptive of rural settlement. As people moved, so did ideas, such as Christianity and Islam, affecting how people regarded ancestral forests. These movements have often ruptured memories of the historical significance and cultural role of specific forests. Of fourteen elderly men interviewed shortly after their midday prayers in the mosque in Mlamleni village of Vikindu Forest in 2004, for example, only two had been born in the area, the others arriving in the 1950s to work on nearby sisal plantations. This is a significant point in considering long-term knowledge and use of forests, the degree to which people recognize forests as sites of sacred ancestral groves that they are willing to protect, or whether the forests are viewed merely as sources of charcoal, poles, and land. While Islam displaced ancestral traditions at a place like Vikindu because of these population movements, Muslim elders at Kinjumbi village, near Naminangu Forest, south of the Rufiji River, still maintain ancestral shrines at the edge of the forest and retain a better collective memory of the forest's history as a result. There appears to be an association between such local collective memory and the survival of forests. After a century as a state forest reserve, Vikindu has virtually disappeared as a forest, while Naminangu, demarcated at the same time, remains intact. Proximity to Dar es Salaam is surely a factor here. Yet oral testimony suggests that local long-term historical identification of people with forests is more important to forest survival than are state policies of reservation, which inaugurated their concerted exploitation and degradation. This should be a warning in the era of biodiversity preservation, which seeks to make coastal forests into nature museums and genetic or carbon banks, severed from their human populations, whose presence is regarded as an inconvenience rather than as an integral part of forest history.

Acknowledgments

Research for this book has been generously supported by several sources from Colorado State University. In particular I thank the Department of History and the College of Liberal Arts for annual professional development funds for overseas travel to Germany, Britain, and Tanzania from 2000 to 2006. The College of Liberal Arts also supported my research with Academic Enrichment Fund and Faculty Development Fund grants in 2006 that helped me finish writing. The German Academic Exchange Service (DAAD) supported two research trips to German archives in 2002 and 2006 that made this book's genesis and completion possible. The Tanzania Commission for Science and Technology (COSTECH) granted me research clearance to conduct archival and field research in Tanzania from 2000 to 2004. I am grateful to the staffs of the Tanzania National Archives, the German Federal Archives in Berlin, the British National Archives, and the Plant Sciences Library at Oxford University for their help. Interlibrary Loan Services of Morgan Library, Colorado State University, deserves special thanks for obtaining books and manuscripts needed to complete this book.

I am indebted to Bertram Mapunda, Elieho Shishira, and Yusufu Lawi for facilitating research clearance in Tanzania on several occasions. Fieldwork in Tanzania would not have been possible without the help of Esau Godwin, Robert Salie, and especially Edward Kileo, who mediated and transcribed most of the interviews used in this book. Mr. G. Mbonde of the Tanzania Forest and Beekeeping Division granted me access to Vikindu Forest. Michael Tuck participated in some of the interview trips, and has always been an invaluable sounding board for all manner of discussion on African history. My deepest thanks go to the many Tanzanians who agreed to talk to me about forests and history, always receiving me with an amazing generosity and hospitality. This is their story. This book would not have been written without the inspiration of historians of the African environment whose work preceded mine. I especially acknowledge Edward Alpers, David M. Anderson, Christopher Conte, Steven Feierman, James L. Giblin, Helge Kjekshus, Juhani Koponen, Lorne Larson, Yusufu Lawi, Gregory Maddox, James C. McCann, Jamie Monson, Roderick Neumann, Thomas Spear, and James L. A. Webb for their work. Jim Giblin, James C. McCann, Thomas Spear, and James Webb have been especially supportive of my attempts to write a social history of the Tanzanian forests. Gillian Berchowitz, James Webb, and Rick Huard at Ohio University Press have made the editing process a good experience and have helped me improve the manuscript greatly. Two anonymous reviewers for Ohio University Press made invaluable suggestions that have improved this book. I alone am responsible for any remaining flaws. My colleague at CSU, Jared Orsi, read parts of what became chapter 3 and offered bibliographic suggestions. And I thank M. J. Maynes for continuous encouragement and friendship.

My sister Janice Sunseri, who spent many years working in the forests, has often encouraged my writing by asking to read my work, going far beyond the expectations of sibling loyalty. I thank my entire family for their ongoing camaraderie. My greatest debt is to my wife, Elizabeth Bright Jones, who helped me formulate many of the ideas in this book on our walks, which are the high point of every day. To her I dedicate this book.

Author's Notes

Currency

The most widely used currencies in East Africa during the nineteenth century were the Maria Theresa dollar, generally exchanged at par with the U.S. dollar, and the rupee, valued at 2.125 to the dollar. In German East Africa the rupee was the common currency, valued at 1.33 German marks. Before 1904 the rupee was divided into 64 pesa; thereafter to the end of German rule it was divided into 100 heller. The main currency of Tanganyika under British rule was the shilling, equivalent to the British shilling but divided into 100 cents. Twenty shillings made one pound.

Swahili and Bantu Spelling

Most trees and tree-related objects are in the same noun class (often called the "tree class"), members of which generally start with "m" and form their plural with "mi-" as a prefix: *mti* = tree, *miti* = trees; *msitu* = forest, *misitu* = forests.

Forest Administration

There was no autonomous Forest Department in German East Africa. Forest policy was coordinated by the Office of Agriculture, Forests and Surveying (called Referat VIII) and implemented by local forest administrations (*Forstverwaltungen*). After 1907 these were reorganized into multidistrict forest offices (*Forstämter*), which in turn were subdivided into forest districts (*Forstbezirke*). Colonywide forest policy was coordinated by the forest director (*Oberförster*) in Dar es Salaam after 1906. The British inaugurated a Forest Department in Tanganyika in 1920. From

1948 it was known as the Forest Division of the Agriculture and Natural Resources Department. After Tanzanian independence in 1961, the Forest Division has been housed in various ministries, most recently in the Ministry of Natural Resources and Tourism.

Abbreviations

DOAG	Deutsch-Ostafrikanische Gesellschaft (German East Africa Company)
FAO	Food and Agricultural Organization
IUCN	World Conservation Union
PFM	participatory forest management
TFCG	Tanzania Forest Conservation Group
WCST	Wildlife Conservation Society of Tanzania
WWF	Worldwide Fund for Nature/World Wildlife Fund

CHAPTER 1

The Ax and the Copal Tree

Forests and Political Consolidation in the Coastal Hinterland, ca. 1820–90

IN 1845 the French explorer Maizan proceeded inland from the eastern African coastal port of Bagamoyo into Uzaramo, seeking to open up the mainland opposite Zanzibar to French trade.[1] For some time French at Zanzibar had despaired of their secondary trade status in relation to Americans, and resented the sultan of Zanzibar's monopoly over ivory and copal, the most important mainland trade commodities. Maizan's excursion threatened an established trade balance that had been achieved between the sultan of Zanzibar and Zaramo suppliers of copal, the most important export product of the coastal hinterland. As Maizan passed through a palisaded forest village called Dege la Mhora, its *pazi* (chief), Mazungera, apprehended Maizan, accused him of violating local authority over the land by trading with other chiefs, and dismembered him. French efforts over the next decade to compel the sultan to apprehend Mazungera came to nothing, perhaps because the sultan was complicit in Maizan's murder, but more clearly because the sultan lacked authority over hinterland chiefs and depended on them to allow an unhindered flow of trade to and from the interior.

The Maizan case shows that at midcentury Zaramo chiefs held undisputed authority over the coastal hinterland opposite Zanzibar because of their monopoly of the copal trade. Copal was a product of the region's dry lowland and hillside canopy forests, sandwiched between the Indian Ocean littoral and the Eastern Arc rain forests. The coastal hinterland was home to diverse Bantu-speaking farmers who came to identify themselves as Zaramo, Rufiji, Ndengereko, and Matumbi during the nineteenth century. The ability of hinterland chiefs to form cohesive communities during a turbulent century marked by slave traders from the coast and raids for people and grain by societies further west owed in part to their control of the vichaka (dense coastal forests) and their resources. From Bagamoyo in the north to Lindi in the south the copal trade was paramount for most of the nineteenth century.[2]

The vichaka forests and the copal trade were intimately tied to the emergence of chiefly authority and political coalescence in the coastal hinterland during the nineteenth century. The best evidence of this comes from the Uzaramo region, where newcomer chiefs from Ukutu and Uluguru to the west, called mapazi, asserted authority over less powerful local lineage heads (*wandewa*) and their copal-bearing forests.[3] The title *pazi* stemmed from *mhaazi* (or *mabazi*), the term for a ceremonial ax that symbolized chiefly power over forests.[4] Displaying the ax over the left shoulder, the common method of carrying the ax while working, suggested that power stemmed from the ability to clear the forests.[5] Zaramo chiefs were not alone among eastern and central Africans in carrying a ceremonial ax, but were unique in privileging the ax as coterminous with chiefship and societal identity.[6] As the *wenye mabazi*, "wielders of the ax," numerous local men emerged as chiefs and headmen by asserting the right to control the vichaka forests and trade their products for imported cloth, beads, and guns.[7] Control of the coastal forests in the nineteenth century allowed hinterland communities to find refuge from warfare, to farm fertile forest lands, to exact tolls on passing caravans, and to extract copal and sometimes ivory to market on the coast. From the 1820s the copal trade linked coastal hinterland communities to world markets, attracting Western and Indian traders with their cargoes of cotton textiles and other manufactures to Zanzibar. The copal trade commodified the coastal forests, empowering mapazi ax wielders, who controlled forest access.

Figure 1.1. Luguru lineage head with a ceremonial ax. Reprinted by permission from Roland Young and Henry A. Fosbrooke, *Smoke in the Hills: Political Tension in the Morogoro District of Tanganyika* (Evanston, Ill.: Northwestern University Press, 1960), facing p. 68.

The wealth generated by copal and, by the 1870s, a new forest product, wild rubber, attracted Western traders and encouraged the sultan of Zanzibar to shake off his tributary relationship with Zaramo chiefs. In 1877 William Mackinnon's company began a road from the sultan's port

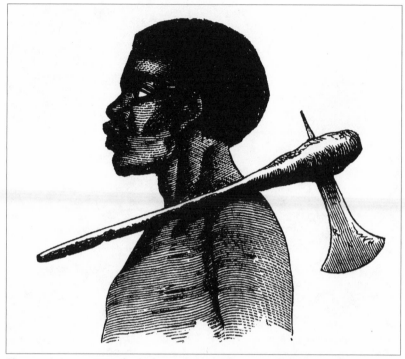

Figure 1.2. Common method of carrying an ax. From Richard F. Burton, *The Lake Regions of Central Africa* (New York: Harper and Brothers, 1860; repr. New York: Dover Publications, 1995), 489.

of Dar es Salaam into the hinterland, cutting a swath through the forests that challenged Zaramo dominance of local trade. The factory-made axes imported by the British firm to build the road are an apt metaphor for the Western challenge to Zaramo authority, which ushered in German colonialism in the next decade. Colonial rule brought a new forest order—a new way of seeing the landscape, regulating forest use, and distributing authority.

Colonizing the Vichaka Forests

The Tanzanian vichaka forests are sandwiched between the mangroves of the Indian Ocean littoral and the Eastern Arc rain forests that begin about 150 kilometers from the coast. Classified by biologists as coastal forests, the vichaka are distinct from rain forests because of their annual three-to-five-month dry season.[8] In this environment endemic plants

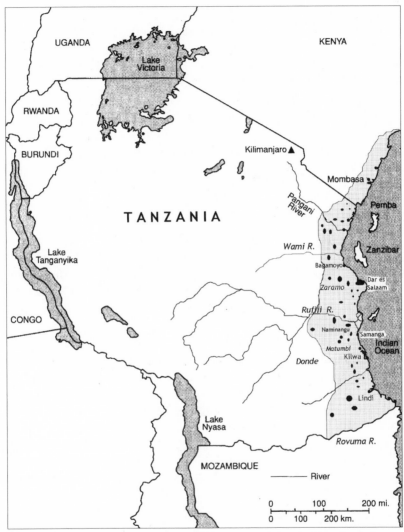

Figure 1.3. Tanzanian coastal hinterland and forests. Map by Thaddeus Sunseri.

and animals have adapted to water scarcity, making for a large number of unique species, including *Hymenaea verrucosa,* the copal tree. There are some sixty-six coastal forests in Tanzania and over two hundred along the East African coast from Somalia to Mozambique, surrounded by savanna woodlands, called miombo, and cultivated land. Coastal forests are continuous stands of trees ranging in altitude from sea level to 750 meters.

The rising of the Central Tanganyika Plateau isolated the coastal forests 20 million years ago, severing their connections to the rain forests of central and West Africa. During long dry periods in Africa's past, coastal forests retreated, advancing again during wet periods.[9] Farming over hundreds of years, especially annual field burning, made these forests "richer in fire-tolerant, pioneer and other sun-loving species" that typified the surrounding woodlands.[10] Farmers have occupied the coastal belt for at least two thousand years, using the forests for fuel while cultivating adjacent lands.[11] They practiced shifting agriculture owing to land abundance, poor soils, and low population densities that made labor scarce in the production process.[12] Farmers thus became fairly mobile and decentralized out of necessity, which in turn enabled forests and adjacent woodlands to recover from or adapt to human use.

During the nineteenth century the Zaramo and their neighbors faced pressure from Zanzibar-based traders to the east and inland slave raiders to the west. In response they moved deeper into the coastal forests, where they adapted copal extraction to their survival repertoire. They cleared parcels to plant maize, rice, and sorghum, using a coppicing technique that enabled trees to regenerate quickly. The burning of fields between rainy seasons, when foliage was moist, prevented uncontrolled conflagrations.[13] After a few years farmers opened up new fields nearby, allowing used lands to regenerate to kichaka coastal forest after several decades. With the coming of colonial rule in the next century, pressure to grow cash crops would strain the ability of the forests to recover.

As Zaramo colonized the coastal forests, they introduced fruit trees to supplement their diet and establish land ownership.[14] They planted coconut palms as far as the soils allowed, as well as mangoes, oranges, bananas, and fire-tolerant fruit trees, such as dum palms (*Hyphaene thebaica*).[15] The explorer John Hanning Speke believed that the end of the dum palm frontier marked the end of the copal lands, which suggests that farmers settled forests wherever copal deposits were prolific.[16] Planting fruit trees bestowed rights to the land, implied permanence of settlement, and sometimes was a means for women to have de facto land ownership. Coastal forests also contained edible roots, mushrooms, and other plants that could be used as famine food, including the fruit of the copal tree. Land and trees provided security, which stemmed from the power of the pazi ax wielder, who oversaw forest settlement and clearance.[17]

In the nineteenth century almost all travelers noted the importance of stockaded forest settlements for coastal hinterland societies.[18] The Zaramo built palisaded villages called *pongonos* in dense bush or forests as protection against raiders.[19] Pongonos were strategic sites to stop caravans and make traders pay *hongo* (transit tolls). One such forest fortress still existed under early German rule at Dunda, just outside Bagamoyo, and was once a major site of copal digging.[20] These havens from warfare in the nineteenth century became refuges from tax and labor demands under colonial rule, motivating colonial officials to drive people out of the forests in the twentieth century.

For Bantu speakers of the coastal hinterland, forests were sites to honor ancestors and perform initiation rituals.[21] They were locales where spirit possession took place and sometimes were abodes of malevolent spirits. The Zaramo believed the forests to be domains of benign spirits called *vinyamkela* (sing. *kinyamkela*) and more powerful and malevolent spirits called *wenembago* (sing. *mwenembago*), "masters of the forest," who interfered in human affairs or influenced natural events.[22] There is good reason to believe that the latter term really meant "master of the ax" (the same as pazi), conflating ancestral spirits with living chiefs.[23] Marja-Liisa Swantz identifies wenembago as male spirits who discouraged women's presence in forests.[24] Spirits selected individuals to become mediums by possessing them in the forests.[25] Seven principal tree species, including mvule (African teak, *Milicia excelsa*), the most sought after timber species under colonial rule, were likely sites for spirit possession.[26] Spirit mediums who derived their authority and power from the forests were called upon to heal physical and mental illnesses.[27] Forests were also the abodes of malevolent spirits that often resided in the hollows of large trees, such as baobabs.[28] Social norms prohibited people from felling spirit trees, lest spirits follow one home. Mediums therefore built "spirit huts" near trees where people made *tambiko* (offerings to ancestors).[29] Common people also buried their ancestors in forests, and honored them with wooden figurines and by placing replicas of spirit huts in their fields, ensuring agricultural fertility. Forest spirits were thus guardians of fields and of social health.[30] Rainmaking shrines were also fundamental to maintaining fertility of the land. The Zaramo believed that the most important shrines were in the Luguru and Nguru mountains, to the west, to which they made pilgrimages in times of drought.[31] Yet chiefs and elders also presided over local rain shrines located at forest springs, caves, or river pools.

The Emergence of the Copal Trade

During the nineteenth century Bantu speakers of the coastal hinterland came to be ruled by immigrant leaders who offered them protection. A dominant theme of immigrant traditions is that these "big men" came from the west seeking to control the ivory trade in collaboration with Swahili or Arab traders of the coast, with whom they formed alliances through marriage.[32] The most common Zaramo tradition holds that an elephant hunter named Kibamanduka migrated from Ukutu just west of the coastal hinterland and agreed to protect coastal people from Kamba invaders in exchange for his recognition as pazi (paramount chief), and for a tribute that included imported cloth.[33] Descendants of Kibamanduka also assumed the title of pazi, and many of the region's subchiefs claimed him as their ancestor and maintained reputations as elephant hunters long after the region's elephant population had declined. A migration tradition of the southern Zaramo for the first time historicizes the copal trade. There an elephant hunter named Kibasira migrated from Ukutu and settled at Kisangire, where he traded "gum" to coastal Arabs at Kisiju, garnering great wealth that enabled him to found a ruling lineage.[34] Kibasira's power as pazi coincided with the emergence of copal as the most valuable forest commodity of the coastal hinterland.

The copal trade paralleled the rise of Zanzibar as an Indian Ocean commercial entrepôt. The mercantile Busaidi dynasty of Oman established control at Zanzibar by the mid-eighteenth century in concert with Swahili efforts to dislodge the Portuguese from the region.[35] In the first quarter of the nineteenth century the Omanis created a loose hegemony over many coastal Swahili trade ports, and many Omani merchants gravitated to the mainland to trade in slaves and ivory. At the same time, British antislaving efforts curtailed the southern Indian Ocean slave trade to the Americas and the Mascarene Islands, leading many Omanis to shift from slave trading to using slave labor for the production of cloves, coconuts, sesame, sugar, and grain on the islands of Zanzibar and along the mainland coast.[36] Although plantation-produced cloves became the major Zanzibar export after about 1840, ivory from the mainland was the life blood of the long-distance caravan trade. Ivory and other mainland products, including copal, leather, and dyestuffs, accounted for more than three quarters of Zanzibar's exports in the 1860s.[37]

Polities of the coastal hinterland, sandwiched as they were between coastal trade ports and the inland trade frontier, were not significant suppliers of ivory or slaves at midcentury. Yet they nonetheless became steady consumers of manufactured goods and currency that passed through Zanzibar, owing to their ability to extract copal from the region's forests and enforce payment of transit tolls. For much of the century an accord existed between hinterland communities and leaders of coastal ports that guaranteed the free flow of trade in exchange for an annual tribute. According to a Zaramo historical tradition, the sultan's men were allowed to administer Dar es Salaam and Kisiju ports in order to protect trade.[38] Breaches of this agreement, such as the granting of land and transit rights to Europeans without Zaramo approval, led to immediate repercussions, including Zaramo attacks on coastal communities, disruption of caravan traffic, and refusal to supply coastal ports with copal. When this happened, trade at Zanzibar dried up, and Western traders, led by Americans for most of the century, suffered vastly diminished returns as copal prices escalated dramatically while they were unable to sell their cargoes of cloth and other manufactures.[39]

The copal tree, called *msandarusi* by Swahili and *mnangu* by inland Bantu speakers, grew only in the vichaka forests of East Africa and nearby

Figure 1.4. *Misandarusi* or *minangu*—copal trees. From Heinrich Schnee, ed., *Deutsches Kolonial-Lexikon,* 3 vols. (Leipzig: Quelle und Meyer, 1920), vol. 2, plate 108.

Indian Ocean islands.[40] Ninety-five percent of East African copal lay in the red sandy soils of the coastal hinterland forests between Bagamoyo and Lindi, significantly empowering the chiefs and incoming big men who controlled these forests to break into Indian Ocean trade networks.[41] For hundreds of years Africans had traded copal into Indian Ocean networks in small quantities as an incense.[42] By the eighteenth century Europeans had discovered that copal made a varnish that could rival Chinese and Japanese lacquers in beauty and hardness.[43] The copal trade took off with European settlement in Asian trade ports by 1800, which created a demand for varnish for carriages, palanquins, and furniture.[44] Small quantities of East African copal—a little less than $500 worth (approx. 2,000 kg.)— found a market in Bombay in 1802.[45] The next year ten times that amount was traded at Bombay, doubling again by 1815, by which time the Bombay market was well established. In the 1840s East Africans traded some 190,000 kilograms of copal per year to Bombay, which might have been the height of the Indian branch of the copal trade. Indian immigrant traders to East Africa from the mid-eighteenth century facilitated the Bombay trade, becoming essential middlemen of the copal trade on the mainland and at Zanzibar.[46]

The boom in the copal trade came with the rise of a Western middle-class culture and the demand it created for finished furniture, household ornaments, pianos, and most important, carriages, all of which required large quantities of varnish. From the late eighteenth century commercial varnish makers emerged in England, the first in Surrey in 1791. The first American commercial varnish manufacturer was founded in 1815 in Philadelphia, and others followed shortly thereafter in New York and Boston to supply a rapidly expanding carriage industry.[47] By midcentury an emergent railway industry created a new demand for copal for railway car varnish that sustained the trade well into the twentieth century.

The properties of East African copal made it more valuable than resins and gums found in other parts of Africa and the world. "True copal," resembling amber, was a fossil found one or two meters below living copal trees or in the red laterite soils where living trees once had stood, perhaps thousands of years before.[48] Although some fossil copal contained trapped insects, suggesting it once was exuded from living trees, most came from the decayed roots of copal trees.[49] Fossilized copal is not soluble in water or alcohol but had to be melted to produce varnish, excluding so-called gum copal from the category of gums. Copal found at the greatest depths was the most fossilized, thus the hardest, the most

Figure 1.5. Sorting copal in an English varnish factory. From Louis Edgar Andés, *Die Fabrikation der Kopal-, Terpentinöl-, und Spirituslacke* (Vienna: A. Hartleben, 1909), 155.

valuable, and the most labor intensive to extract. Fossil copal exposed to air contracts, giving a surface that resembles gooseflesh. This and its amber shade distinguish it from fresh copal resins tapped or exuded from living trees, called *msandarusi mti* and *chakazi*.[50] This inferior "white" copal still had a market for lesser-grade varnishes, typically fetching half the price of fossil copal. About three and a half kilograms of copal mixed with turpentine and linseed oil produced from twenty to thirty liters of varnish. The best carriage varnishes had high melting points, dried quickly, resisted cracking with temperature changes, were elastic, and had pleasing shades.

The entry of American traders from New England into East Africa was the major stimulus of the copal trade.[51] The first Salem ship arrived in Zanzibar in 1826, and the second returned home in 1827 "carrying a valuable amount of gum copal."[52] In 1832 the *Black Warrior* returned to Salem from East Africa, "bringing the largest cargo of gum copal yet received. Makers of fine varnish and lacquers gobbled it up so greedily."[53] By 1845 Americans dominated the Zanzibar copal market, by that time taking 42 percent of Zanzibar's annual production, compared to Bombay's 28 percent and Britain's 24 percent. In that year a total of 42,500 *frasila* (approx. 676,000 kg) of copal were traded from Zanzibar, all com- ing from the mainland's *vichaka* forests.[54] In 1859 Americans took 68 per- cent of "Zanzibar" copal, Germany took 24 percent, and India took most of the rest.[55] Supply disruptions caused by the American Civil War dis- placed Americans as the dominant traders in copal and other East African products. By the end of the war the American share of copal dropped to less than 20 percent, compared to Germany's 45 percent and France's 35 percent.[56] Moreover, the opening of the Suez Canal, in 1869, gave European traders an advantage over the Americans in the import of copal and other goods.[57] In 1870 the last Salem ship returned home with a load of copal from Zanzibar.[58] By the 1880s Germany, India, and Hong Kong were the most important destinations for East African copal, although copal trans- shipped through British ports still accounted for 10 percent of American imports from East Africa.[59]

The sultan of Zanzibar capitalized on the growing importance of Western trade by exacting tolls on products traded to and from the coast. This entrepôt role launched the sultan's claim of authority on the main- land, backed by garrisons in coastal towns and along caravan routes into the interior.[60] From 1839 the sultan prohibited Westerners from trading directly on the mainland so that the export trade could be forced through customs officials in coastal towns. The sultan claimed a monopoly on ivory and copal from the coast opposite Zanzibar, imposing a fixed 20 percent duty until late in the century, when it was lowered to 15 percent.[61] In 1848 some 850,000 kilograms of copal were exported from East Africa. Be- tween 1859 and 1865 copal exports averaged between 360,000 and 545,000 kilograms per year.[62]

Whereas European reports before 1820 mentioned copal only inci- dentally, after midcentury one of the aims of explorers was to identify its sources.[63] J. F. Elton's observations from the 1870s are by far the best on the nature and extent of the copal trade between Dar es Salaam and Kilwa.[64] He noted that virtually all villages from Dar es Salaam to the Rufiji River extracted copal, creating a pockmarked landscape that endangered pack donkeys.[65] Villagers informed Elton that the entire range of hills and forests between the Swahili Coast and its hinterland had abundant copal diggings. Copal was the most lucrative commerce of Indian traders be- tween Dar es Salaam and the Rufiji River to the south.[66] Elton noted that "everywhere signs of copal diggings were visible. In fact we were passing through the main fields from which the Zanzibar market was once al- most entirely supplied."[67] Eleven distinct trading towns formed south of

Figure 1.6. Elton's map of the coastal hinterland showing copal deposits. From J. F. Elton, *The Lakes and Mountains of Eastern and Central Africa* (London: John Murray, 1879; repr. London: Frank Cass, 1968), facing p. 72.

Dar es Salaam to trade copal in the 1870s, at a time when the copal frontier had already begun to favor the southern coastal hinterland.

The scattered location of coastal forests meant that no single chiefdom could monopolize copal extraction, yet hinterland chiefs readily united to defend the copal diggings from outside intruders.[68] Local notables, *watu wakuu*, led each gang of diggers and negotiated trade terms with Indian buyers.[69] At Tuliani coastal forest Elton observed, "In the early morning, strings of natives are seen on the paths, each party led by a few men armed with old muskets and bows and arrows, and consisting of women and lads carrying copal baskets, and, except during the very dry season, these arrivals take place daily."[70] Copal digging usually followed the harvest and rainy seasons, as attested by an American merchant in June 1845 who wrote, "At present there is no Gum on hand as it is the harvest of Corn [grain], after which Gum is collected."[71] Diggers used modest technology—iron hoes and wooden digging sticks—first prospecting test holes beneath copal trees, and if they located fossil resin, they dug up a pit to a depth of about a meter. Once it was exhausted, they started a new pit until they completely excavated the ground beneath the tree. After collecting sufficient copal, chiefs' agents began a lengthy price negotiation with Indian traders. Extractors mixed fossil copal with fresh, or tree, copal and other adulterants like sand and gravel in order to increase their profit margin. In the late 1850s copal fetched $1.50 to $2 per frasila on the mainland, rising to about $3 to $5.50 per frasila in the mid-1870s.[72] Western merchants in Zanzibar paid $7 to $9 per frasila, which included the sultan's duty of 20 percent and a share to Indian merchant houses and their agents. They then sold their cargoes for as much as $21 per frasila in Salem.[73]

The high world demand for East African copal ushered in conflicts over control of the coastal forests that challenged the power of mapazi ax wielders. This challenge was set in motion by a hurricane that hit Zanzibar in 1872, which destroyed clove and coconut trees as well as Western steamships and hundreds of dhows used for the transit trade between the mainland and Zanzibar.[74] Many cargoes were lost and trading firms went bankrupt. Some traders, including Sultan Barghash bin Said al-Busaid, moved to recoup their losses as quickly as possible by garnering a greater share of mainland trade. At the same time, the British pressured Sultan Barghash to sign a treaty banning the slave trade from the mainland. The pressure to end the slave trade was also a challenge to the sultan's control over coastal trade outlets. This period saw the erosion of the tributary relationship between the sultan's coastal trading towns and chiefdoms of the hinterland that supplied copal and grain and granted transit rights to long-distance caravans.[75] Traditions recall myriad conflicts between inland chiefs and Zanzibar agents, which are best read as a struggle over the copal trade. Elton reported a state of turmoil in the far south, near Lindi, as interlopers waylaid villagers seeking to trade copal at coastal towns, leading to a temporary cessation of trade.[76] Camped just south of the Rufiji, a crowd of some eight hundred men, more than half armed with muskets, confronted Elton, believing that he was there to disrupt the caravan trade. The leader said that "they heard there was to be a fight, and they would join the fight."[77] Peace was established when Elton gave a tribute of cotton cloth in exchange for rice, although an elderly chief muttered that evil days were about to befall the Rufiji.

By the late 1870s the British Mackinnon firm spent a year negotiating a mainland concession with Sultan Barghash that, before it was abandoned, would have supplanted the sultan as the dominant authority over coastal trade while giving the company extraordinary, unheard-of economic privileges, including rights over minerals and forests.[78] As a prelude to the concession, Mackinnon built a road from Dar es Salaam that cut 117 kilometers into the coastal hinterland, well into Zaramo territory, wide enough for two wagons side by side, before it was abandoned in 1881. The Mackinnon Road presaged the rival German efforts to gain a mainland concession a few years later.[79] At the same time, the sultan was busy clearing land to expand his coconut plantations around Dar es Salaam, pushing inland into the coastal hinterland, clearing copal- and rubber-bearing trees in the process.[80] These challenges made mapazi and other elites even more dependent on trade imports, especially cloth and firearms, in order to maintain patronage networks and preserve their social standing and reputations as hunters.

Trade and the Transformation of Coastal Hinterland Societies

The political power symbolized by the ceremonial ax was manifested in the ability of chiefs to attract followers who provided labor for their fields, force of arms in times of conflict, and free hands to dig copal during the rainy season. Chiefs gained followers by building fortified villages in forests during times of insecurity, by managing a healthy agrarian economy that made use of diverse fields and crops, by protecting crops and people from animal predators, by honoring ancestors to provide fertility and rain, and by rewarding followers with valuable commodities, especially cotton cloth. The African demand for cotton cloth fed the copal trade, since Americans needed to market cottons to pay for the long, expensive, dangerous trip to the Indian Ocean, and without cottons Africans had little incentive to extract copal.[81]

For much of the nineteenth century the staple cloth that East Africans most demanded was American cotton cloth, known as *merikani* in Swahili. From the 1780s the New England textile industry combined cotton spinning and weaving in a single factory to produce a uniform, strong cloth, a "plain, coarsely woven, but durable fabric" that could compete with hand-woven Indian cottons in the American domestic market.[82] This strong, inexpensive cloth went on to outcompete Indian textiles in East Africa at a time when the British were preoccupied with supplying a multitude of domestic and international tastes in cotton cloth. By 1859 Americans supplied 51 percent of cotton cloth imports into Zanzibar, compared to 29 percent from British-ruled India and 21 percent from Britain.[83] American cotton imports to Zanzibar rose steadily from 4,250 bales (1 bale equaled 750 yards), worth $239,655, in 1848 to 6,950 bales, worth $421,850, in 1856. In that year American purchases from Zanzibar totaled $565,925, 63 percent of which was copal. And it was New England production of textiles, varnish, and carriages that led Americans to East Africa to purchase copal and sell cloth.[84]

The value of cotton cloth for East Africans went far beyond clothing, allowing men and women, commoners and elites, to express status and identity.[85] Chiefs presided over cloth distribution according to established hierarchies of patronage. Thus, the copal-cloth networks of the coastal hinterland "helped to consolidate many a political system" at a time of rapidly shifting ethnic identities in East Africa.[86] The ability of a chief to accumulate cotton cloth (and other commodities, including beads, copper and brass wire, and grain) to attract a following was a key factor in the coastal hinterland, where other commodities, such as cattle and ivory, were scarce owing to sleeping sickness or overhunting of elephants.[87] Burton noted that almost all Zaramo men and women wore cotton cloth, making them distinct from peoples further west beyond the copal belt, who were not able to corner the caravan routes or trade their own products. Zaramo women expected their husbands to provide them with cloth, and Speke considered the Zaramo the best-clothed people of the inland.[88] Cloth also allowed Zaramo, Rufiji, and other coastal hinterland peoples to establish trading links with people further inland. At midcentury traders at the coast could obtain a two-meter length of merikani sheeting for twenty-five cents and sell it in the interior for one dollar.[89] At about that time one copal digger's daily labor—as much as four to five kilograms—might earn one dollar in the hinterland, and three times that on the coast.[90] The copal-cloth networks were important for survival, since cloth could be traded for food in times of famine. American traders were well aware of this connection; one wrote (in reference to the trade at Madagascar), "it is the beginning of the rice season & they want Cottons to buy rice with."[91] William Beardall noted in 1880 that people traded copal down the Rufiji River for rice and cloth.[92] Accumulated cloth also enabled hinterland communities to retain their food reserves for their own use. Joseph Thomson noted of the Makonde in 1882, "Owing to the large amount of rubber and copal which they are able to collect each year, they have become exceedingly saucy and difficult to deal with. We found it almost impossible to buy food from them, as at that time they did not choose to dispose of their surplus grain and, indeed, prefer to turn it into native beer."[93]

The adoption of cloth transformed perceptions of style and status, influenced by coastal Swahili material culture and the penetration of Islam into the hinterland.[94] The association between cloth and status affected men before women, since male porters and traders had earlier contact with coastal culture and Islamic norms and prior access to cloth. Elton observed in 1873 that many Rufiji men, but few women, wore cotton cloth.[95] As the possibility of obtaining cottons through trade increased during the nineteenth century, social traditions changed to reflect this new commodification. Bley noted that all Zaramo women wore a large cotton cloth once married.[96] In the southern hinterland in the 1890s the bride price paid to a woman's father could be as high as $50, half of which went to the wife as marriage cloth.[97] By then a husband's absence for three years without providing his wife with food or cloth was grounds for divorce. These social transformations created steady pressure to maintain trade links in order to obtain cotton cloth and other prestige goods.

While cloth allowed chiefs to solidify social relations, imported firearms and gunpowder empowered them to protect their people. They purchased firearms in fairly large numbers for defense against inland and coastal slave raiders. Elton observed men using firearms to guard copal diggers at work and estimated that half the eight hundred men who confronted him in 1873 carried firearms.[98] In 1859 Americans traded eight thousand muskets and eleven thousand eleven-kilogram barrels of gunpowder to Zanzibar, and other nations traded an additional sixteen thousand muskets.[99] The Sultan exacted a high duty on imported gunpowder and a 5 percent duty on firearms and made it clear to the American consul that he desired to see this trade continue.[100]

Although numbers of imported modern rifles increased during the nineteenth century, muskets manufactured specifically for the African market effected the most far-reaching changes on African societies. Widely disparaged by modern armies, trade muskets were "ideal for Africa" because they were simpler in construction, thus more easily repaired by African smiths than modern rifles.[101] Muskets were more important than rifles for hunting because accuracy at a distance was not important in the bush or forests, where "an ounce musket ball is more likely to stop the animal in its tracks" than was a small rifle bullet.[102] Rochus Schmidt noted that, in the absence of imported lead bullets, Zaramo smiths made their own iron bullets for elephant hunting.[103] Muskets facilitated the hunting of elephants for their tusks, hippopotami for their teeth, and buffaloes for their horns. They supplemented or replaced spears, axes, and traps, easing the acquisition of game meat, an important addition to the diet in the cattleless coastal hinterland.[104] In times of famine, game meat could be a matter of group survival. Perhaps most important, firearms provided an edge in eradicating crop predators, particularly wild pigs, baboons, monkeys, hippopotami, and elephants, all of which could devastate whole fields overnight, forcing entire villages to relocate.[105] Muskets were cheap enough to be owned by commoners, altering the balance of the hunt in favor of farmers. On some islands of the Rufiji Delta firearms allowed the virtual eradication of wild pigs by late in the century, allowing people to colonize the delta and grow rice and cassava.[106]

Imported beads, brass wire, and coins also empowered hinterland polities to foster exchange and prestige relationships with neighboring peoples that could be a matter of group survival.[107] During the Civil War, American merchants at Zanzibar were suddenly faced with a shortage of cotton cloth, muskets, and powder needed to acquire ivory and copal.[108] They reluctantly paid for these goods with gold coins in order to maintain their trade ascendancy on the East African coast. Fifteen years later, at a time of famine in the coastal hinterland, villagers of the upper Rufiji approached the explorer Beardall seeking to buy rice with dollars.[109]

The coastal forests were at the heart of transformations in wealth, status, and survivability as the sole source of East African copal, which varnish manufacturers regarded as exceptional among resins and gums found in Africa and the world. As Zanzibar and Western traders targeted mainland sources of copal for direct control in the 1870s, another threat to hinterland trade autonomy appeared with the emergence of wild rubber as a mainland product, whose demand quickly outdistanced copal in Western markets. In contrast to copal, sources of rubber stretched far beyond the coastal hinterland, threatening the geographic monopoly of mapazi ax wielders.

The Ax and the Vine: Rubber and the Decline of the Copal Economy

Chiefs' control over coastal forests after 1870 was first aggrandized and then undermined by the burgeoning Western demand for wild rubber.[110] Although rubber trees and vines grew in coastal forests, dozens of Tanzanian tree and vine species found in myriad forest and woodlands environments produced rubber latex.[111] Chiefs of the coastal hinterland thus did not have a geographic monopoly over rubber as they did with copal. Coastal forest communities initially took advantage of rubber's accessibility, its symbiosis with copal extraction, and high prices before the rubber frontier moved westward, superseding the copal networks on the eve of colonial conquest.[112] At the same time, there is some evidence that fossil copal deposits were declining by the late 1880s, increasing the relative importance of rubber. The escalating value of rubber and declining availability of copal convinced Western traders, led by Germans in the 1880s, that they needed to rationalize the process by which both products were extracted and traded.[113] To do this they needed to control the mainland directly.

Most studies of the wild rubber economy of Tanzania have focused on the colonial period, when the terms of exchange had already turned against rubber tappers.[114] Yet in many parts of Africa the rubber boom initially created a moment of prosperity for tappers, allowing them to

Figure 1.7. Drying rubber in German East Africa. From Heinrich Schnee, *German Colonization: Past and Future* (Port Washington, N.Y.: Kennikat Press, 1926), facing p. 153.

participate in commodity networks and enhance their standard of living.[115] Robert Harms's analysis of west-central Africa is useful in distinguishing between concession regions, like King Leopold's Congo, and "free trade" regions, such as East Africa. In the former, monopolist companies forced people to collect set quotas of rubber by threat of violence. Although this clearly led to overexploitation of rubber trees and vines, the companies eased production when world prices declined, not having to worry about overtapping of rubber trees by rival companies in their concessions.[116] In free-trade regions, where extraction was largely in the hands of local chiefs, high prices and ubiquitous trade competition led people to collect rubber quickly and destructively. Before the onset of German rule the pattern of rubber extraction in East Africa was much the same as for copal. People spent days in coastal forests, slashing trees and allowing the sap to coagulate, whereupon it was rolled into balls the size of an orange and taken to Indian traders.[117] In the 1870s and 1880s, when raiders from the interior, collectively called Mafiti, threatened the coastal hinterland, security dictated that rubber collection be confined to dense forests. In the 1870s a frasila of rubber fetched $9 to $10 at Dar es Salaam, and, unlike copal and ivory, was not initially subject to the sultan's export monopoly and thus was a more lucrative commodity than copal. Rubber was also more easily extracted than fossil copal and could be collected during the dry season, when copal was not dug owing to the hardness of the ground.[118] As rubber surpassed copal and even rivaled ivory in value by the 1880s, the sultan subjected it to a 15 percent export tax.[119]

The most favored East African rubber came from *Landolphia* shrubs and vines found in coastal forests, rain forests, woodlands, and even in intermediate scrub lands.[120] *Landolphia* rubber fetched higher prices than many African rubbers because it coagulated fast, making unnecessary the use of artificial coagulants, which devalued the product.[121] Peasants tapped shrubs and vines by making incisions in the bark or by stripping the bark to obtain more latex, a method that also killed the plant. Because *Landolphia* vines often used other trees, such as copal, as hosts, tappers sometimes chopped down the host trees for easier access to vines.[122] By the late 1880s the most sought after East African rubber came from *Landolphia dondeensis*, named after the Donde region of the Ngindo people, just west of the coastal hinterland, a region dominated by miombo woodlands punctuated by dense forests.[123]

Already in the 1870s people of virtually the entire coastal hinterland tapped rubber, leading to shifts in power relations as armed interlopers, often Ngoni and Mbunga slave raiders and elephant hunters from the west, occupied or raided lands rich in rubber trees. The Mbunga established an outpost at Kisaki near the upper Rufiji River by 1880, where they threatened the central caravan routes and frequently raided down the Rufiji and into Uzaramo for grain and captives, whom they often put to work tapping wild rubber for trade to the coast.[124] In the far south a Yao elephant hunter named Machemba dominated the Makonde Plateau in the 1870s and became powerful over the next decade by making the southern coastal hinterland into one of Tanzania's main rubber export zones.[125] According to a British missionary, Machemba was willing to trade anything—slaves, copal, rubber, ivory—that would bring him gunpowder, cloth, and beads.[126] Whereas the chiefs who controlled the copal diggings had long established a lineage and ritual authority, the new era of big men and "migrant adventurers" who controlled the rubber networks had no pretense of ancestral right to the forests and the land.[127]

Although raids from the western frontier were an ongoing threat to chiefdoms of the coastal hinterland, the greatest threat to their autonomy by the 1880s came from European traders seeking a greater share of trade wealth. Europeans had long believed that Africans exploited copal and rubber irrationally, undermining potential profits. For example, as with tree copal, Africans adulterated rubber with sand and other waste to inflate the weight of the product before it was traded. Africans furthermore prioritized farming over copal and rubber extraction, creating seasonal fluctuations in the market. European traders also resented their exclusion from mainland trading by the sultan's "Mrima monopoly," which favored Indian agents at their expense. Motivated by these considerations at a time of pronounced European competition throughout Africa, in 1884 German traders based in Zanzibar took the lead in asserting a permanent presence on the mainland. With a guarantee of protection from the German government, the German East Africa Corporation (DOAG) undertook a series of expeditions on the mainland to obtain treaties from chiefs that purportedly gave the company rights of authority, creating a de facto German colony.[128] The language of these treaties conferred on the DOAG "the sole and unlimited right to exploit mines, rivers, forests, the right to exact tolls and raise taxes, to administer and impart justice, and to maintain an armed presence."[129] It is unclear what the chiefs of the coastal hinterland thought they were agreeing to, if anything, when they accepted money, cognac, and other gifts from treaty collectors, but they seemed to expect German aid against the Mbunga attacks that plagued the region.[130]

The treaty-making phase of 1884–85 was followed by an effective DOAG takeover of the coastal ports, which had long been the domain of the sultan of Zanzibar. In 1888 the German consul in Zanzibar pressured the new sultan, Khalifa bin Said, to transfer the concession to collect custom duties to the DOAG.[131] This allowed the company to station its men in some thirty toll stations along the coast and in the interior in place of the Indian traders and Swahili notables who served as the sultan's customs agents, and who had established personal trading relationships and marriage affiliations with chiefs of the hinterland.[132] The 1888 treaty empowered the DOAG to take over garrisons and unoccupied buildings, to exact taxes and duties, to take over "unoccupied" land, and to negotiate separate treaties with African chiefs.[133] Because the DOAG was to collect revenue on behalf of the sultan under a fifty-year lease, its only real profits would come from increasing the total extent of trade from the interior and by rationalizing collection of duties, particularly for rubber, ivory, and copal.

A sign of the novel intrusion that the DOAG brought was the founding of a trial plantation at Pugu, outside Dar es Salaam, located in a kichaka forest previously under Zaramo control, where copal and rubber had long been extracted. The DOAG agent at Pugu, August Leue, set up a copal washery in Dar es Salaam and attempted to domesticate *Landolphia* rubber at Pugu.[134] Although the plantation showed no early success, within twenty years plantation rubber would make wild-rubber extraction unprofitable. By 1888 the DOAG sold Pugu to Benedictine missionaries, who continued to fly the DOAG flag and trade copal and rubber.

All along the coastal hinterland similar usurpations of chiefs' rights over land and forests took place. DOAG agents pulled down the sultan's flags in coastal and some inland ports and asserted control over trade, often in a heavy-handed manner that offended local customs and deprived African traders of any negotiating leverage. Zaramo attacked two of the three DOAG stations in Uzaramo in 1887, a prelude to a general coastal rebellion in 1888.[135] Meanwhile, lands further west were in a state of war owing to the inability of the DOAG to assert authority as the sultan withdrew his garrisons, undermining the stability needed for caravan traffic to flow and encouraging a variety of armed interlopers to fill the vacuum.[136]

The ensuing rebellion against the DOAG united coastal notables and inland mapazi, as well as Mbunga raiders and big-men traders such as Machemba.[137] Beginning in August 1888 this coalition drove DOAG agents out of all the coastal ports except Bagamoyo and Dar es Salaam, where the agents hunkered down and where trade virtually ceased for the duration of the war. The pazi of Kunduchi ordered the destruction of the Benedictine rubber plantation at Pugu.[138] On the southern coast at Kilwa the *liwali* (governor), Mataro, other town notables, and fifteen to twenty thousand armed Africans, many of whom were Yao ivory and rubber traders, killed two DOAG agents and occupied the town then sought to find an outlet for a large ivory caravan that had just reached the town.[139] They rehoisted the sultan's flag and prevented some two hundred Indian traders from departing while making it clear that what they really wanted was "to carry on trade and to export all goods save the necessities of life."[140]

In January 1889 the Reichstag in Germany voted 2 million marks to finance a military expedition to put down the East African uprising.[141] This marked the end of the DOAG's failed attempt to administer the mainland, as power was transferred to the commander of the German expedition, Hermann von Wissmann. Aided by a growing food shortage along the coast and the gradual fractioning of the resistance movement, Wissmann's forces burned villages and moved from the northern coast to the south prosecuting the war. German conquest of the mainland, which took a decade, inaugurated formal colonial rule in East Africa. The most urgent goal of the colonial administration after pacification was to rationalize production and trade of the most important commodities, especially rubber, while finding new sources of profit that could support a colonial infrastructure.

Rationalizing Rubber, Marginalizing Copal

From the start of German rule, colonial officials asserted control over rubber from the point of production to the point of trade, while they effectively marginalized copal networks. An 1890 ordinance prohibited trade in rubber adulterated with stones, sand, and other fillers in order to improve its desirability on European markets.[142] In 1893 Germans founded a military post at Barikiwa, in the heart of the Donde rubber zones, to ensure security from Ngoni and Mbunga raids.[143] Pacification of the inland encouraged German merchant houses to penetrate the rubber frontier, offering cloth and other commodities to African peasants to fan out and collect rubber, usurping the middleman trading role that Zaramo, Matumbi, Rufiji, and other coastal hinterland chiefs once were able to guard through force of arms.[144] The frenzy of rubber tapping that was unleashed killed vines and shrubs in closest proximity to the coast, pushing the rubber frontier ever further west. During the 1890s, drought and locust plagues created famine conditions that impaired grain production and decreased the productivity of *Landolphia,* leading people to overtap rubber vines by digging them up by the roots, cutting them into pieces, and boiling them to extract every drop of latex.[145] The deficient product that came to the market as a result of these practices led German merchants in 1893 to demand greater state oversight over rubber extraction and marketing. Ordinances that followed prohibited the trade in *mpira ya chini* (rubber from vine roots) and *mpira ya kuponda* (rubber obtained by pulverizing the plant), and ordered that all deficient rubber be confiscated and their owners fined up to three hundred rupees.[146]

The instability of the early colonial rubber market created tensions between local communities and Indians traders, each trying to gain advantageous terms of trade. In 1897 near Samanga, an important southern coastal trade port formerly dominated by the copal trade, Africans reportedly lynched Indian traders, drove some into the bush, and plundered their shops. The tension was persistent enough that the German regime stationed a garrison at Samanga and forbade Indian and Arab traders from residing or trading in villages of the coastal hinterland. German rulers set up official market halls in many towns of the region, where they sold products of the land at public auction "in order to decrease the trade advantages that Indian traders have over Africans."[147] By 1898 the German administration mandated a price of about two rupees per kilogram of "clean" rubber at a time when rubber fetched about fourteen rupees per kilogram in Hamburg.[148] Gone was the ability of rubber tappers to bargain the price of their product upward. Although rubber surpassed ivory to become the most important export product of German East Africa in the 1890s, the terms of trade had decreased dramatically for East African rubber collectors. The 13 to 15 percent of world rubber that they supplied in 1870 dropped to less than 1 percent by 1898.[149]

Over the next decade competition from European plantations growing exotic ceara rubber (from the tree *Manihot glaziovii*) virtually eliminated the wild-rubber trade.[150] Plantation rubber was concentrated near roads, railways, and water sources and thus was easier to market and less vulnerable to drought. On top of these advantages, colonial officials exempted plantation rubber from export tariffs, in contrast to the 15 percent tariff on wild rubber.[151] Most important, in a colonial economy with limited supplies of labor, the German vision of economic development was for African men to work as wage laborers on rubber, cotton, and sisal plantations and for African women to grow cotton and food on their household farms, and not to extract products of the forests like copal and wild rubber.

The decline of the trade in copal, still the most important commodity exclusive to the coastal forests, is harder to explain, since a worldwide demand for copal continued well into the twentieth century. Schmidt observed many copal pits throughout Uzaramo on his expedition in 1885, and travelers in the 1890s still noticed people digging fossil copal.[152] Yet by then the most obvious fossil sources of copal had been exhausted, so that most copal traded was fresh tree resin with half the value, and which could not compete with vast new sources of fossil copal found in the coastal hinterland of Mozambique.[153] Under German rule, the apex of the copal trade was in the first year of colonial rule, when 282 metric tons (tonnes) were exported.[154] Thereafter about 155 tonnes per year were exported until 1898, when the introduction of the hut tax led to a brief rise to 238 tonnes, as people scrambled to earn cash, since copal was not included among the products that Africans could use to pay taxes in kind.[155] In general colonialists believed that copal and rubber collection competed with African agriculture and thus was detrimental to colonial prosperity.[156] Between 1908 and 1913 copal exported from German East Africa averaged just over 115 tonnes per year worth about $6.50 per frasila, the lowest prices and quantities since the 1830s.[157] By then the great effort needed to dig fossil copal, in light of its scarcity and official discouragement, meant that it was increasingly associated with poverty, a product that came to the market mainly during famine years.[158]

CHAPTER 2

Colonizing the Mangroves of German East Africa, 1890–1914

IN MAY 1891 the new German government in East Africa issued an ordinance that regulated tree cutting throughout German East Africa, even before most of the mainland had been conquered.[1] The ordinance aimed primarily to rationalize fee collection on the most profitable export timber, especially mangrove poles, which had for centuries been a mainstay of Indian Ocean trade. In addition, it included firewood in the 10 percent export toll on timber, which the sultan of Zanzibar had previously maintained, and introduced a cutting fee of 30 percent on all commercial timber.[2] The ordinance launched state forestry in German East Africa, replacing the authority of chiefs and elders over forests with that of colonial officials, foresters, and customs agents.

State forestry, often called scientific forestry, was an ideology of forest use that had evolved alongside European states themselves. Originating in medieval Europe when monarchs claimed exclusive rights over many forest parcels for hunting and household use, by the eighteenth century forestry was a means of rationalizing forest use so that emergent states had adequate long-term wood supplies for shipbuilding, town construction, and fuel. State forestry curtailed peasant use of forests, which officials deemed to be destructive and wasteful, ending long-standing use of the forests as a commons. Peasants frequently rebelled against the loss of forest resources needed for survival or simply ignored forest laws by poaching wood and game. State forestry therefore included a policing bureaucracy to guard the forests. Foresters replaced diverse, unprofitable, slow-growing deciduous hardwood trees with fast-growing softwoods that had proven market value and industrial demand, rationalizing and homogenizing the forest landscape into monocrop tree plantations.

As Europeans colonized the world, they adapted their vision of state forestry to tropical forests that were far more diverse than those of the Northern Hemisphere. Among these were mangrove forests that fringed the coastal littorals of virtually the entire tropical world, bringing problems of species diversity and landscape inaccessibility that challenged existing principles of forestry. Recognizing the value of mangroves for Indian Ocean commerce, German rulers in East Africa lost no time in bringing the mangroves under state control, desperate to make the colonial venture profitable. Yet East African conditions—including terrain, mangrove diversity and limited marketability, and labor shortages—thwarted the introduction of scientific forestry. Curtailing peasant rights to mangroves led to ongoing resistance that included both organized protest and hidden struggles, such as mangrove poaching and refusal to work in mangrove stands. Germans failed to rationalize the mangrove economy with modern sawmills. The result was a subversion of German ideals of scientific forestry, seen in the proliferation of private concessions for mangrove bark exploitation. Nevertheless, scientific forestry undermined African control over the mangrove economy, introducing a new structure of power and radical ideas about forest ownership.

The Precolonial Political Ecology of the Tanzanian Mangroves

Germans first intruded into the mangrove economy in 1888 when the sultan of Zanzibar granted a treaty concession to the German East Africa Company (DOAG) to collect tolls and administer the sixteen-kilometer-wide coastal strip. The treaty allowed the company to use coastal trees for ship repair, construction, and administration, and to occupy coastal ports in order to increase tolls and prosecute mangrove smuggling. The ensuing DOAG occupation of the Rufiji Delta, the biggest source of mangroves for Indian Ocean commerce, in addition to smaller ports, threatened the African side of the mangrove business, leading coastal people to support the Bushiri rebellion, which aimed to end DOAG administration and restore the sultan's customs officials. Rebel forces occupied the Rufiji Delta and other coastal ports until the German government landed troops and took control of the mainland in 1890.[3] The German colonial government lost no time in occupying river deltas and coastal lagoons and bringing the mangrove trade under its control.

Mangroves had long played a fundamental role in the history of coastal polities and Swahili civilization, drawing East Africans into Indian Ocean trade networks for almost two millennia. Bantu-speaking, iron-using farmers had settled at the northern periphery of the Rufiji Delta by the first century CE, and traded with India, the Middle East, and the Mediterranean between the fifth and seventh centuries, and probably much earlier.[4] Seasonal monsoons facilitated Indian Ocean trade, shaping a distinctly Bantu-speaking and Islamic Swahili civilization after 800 CE.[5] The export of mangroves to the timber-scarce Arabian Peninsula, Persian Gulf, Gujarat, and eastern Mediterranean incorporated East Africa into Indian Ocean and Red Sea trade networks. The mangrove trade paralleled the gold transit trade from Great Zimbabwe, centered on the Swahili island entrepôt of Kilwa Kisiwani, eighty kilometers south of the Rufiji Delta, which was also an important source of mangroves.[6]

Mangroves are a feature of tropical ocean topographies.[7] In East Africa they are formed by the actions of the South Equatorial Current of the Indian Ocean, which distributes organisms and nutrients into protected areas of the coast, such as the deltas of the Wami, Ruvu, Rufiji, and Rovuma rivers. The motion of two high and two low tides each day help form mangroves by drawing in nutrients and flushing out salt accumulations in river deltas and lagoons.

The most extensive mangroves of East Africa are located in the Rufiji Delta, making up almost half of modern Tanzania's 1,335 square kilometers of mangroves. The Rufiji is the biggest waterway of East Africa, draining 180,000 square kilometers.[8] Nine major arms form the delta about thirty kilometers from the coast, creating forty-three islands within about 53,000 hectares. Seasonal monsoons coupled with hot, humid air between 25° and 35°C shape the delta ecology, as do two annual rainy seasons, March through May and October through December. Although these rains create severe, unpredictable flooding upriver, the many rivulets and tributaries of the delta usually absorb high waters. Coupled with the influence

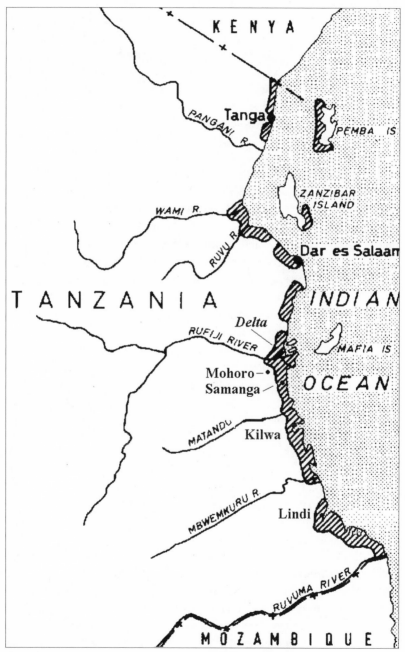

Figure 2.1. Mangroves of Tanzania. Map by Thaddeus Sunseri.

of Indian Ocean tides, the rains and water flowing from highland forests of the southwest interior create a swampy delta environment that is often inaccessible from the mainland. The northern delta channels are navigable by dhow and small transport craft, while the southern delta tributaries favor the dugout canoes that are still the mainstay of Rufiji River transport. The Rufiji and its tributaries deposit silt and mud that create an environment favorable to the growth of eight of the eleven mangrove species of East Africa.[9] The mangroves form a barrier against ocean wave erosion, while anchoring delta sediments to create a habitat for prawns, fish, mollusks, animals and people.

Swahili civilization was identified materially by trading towns that used mangrove poles and coral in construction. Artisans used mangrove wood to burn coral and shells for the lime used to cement the stone-and-coral houses of town dwellers and for the hundreds of stone mosques that dotted the coast after about 1000 CE.[10] Swahili town architecture used mangroves to build multistory houses called *viunga* that relied on supports and crossbeams of uniform length. Mangroves furthermore provided poles of various widths and lengths for the frames, walls, and rafters for common people's houses, an average house consisting of some fifteen hundred poles.[11] A German district official estimated that a village of sixty-six houses required thirty hectares of mangroves for its construction needs alone. Traders graded mangrove poles according to length, width, and use, and usually sold them in lots of twenty, called *coria*. One Zaramo-style house required two hundred poles (*majengo*), sixty support pillars (*nguzo*), forty rafters (*makombomoyo*), two hundred cross-rafters (*mapao*), and one thousand cross-poles (*fito*). Exported rafters were even more costly and elaborate.[12] The most common were support beams (*maboriti*). The rafter market was varied and depended on consumer demand that changed seasonally.

Although almost all travelers mentioned the mangrove trade, figures on the extent of mangrove exports before the twentieth century are rare. In 1859 Zanzibar recorded twenty thousand rafters among its exports, one-fifth destined for India and three-fifths to Arabia.[13] It is likely that many more rafters bypassed Zanzibar as dhows slipped into river deltas and coastal lagoons to load mangroves covertly, in violation of the sultan's tolls at a time when mainlanders still contested his authority along the coast. Furthermore, unlike copal, ivory, and rubber, which merchants transshipped to other parts of the world, Zanzibar itself was the final destination for many mainland rafters. In the late 1850s a score of rafters fetched two to three dollars at Zanzibar and as much as twenty dollars at Jidda in Arabia.[14] In 1878 the Rufiji was the major source of rafters bound for the Red Sea and Arabia.[15] In the mid-twentieth century the mangrove trade, still carried primarily by dhows, was the focal point of commerce to the Arabian Peninsula.[16]

Mangroves were even more important for mainland industries. Artisans along the coast constructed and repaired dhows and other ocean craft using a variety of mangrove species and hardwoods from nearby coastal forests.[17] Hassan Juma of the coastal town of Mbwa Maji, who built smaller outrigger canoes (*ngalawa*) that were used for coastal trade and fishing,

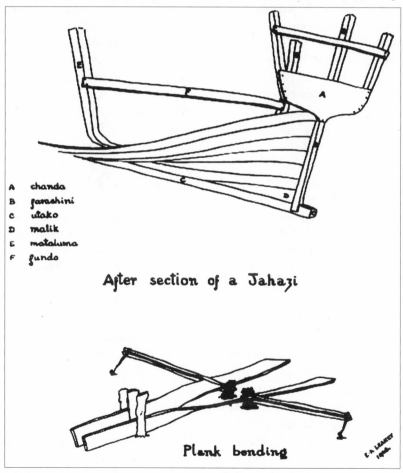

A   chanda
B   farashini
C   utako
D   malik
E   mataluma
F   fundo

After section of a Jahazi

Plank bending

Figure 2.2. Dhow construction. Tanganyika District Books, Mtwara District, Native Industries, Boat Building.

recounted how even this smaller vessel required many types of wood for the prow, the outriggers, and the hull.[18] Besides ship construction, mangroves had for almost two thousand years been used for iron smelting and for sugar and salt production.[19] Coastal dwellers traded these goods to hinterland people for rubber or copal, which they then used to buy imported cloth, beads, and firearms.[20] People used mangrove wood to burn lime for house construction and for a variety of other daily needs—firing pottery, processing coconut oil, and cooking.[21]

By the nineteenth century, and in all probability centuries earlier, the demand for mangroves led people to occupy the islands of the Rufiji Delta in some fifty settlements to farm the land, to fish, and to cut trees for sale. There is every reason to believe that the headmen who presided over each settlement possessed the same kind of authority over mangroves as the mapazi ax wielders did in the coastal forests a few kilometers inland. By the 1870s delta residents included refugees from Mbunga invasions down the Rufiji River that plagued the region until the 1890s. Although some people farmed land located in the middle of delta islands, others, such as the villagers of Bumi, grew rice adjacent to the river and maize and millet down to the river banks, relying on floods to develop a semi-intensive cropping regime.[22] Farmers interspersed their fields with banana groves and coconut and mango trees.[23] Fruit trees bestowed land ownership, an important fact in light of eventual German conversion of the delta into a forest reserve by claiming the land to be ownerless. Throughout the delta farmers built cutting stations on riverbanks, where they stockpiled mangrove poles in advance of the seasonal dhow arrival. By the 1870s the sultan of Zanzibar laid claim to the mangrove trade, building a toll station at Simba Uranga on the Saninga arm of the Rufiji in order to exact a 10 percent toll on rafter exports and to supply his own extensive household needs.[24] He enticed Rufiji woodcutters to the station by exterminating wild pigs on delta islands to make the region habitable.

Although the Rufiji Delta was the most extensive site of coastal mangroves, villagers made use of mangrove stands in lagoons and river mouths all along the coast. Mangrove stands surrounded the coastal settlements of Samanga, Matapatapa, and Marendego just south of the delta, where the Suni, Kiperere, and Mpumula rivers emptied into the ocean.[25] People reached these lagoons only by dugout canoe or on foot at low tide. Dhows sailed in at high tide, were beached—to be loaded with rafters, ivory, copal, wax, and grain at low tide—and then set sail again at high tide. Some of these villages specialized in dhow repair. Indian traders set up posts nearby. The authority of the sultan of Zanzibar was nominal at best along the southern corridor between the delta and Kilwa. The German arrival in the 1890s, advancing an ideology of scientific forestry, was therefore an especially abrupt and unwelcome usurpation of local authority.

The European and Asian Origins of Scientific Forestry

State forestry emerged in eighteenth-century Germany as an applied science meant to solve the problem of timber and fuel shortages at a time of early industrialization.[26] It was premised on the belief that forests were scarce resources that were essential for state revenue and economic growth. Therefore, it was necessary for the state to regulate forest use by sharply circumscribing rural people's access. Because state forestry entailed cutting and potentially depleting forests, early forestry aimed to quantify wood availability in a given forest so that timber harvesting could mesh with long-term fiscal and economic needs. Believing that wood consumption was outstripping supply, German foresters spearheaded silviculture by dividing forests into plots that could be harvested and replanted in long-term rotations using fast-growing species, especially pines. This method of rotational planting and harvesting viewed trees solely as an economic resource and aimed to create uniform, nondiverse forests that could be methodically and easily quantified and harvested with the needs of the wood market in mind. From the mid-eighteenth century scientists began to see forests as important for protecting watersheds and moderating climate.[27] By the nineteenth century some foresters criticized the focus on monocrop forests, arguing for the aesthetic and ecological value of mixed forests.[28] Yet economic considerations trumped this early environmentalism, since rotational forestry brought significant revenue to German states in the form of wood sales.[29] It also required training a bureaucracy of foresters and employing thousands of workers to plant, harvest, demarcate, and protect forests. At the end of the nineteenth century German forest departments employed some quarter million people in forest work, whose upkeep was "more than repaid by the sales of timber."[30]

German scientific forestry favored a *Hochwald* (lit., high forest) model, which was a policy of reforestation using decades-long rotations in order to obtain as much construction timber and firewood as possible over the long term. This contrasted with the French predilection for *Niederwälder*, short-term rotations to obtain fuelwood as quickly as possible.[31] The Hochwald path, which was applied to Germany's overseas colonies, required a permanent state and forest bureaucracy in order to oversee forests over many generations. It discouraged private forests and forest concessions and aimed to replace local, communal stewardship of forests with central state control. The Hochwald path strictly regulated peasant access to forests and forest resources, prioritizing state and industrial interests.[32]

Long before the advent of Germany's empire in Africa, German foresters studied forest and social conditions in South and Southeast Asia and South Africa, bringing that knowledge back to German forestry schools, while they brought new tree and plant species to the royal botanical gardens in Berlin for study.[33] In Asia, German foresters were first confronted with mangrove forests as they helped found the forest departments of Burma, India, and Indonesia.[34] Germans adapted their traditions of scientific forestry to colonial and tropical conditions, learning to manage far more diverse forests and landscapes than were found in Europe. Yet the major goals remained the quantifying of timber for fiscal and commercial exploitation and curtailing peasant access to forests. As Dietrich Brandis, German-born inspector general of forests in India after 1863, wrote, "Climate and species of trees are different in India but the principles upon which systematic forestry is based, are the same in all countries."[35]

Although European colonizers adapted their principles of forest management to Asia, dictates of social control were new to European foresters in Asia. In particular, Asian peasant and pastoralist use of fire to clear fields or renew pasture, broadly called shifting agriculture, was practiced widely.[36] More than simply a means of clearing the land or grazing animals, shifting cultivation was a way of life bound up with spiritual beliefs, cropping regimes, and seasonal rituals. Foresters viewed shifting cultivation and other human use of fire as the most pressing threats to rational forestry.[37] Peasant resistance to forest laws led colonial foresters to create forest police, as they did in Germany, as a permanent feature of state forestry.[38]

Colonial forestry in Asia focused on teak and other tropical hardwoods that provided a known resource for shipbuilding and construction. Yet European foresters also undertook the rationalization of Asian mangroves, particularly in the Sundarbans of the Brahmaputra and Ganges Delta of Bengal and the Irrawaddy Delta of Burma. William Schlich, a German who was conservator of forests in Bengal in 1875 and later inspector general of Indian forests, and who wrote an influential multivolume manual of forestry, initiated the reservation and managed exploitation of the Sundarbans to prevent their wholesale depletion by woodcutters and rice farmers, who had been encouraged to settle in the delta just a few decades earlier to cut mangrove fuel for Calcutta mills. In such aquatic environments, foresters learned about mangrove growth patterns, commercial uses for mangrove wood and bark, and the interplay between peasant rice production and tree cutting. The introduction of state forestry into the Asian mangroves, and the social control and population removals that it entailed, provided a blueprint for the German conquest of the Rufiji Delta after 1890.

Colonial Transformation of the Rufiji Mangroves

Although German foresters arrived with a preexisting vision for controlling forests and their inhabitants, they encountered unique landscapes and conditions in East Africa that shaped colonial forest policies and the colonial state itself. The major difference was a pronounced shortage of human and animal labor power in German East Africa compared to Europe and Asia, which proved to be an obstacle to scientific forestry and other colonial development projects.[39] Sleeping sickness and other animal diseases killed oxen and horses, in contrast to South and Southeast Asia, where elephants, oxen, horses, and water buffaloes were used in forest work.[40] For most of the twentieth century labor shortages hindered the development of scientific forestry in German East Africa, as seen first in efforts to exploit the mangroves.

The mangroves were a natural target for early forestry. No railway or road network was needed to exploit them owing to established shipping outlets, and they had a ready demand from Indian Ocean traders and Zanzibar consumers. Networks of mangrove cutters had long settled along the coast and in the Rufiji Delta. Germans hoped that a long-standing mangrove industry would aid colonial efforts to raise revenues quickly so that colonialism could pay for itself. The colonial state had a substantial debt to the sultan of Zanzibar for his loss of the mainland, in addition to some 6 million marks owed the DOAG for relinquishing its concessionary rights to the mainland.[41] Colonial officials lost no time in raising prices for mangroves in order to service these debts, which backfired when many buyers turned to the black market for their rafters or to non-German sources elsewhere along the East African coast.

A further drain on mangrove revenues stemmed from the sultan's overlapping treaty rights to the Rufiji Delta for timber and fuelwood for his household use.[42] The sultan retained the right to take mangroves from two delta forest parcels totaling one hundred hectares, and was also allowed 100 coria (score) of firewood monthly, for which he paid the nominal fee of 36 pesas per score, less than half the official price. German toll officials complained that the sultan took far more wood than he actually needed for household use, marketing the excess at a good profit.[43] In 1897–98, for example, the sultan sent fourteen dhows to the Rufiji, two alone returning with 2,130 and 1,750 rafters, respectively.[44] The sultan in turn protested that he was given inferior wood and that German forest officials interfered with his dhow captains. In 1903 the German government ended the sultan's free wood subsidy.[45] Although the export value of mangroves did not rival ivory, rubber, or copal, it was nevertheless substantial, averaging about seventy thousand rupees per year during the 1890s.[46] Officials hoped to increase this amount by rationalizing mangrove extraction and finding new customers. Unlike other extracted exports, mangroves were sustainable if foresters maintained cutting and replanting schedules. Their importance for export revenues led officials in 1894 to ban peasant use of mangroves in the Rufiji Delta for firewood, which was the first stage of the introduction of regulated forestry.[47]

The colonial intrusion into the mangroves upset established patterns of peasant subsistence and chiefly authority. Although villagers used different mangrove species selectively for different purposes—such as fuel, house construction, tools and canoes—colonial foresters justified their intervention by portraying African use of the mangroves as destructive and irrational. Africans, wrote the first forest assessor, Eugen Krüger, in 1893, cut down ten mangroves in order to acquire one, destroying saplings needed for forest regeneration.[48] Villagers cut mangroves from the edges of delta islands rather than from the center, causing erosion and denuding plant cover. Over time this led to the silting of delta rivers, creating a swampy environment that spread fever and made large tracts of land uninhabitable. State forestry, Krüger argued, would enable two to four times as much wood to be extracted without damaging mangrove stands, and over time rotational planting would double their extent. Instead of a few thousand marks paid to the state through cutting fees, six hundred thousand marks per year could be earned if the state used fifteen-year cutting and planting rotations in the estimated sixty thousand hectare of mangroves. In order to control wood cutting directly, forest officials prohibited dhow captains from entering the delta to purchase rafters directly from African cutters or Indian brokers, while they courted German firms for sawmill concessions in the delta.[49]

Figure 2.3. Mature mangroves (Bruguiera), Rufiji Delta. From Heinrich Schnee, ed., *Deutsches Kolonial-Lexikon,* 3 vols. (Leipzig: Quelle und Meyer, 1920), vol. 2, plate 123.

The colonial forestry blueprint was launched in 1898 with the creation of a forest administration over the Rufiji Delta, the first part of the colony to be so regulated.[50] This divided the delta into three forest districts based at the ocean stations of Salale, Msalla, and Yaya, European foresters overseeing the first two and an African agent in charge of Yaya. A trial plantation at Usimbe in the inner delta experimented with mangrove silviculture. Toll stations at Simba Uranga for the north delta and Mohoro south of the delta monitored mangrove exports, and in 1900 Mohoro was made the capital of the newly created Rufiji District.[51] The forester Karl Grass, who became the first Rufiji district officer, wrote that the goal of the forest administration was to eliminate the destructive African use of the forests and replace it with rational economic management.[52] By eliminating an independent African mangrove economy, the forest administration henceforth employed Africans to cut mangroves and transport them to collection sites for sale to foreign dhows or other customers. Toll officials set prices for a variety of wood grades, which they intended to be low enough to attract business yet high enough to increase revenues. Prices included a 30 percent cutting fee on top of wage costs and a 10

Figure 2.4. Working the Rufiji mangroves.

percent duty for exported poles. These changes made mangrove rafters far more expensive than in times past and diverted some dhow captains to other sources in Zanzibar and the Kenya coast.

Forest officials hoped that the decline of the rafter business would be made up by introducing sawmills to diversify mangrove use. In 1898 they granted a consortium of German businessmen a thousand-hectare concession to found the Rufiji Industrial Corporation at Saninga to mill mangroves in the first steam-powered sawmill in the colony.[53] Milling mangroves into boards and planks was a major innovation, using a variety of mechanical saws, planers, and groovers to even out the interlocking grain of the wood.[54] Mangroves were notoriously dense and difficult to saw, and saw blades required continuous sharpening, maintenance, and replacement. To help the company achieve a sound footing, the government reduced the cutting fee by half for ten years and agreed to supply the mill with mangroves cut from government land. The government expected the sawmill to market 4,800 cubic meters of mangroves annually.[55] However, this early experiment with managed forestry ended abruptly in 1901 when the RIC was liquidated because it was unable to compete with imported European softwood timber for colonial construction needs, which, although more expensive, was far easier to work than mangrove timber.

The RIC was also unable to replace the established mangrove market. Arab, Indian, and African consumers favored rafters and poles over sawed boards. Construction poles for African houses were in highest demand because they were cheaper than sawed boards and imported timber, were not susceptible to white ants and other insects, were more durable, and were far stronger in supporting heavy loads.[56] External demand for mangroves poles also remained strong despite price increases under German rule. Arab and Indian dhows arrived with the northeast monsoons from February to April, loaded up, and returned with the southwest monsoons, some carrying as many as eight thousand rafters with a value of up to two thousand rupees. Other buyers arrived to take wood back to Tanga, Kilwa, and Dar es Salaam for the internal market. Smugglers remained a problem that toll officials failed to curb effectively.[57]

After the liquidation of the RIC, the forest office maintained the Saninga sawmill while seeking to sell as many varieties of mangroves as possible to clear a profit "at least as fuelwood."[58] Colonial officials monitored mangrove prices in the British possessions of Zanzibar and Kenya and publicized Rufiji mangrove prices in Zanzibar newspapers. The Zanzibar market was frequently disrupted by German fears that bubonic plague and other "Indian" diseases would spread from Zanzibar to the mainland.[59] Although the forest office set minimum prices for thirteen categories of wood, it responded to sudden fluctuations in mangrove demand with flexible pricing but allowed prices to climb if many dhows arrived at once to create a sudden demand. German officials pursued South Africa as a market for mine shoring and railway ties, hoping to compete with established timber supplies from the Dutch East Indies.[60] In these ways, the Rufiji forest economy cleared a profit of 78,285 rupees after its first five years of operation.[61]

After the turn of the century the major demand for Rufiji mangroves came from the capital of Dar es Salaam, one hundred kilometers to the north.[62] As Africans migrated to the city for work, the town's population grew from about ten thousand in 1894 to twenty-five thousand at the outset of World War I, creating a demand for cooking fuel and construction poles.[63] Wood was needed for harbor construction and after 1905 for trestles, railway ties, and fuel for the construction of the Central Railway. Steamships, private industries, and government hospitals all consumed great amounts of wood fuel, demands that could not be met from coastal forests or mangroves near the capital. Wood shortages in the 1890s meant that in order to construct the capital "every board, every strong beam has to be imported from Europe at high prices."[64] Colonial officials hoped that the mangroves of the Rufiji Delta would lessen this need for timber imports.

The wood demand from Dar es Salaam quickly strained the Rufiji forest office. In 1899 the government flotilla converted its steam engines to burn mangroves rather than expensive imported coal, creating an ongoing, extraordinary demand while obtaining the wood at below market value as a government sector. In a five-month period from 1902 to 1903 the flotilla consumed some fourteen thousand coria of mangrove poles— altogether 280,000 logs of varying lengths. By January 1903 the Salale forest district, encompassing about half of all Rufiji mangroves, worked exclusively to supple firewood to the flotilla, with a standing order for twelve hundred coria per month.[65] Rufiji also supplied firewood to government trial plantations at Kurasini in Dar es Salaam and Usimbe on the delta periphery and to the hospitals in Tanga and Dar es Salaam. Three quarters of Rufiji wood used by the government was for fuel. The Schultz beer brewery in Dar es Salaam also demanded a steady supply of fuelwood—eighty to one hundred cubic meters per month—that the Rufiji forest office was anxious to supply.

Labor shortages made it impossible to provide mangrove wood to government and private buyers at these levels. In 1902 the forest office reneged on an order to supply twenty thousand rafters for mine shoring in South Africa and strained to meet the flotilla's orders for fuel.[66] Yet wood that was already cut and stored often rotted on the ground before buyers could be found, and buyers often demanded wood grades that had not been stockpiled.[67] The Prussian minister of public works sought East African mangroves for ties for the Prussian state railways in order to encourage economic links between the metropole and colony, but the Forest Department could not supply the requested fifty thousand ties at a low enough price.[68] The shortage of labor emerged as the major obstacle to a successful Rufiji forest economy, challenging the success of scientific forestry in German East Africa.

Working in the Mangroves

The German colonial state created Rufiji District in 1900 in part to give forest personnel the authority to regulate working and living conditions in the delta and along the river. This meant converting Africans living in the delta into wage laborers, aided by the introduction of hut taxes in 1898, which created pressure to work.[69] Transforming the mangrove business from a peasant economy into a government monopoly made the state both landlord and employer and reshaped power relations in the delta. The forest office co-opted headmen to collect taxes, pressure people to work, and punish those who broke forest laws. A 1904 ordinance declared all Tanzanian mangroves to be state forest reserves, defining them as "ownerless and unoccupied," which provided the legal device needed to evict peasants from delta islands and move them to cutting stations where their labor could be controlled. At the same time, the new forest economy exposed the forest office to African labor leverage for the first time, which made foresters reluctant to expel peasants from the delta prematurely.[70]

Delta work required people to locate mangrove species for different consumer demands—house construction, rafters, firewood, ship and canoe building, fish traps, and tools. Early forestry therefore relied on African knowledge of the various kinds of mangroves and their uses. Consumers favored *mchu* (*Avicennia*), which made up as much as one-third of delta mangroves, for dugout canoes, but rejected it as fuelwood because it emitted too much sooty smoke. Africans preferred *mkandaa* (*Ceriops*) for fuel but required that it be cut to specified lengths and be neither too light nor too dense.[71] The riverine labyrinth of the delta forced workers to use dugout canoes at high tide to reach inaccessible stands. Eight to ten men were needed to transport large logs in a difficult terrain of mud and tangled roots and vines.[72] The forest office spent a hundred and fifty rupees each year building bridges over delta creeks and sometimes laid a "forest rail" as long as eighteen hundred meters, which took a great deal of time to assemble, often had to cross several rivulets, was expensive, and thus was used sparingly. Because mangroves were too dense to float, the

Forest Department built two flat-bottom barges to transport wood from cutting points to toll stations.

The labor question was the major challenge to a German-style regulated forestry in the mangroves. Delta farmers refused to work regularly, staying for only two to three days per week before returning to their household farms.[73] In 1898 the Forest Department recruited migrant workers from the upper Rufiji for mangrove work, but the migrants deserted after experiencing the harsh working conditions of the delta. Foresters complained in 1900 about the high wages (five and a half to nine rupees per cubic meter) needed to entice local men to do mangrove work. The forest office lowered this rate to five rupees per cubic meter by applying the hut tax strategically, by putting pressure on headmen to supply workers when mangrove demand was highest, and through "judicious use of the whip," as the district officer Grass admitted.[74] Yet even the reduced wage rate enabled a worker to pay his annual taxes by cutting and transporting one cubic meter of wood and still have two rupees left over. If conditions were too harsh, or if wages were pushed too low, workers deserted. When wages for casual labor declined from sixteen to twelve pesas (from one-quarter to one-fifth of a rupee) per day in 1903, many regular forest workers quit coming.[75] In 1906 twenty-nine contracted Rufiji woodcutters deserted to Dar es Salaam with their wage advances.[76] Rufiji foresters had difficulty finding workers at planting and harvest times and during postharvest rituals. Many Rufiji villagers evaded delta work by moving to Dar es Salaam for better-paying work. Foresters frequently complained that they could not enlist sufficient workers despite frequent wage increases. As a result the forest office had to turn down standing wood orders. Although the Rufiji forest office supplied fuelwood for some sixty locomotives on the Central Railway after 1905, it could not supply enough to compete with imported steel ties for railway repair.[77]

While the labor shortage impaired the forestry business, it also prevented the Forest Department from practicing sustainable forestry. The Rufiji forest office intended to reforest cut out parcels with new mangrove plantations growing only species with a proven market. With this in mind, foresters surveyed delta mangroves, learned their African names and local uses, their growth rates and favored conditions. They discovered that the total extent of Rufiji mangroves was not the sixty thousand hectares once projected but only sixteen thousand. This meant that fifteen-year planting-and-harvesting rotations would bring in only a quarter of the profits formerly estimated, creating pressure to exploit the stands much sooner or reforest faster. Reforestation relied on casual laborers from delta villages, women whose primary task was to weed young mangroves in selected parcels, which would otherwise be choked off by the fast-growing delta grasses.[78] They also planted and tended saplings, and guarded tree stands from field fires, wild pigs, rats, and antelopes. These efforts at silviculture suffered from the same labor shortages that beset the tree-cutting market. Despite frequent wage increases, in 1912 the Rufiji forest office complained of insufficient casual workers and as a result, according to one report, "this year once again no new planting can be undertaken in the mangrove stands."[79] Sixty percent of the Rufiji forest office's costs were for its workforce, and it was perpetually faced with production bottlenecks as people simply refused to work.[80] The forest office cut down far more trees than it was able to replant yet never enough to make the mangrove economy viable.

Conceding Mangrove Forests

The failure of the mangrove economy to put colonial forestry on a sound footing led the colonial government to grant concessions to private entrepreneurs to exploit mangroves for their bark. German foresters were familiar with the use of mangrove bark for leather dye from their experiences in the Asian mangroves, where the cutch industry, as it was called, was well established.[81] In 1896 the Denhardt Brothers firm, which traded mangroves from Lamu on the Kenyan coast, discovered that the bark of two East African mangroves, *Rhizophora* and *Bruguiera*, contained extraordinarily high levels of tannic acid, making them suitable for leather dye despite a red tint that some dyers found undesirable. Because bark from German East Africa could be imported into Germany toll free, it had a competitive advantage over bark or dyewoods from non-German lands, and could also help foster economic ties between colony and metropole.[82] Furthermore, the botanical garden in Berlin reported that leather dyestuffs were in short supply.[83] The dye industry therefore offered a way to make the mangrove economy profitable, especially since the trees had to be stripped before being sold as poles or fuel, making the bark simply a byproduct.

Despite this optimism, the bark industry created several obstacles to sound mangrove management. Bark from young mangroves was deficient in tannin. Yet, as the sawmill industry that had used mature mangroves collapsed after 1900, the forest economy focused on immature mangroves used for the rafter and pole market. Foresters recognized that the rafter and bark economies were dysfunctional. Karl Grass wrote, "The goal of the [forest] economy is the production of timber, and the bark is a byproduct. An industry that has bark as its main use is not compatible with the principles of a regulated forest economy."[84] Yet concessionaires, led by Denhardt Brothers, had no desire to trade in rafters or fuelwood since the government exacted high tolls and cutting fees on these products and dominated the major trade outlets through its own forest economy. The rafter market furthermore incurred much higher labor costs than the bark trade. It was far cheaper to pay African villagers on a weight basis to peel bark from living mangroves, much as they had tapped rubber or dug copal in times past, than to hire and manage wage laborers, especially in an era when wages were rising. Bark merchants viewed the 85 percent of the tree that was wood mass as the byproduct, which they preferred to leave in the forests to die and rot.[85] This made the mangrove bark business anathema to professional foresters.

In spite of these problems, the Colonial Office directed that bark concessions be granted in all the mangrove forests, from Tanga, in the north, to Mikindani, in the far south. This was in part because concession agreements required mangroves to be exploited sustainably. Forest officials expected bark firms to practice rotational forestry, dividing their concessions into five divisions, one-fifth of which could be exploited annually—still far less than the minimum ideal of fifteen-year rotations. Within two years each exploited parcel was to be reforested. Furthermore, concessionaires had to exploit mangroves for both bark and timber so that they would contribute to colonial wood needs, while ensuring that stripped trees not simply be left to rot. This provision increased the labor costs tremendously, as concessionaires not only hired local female casual labor but also expensive male contract workers. The colonial state was poised to profit immensely from the bark concessions. Apart from paying annual leases in the range of twenty thousand rupees for two thousand hectares, concessionaires paid the government two to three rupees for every tonne of bark and three rupees per cubic meter of timber exported, as well as a 10 percent export duty for timber. Since the Forest Department was not in a position to exploit all the mangroves itself, owing to its own labor shortage, it leased what otherwise would have been a wasting asset. In 1906 Denhardt Brothers leased 16 percent of all of the mangroves of German East Africa, about 5,500 hectares (of a total of 34,600 hectares).[86] Seven years later Denhardt controlled 24,300 hectares, 70 percent of the total, with another 8 percent going to other concessionaires, leaving the Forest Department the remaining 22 percent for its own mangrove rafter and fuel economy.

The bark concessions caused a massive destruction of the mangroves, confirming professional forester's worst fears of privatization.[87] Denhardt Brothers was found to be far too undercapitalized to exploit their concessions for both bark and timber. The company made no effort to cut mangroves in rotations. Rather than paying workers to transport logs to collection sites to be stripped, the Denhardts paid local villagers, men and women, for bark according to weight. Bark collectors usually did not fell the trees, rather they stood on the exposed tree roots and stripped the bark as high as they could reach—about two meters—before moving to another tree.[88] Five to six meters of bark was thus left on the trunk to dry out and die along with the tree. If workers first felled the trees before stripping the bark, they left them decaying on the ground, obstructing reforestation. Characterizing this method of exploitation as *Raubwirtschaft*—the term commonly used to castigate peasant use of the forests—one forester wrote, "The formerly very good, closed [canopy] stands of forty-to-fifty-year-old trees now make a thoroughly discouraging impression with standing, half-stripped, dried-out trunks."[89] Governor Rechenberg called the Denhardt firm one of the biggest swindlers in German East Africa.[90]

Rechenberg furthermore condemned the firm for its labor relations, a sore issue because he viewed labor abuses as a cause of the 1905 Maji Maji rebellion. Workers deserted the Denhardts' Lindi concession a few months before the war broke out because the firm owed wages already in its first year of operations.[91] The following year the dispute still had not been settled, so no workers were forthcoming. In the northern coastal concessions at Tanga and Pangani, where workers had greater opportunities for higher-paying jobs on plantations, railways, or as porters, the Denhardts imported mangrove workers from Lamu until the British prohibited labor to be exported from their colony.[92] Rechenberg viewed the company as detrimental to sound forest management in the colony and recommended against extending its contracts.

Overruling these objections, the Colonial Ministry not only upheld the Denhardts' privileged access to mangroves but reduced their required annual payments in light of the firm's inability to obtain sufficient workers.[93] Many in the colonial administration regarded the Denhardts as heroes of early German colonialism because their early operations at

Lamu on the Kenyan coast had given the German government leverage in negotiating colonial borders with the British in 1890. The Denhardts' near monopoly of mangroves had come at the expense of competitors such as the Feuerlein firm of Stuttgart, which had mastered the extraction of leather dye from mangrove bark.[94] Despite greater capital, better labor relations, more direct profits to the colonial government, and apparently sounder forest management on its small sixteen-hundred-hectare Rufiji concession, the Feuerlein firm was unable to expand its concession because most of the available mangroves were controlled by the Denhardts.

Mangroves and Rural Protest

Villagers living near the coast organized protests against colonial forestry in response to their loss of access to mangrove lands and resources. This loss of access was urgent after 1904, when the German government declared all mangroves of coastal Tanzania to be forest reserves, empowering district officials to expel villagers from settlements within mangrove boundaries.[95] The reserve declaration set in motion a gradual relocation of Rufiji Delta villagers to the western delta periphery, where the state could tax them, pressure them to work for a wage or grow cash crops, and control their wood use. Similar patterns of population removal followed in many coastal mangroves. In 1911 a land commission declared a separate forest reserve at Bumi, a long-standing settlement in the delta, pronouncing the village to be uninhabited despite the presence of rice fields and palm plantations. The reserve declaration prohibited all field burning and wood extraction within the reserve.[96] In 1912 forest reserve declarations followed at Kikale on the northern Rufiji Delta and in the adjacent mangrove lagoons at Mchungu.[97] District officials asked villagers who showed up at the public reserve declarations to produce tax certificates, effectively silencing claims to land in the forests except in the case of one resident, who claimed two palm trees in the new forest reserve.

Villagers protested loss of access to the mangroves. The most dramatic example of protest was the Maji Maji War in 1905, which, because of its connections to coastal forest reservation, is discussed in the next chapter. Less violent, but more persistent, protest was seen in letters and petitions from local elites who were charged with guarding the mangroves from their people. In Tanga District, on the northern coast, Denhardt Brothers held a mangrove concession after 1903 that required villagers to obtain company permission to cut mangroves even for subsistence use.

The German-appointed akida, Hamisi bin Mshangamwe, protested to the district office the ensuing shortage of construction poles, writing that some four hundred of his people had no houses in which "to live or rent to others" as the rainy season approached.[98] He wrote that they had no trees for building, axes or saws for felling trees, dhows for transport, or food to feed forest workers. Mshangamwe then requested a two-thousand-rupee government loan to build 150 houses, which he hoped to repay by selling timber, lime, and planks for dhows. The government response does not survive, yet the case attests to the dramatic undermining of the local mangrove economy that came with colonial forestry.

Elsewhere along the coast villagers who once had unbridled access to mangroves for household use and trade organized against the new forest economy. In 1912 headmen of the coastal towns in Kilwa District south of the Rufiji Delta assembled at a land commission and demanded that their people be given access to the mangroves for basic household needs, required by law, but not allowed in practice.[99] District officials admitted that subsistence use of the mangroves had caused no damage to the stands and acceded to the demand for free access as long as people first obtained a permit from the district station and agreed not to sell their wood on the market. Despite these warnings, the black market in mangroves continued, as villagers used dugout canoes under cover of night, even in the Rufiji Delta, where oversight was strongest, to sell illegally cut rafters to ocean-going dhows.

The Closing of the Mangroves

In 1912 a German forester toured a stretch of mangroves around Samanga, south of the Rufiji Delta, to assess the results of almost two decades of colonial forestry and found a scene that belied colonial stereotypes of African forest misuse.[100] He toured a handful of villages located on creeks that flowed down from the nearby Matumbi hills, forming a complex of mangrove lagoons. The sultan of Zanzibar had once maintained a single agent at Samanga to collect duties on mangroves, as well as on the copal, rubber, and ivory that was traded from the nearby coastal hinterland. In those days dhows had landed at low tide to unload their cargoes and to take on mangrove poles and other goods and often remained for extended periods for repairs. By the turn of the century German customs stations at Kilwa, the Rufiji Delta, and Dar es Salaam monopolized the legal mangrove trade. In 1912 half a dozen different mangrove species still dominated the lagoons, and villagers had recently asserted their right to use the mangroves for housing construction, firewood, boat building, and fish traps. Villagers favored one mangrove species for firewood, *mkandaa* (*Ceriops*), which was a minor part of the stands, therefore its extraction caused little damage. Nor was their use of *mkaka* (*Rhizophora*) for housing destructive, since they used only trees that had reached construction size. The forester concluded that local use didn't threaten the mangroves. To the contrary, by thinning selected parcels, local use promoted the growth of young trees by exposing them to sunlight.

On top of this apparently benign local use of the mangroves was an overarching structure of colonial forestry. This structure divided the Samanga mangroves into two forest districts, which were further divided into compartments, and further into subcompartments for the purpose of reforestation using "plantation-style high forest rotations" of eighty to ninety years. These rotations favored *Rhizophora,* the most marketable of the mangrove genera for rafters, which offered "a nice potential profit for the treasury." The forester Eduard Haberkorn noted that some of the stands could be left standing for another decade but that others were overmature and needed to be exploited soon, after which they could be brought into regular planting and harvesting rotations. Of concern were the region's low population and the opportunities provided by the fishing industry, which made villagers loath to do wage work reforesting mangroves. A much greater threat to the mangrove ecology was the Denhardt firm's proliferation of bark stripping, which impaired mangrove recovery and sound forestry.[101]

The colonial introduction of scientific forestry into the mangroves forced coastal people to reorient their working lives. A boatbuilder from Mbwa Maji, on the coast, who was about seventy years old in 2004, recalled that in the past all the trees needed to construct an ngalawa (outrigger canoe) were available nearby, but it was now necessary to go far inland for suitable trees.[102] Free access to mangroves had been eliminated when colonial rulers leased the most important stands to "foreigners" for pole or bark extraction. The direct result was that boat builders had to find new trees for their craft, such as mangos and even mnangu, the copal tree. Yet many of these trees were unsuitable for boats. "Trees like *mfuru* and mnangu aren't good because they are too brittle, and all day long it is necessary to pour water over them, but they constantly crack." Other trees, such as *mzambarau,* the Javanese plum, were simply too heavy. "If you use it for ngalawa construction it sinks easily in the water." When asked why people did not protest removal from forest reserves, the boat-builder responded, "Who is able to resist the government?"

Scientific forestry introduced a totally new discourse of power into German East Africa, one that asserted state rights over the mangroves and other forests where people once had fairly unbridled access mediated by local headmen and chiefs.[103] The new forest order fundamentally transformed the relations between local villagers and their landscape. It prioritized some mangrove species over others and sought to remake the forest landscape by simplifying it through regularized planting and harvesting. Villagers once engaged in myriad local activities were henceforth valued only as forest workers who planted and cut mangroves for a wage or stripped trees for their bark. Although villagers often successfully resisted the state's labor demands and often subverted their exclusion from the mangroves, colonial forestry ushered in ongoing conflicts over forest resources that outlasted German rule. After 1904, German foresters extended the laboratory of scientific forestry that had begun in the mangroves to the forests of the coastal hinterland, with far greater repercussions.

CHAPTER 3

Insurgency in the Coastal Forests, 1904–14

IN JULY 1905 several hundred Matumbi insurgents emerged from Naminangu Forest, recently designated a colonial forest reserve, to attack Samanga town, south of the Rufiji Delta. They burned the plantations and property of influential Arabs, Indians, and a German settler and threatened the area for about two weeks.[1] Other Matumbi attacked the Kilwa District substation at Kibata, in the midst of vichaka coastal forests about thirty kilometers inland, killed Arab and Indian traders and a German settler, and forced the German-appointed Arab akida to flee to Kilwa for safety. Rebels drove out other Arab and Indian traders ensconced in the Matumbi hills in Namakutwa and Nyambawala forests and burned their houses and possessions.[2] These attacks launched the Maji Maji War in southeastern Tanzania.

Although an established and growing literature has attributed the war's genesis to a variety of colonial grievances, including forced labor, forced cotton production, and the abuses of German officials and their surrogates, attentiveness to the sites of conflict in the coastal hinterland shows that colonial scientific forestry, especially the reservation of mangroves and coastal forests after 1904, played a fundamental role in the outbreak of the rebellion. In many respects the war was a reaction to colonial usurpation of the authority that mapazi and other chiefs and headmen once had over the forests and their resources as ax wielders. Forest policy acted in concert with other colonial conservationist intrusions, including attacks on shifting agriculture, bans on hunting, and the creation of wildlife reserves, all of which endangered peasant subsistence. These intrusions furthermore usurped the trade in forest products—ivory, rubber, copal, and mangroves—that had once been important to coastal hinterland societies.

Apart from its role in the outbreak of the Maji Maji War, colonial forestry also shaped German reconstruction policies following the war. Scholars have viewed Maji Maji as a break between a prewar era of abuse and a postwar era of improvement. Although colonial rulers ameliorated some abusive policies, such as forced labor and forced cotton production, they intensified state forestry following the war. In the greater Rufiji region there was a close connection between Maji Maji battle sites and postwar patterns of forest reservation. Forest policy was a tool for social and spatial control, used to force rebels and peasants alike out of forests into open villages, where labor could be tapped, taxes assessed, cash crops promoted, and behavior shaped. Forestry prioritized economic development in an era when railway expansion created a much greater demand for timber and fuel. German foresters, aided by salaried African rangers and forest police, emerged as the main power brokers over the use of forests and trees. The ceremonial ax that once symbolized chiefly authority over forests was replaced with the forester's marking ax, which inscribed valuable trees and timber with colonial insignia as it readied them for export.

Forestry and the Attack on African Subsistence

German colonialism aimed to replace African shifting agriculture with intensive land use by applying fertilizer, technology, labor management, and new crops to East Africa. Colonial rulers also assumed that Germans would settle in the colony in fairly large numbers, bringing an agricultural expertise and capacity to transform the land. Forestry's role would be to create a European-style landscape in a territory believed to have been devastated by African misuse. Intensively cultivated fields would have their counterpart in a cultivated forest landscape, called the *Kulturwald,* or *Plänterwald,* where foresters would plant valuable tree species, especially pines, that could be harvested in perpetuity. Such a cultivated forest landscape represented what it meant to be German.[3] As one forester advised the Foreign Office even before the start of formal German rule in East Africa, German immigration to the colonies was unthinkable without a properly forested landscape that would protect not only the soil and climate but the "health and well-being of the settler."[4]

A secondary goal of colonial forestry was to identify indigenous trees that could contribute to colonial revenues. Most early forestry focused on the northeast highlands, where most of the territory's few rain forests were concentrated. These supposed *Urwälder* (primeval forests) contained exploitable softwoods, especially evergreens such as cedar and *Podocarpus.* Although forestry called for the protection of trees on mountain ridges and watersheds to prevent soil erosion and moderate the climate, there was no thought given to preserving rain forests for their species diversity. The forest assessor Eugen Krüger wrote in 1893, "Only systematically managed timber forests are of use to us, not primeval forests."[5] A decade later Chief Forester Otto Eckert still concurred: "The view of the forest administration is that all these primeval forests are ripe for harvest. Postponing their exploitation until a later date thus means a loss of state property."[6] Once German foresters cut these forests down, Eckert claimed, they would replant them with economic species able to produce five times as much wood mass with a profit of some 5 million marks annually if harvested on long-term cycles. A regulated forest economy would help reverse the negative balance of payments that plagued the colony and emancipate it from dependence on the often anticolonial parliament in Germany.

On the savanna woodlands that characterized most of the coastal hinterland and half of German East Africa, marketable trees were too few and scattered to interest German foresters. Foresters had little incentive to master this environment, since in Germany there was no wood shortage, thus little demand for diverse tropical timbers whose characteristics and uses were unknown. Forestry aimed to eliminate African shifting agriculture around the scattered coastal forests, which they viewed as wood reserves for the construction of colonial towns like Dar es Salaam. Officials condemned Africa shifting agriculture as "wild burning," and therefore "hostile to civilization" (*kulturfeindlich*) because it created a scarcity of wood and water and an arid environment antithetical to commercial agriculture. Forester Krüger claimed that African farmers set fire to as much as a thousand hectares of forest in order to prepare a tiny parcel for sowing, burned large swaths of bush in order to drive antelopes into snares, and cut down a whole tree just to obtain one plank.[7] Germans imagined that East Africa was once as heavily forested as Germany and attributed the general lack of high forests to shifting agriculture. African land use allegedly deprived colonial towns of construction and fuelwood, necessitating expensive lumber imports from Europe.

The first forest ordinance, in 1893, addressed these suspicions by prohibiting Africans from burning fields near towns and along rivers. After the turn of the century colonial ordinances prohibited all field burning.[8] Instead peasants had to cut and rake brush into piles before burning, which significantly increased the labor burden while depriving most of the farmland of ash fertilizer. The forest ordinance required Africans to purchase a five-rupee permit to cut wood for household and commercial use, while officials closely monitored wood markets for illegal use. District officers conscripted African headmen to enforce these laws and police the forests.[9]

In contrast to the strict controls on African forest use, colonial officials gave European settlers and missionaries fairly unbridled access to forests. In the 1890s policymakers had assumed that the colony was destined for white settlement, particularly in the northeast highlands, where the climate and altitude seemed healthy for European settlers, and the landscape favored coffee, rubber, and sisal as cash crops. Settlers cut down forests to make way for plantations with only modest provisions for forest protection. An 1895 forest ordinance prohibited settlers from denuding mountain ridges and river valleys and required that one-quarter of their lands be kept under forest cover.[10] Yet planters generally ignored these laws, and colonial officials, favorably disposed to settlement, usually did not enforce them.[11] Missionaries also exploited forests rapaciously, using saws and sawmills on a wide scale to work Tanzania's hardwood timbers to construct schools and churches.[12]

Misitu ya Serikali: Reserving Forests

In 1903, Moravian missionaries reported to the Foreign Office that many forest parcels in German East Africa were being destroyed with no effort to reforest.[13] Governor Adolf Graf von Götzen acknowledged that a true regulated forestry had not yet been introduced in German East Africa, even though "the forest question is a life-and-death matter for the colony."[14] He responded with a new forest ordinance that aimed to end "the destructive influences of the human hand" by introducing forest reserves throughout the colony. Drawing on the 1895 Crown Land Ordinance, which allowed the colonial state to assume control of all "ownerless" land in the colony, Götzen promulgated the 1904 Forest Protection Ordinance, which empowered the administration to declare forest reserves.[15] The new policy aimed "to occupy as state property with all due haste as much reserved [forest] land as possible."[16] It prioritized montane and other canopy forests that enclosed watersheds and known valuable timbers. Foresters also protected mountain ridges and unforested areas around river sources by prohibiting tree felling in these locales. African access to forest reserves was allowed only if there was no other means of procuring wood for domestic needs, and then only with strict oversight. Götzen wrote, "I consider the retention of forests, as well as the founding of new forests in denuded regions, to be the most urgent task of government."[17] If done promptly with sufficient trained foresters, he believed, forests reserves would bring the government a "perpetual source of income."

The colonial assertion of authority over coastal forests preceded reservation. Germans appointed *maakida* (subdistrict officials) in many areas, whom they paid twenty to forty rupees monthly, with authority over taxation, labor conscription, land use, and law enforcement. Maakida thus "in no way represented the interests of the people."[18] In Uzaramo, Germans appointed elders of the Kawamba clan, who claimed traditional authority as mapazi (ax wielders) and as elephant hunters, as maakida at Vikindu and Kisserawe, and installed other members of the clan as *majumbe* (headmen).[19] Majumbe had been a common title under Zanzibar rule of the coast, and now German officials applied the term to most local elites except in the most centralized societies.[20] They paid majumbe nominal salaries or a portion of taxes they collected or wood-cutting permits they issued. Those who enforced German policy received benefits, such as concessions to collect rubber in forest reserves. Although many headmen had traditional legitimacy, they were made to enforce burdensome colonial laws at the cost of loss of local prestige. Many sat on the land commissions that declared their ancestral forests to be state reserves.

The 1904 forest ordinance directed that district officials throughout German East Africa identify suitable forests for state control.[21] Although the first forest reserve was the entirety of the coastal mangroves (see chapter 2), early forest reservation also targeted the vichaka forests, the several score of dry canopy forests of the coastal hinterland, especially those near colonial towns that were needed as timber and fuel reservoirs. Some contained valuable rare woods such as mpingo (blackwood) or were important sources of rubber. Others acted as watersheds, particularly for rivers and streams that irrigated plantations. Forest reservation was a tool for the state to assert power over the countryside by moving people from places where they were insufficiently controlled to locales where they were desired as farmers, workers, and taxpayers.

The first forest reserves in Dar es Salaam and Kilwa districts illustrate these multiple aims. In 1904 forest officials reserved four coastal forests near Dar es Salaam and demarcated another thirteen forests along roads leading to Dar es Salaam and coastal ports.[22] Sachsenwald Forest, on the southwestern outskirts of Dar es Salaam, which had been designated a forest district (*Revier*) in 1898 to supply the town's wood needs, was reserved in April 1904.[23] Next was Pugu, just west of Dar es Salaam along the planned route of the Central Railway. Long exploited for its wild rubber and copal, Pugu was interspersed with African settlements and several European rubber and coconut plantations. In 1904 a land commission that included District Officer Carl von Winterfeld, a government surveyor and forester, akida Kawamba bin Kawamba Mschale of Kisserawe, and the headmen of Pugu and Kisserawe declared Pugu to be a reserve.[24] This first of inland forest reserves was unusual in allowing peasants to remain on two land parcels within the forest. Ten residents, including a pazi of Kisserawe and the *jumbe* Sogorro, received between three and twenty rupees for the loss of their farms. Forest officials followed Pugu with the declaration of Vikindu, Sachsenwald, and Massangania forest reserves.[25] All these forests were surrounded by villages and enclosed farms, fruit trees, wells, and ancestral graves. Vikindu, for example, just ten kilometers south of Dar es Salaam, included over one hundred houses, maize fields, and a forty-hectare coconut plantation. The state compensated evicted farmers with nominal sums—less than half the annual three-rupee hut tax—for cleared land and up to six rupees for houses. Foresters evicted ninety-four people from Massangania after compensating them for their maize fields, huts, and palm and fruit trees. Forest reserve protocols granted villagers continued use of springs and the right to bury the dead and care for ancestral graves in the forests.

Forest reserve declarations followed an established template. This included a public ceremony whereby government officials, accompanied by local elites, announced in Swahili that free access to the forest was subsequently prohibited. Hundreds of people usually witnessed the proceedings and could theoretically claim ownership of land or fruit trees in the forests, which rarely occurred. At least once officials used the occasion

Figure 3.1. Sachsenwald Forest Reserve. From Heinrich Schnee, ed., *Deutsches Kolonial-Lexikon,* 3 vols. (Leipzig: Quelle und Meyer, 1920), vol. 3, plate 177.

to check that people had paid their taxes.[26] If no claims were made, district officials declared the forest to be the property of the colonial treasury and specified its boundaries, often following natural markers such as rivers, termite mounds (which could project two or more meters upward), or mountain ridges. If no natural markers were evident, foresters erected stone or wooden posts with state insignia, and sometimes planted exotic trees to mark the new forest, itself a dramatic representation of state ownership. Protocols mandated that local headmen guard the forests from peasant use—a public reversal of their past roles—and that violators be punished with imprisonment or heavy fines. Forest authority now lay in the hands of German forest wardens, the *mabwana misitu,* assisted by African rangers and police, who guarded reserves against all forms of unapproved African use.

Alongside forest reserves, after 1903 German policy was to create massive wildlife reserves in every district in German East Africa.[27] In the coastal hinterland officials laid out three reserves by 1903: two on the upper Rufiji that together formed the core of the future Selous Game Reserve, and one along the Matandu River in Kilwa District that extended from Liwale almost as far as Kilwa on the coast. Wildlife reserves protected large game and small crop predators alike, at a time when European hunters believed that Africans hunted animals destructively and unfairly. Game laws created additional burdens on African hunting. They mandated permits to hunt large game, especially elephants; limited the size of African hunting parties; curtailed African use of firearms; and prohibited hunting with nets, fire, and traps. Villagers saw no difference between forest and wildlife reserves.[28] Both protected animals that destroyed crops and killed people, and both prohibited Africans from residing within their borders. Together forest and wildlife reserves unleashed a crisis in the rural economy that people sought to redress by rebelling against German authority.[29]

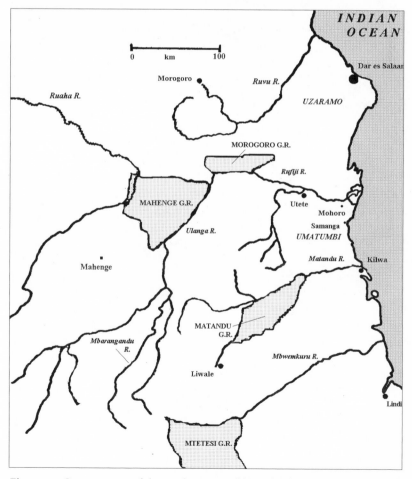

Figure 3.2. Game reserves of the southern coastal hinterland, c. 1904. Map by Thaddeus Sunseri.

Forest Reserves and Rebellion

The Maji Maji War, named for a water medicine (*maji*) that supposedly provided rebels immunity from German bullets, broke out in the Rufiji-Kilwa coastal hinterland in July 1905.[30] Until recently scholars have viewed Maji Maji as a protonationalist uprising against German oppression, a unified movement that was the brainchild of spirit mediums of the Rufiji region who spread a message of resistance to neighboring peo-

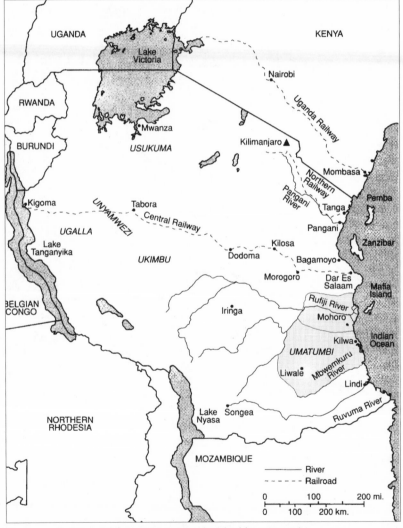

Figure 3.3. Rufiji and Kilwa districts. Map by Thaddeus Sunseri.

Figure 3.4. Nyamwezi elephant hunters in German East Africa, c. 1912. Bildarchiv der Deutschen Kolonial-Gesellschaft, University of Frankfurt.

ples by distributing water medicine.[31] Most cite German development policies, especially forced cotton growing, as the cause of the rebellion. Missing in these analyses are the intrusive forest and wildlife policies that undermined rural subsistence and the power of chiefs and headmen, who became the prime movers of the rebellion in order to recoup their prestige.[32] Maji Maji was furthermore a reaction to the colonial attack on the copal, rubber, and ivory trades, whose demise eroded the ability of chiefs to accumulate wealth and attract followers. The rebellion spread through ivory and rubber trade networks, which connected coastal hinterland peoples to Mbunga and Ngoni allies far inland and to others south of the Rovuma River in Portuguese territory.

The rebellion paralleled the creation of forest and wildlife reserves. Coastal mangroves, declared to be forest reserves in 1904, were early sites of rebel attacks at Kisiju, Mohoro, Samanga, Kilwa, and Lindi. The loss of access to mangroves led people to support rebellious chiefs.[33] Rebels operated from nearby coastal forests targeted to become forest reserves. One was Naminangu Forest, named after the copal trees (*minangu*) that were crucial to the nineteenth-century economy. In September 1904 a land commission declared Naminangu the first high forest (Hochwald) reserve in the Rufiji-Kilwa region, just ten kilometers inland from Samanga.[34] The creation of Naminangu Reserve, which enclosed an ancestral shrine, signaled to the Matumbi people that colonial forest controls would not be confined to the coast.[35] The land commission noted valuable timbers in the forest, especially mpingo, which had a market in Europe for clarinets and other woodwind instruments. Rebels attacked the property of German and Arab members of the land commission based at Samanga in one of the first actions of the war.[36] Rebels also drove from power the akida of Kibata, in the Matumbi hills, and forced Indian and Arab rubber traders to the coast for refuge.[37] Further south, rebels attacked members of the Kilwa land commission who had asserted control of the mangroves around that town. German military strength at Mohoro prevented rebels from penetrating the Rufiji Delta.

In southwest Kilwa District, rebels attacked the German military station at Liwale, where a forest reserve and game reserve had recently been created. This region had once been the locus of the wild-rubber trade, which now competed with a German plantation growing ceara rubber.[38] The Ngindo people believed that the creation of Liwale Forest Reserve in 1904 was a ruse for Germans to expand the plantation into the forest and assume control over woodlands rich in *Landolphia* rubber shrubs.[39] Liwale was also the gateway to the Matandu River Game Reserve, created in 1903, which protected elephants, hippos, and other destructive animals. A governor's ordinance in 1901 had banned elephant hunting in Kilwa District.[40] The Matandu Reserve encompassed the village of Kitandangangora, home of the elephant hunter Abdullah Mapanda, who led the rebellion around Liwale.[41] In mid-August 1905, Mapanda's forces attacked the German fort at Liwale, killing the two German members of the land commission that had demarcated Liwale Forest. One was killed by two sons of Jumbe Rihambi (Lihambe), who also sat on the Liwale land commission.[42] Rebels destroyed the Liwale rubber plantation and plundered its rubber stocks.[43] These early battles of the Maji Maji War showed that rebels had clear targets of attack that intersected with colonial forest and hunting controls.

The center of the war on the Rufiji River was a forest reserve at Utete, which was the site of a hot spring used for trials by ordeal.[44] It is likely that Utete was a distribution point for water medicines used to ensure agricultural and social health and to protect hunters. In April 1905 a land commission declared Utete a forest reserve, specifically encompassing the hot spring.[45] On 3 August, Governor Götzen prohibited African use of the reserve, even as the rebellion was breaking out to the south. In the next few months thousands of rebels led by a renowned hunter based in the forests around Utete engaged German forces in ongoing battles that crossed to the north side of the Rufiji River.[46] They attacked Akida Melicki, who sat on the Utete land commission, and burned down his village of Mayenge. Melicki provided irregular troops to German forces, which together combed the forests north and south of the Rufiji, burning huts and confiscating grain, cassava, and other food to deprive suspected rebels of supplies. Throughout the Rufiji region, coastal forests were simultaneously battlegrounds of the conflict and havens for women, children, and the elderly, whom Germans treated as rebel supporters.

North of the Rufiji, the most prominent Zaramo rebel was Kibasira, a pazi descended from a line of elephant hunters.[47] The forests near Kibasira's village had been mapped as a reserve in 1904, and the nearby

Figure 3.5. German irregulars plunder a forest village during the Maji Maji uprising. From Hans Paasche, *Im Morgenlicht: Kriegs-, Jagd- und Reise-Erlebnisse in Ostafrika.* (Berlin: C. A. Schwetschke und Sohn, 1907), facing p. 118.

upper Rufiji Game Reserve enclosed his ancestral homeland. Africans cited animal depredations emanating from the reserve as a wartime grievance.[48] Another Zaramo arrested as a rebel was Pazi Kitoweo of Msanga, whose village lay near the projected Maneromango forest reserve.[49] Zaramo living around Vikindu Forest also cited grievances over forest and hunting laws as a cause of the uprising.[50] In the far south the picture was much the same. An elder from Lindi District recalled in 1968 that the need to buy elephant hunting permits was one of the incitements to war. Others were angered at the closing of the Lindi mangroves.[51] Southwest toward Songea, hunters were prominent rebel leaders in a region where Governor Götzen had outlawed elephant hunting in 1901.[52]

Throughout southern Tanzania rebels attacked mission stations, which the 1904 forest ordinance had granted extraordinary rights to timber for schools and churches.[53] Mission stations were notorious consumers of timber in their sawmills, and had access to timber that was denied to Africans. They condemned African spiritual use of the forests, and sometimes felled trees considered to be abodes of spirits.[54] In late August 1905 rebels attacked the Benedictine mission at Nyangao in Lindi District, shattering its doors and pulling off its ironwork, probably to be refashioned into weapons, before burning down all the buildings.[55] Missions near the forest reserves outside Dar es Salaam, in contrast, were spared because of the quick and brutal intervention of German forces at the outset of the war.[56]

The commission sent to investigate the causes of the uprising collected testimony verifying that colonial forest and hunting restrictions led people to rebel.[57] It is notable that in Mikindani Subdistrict, which was calm during the war but had recently experienced a serious harvest shortfall, people were able to pay taxes and weather the crisis by collecting rubber and copal in coastal forests that were not yet state reserves.[58] Recognizing the connections between forest and wildlife laws and African discontent, the German government temporarily relaxed the laws in 1906 until the rebellion had been put down.[59]

Following the war, the German government set out to reassert its authority over people and forests. It demanded indemnities from rebel districts that included "fruits of the land . . . especially those of the forest and valuable forest products like rubber and ivory."[60] Refugees from wartime violence occupied the forests, seeking to escape postwar indemnities and a resurgent German development agenda. Germans viewed postwar forest habitation as undermining colonial reconstruction, and they aimed policy at rooting people out of the forests. Maji Maji shaped postwar forest policy by creating a connection in the colonial mind between conservation, development, and social control.

Postwar Forest Policy and the Development Agenda

Following the war, the new German colonial administration pursued a development agenda that included railway expansion, peasant and plantation cash crop promotion, and regulated wage labor, abandoning the outright labor compulsion and forced cash crop production that preceded the war. Governor Albrecht von Rechenberg discouraged continued white settlement while seeking ways to provide concrete benefits to Germany, including revenues to help the colony pay for itself. Scientific forestry played an important role in these objectives. Managed forests would provide the timber and fuel needed for colonial development, offsetting the need for expensive timber imports from Europe. The expansion of plantations created a demand for fuelwood for sisal processing, cotton ginning, and steam tractors. Both the Usambara and Central railways consumed immense quantities of fuelwood as well as timber for railway ties and trestles. Some timber industrialists in Germany recognized a growing shortage of hardwood in Europe, which they hoped to substitute with tropical timber. Reserving forests would furthermore drive out refugees who resisted the development agenda, making their labor power available for colonial pursuits. Working against these goals was a poor German knowledge of the Tanzanian forest landscape and the characteristics of its trees. As forests became more valuable for colonial development, African use was castigated all the more, leading the colonial state to expedite forest reservation.

Rechenberg's administration promulgated a new forest ordinance in 1909 that clarified the state's authority to declare forest reserves and profit from forests and their products, "especially wood, bark, fibers, resin, rubber, leaves, blossoms, and fruits."[61] The 1909 ordinance empowered the state to grant forest concessions and regulate forest use (such as bark extraction or rubber tapping), while requiring that reforestation follow exploitation. The law ended African and missionary rights to free wood from crown lands for domestic use. As seen in the last chapter, this provision elicited widespread protest from rural communities accustomed to such access. Although German policy changes ameliorated labor conditions following the war, they intensified forest policy and the burdens it placed on rural society.

The colonial state also reined in European settler exploitation of the forests with an accompanying forest decree in 1908. Most German settlers had denigrated the East African forests as "unpleasant obstacles to communication and agriculture," and had cut down the forests freely to make way for coffee, cotton, rubber, or sisal plantations.[62] The 1908 ordinance forced planters on estates larger than one hundred hectares to retain all trees less than twenty-five centimeters in diameter and one-fourth of all trees over twenty-five centimeters. New settlers leased land through long-term contracts, which required improvements in the land, including reforestation, before they could own estates outright.[63] Planters were hostile to such provisions and voiced a complaint common among Africans that forests harbored crop-destroying vermin that impaired production.[64] Some, such as the cotton planter Heinrich Otto, resented their inability to expand plantations onto forest land or to use nearby forests freely to fuel their steam tractors.[65] Forest policy, like labor policy, emerged as an arena of conflict between settlers and the Rechenberg regime.

That the state asserted control over the forests did not mean that it opposed their exploitation. The mission of forestry after 1907 was the "rational assessment of all forest products and management of forest income for a continuous source of income for the treasury."[66] Toward this end, the Forest Department contracted private entrepreneurs to set up sawmills near government forests, as it had done since 1900 in the Rufiji mangroves. The major obstacle to a timber industry was the European preference for softwood imports for the bulk of construction. In 1908 German East Africa exported two thousand tonnes of wood of all kinds—mangroves, firewood, blackwood, and timber—worth eighty thousand marks.[67] In the same year the colony imported over two thousand tonnes of wood and wood products worth three hundred thousand marks. This import dependency, and poor financing of the Forest Department, delayed assessments of colonial forests and their timbers. Biological research institutes, including Amani in East Usambara, Kurasini in Dar es Salaam, and Usimbe in the Rufiji Delta, collected seeds and blossoms of indigenous trees and experimented with their regeneration, but it was far easier to plant known profitable exotic tree species—Asian teak, eucalyptus, ironwood—than to learn how to mill and reforest East African hardwoods. Forest academies in Germany also neglected study visits to the African colonies, most of their tropical forest knowledge being derived from Asia, especially the Dutch East Indies. In 1909 the German minister of agriculture, crown lands, and forests lamented that German tropical foresters knew very little about the most common and valuable African timbers, their growth patterns, technical characteristics, and value to either colony or metropole.[68] Equally deficient was knowledge of forest composition, methods of reforestation, climate, biology, and plant diseases. Colonial foresters relied on European techniques of forest regeneration and silviculture but had not mastered the far more diverse African environment.

Germany's lack of demand for tropical timber also hindered colonial forestry. German softwood plantations, and suppliers from eastern Europe, Scandinavia, and the United States, supplied all its needs.[69] Hardwoods from German colonies were expensive, as they incurred export and import tolls and shipping costs over long distances.[70] In 1911 the Colonial Office aimed to change this resistance to using African trees by mandating that government ministries find ways to use colonial timber. The government pressured German pencil manufacturers to substitute East African for American cedar, even though most considered African cedar to be too dense and expensive. The Colonial Office asked the Ministry of Public Works to substitute tropical hardwoods, especially mvule, for walnut, ash, oak and mahogany imported from eastern Europe and the United States.[71] Industrialists informed the Colonial Office that most imported African mahogany and mvule came from non-German colonies in West Africa. With the European market all but cut off, German East African officials hoped to market their timber in South Africa for construction, mine shoring, and railway ties, but could not compete with Indonesian hardwoods or Baltic and North American pines, which were cheaper to transport over long distances because of their lighter weight.[72] These problems meant that German East Africa had to be its own market if scientific forestry were to pay for itself.

The East African Railway Corporation (OAEG) was a major consumer of timber for ties, bridges, trestles, and fuelwood, enabling the Forest Department to accrue revenues to maintain forest reserves through reforestation, silviculture, and protection. Altogether Germans ran 120 locomotives on the Central Railway, and after 1910 some sixty new locomotives all consumed wood instead of imported coal.[73] The railway used a combination of imported steel and local wood for its ties, and the reconstruction of the Dar es Salaam–Morogoro branch after 1912 used only East African timber for its ties.[74] The extension of the Central Railway allowed the Forest Department to exploit timber stands far from the coast, while timber provided the railway with the traffic needed to make it a viable economic enterprise.

Despite their mutual interests, the relationship between forestry and railway development was sometimes antagonistic. The Forest Department was often unable to supply sufficient timber and fuel to the railway. The OAEG therefore asserted its right to forests along the railway, contracting Africans to work these forests in ways that the Forest Department considered to be destructive.[75] The Forest Department had to stay a jump ahead of the railway as it pushed inland, reserving forest parcels before the OAEG claimed prior rights.[76] Forest reservation in Dar es Salaam District after 1907 thus concentrated on parcels along the route of the railway, rather than outlying forests important for water catchment. In 1910 the department marked four reserves along the railway line at set intervals and interspersed so as to allow the OAEG access to forests and woodlands in between.[77] The department disputed the OAEG's rights over Pande Forest, on the coast in the Kunduchi *akidat* (subdistrict), arguing that wood cutting in Pande endangered water supplies in Dar es Salaam, created a flood risk and impaired the region's agriculture. Although the government relinquished control over Pande, it invoked the 1908 forest ordinance that prohibited wood to be cut in the forest for the common good.[78] In the rest of Dar es Salaam District the Forest Department created only three other forest reserves after Maji Maji, demonstrating the degree that railway policy shaped patterns of forest management in the central coastal hinterland.

Forest Reservation as Counterinsurgency

In southeastern Tanzania the legacy of the Maji Maji War led colonial officials to use forest reservation as a tool for social transformation, discipline, and counterinsurgency.[79] The continuing refugee occupation of the forests in a region targeted for a peasant cotton campaign, the ongoing need to convert peasants into wage laborers for work of all sorts, and the lingering fear that the forests were used as spiritual grounding for a future rebellion intersected with the "science" of forestry and the economic goals of colonialism. Between 1907 and 1914 foresters reserved seven new coastal forests in Lindi District, four in Kilwa District, and nineteen in Rufiji District.[80] Although many of these forests protected water catchments and contained valuable timber, the German administration was scarcely able to manage them effectively, owing to insufficient personnel, a general labor shortage, and a poor knowledge of their timbers. The main goal of these reserves was to bolster colonial authority in the eyes of subjugated peasants.

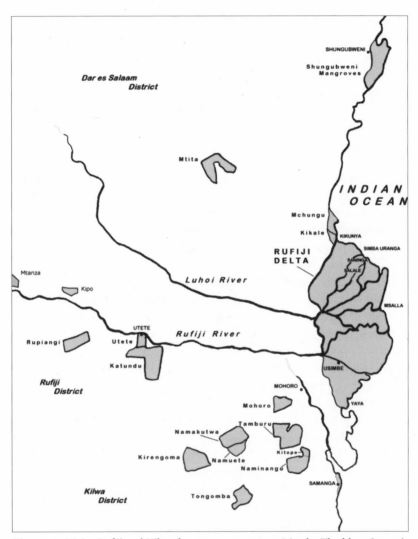

Figure 3.6. Major Rufiji and Kilwa forest reserves, c. 1914. Map by Thaddeus Sunseri.

Many forests that were reserved in Rufiji District had served a spiritual role for Maji Maji rebels. This was true of Mpanga Forest, on the upper Rufiji far from German centers of control and not of particular significance as a water catchment or as a source of timber. Germans believed that a hot spring north of Mpanga had been the main source of maji medicine.[81] Mpanga furthermore lay at the intersection of three districts of rebellion (Mahenge, Rufiji, Morogoro) and therefore was a colonial

Grenzwildnis (frontier) whose isolation made it favorable for rebel organizing. Germans first declared crown land on both sides of the Rufiji at Pangani Falls in 1905, but the war delayed creation of the forest reserve until 1910. Thereafter debates ensued about the use of the reserve and its environs. The upper Rufiji wildlife reserve dominated the north bank, where East African officials planned an electricity generator and a hotel for tourists to view the "wild romantic beauty of the Pangani Falls," perhaps influenced by British plans to develop Victoria Falls for tourism.[82] Against these plans for development, the Prussian State Office for the Protection of Natural Monuments moved to declare a nature park over the falls. Of these plans, only Mpanga Forest and the Rufiji wildlife reserve survived World War I.

Foresters took over other "spirit" forests as reserves, and new declarations omitted villagers' rights to tend ancestral graves in the reserves. In 1911 a land commission declared Mtondo Forest, near Mohoro, as a reserve, although it protected no water catchment and was clearly part of peasant farming systems.[83] On the eve of the war Mtondo had been an active site of medicine distribution and *ngoma* (dance) rituals that people used to ensure agricultural fertility. District officials increased the extent of Utete Forest Reserve in 1914, whose hot spring was a probable site of maji distribution during the war. A further suspected source of maji medicine was a cave complex located in the Matumbi hills near Ngarambe, which was capable of hiding several thousand people and possessed a permanent source of water.[84] In 1912 the central government directed that the cave be declared crown land, presumably because its immense amounts of guano could be marketed as fertilizer, although published reports at the time identified it as a rebel hideout.[85] World War I delayed its declaration until the 1950s when, under British rule, it was gazetted as Mbinga Forest Reserve.

A major goal of forestry following Maji Maji was to force villagers out of the forests, channel them into colonial pursuits, and deprive them of future bases of insurgency.[86] Colonial foresters took over Kipo and Mtanza forests, on the north bank of the Rufiji, between 1908 and 1910, which had been areas of intense fighting and peasant refuge during Maji Maji.[87] In 1911 foresters demarcated a vast highland forest complex along the Rufiji-Kilwa border as Namuete, Nerumba, Kumbi, and Nandunda forest reserves.[88] Incorporating nine forested mountains surrounded by settlements that had been used as a refuge during the rebellion, the forest declarations forced people to resettle along open roads under colonial control. This pattern continued in Kilwa District, where the Kibata station chief, Albert Thurmann, who led the German forces against Maji Maji rebels around Liwale, marked out forest reserves.[89] A policeman rather than a trained forester, Thurmann reserved forest parcels that were battlegrounds during the war, including Kitope, Kisangi, and Tongomba forests.[90] District officials mapped Rondo Forest in Lindi District before Maji Maji, but did not declare it as a reserve until 1910, by which time it was well known as a wartime rebel assembly point.[91] A German report cited the uncompensated eviction of villagers from Rondo Forest as a cause of the rebellion in Lindi District. Although forest reservation aimed to empty forests and thereby make them safe, they continued to be suspicious places. In 1913, for example, Rufiji planters claimed that African conspirators used the forest reserves of the Rufiji-Kilwa border region to plan another rebellion, which the quick action of the district office prevented.[92]

Colonial officials rewarded loyal African headmen by granting them rubber concessions in forest reserves, showing that the postwar development agenda did not exclude the economy of extraction. Jumbe Timtim bin Giay of Marendego, who sat on the land commission that created Tamburu Forest Reserve in 1912, received a concession to tap rubber in the reserve.[93] At least five other headmen profited from rubber concessions in forest reserves in the Matumbi hills.[94] Occasionally forest protocols granted local villagers and their descendants subsistence wood rights in forest reserves.[95] Even though Pindiro Forest had been an area of intense wartime conflict, the Kilwa district office opposed making it into a reserve, believing that local prosperity and peace depended on peasants farming and tapping rubber in the forest.[96] Yet the central government demanded that Pindiro be declared crown land "as soon as possible" owing to fears that the border region was a refuge for unruly vagabonds who avoided labor and taxes, hunted without licenses, and plotted another rebellion.[97]

Working the Forest Reserves of the Coastal Hinterland

Even though the Forest Department reserved only 1 percent of the landscape of German East Africa as forests by 1914, that was far more than it was able to manage. Scientific forestry demanded capital and labor to demarcate forest boundaries; to police forests against wood theft, game poaching, and illegal incursions; to identify timber for exploitation; and to reforest cut parcels. It needed workers to cut firebreaks around each reserve, weed them at least once annually to prevent field fires from jumping their borders, and fell trees and transport timber to sawmills. Forestry was a labor-intensive enterprise in a colony short of people, where fear of another rebellion made colonialists reluctant to use too much force.

The Forest Department itself lacked sufficient trained personnel for such a large territory. In 1910 seventeen European foresters, seventy-five African forest rangers, and ten forest police oversaw about three hundred thousand hectares of reserves, an extent that more than doubled by 1914.[98] Most European foresters were assigned to the northeast highlands, where the dense rain forests, more workable softwood species, and greater concentration of sawmills allowed for a more familiar European model of scientific forestry.[99] The coastal hinterland, divided between the Dar es Salaam forest office (including Dar es Salaam, Bagamoyo, Morogoro, and Dodoma districts) and the Rufiji forest office (overseeing Rufiji, Kilwa, and Lindi districts) had just a handful of trained foresters and African rangers.[100] Only eleven African rangers oversaw forty reserves in Rufiji, Kilwa, and Lindi districts.

The main task of German foresters was to identify closed stands that encompassed watersheds or that had rubber or valuable timber in sufficient concentrations for eventual exploitation. They marked reserves with stone or cement beacons, cut firebreaks, and sometimes planted exotic trees on forest borders. They recruited and oversaw labor for these tasks, enlisting local headmen to mobilize their people, often as a corvée obligation.

On a daily basis, African forest rangers were the main faces of colonial authority. Dressed in the uniform of a policeman (*askari*)—khaki, a black belt, and a red fez with the German eagle—and armed with the forester's marking ax, they patrolled the reserves against prohibited use or peasant field burning near forest stands.[101] They checked that people had permits for any wood use, even outside reserves, often in a heavy-handed manner. Yet a paucity of rangers meant that oversight was sporadic and transgressions were frequent. The two rangers of Rufiji District were preoccupied with the trial tree plantation at Mohoro and guarding the borders of the Mohoro Forest Reserve, all but ignoring twenty inland reserves. Two of the four rangers in Kilwa District oversaw the Denhardt mangrove bark concession, while the other two managed the Liwale rubber forest. In the absence of rangers, forest protocols required that headmen guard reserves against violations.

The most arduous task of forestry was to cut and maintain firebreaks around reserves to protect trees from peasant field fires during the dry season. After Maji Maji the government suspended the prewar ban on peasant field burning, which peasants had cited as a cause of rebellion. As a result it was necessary to cut firebreaks five to seven meters wide around reserves, except where watercourses formed natural borders.[102] In 1912 field fires burned through the unprotected Namakutwa Forest Reserve, while firebreaks saved the neighboring Namuete and Tamburu forests. Yet even protected forests were vulnerable to field fires, as happened when a fire that spread from a farmer burning weeds around his mango trees in a high wind ignited and destroyed the entire Mohoro teak planta-tion.[103] In 1910 district officials sentenced a woman to one month in chains for negligent arson after starting a fire in the Kurasini Forest Reserve, near Dar es Salaam.[104] Maintaining firebreaks was expensive. The Rufiji forest office paid almost a thousand rupees in 1911 just to cut firebreaks. The 2,350-hectare Mohoro Forest Reserve, one of the smallest in the coastal hinterland, had a twenty-kilometer border that took fifty people ten days to clear. It was necessary to recut firebreaks annually and patrol them frequently against illicit field burning.

Rufiji officials timed tax collection to coincide with the labor needs of the forest office. They pressured headmen to muster casual workers for the unpopular forest work, which was low paying, extremely ardu-ous, and dirty. Four days of backbreaking labor earned only one rupee, about half the wage rate of plantation work that also included a food ration. It is likely that women were the primary workers for cutting firebreaks, as they predominated as casual laborers and did similar work on the few Rufiji-Kilwa cotton plantations; most able-bodied men worked for higher wages in other parts of the colony. Yet forest work conflicted with planting time on household fields. In the absence of ca-sual workers, the Mohoro forest office used a handful of penal laborers for its trial tree plantation.[105] The high cost of forestry in a territory lacking sufficient labor meant that most forest reserves went unprotected and unworked.

In most of the coastal hinterland, lack of capital and labor meant that foresters were unable to harvest and replant economic tree species in long-term rotations, which was the basic task of forestry. They focused their efforts at silviculture on the Rufiji Delta mangroves (see chapter 2) and exotics on the Mohoro and Kurasini trial plantations. This meant that more trees were cut down under state auspices than could be re-planted, making some regions, such as the outskirts of Dar es Salaam or the line of the Central Railway, noticeably deforested.[106]

Insurgent Peasants in the Coastal Forests

Colonial forestry was a burdensome intrusion into the peasant economy and culture.[107] It undermined the central role of chiefs in presiding over circumcision rituals and honoring ancestors buried in forest reserves, transforming them instead into agents of the state. Because officials deemed spirit mediums to have inspired Maji Maji, they separated them from their forest shrines through reservation.[108] Peasants often complained that they lacked building poles and fuelwood for basic subsistence. Along the Rufiji it was difficult to make the dugout canoes needed to traverse the river and floodplain. The strict ban on using fire in forests thwarted wax and honey collection. Forestry prevented villagers from collecting medicines and roots, mushrooms, fruits, and insects, which were used as famine foods.[109] Only colonial elites obtained concessions to collect rubber and earn cash, while copal digging was a thing of the past. Corvée labor to cut forest borders conflicted with subsistence farming. Forest reserves hemmed in villagers, preventing them from expanding their farmland in natural rotations.[110] Forests harbored crop predators and other animals that killed people. Despite the validity of these grievances, colonial officials concluded that "the discomforts caused by the forest reserves must be borne for the common good."[111]

These circumstances meant that resisting scientific forestry was a matter of survival. Avoiding outright rebellion after 1907, peasants nevertheless attacked forestry in complex ways. They sometimes removed or destroyed forest border markers, encumbering the Forest Department with additional costs and limiting its reach. Arson was an ideal weapon of resistance, since it was largely anonymous and difficult to verify as either intentional or negligent. The Kilwa penal records for 1908–9 include seven cases of arson, without detailing their circumstances.[112] In 1909 fire that authorities believed was "premeditated arson" hit Kipo Forest, on the north bank of the Rufiji River.[113] A Maji Maji battleground and haven, the creation of the twenty-five-hundred-hectare Kipo Reserve left only eighty hectares for peasants. In 1911 Rufiji officials reported that "in the last year no forest reserve has been completely protected from fire. Some of these fires originated outside the reserves and jumped into the forests, but others seem to be premeditated or set negligently inside the forests, yet we have been unable to capture any malefactor."[114]

Less dramatic were peasant violations of forest borders by grazing livestock, clearing fields, hunting for honey or beeswax, and poaching wood. In 1910 a lone woman was found living and farming in Sachsen-wald Forest, outside Dar es Salaam, and was evicted after a reprimand.[115] In Bunduki Forest Reserve of Morogoro District in 1910 officials convicted six men, three women, and one child for setting fires negligently near the forest, fining them each one rupee or one day of labor in chains. In 1911 officials fined thirty-five people two rupees each for farming in the forest reserve.[116] This included fining a twelve-year-old child two rupees and one day in chains for grazing goats in the forest's firebreak.

Peasants resisted the colonial forest agenda most effectively by refus-ing forest work.[117] The Forest Department lacked labor for all aspects of scientific forestry. Contracted forest workers often deserted the work site for jobs on plantations or railways, or demanded pay increases when they saw better opportunities elsewhere.[118] The Denhardt mangrove conces-sions were chronically crippled by lack of labor.[119] Casual forest workers neglected to show up when their household fields needed tending, and some people refused to do corvée work on forest roads.[120] The Forest De-partment never overcame its "burning labor question."[121]

At the end of German rule much had been achieved in the direction of scientific forestry.[122] The Forest Department had identified some 250 for-est reserves and had begun demarcating their borders. German foresters identified a few African tree species that had a market value, even though they favored more familiar, marketable Asian exotics. Africans learned that the colonial state and its surrogates, not their own chiefs or ancestral spirits, now had authority over trees and forest products, even outside forest reserves. Peasants understood that they would be called upon an-nually to do corvée forest labor and that they risked fines or imprison-ment if their field fires jumped into forest reserves. Missionaries taught that "spirit trees" were proper targets of the ax and the saw, and forest rangers harassed people who entered reserves to make offerings to ances-tors.[123] Sawmills competed with the ax as a means of forest exploitation. An entirely new discourse had emerged that viewed the forests as cultur-ally dead but economically valuable domains under colonial authority.

Yet it would be incorrect to reify the power of the state, capital, and colonial science as forces capable of transforming forest relations accord-ing to the European template. African-organized resistance and day-to-day struggles shaped colonial forestry in concrete ways that preserved some rural autonomy. Forest laborers remained insurgent and undisci-plined. Forestry's goal of remaking the Tanzanian landscape into one conducive to European settlement died with the Maji Maji War, and the state even reined in settler exploitation of the forests after their role in the colonial economy was devalued. Although foresters had reserved virtually all rain forests and dryland canopy forests at the end of German rule, these amounted to only 1 percent of the total landscape, and most remained terrae incognitae. Germans made no effort to reserve as forests the approximately 50 percent of the land that was miombo woodland. Colonial knowledge of African trees—their names, locations, characteristics, growing patterns, and uses—was fragmentary at best. Finally, Germans failed to end the use of forest reserves as sanctuaries from the colonial development agenda or as places of cultural grounding. Elders in the coastal hinterland in 2004 could still point to ancestral shrines in forest reserves that were a reminder of the cultural centrality that the forests once had.[124]

CHAPTER 4

State Forestry in a Colonial Backwater, 1920–40

IN 1933, Yusuf Mlanzi cut down a *mninga* tree to make a "fancy bed and table legs."[1] Because mninga was a first-schedule species, protected on account of its high value, Mlanzi needed a permit to cut it, even outside forest reserves. Mlanzi refused to tell the African forest guard who apprehended him where he felled the tree, creating suspicion that he cut it in a forest reserve, which would make it a more a serious offense. The Rufiji district forester suspected that Mlanzi intended to sell the furniture and demanded that the district office fine him heavily for wood theft. The magistrate refused to prosecute, arguing that it was not proven that the furniture was meant to be sold and that Mlanzi, like all Africans, had a right to wood for household use. Since Mlanzi lived 160 kilometers by footpath and canoe from the forest station at Salale, the magistrate ruled that obtaining a wood permit, even though it was free, was unduly burdensome, and dismissed the case.[2] This decision confirmed an ongoing suspicion of colonial foresters in Tanganyika that political officers did not take forest infractions seriously. As a result, "the local natives make a laugh of it and boast how easy it is for them to get off with theft of poles and Timber."

The Mlanzi case shows that the forestry agenda under British rule in Tanganyika often clashed with administrative priorities that included trade in forest and agricultural commodities and the incorporation of Africans into the colonial state as taxpayers. In theory forestry shared these goals, its principal task being to identify marketable tree species to be harvested and reforested on long-term rotations.[3] Moreover, as a supplement to agriculture, forestry had a mandate to protect watercourses and moderate the climate. The rise of ecology as a science during the interwar years bolstered this mandate, as scientists learned of the connections between plants, soils, insects, animals, and people.[4] "Trees are the soil makers," wrote the chairman of the Empire Forestry Association. "It follows that afforestation may be used as a means of refertilizing lands which have become exhausted."[5] Yet during the interwar years, the lofty as well as base material goals of forestry in Tanganyika were unrealized. Tanganyikan timbers failed to find a wide international market, depriving the Forest Department of revenues needed to expand its activities. While forest and political officials alike wanted to move Africans out of forests and integrate them into the colonial economy, they clashed over forestry's opposition to independent African use of forest products, which administrators saw as a means for Africans to pay taxes and contribute to export revenues. Africans exploited these divisions in government to return to the forests to farm and to extract natural products, especially copal, poles, timber, and fuelwood. Especially after the Great Depression impaired colonial revenues, administrators encouraged actions that foresters viewed as insurgent.

Although the revival of copal extraction suggests a return to precolonial patterns of African forest use, peasant innovators—men and women—whose obeisance to chiefly authority had eroded after several decades of colonial rule, spearheaded the new forest economy. Characteristic of this new generation were African pitsawyers, who penetrated the recesses of the landscape in search of marketable timbers that could be sold in colonial towns. While some of these men were local, and subject to Native Authority bylaws, most roved the land like elephant hunters of old, not bound by the reverential awe with which the forests were once regarded and initially encouraged by colonial foresters seeking to open up the vast woodlands for colonial benefit. Pitsawyers and other peasants, such as Yusuf Mlanzi, demonstrated an insurgent individualism in their use of the forests, seeking to supplement farming with marketable products of the forests. The Forest Department's response to this challenge was to create Native Authority forests as an additional layer of social control. Yet interwar forest use in Tanganyika demonstrates the limits of imperial forestry, indeed of imperial science in general, operating in a periphery of the British Empire at a time of world economic instability. This weakness enabled Africans to return to the forests in order to survive the burdens of colonialism.

World War I and Tanganyikan Forestry

British rule in Tanganyika began with a German forestry template on maps and in files, but not on the ground. World War I erased the German structure of forest controls and inflicted tremendous violence and economic and social burdens on Africans, leading many to use the forests for refuge and survival. The coastal hinterland forests were wartime battlegrounds and material resources. The German strategy of tying down British forces by eluding capture meant in large part occupying forests and woodlands in order to fight a guerrilla war. The dense forested hills of Rufiji and Kilwa districts were ideal for this strategy. By December 1916, German forces had encamped at the district station of Kibata, then moved through the forests toward the Rufiji to avoid British encirclement.[6] With tens of thousands of British and German troops occupying the region, food was in short supply, exacerbated by prolonged rains and Rufiji floods between January and May 1917. Both sides scoured the region for food, including crops in the field and game meat, forcing villagers to use the forests for famine food such as roots, wild fruits, and mushrooms. Bubonic plague hit the region at the outset of the war and meningitis swept the region in 1916.[7] Forced conscription of some fifteen thousand porters and bombardment of villages along battlefronts drove villagers away from roadways and river valleys into the recesses of the landscape to survive as best as they could for the duration of the war.[8] British officials struggled after the war to draw people out of the forests, as the Germans had after the Maji Maji War.

The war left the Tanganyikan forests in a sorry state. First Germans, then the British, denuded the Sachsenwald and Pugu forests and nearby mangroves outside Dar es Salaam for town defenses and steamship fuel. They cut wood along the Central Railway to rebuild trestles, to supply ties, and to fuel locomotives.[9] Tens of thousands of soldiers and porters extracted poles and firewood for temporary housing and cooking fuel.

Combatants took wood for trenches and cut paths through forests to make way for motorized transport.[10]

At the level of imperial policy, the war led many to conclude that the world was on the verge of a "timber famine."[11] This affected the British particularly, whose country had few forests after generations of industrial exploitation and a poor forestry infrastructure. Overseas timber sources accounted for 95 percent of Britain's wartime needs.[12] This dependency continued after the war. In 1926 Britain imported £56,000,000 worth of timber, only one-fifth of which came from the empire.[13] In order to address these ongoing shortages, the government created a Forestry Commission to reforest Britain and to secure timber supplies overseas.[14] In 1920 the first Empire Forestry Conference inaugurated the Imperial Forestry Institute at Oxford to coordinate empirewide forest management and prepare for the possibility of another national emergency.[15] This imperial and metropolitan focus substituted the hegemony of British scientists and foresters over colonial forests for the authority of African chiefs.

The British, like other Europeans, had become dependent on softwoods for their domestic timber needs. Softwoods made up 80 percent of the world's sawed timber and 90 percent of British timber imports.[16] The world's so-called timber famine thus created no immediate market for Tanganyikan hardwoods, preventing the revenues needed to pay for forest management. The bulk of imported European hardwoods were North American oak and Asian teak, with little African mahogany and mvule. African hardwoods that found a European market originated in British and French West African colonies.[17] Tanganyika's peripheral location challenged British foresters to create a market for its hardwood timbers, which was a prerequisite for forest reserve expansion.

Reserving and Unreserving Tanganyikan Forests

Building on the prewar German template, the British created a Forest Department in Tanganyika in 1920, staffed with eleven European foresters and one hundred African forest guards, fewer than the forestry personnel at the end of German rule.[18] The conservator of forests, D. K. S. Grant, concluded that wartime devastation had rendered some German-era forest reserves unviable, with little usable timber, while elsewhere Germans had overlooked forests that should be reserved. In 1923 about 230 German-era forest reserves encompassed approximately 1 million hectares, just 1 percent of the landscape. Grant accepted that these reserves protected most water catchments but decried that German foresters had done little in the way of reforestation and silviculture.[19] He lamented that only 36 percent of the forest estate had marketable trees. The immediate goal was therefore to harvest the overmature trees rapidly and replace them with "more economic species," especially Asian teak and other exotics. Economic priorities meant that foresters focused on mangroves and forests along transport and railway routes and near towns. Successful exploitation depended on private sawmills. In 1926 there were only five commercial sawmills in Tanganyika, all located in the cedar forests of the northeastern highlands.[20] Foresters and commercial millers saw little profit in lowland forests and woodlands, creating space for Africans to reassert their own use.

With these considerations in mind, British foresters reassessed the inherited map of forest reserves, taking into account wartime encroachment, economic potential, and colonial development priorities. Forest personnel were insufficient to manage all existing reserves, so the department focused on those with known marketable timber. The 1920s therefore saw the excision of reserves if they were deficient in timber, if they had potential for cash crop production, or if peasant opposition was strong.[21] The overall extent of forest reserves decreased between 1923 and 1926 and increased modestly until 1931. The department retained on paper some reserves that existed in name only. British foresters also reserved some closed forests that the Germans had overlooked. When the reshuffling was over, by World War II the total extent of the forest estate had barely changed.

Forest reservation in Rufiji and Kilwa districts illustrates the interwar patterns. The economic importance of the mangroves led the Forest Department to concentrate on the coast, neglecting most of the twenty-seven inland forest reserves. In 1925 the chief secretary underreported, "There are twenty-one Forest Reserves outside the Delta. . . . I have toured through most of them and have not yet discovered anything worth preserving as Forest."[22] In 1934 the Rufiji district office recorded only fourteen forest reserves, and foresters did not even know many of their names. In the 1930s fire damaged most of the coastal forests because foresters could afford to maintain firebreaks only in reserves closest to the Rufiji Delta.[23] This neglect stemmed from the conclusion that the coastal forests had "not much timber of commercial value."[24] Furthermore, as under German rule, transport was difficult, workers were expensive and scarce, and it was cheaper to grant private concessions to exploit marketable products like mpingo, mangrove poles, and bark than to finance regulated forestry.

Africans took advantage of this neglect by breaching the boundaries of forest reserves, often seeking more land for cultivation. In Kilwa District, for example, villagers requested permission to farm in Tongomba Forest Reserve. The district officer agreed that the reserve hemmed in the people and that it was "imperative that these people should be allowed more land for cultivation purposes."[25] He feared that the villagers would move away if they didn't have adequate land, which would undermine efforts to amalgamate villagers close to the district station at Kibata. The conservator of forests acceded to the decision, transferring 122 hectares of Tongomba Forest to the village.[26]

African elites were caught between the popular interest in returning to the forests and the government's desire to use land and forests for market production. After 1926 British policy in Tanganyika was to create African native authorities with local legislative, administrative, and judicial powers under colonial supervision.[27] In theory native authorities (NAs) had historical legitimacy as descendants of clan and lineage founders, thus wielded authority over people, land, and forests. In reality the British engineered rural societies in thoroughly artificial ways, lumping people together based on their understanding of past histories, language affinities, and residence patterns, creating local structures of power that often evoked popular opposition. In place of the mapazi chiefs of old in Uzaramo, for example, the British created eleven *wanyemzi* (executive officials), each with authority over an "arbitrarily fixed geographical division" that had no local legitimacy.[28] In Rufiji District they reconstructed chiefly authority three times in the interwar years, ending with eighteen *watawala* (chiefs) after 1933 presiding over some two hundred majumbe (headmen).[29] NAs enforced burdensome colonial policies, including mandatory cash cropping and wage labor, population removals, and prohibitions on forest or tree use. These authorities acted as "local foresters," prohibiting use of scheduled trees and mustering people to cut firebreaks, fight forest fires, or build forest roads.

Understanding their precarious position, native authorities looked for ways to increase their popularity by couching reform in language that addressed the colonial agenda. In 1936 the headmen of Liwale and Makata towns requested the abolition of the Liwale Forest Reserve.[30] They argued that more land was needed for cash crops, and that they desired to "link up their two countries near District Headquarters," both of which were colonial priorities. District officials agreed with local people that the reserve's original purpose had been to expand a German rubber plantation, since the forest had no timber of fiscal value.[31] Despite arguing just a few years earlier that the forest was needed to protect the Liwale River and valuable mvule trees, the conservator of forests assented to the excision in order to encourage development, trade, and village amalgamation, a decision that was met with "much local satisfaction."[32] Popular pressure led to the elimination of reserves elsewhere in the coastal hinterland. In Lindi District the conservator excised the 3,077-hectare Nagapemba Forest and the 12,146-hectare Ruangwa Forest. He acknowledged that land shortages made it necessary for peasants to farm in the reserves in order to contribute to the colonial priority of growing marketable cash crops.[33]

Although the total forest estate declined in the coastal hinterland, elsewhere in Tanganyika foresters marked out new reserves for reasons that included protection of water catchments, prevention of soil erosion, countering peasant or pastoralist encroachment, combating sleeping sickness, and the desire to exploit timber. Yet Tanganyikan forest reserves increased by only about 80,000 hectares by 1940, while another 300,000 hectares "awaited reservation" at the outset of World War II as part of a ten-year forestry development plan.[34] Colonial officials created Native Authority (or clan) forest reserves between the two world wars to bolster the power of chiefs. This was done by preserving small sacred forests that had local spiritual or rainmaking significance.[35] They surrounded these with tree plantations meant to provide fuel and poles for village needs and keep peasants out of state forests.[36] Chiefs required villagers to cut firebreaks around plantations, to fight forest fires, and to plant and tend exotic trees. Peasants viewed "government trees"—exotics such as eucalyptus, ironwood, and black wattle (*Acacia mearnsii,* harvested for its tannins)—as a prelude to the loss of farm land to forest reserve expansion.[37] NA forests grew outward from state forest reserves, creating buffer zones that displaced peasants from forest fringes.[38] In some localities foresters required that peasants plant exotics in their fields as part of onerous antierosion schemes. These policies and perceptions made NA reserves, which peasants called *mashamba ya bwana* (the King's plantations), highly unpopular, as seen in frequent arson attacks. Such opposition and unpopularity slowed development of NA forests. In 1937 there were only 27,750 hectares of NA forests, only 2.5 percent of all reserves. By then the Forest Department had all but abandoned the NA forest experiment, concluding that chiefs "showed little sense of duty in managing or conserving natural forests."[39]

Forest Crimes and Protected Trees

The Tanganyikan Forest Department moved beyond German-era forestry by categorizing marketable tree species as protected or "scheduled" trees. By making it illegal to cut down scheduled trees without a permit in and outside of forest reserves, the Forest Department extended its authority onto peasant lands for the first time.[40] Although anyone could cut unscheduled trees outside of reserves for household use or to clear land, a permit and royalty was required if they were sold.[41] Each year the Forest Department scheduled new trees based mainly on market value, extending its authority progressively. The most prized hardwood timber trees were mvule and mninga, which grew in the coastal forests, woodlands, and in the Eastern Arc rain forests.[42] Both were teaklike hardwoods, valued for construction and furniture because they were strong, durable, resistant to shrinking and warping, and easy to work. Colonial foresters encouraged the commercial exploitation of mvule and mninga by offering private concessions, but they found few takers because these trees were scattered across the landscape, far from roads or railways, making them unprofitable to extract. Mninga rarely exceeded twenty-five mature trees per square kilometer, and sustainable exploitation, which prevented overcutting or the felling of immature trees, decreased the yield to scarcely one tree per square kilometer annually.

Besides the colonywide schedule of protected trees, district and Native Authority bylaws protected trees locally. In Liwale Subdistrict a permit was needed to cut mpingo, mninga, msandarusi, *mbarikwa, mtondo,* and miombo, the last being the most common woodlands tree genus. Local tree schedules therefore empowered administrative officers to shape farming patterns and to circumscribe settlement on lands outside forest reserves. Although growing cash crops was a higher priority than protecting scheduled trees, peasants were often caught between the colonial demand to plant more crops and forest rules that protected specific trees. In Kilwa District mninga grew on land that peasants considered particularly fertile.[43] The protected *mnepa* tree grew too profusely for peasants to clear their fields adequately. Scheduled trees created overlapping authority between the Forest Department, administrative officers, and headmen, confusing local power dynamics. Farmers constantly had to seek permission from colonial elites as to where they could plant crops. As a result, many peasants moved away from administrative towns or roadways, where they could ignore tree schedules and other burdensome colonial laws.

Scheduling trees created a new framework for criminalizing behavior. Most of the evidence for African illicit tree cutting shows this activity along the Central Railway, where scheduled trees were most accessible and marketable. Most forest offenses included cutting or burning scheduled trees without permits in order to clear land for agriculture or grazing, with just a handful of perpetrators selling the timber.[44] Of eighty-three cases of illegal tree cutting in Dar es Salaam District in 1930, virtually all involved one species, mvule.[45]

Pitsawyers and the Opening of the Miombo Woodlands

Recognizing the growing importance of mvule and mninga for Tanganyikan construction and revenues, British foresters reassessed the woodlands where many scheduled trees grew. Named for the dominant tree genus, miombo (*Brachystegia* spp.), these woodlands made up as much as half of Tanganyika, and a far greater percentage of the coastal hinterland. Woodlands are a savanna landscape, where a single rainy season brings 75 to 100 centimeters of rain, followed by a four-to-six-month dry season.[46] Miombo woodlands are covered with a tree canopy of between 20 and 60 percent that rarely exceeds fifteen meters in height. They transform from a "forest of the freshest green carpeted with legions of flowers" in the rainy season to a leafless scrubby landscape punctuated by grasslands in the dry season.[47] Miombo seeds require fire cracking to germinate and therefore have adapted to hunters' and farmers' use of fire over thousands of years. The shallow, acidic, and nutrient-leached woodlands soils are unsuitable for sedentary, intensive farming. Woodlands farmers therefore favored dispersed dry lands or river valleys for their fields. German and British foresters rejected miombo as forest because of its partial tree cover, because of its dearth of marketable trees, and because it harbored the tsetse fly, a vector of sleeping sickness, which killed cattle and prevented plow agriculture.[48] Conservator Grant wrote of miombo woodlands in 1924 that "their merchantable timber is scattered to such an extent that the savannah cannot be considered at all from a forestry point of view."[49] Yet by the late 1920s ecologists began to view miombo as part of a forest succession that, if separated from people, would reach a climax as closed forests.[50] However, in the interwar years the colonial obsession with sleeping sickness was a far more powerful landscape priority, which saw woodlands as a development threat to be eradicated or separated from people.

With commercial sawmillers reluctant to operate in the woodlands, the Forest Department turned to African pitsawyers. During the 1930s, when many sawmills suspended operations due to the Depression, pitsawyers were the sole timber suppliers in many regions. Pitsawyers first emerged when Europeans introduced hand saws (*misumeno,* lit., tooth knives) into East Africa at mission stations, administrative posts, and on plantations. Saws cut boards and beams for European houses, while African rafter-and-pole houses relied on axes.[51] Saws gave a more even and uniform cut with less wood wastage than axes—used, for example, to split planks for dhow construction. Railway construction made pitsawing into a specialized profession when engineers contracted tasks to teams of workers under their own leaders. These teams, called *vyama* (sing. *chama*), searched the landscape for suitable trees for ties or trestles. In the coastal hinterland these were hardwoods like mninga, whose density required that they be sawed into boards before being carried to the railway for collection. Sawyers did this by digging a pit below a felled tree, supported by crossbeams on which the tree rested. Using a two-handled saw, one man stood in the pit and pulled downward, while his partner stood atop the log and pulled upward, directing the blade into premeasured niches for a

Figure 4.1. Mission carpentry shop, German East Africa. From Heinrich Schnee, *German Colonization: Past and Future* (Port Washington, N.Y.: Kennikat Press, 1926), facing p. 160.

Figure 4.2. Pitsawyers, German East Africa, c. 1910.

uniform cut, working it free whenever it became stuck. Hardwood sawing was especially arduous, requiring pairs of sawyers to take turns. As town
construction demanded sawed timber, Indians and Greeks responded as
lumber entrepreneurs who contracted pitsawing teams. With the increase
of colonial roads in the interwar years, they invested in trucks to pick up
sawed lumber ever further from trunk roads, opening up the woodlands
to greater exploitation.

Despite creating value in otherwise despised woodlands, foresters saw pitsawyers as a necessary evil and temporary expediency. Pitsawed timber was satisfactory for the domestic market, but its uneven cut and lack of seasoning made it unsuitable for export.[52] By the late 1930s, when there was an emergent export demand for mninga and mvule, foresters feared that pitsawed timber would damage the overseas reputation of Tanganyikan timbers. Mvule exports rose from 14.5 tonnes in 1932 to 772 tonnes in 1936. By that time the Forest Department had painted a negative picture of pitsawyers: "[They] have little or no capital at stake, operate in remote and widely scattered localities in the bush; mostly produce inaccurately sawn and unseasoned timber and, it is feared, are often not too scrupulous in adhering to the terms of their licenses. They are content with the minimum of profit and become most active when timber prices show a temporary rise. They undercut the capitalized and reputable sawmiller, who is finding disposal of his second grade lumber already difficult enough."[53] That year the department curtailed casual-tree-cutting licenses in order to assert greater control over timber exploitation. Yet the subsequent boom in gold mining at Lupa and Geita, and increased demand for timber and fuel created by World War II, suddenly enhanced the value of marginal timber, making forestry dependent on pitsawyers well into the 1950s.

Debating Peasant Rights to the Forests

British policymakers clashed over African subsistence rights to forest products, known as the free-issue controversy, which allowed Africans wood for house construction, cooking fuel, tools, fish traps, and furniture. Administrative officers viewed free issue as a supplement to peasant agriculture, which helped peasants pay taxes and become integrated into the colonial economy. The Forest Department, in contrast, viewed free issue as undermining its authority and depriving it of royalties on forest produce. Foresters also objected that it made forest reserves into a commons rather than state property. Peasants resented the need to obtain free permits to cut wood for basic needs, which brought with it colonial scrutiny. The free-issue controversy thus provides a window into interwar forest policy disputes.[54]

The right to free issue stemmed from the Tanganyika Land Ordinance of 1923 backed by the League of Nations mandatory agreement of 1922 that required "native laws and customs" to be considered when formulating land laws.[55] The land ordinance gave Africans the subsistence right to sufficient "land of the Territory and the natural fruits thereof." Some officials, perhaps aware that curtailment of forest rights had been a grievance of the Maji Maji War, feared that ending free issue would upset a customary right and feed resistance to the new regime.

Administrators encouraged free issue in part to increase colonial revenues, blurring the line between subsistence and commerce, the latter of which required royalty payments for wood use. This blurring was seen in the use of timber for dugout canoes. The greater Rufiji River system produced cash crops coveted by the government, mainly rice and cotton, and canoes were the primary means to transport these and other commodities—copal, bark, rubber, ivory, beeswax, hippopotamus teeth—to markets. Before 1936 Rufiji and other district officials allowed free issue timber for canoes (and even dhows), including first-schedule trees, knowing that Africans used canoes for both trade and subsistence.[56] In 1934 Africans cut, free of royalties, 219 mvule, 67 *mkongo,* 15 mahogany, and 180 other trees on the Rufiji and Kilombero rivers to construct some five hundred canoes.[57] The Forest Department viewed this scale of tree cutting for canoes as scandalous. It attributed a fourfold jump in free issue timber from 1933 to 1934 to canoe construction alone and in 1936 convinced the government in Dar es Salaam to impose royalties on canoe timber.[58]

The Forest Department failed to end free issue in other disputed cases. Beeswax collection was an important peasant forest activity, by far the most profitable forest product in the interwar years.[59] In 1927 the total value of timber and mangrove exports was about £15,000, while 506 tonnes of beeswax fetched over £80,000.[60] The Depression increased the export value of beeswax, offsetting revenue losses from tax decreases and falling cash crop prices. Around Liwale, Ngindo placed hives in woodland trees in order to assert clan ownership of groves outside forest reserves.[61] Hives had to be far enough apart so that bees did not compete over the same water sources and blossoms. A hive owner might collect ten kilograms of wax in a good year, which in the mid-1930s might bring in two or three times the annual hut tax.[62] Honey was an important food in famine years.[63] Because wax was treated as free issue despite its export value, forest officials resented beekeeping. They also cited wax collection as the main cause of forest fires and complained that beehives wasted valuable timber, including that from first-schedule trees like mninga. Conservator Grant argued that one mninga "bee barrel" of three cubic feet amounted to twenty cubic feet of sawed timber, thus there was an 85 percent loss of wood.[64] Yet foresters opposed even bark hives, claiming that stripping bark for this purpose killed trees.[65] District officers warned of intense African opposition if free issue for beehives was ended, more so than if taxes were raised. Noting that beeswax was a rare revenue generator in the Depression that also enabled people to pay taxes, the chief secretary retained free issue for beehives.

Africans often flouted forest laws by selling free-issue wood on the black market. In the Rufiji Delta, for example, a farmer named Asmani Kombekini obtained 150 mangrove poles as free issue to build a house. He later pulled down the house and sold the poles to an Arab trader. When the district forester charged Kombekini with wood theft, the district officer refused to find him guilty because there was no proof that his initial intent was to sell the poles. Conservator Grant believed that similar abuse of free issue was widespread. He complained that near Dar es Salaam peasants sold their free-issue timber and fuel to town dwellers, earning about twelve cents (29 pence) for enough wood to cook a meal and considerably more for construction timber.[66] Grant also argued that Africans in Dar es Salaam built houses large enough to rent out to migrant laborers, thus using free-issue timber for profit.[67] Foresters argued that free issue was "a monstrous piece of legislation" that should be replaced with at least a nominal wood royalty.[68] R. S. Troup, director of the Imperial Forestry Institute, toured Tanganyika in 1935 and argued that the 1921 Forest Ordinance, which guided interwar Tanganyikan forest policy, provided no legal basis for free issue from reserves since sufficient wood was available on public lands to meet African needs.[69] Nevertheless, free issue survived British rule and in World War II even helped to provision Dar es Salaam for the war effort.

Before 1926 most free-issue wood was not taken by peasants but by government departments, including Electricity, Public Works, and Railways. In 1925 Forestry issued 159,000 cubic meters of fuelwood, virtually all going to the railways.[70] The mining sector was a major taker of free-issue wood. One-third of free-issue timber and 62 percent of fuelwood went to the gold mines in 1936.[71] Yet peasants were the major takers of free-issue poles for house construction, taking over a million poles in 1930. Forestry attributed this demand to "the native building himself a better and more sanitary dwelling house" than in times past.[72]

Peasants in the Forests: Copal Tapping and Bark Stripping

The interwar years saw peasants return to the forests to tap copal and strip mangrove bark, activities that the colonial administration interpreted as free-issue rights after the onset of the Depression. From the early 1920s the government exempted copal from export duties and royalties to encourage the industry, although it required peasants to obtain free-issue permits. As a result, copal exports grew to about 145 tonnes each year to 1931.[73] Peasants could pay taxes (ten shillings before the depression, seven shillings thereafter) with a half to one kilogram of copal. By the 1930s copal competed with synthetic resins, which dropped prices to £6 to £7 per frasila (16 kg.), down from £9 to £12 in the 1920s. Annual exports averaged only 78 tonnes from 1931 through 1933 and only 22 tonnes per year from 1937 through 1940. Grant argued for copal royalties and greater oversight "to teach the natives rational methods of tapping aimed at producing the maximum sustained yield with the minimum exhaustion of trees."[74] Otherwise, he warned, copal trees would be tapped to death "and the goose that lays the golden eggs will be killed."[75] District officials countered that the generations-old copal industry would not have survived "if native methods of exploiting the gum were ruinous to the trees."[76] The administration concurred and even ended the need for free permits as an obstacle to copal tapping.

The revived copal economy depended on tree tapping rather than digging for fossil copal. Fossil copal was still much more valuable than tree copal, yet most fossil deposits had long been worked out and, unlike tree copal, was not a renewable resource. Mzee Abdalla Kapunga, who knew of copal from his childhood in the Matumbi hills, was hard pressed to remember fossil copal when interviewed in 2004: "Now I recall. It was a type of mineral, with different colors. . . . Some had the color of your shoe [grey]; or were white, like lime; or like a beer bottle."[77] Near the Naminangu "copal forest" in Kilwa District, elders remembered copal only as a tapped commodity. Asked about the interwar copal trade, Mzee Ali Abdalla replied, "There was a big trade. Our elders tapped it and put the lumps in containers to sell in the shops. The shopkeepers sold it to the government, who exported it."[78] In contrast to German rule, when copal digging was associated with poverty, people remembered copal tapping in the interwar years as lucrative. Ali Abdalla recalled, "It was a very good business. Copal helped people to get money to buy clothes. It was a very important trade." Mohammed Abdalla related that in past times, when trees were found "only in the wilderness owned by God," their fathers tapped copal and sold it to Indians who moved in from the coast.[79] Ali Saidi agreed: "People understood that if they sold copal they were able to get money to buy all sorts of things for their families."

Although the copal trade revived throughout the coastal hinterland, from Bagamoyo to Lindi, it was most pronounced in the Rufiji region. The most intense area of copal tapping was Muhamiri Forest, south of the upper Rufiji, sometimes called Kitope Forest.[80] Muhamiri lay at the westernmost edge of the coastal forest belt, the limit of the copal frontier, in both Rufiji and Kilwa districts, but was administered by Liwale Subdistrict. It was thus an administrative no-man's-land that enabled Africans to escape colonial oversight, a region of "unrelieved forest, large tracts of myombo and other trees alternating with large areas of dense *msitu* [coastal forest]."[81] Even though Muhamiri was a water catchment of the upper Rufiji, it had never been declared a forest reserve.[82] As a result, thousands of farmers pushed into the hillsides, collecting copal in a five-kilometer-wide strip on the southern boundary of the forest. Liwale officials, desirous of tax revenues, urged headmen to organize copal collection following the rainy seasons, when tree sap flowed more freely.[83] Foresters feared that farming and copal tapping so far from centers of colonial control amounted to insurgent activity. In 1931 they expelled hundreds of people from Muhamiri before it was realized that it wasn't a forest reserve. The central government overturned the evictions, allowing the people to return in such numbers that in 1933 one African stated that in Muhamiri "there is not room to spit."[84] Copal from Muhamiri allowed Rufiji District to produce about 9 tonnes of copal in 1933 and 52 tonnes in 1934, two-thirds of Tanganyikan copal production that year.[85]

World War II revived copal one last time. The Japanese occupation of southeast Asia in 1942 cut off from the world market resins used for varnishes and paints, leading the East African War Supplies Board to urge people to tap more copal.[86] Copal exports increased from 15 tonnes in 1941 to around 180 tonnes in 1944. The end of the war collapsed the market to 36 tonnes in 1945, and thereafter it virtually disappeared, despite postwar colonial attempts to export it for an emergent American linoleum industry.[87]

The need for Depression-era revenues led British political officers to allow a fairly unbridled peasant access to the forests. An elder in modern Tanzania remembered British rule as a time of extraordinary freedom in the forests, especially compared to modern times. "The British did not bother us—and in fact we thank them because we had a lot more freedom to use the forests than today. These days everything is by order."[88] This freedom was seen in the revived demand for mangrove bark, once again pitting administrative officers against foresters over definitions of free issue and proper use of the forests.

Like the Germans before them, the British valued the mangroves for revenue generation on account of their ongoing importance for foreign trade and domestic consumption. Following World War I, the Forest Department sought new concessionaires willing to exploit mangrove poles and bark in exchange for an annual royalty.[89] The mangrove pole business proved to be risky. Africans had the right of free mangrove access for domestic use. Indian Ocean dhows still arrived to buy mangrove rafters but could often get them directly from peasants on the black market. There was substantial nocturnal illegal cutting of poles that was largely beyond the control of British foresters.[90] When British and Arab concessionaires raised their rafter prices to make up for the loss, dhow captains turned to cheaper sources in Kenya, Zanzibar, and even Madagascar. The high cost of labor also encumbered the rafter market. A Rufiji forester cited the labor shortage as "a serious obstacle to the mangrove industry in the Delta."[91] Rufiji peasants preferred to market their free-issue mangroves or tap copal than work for a wage for private concessionaires or for the Forest Department. Initially under British rule Rufiji foresters imposed a royalty on "free-issue" poles to force people to work, but peasant protests led the central government to end this practice. These burdens on the rafter business led to an export decline from 125,680 poles in 1929 to 34,360 poles in 1933.[92]

The weak rafter market led the colonial administration to focus on mangrove bark, which once again opened a debate over forest conservation versus peasant subsistence rights. In 1927 the export value of mangrove bark, which went to the United States and Europe for leather dye, was over six times that of rafters.[93] While bark exports dropped in the early years of the Depression, in 1937 the trade was still eleven times the value of mangrove pole exports. The most prominent bark concessionaire was M. Ghaui, who from 1926 traded bark from *mkaka* (*Rhizophora*) mangroves around Kilwa.[94] The Kilwa district officer considered Ghaui's bark concession to be essential as an employer of Africans in the Depression, enabling one-fifth of the district's hundred thousand residents to pay their taxes.[95] The Forest Department refused to extend Ghaui's contract when it expired in 1931 because the mkaka mangroves had "suffered heavily as a result of little controllable exploitation" by "unscrupulous concessionaires." Foresters decried the bark stripping that left trees to die, as had been the case under German rule. Conservator Grant concurred: "if the woods are subjected to too great exhaustion they will never properly recover and this forest asset will be lost to the territory for good."[96] Grant instead offered Ghaui a concession to exploit the less desirable mkandaa and *mshinzi* mangrove species (*Ceriops* and *Bruguiera,* respectively), which Ghaui refused.

The refusal to extend the mkaka bark concession could not have come at a worse time. The Depression impaired colonial revenues as commodity prices dropped, while deficient rains and locust invasions damaged both food and export crops.[97] In public assemblies, villagers demanded the restoration of the bark industry. The Southern Province commissioner, A. E. Kitching, agreed, arguing that mangrove use was a free-issue right for coastal Africans at a time of famine.[98] Castigating the mangroves as swamps, not forests, Kitching wrote, "The swamps have no effect upon climate, water-supplies, rainfall, soil erosion, desiccation, and so on and the question of their exploitation should be examined from a business and revenue proposition." Forestry's refusal to extend the Ghaui concession was "conservation run mad," costing the government thousands of pounds in bark royalties and "employment to thousands of natives in need of work." Kitching urged that the concession be extended with no royalty rates so as to "make exploitation really attractive. . . . In any case the extinction of a swamp or two is a matter of no real consequence whatsoever to the Territory." Conservator Grant refused to reverse the closure, pointing out that mkaka needed thirty years to reach "barkable" dimensions. "No forestry expert could challenge my policy," he wrote.[99] The chief secretary sided with district authorities, concessionaires, and Africans in the bark dispute, privileging economic development over forest conservation: "It is of the greatest importance at the present time that no industry which can be made to pay should be impeded; in this case, the receipts from royalty are a minor consideration compared to the importance of putting money into circulation and helping trade."[100] Grant capitulated, while insisting on a law forbidding mangrove bark to be stripped without first felling the tree.[101]

The clear market value of mangroves made them the focus of British silviculture in the coastal hinterland. British foresters replanted mkaka (*Rhizophora*), mshinzi (*Bruguiera*), and mkandaa (*Ceriops*), which had demand for their bark or poles, while ignoring the "almost valueless *mchu* and *mlilana*" (*Avicennia* and *Sonneratia,* respectively), which Africans used for canoe construction.[102] The forest office planted over 240 hectares of mangroves in the north and south Rufiji Delta on forty-two separate plantations.[103] Workers collected mkaka and mshinzi seedlings hanging from mature trees, using canoes to reach accessible stands at high tide. Lined up a meter apart, they planted the seedlings by hand, much like rice paddies, creating rows of monocrop mangroves on selected parcels. They cut down overhanging mchu trees that blocked sunlight. Workers found particularly onerous the need to thin and weed saplings frequently. It took thirty to forty years for a tree to reach rafter girth. "The final crop," wrote Grant, "should be about fifteen score of number-one boriti an acre, and two and a half tons of bark."[104] Yet the Forest Department struggled to find people to work in the mangroves, limiting its ability to extend the plantations. In 1932 the Depression forced the department to suspend mangrove silviculture. In response to these failures at conservation, Grant wrote an article explaining the ecological and economic value of the mangroves for the colony.[105]

Taungya and the Feminization of the Forests

Poor revenues and a weak export market for Tanganyikan timber meant that the Forest Department was not able to pay high enough wages to attract sufficient permanent forest workers. The labor dearth limited forestry's ambitions, prevented expansion of the forest estate, and left many forest reserves unprotected from field fires. Forestry relied on highly unpopular corvée labor, especially on Native Authority plantations, which bred resentment. The department furthermore was forced to tolerate pit-sawyers to open woodlands to timber exploitation and private concessionaires for timber milling and bark extraction. In light of the ongoing labor problem, the Forest Department turned to the Burmese practice of taungya forest cultivation.

Taungya, from a Burmese word meaning hill cultivation, allowed peasant shifting cultivators to reside in forest reserves that had been logged.[106] There they cleared underbrush and planted food crops, which they intercropped with tree saplings that the Forest Department distributed. For a few years peasants tended both food crops and young trees, weeding them and protecting them from wild animals. Then they moved on to another forest parcel and began the process over, expanding the tree plantation over the long term. Often referred to as forest squatters, taungya peasants were licensed cultivators, given de facto rights to land in exchange for forest work. On the face of it Tanganyika was not an ideal place for taungya, since that cultivation method was premised on peasant land scarcity as an incentive to do forest work. In 1923 the Forest Department reported that it was difficult to introduce taungya because there was ample land for peasants outside forest reserves.[107] Even in the densely populated northeastern highlands the Forest Department had trouble recruiting peasants for taungya work, so that from 1925 it recruited landless Kikuyu families from neighboring Kenya.[108] Yet some peasants saw taungya as a means to reclaim access to ancestral forests whose fertility made them desirable areas to farm. Other incentives included better access to water, land for grazing, and steady wages. In interwar Tanganyika the Rufiji forest office employed ninety householders on a taungya basis, each planting one hundred trees annually.[109] Taungya relied on the labor of women, who planted and tended trees while their husbands did wage work elsewhere after helping in the initial clearing of the forest.[110] The Forest Department also used taungya in the forest reserves outside Dar es Salaam for its fuel and pole plantations. On the eve of World War II the Forest Department claimed 2,662 licensed forest cultivators, although many more farmed as unlicensed squatters.[111]

Although taungya allowed peasants to restake a claim to forest land, it is likely that it upset established gendered uses of the forests. In past times men had a hegemony over forest activities, with the exception of rites of passage for girls and spirit possession.[112] Among the Matumbi, ownership of trees was a male prerogative that bestowed de facto rights on ancestral land.[113] Ngindo elders emphasized that women had nothing

Figure 4.3. *Taungya* licensed cultivator on her maize field (Kenya). Reprinted by permission of Oxford Forest Information Service, Oxford University Library Services.

Figure 4.4. Female *taungya* cultivators on a cypress plantation, Tanganyika, c. 1950. Reprinted by permission of Oxford Forest Information Service, Oxford University Library Services.

to do with the beekeeping industry in forests, only helping to purify wax once it was collected.[114] In place of the past authority of chiefs to determine access to forests, taungya brought with it a new symbol of forest access mediated through foresters, a paper contract that spelled out the obligations of licensed cultivators. Because the evidence points to women as the primary taungya laborers, it suggests that a revolution in gender norms was under way as women received de facto title to taungya forest lands. Perhaps for this reason sources from the 1960s assert that male ancestral spirits who resided in forests, ax wielders called wenembago, threatened women especially.[115] The expansion of Tanganyikan forestry that began during World War II and burgeoned in the 1950s witnessed a concomitant growth in taungya cultivation and a reshaping of forest use that continued after independence.

British colonial officials expected that forestry would help to make colonialism profitable by "enclosing" the forests and implementing a regime of intensive, sustainable exploitation that would foster development. Drawing on successful models of forest exploitation in colonial Asia, where teak forests provided timber for construction, shipbuilding, and export revenues, there was no reason to think that British forest expertise could not be replicated in Tanganyika. This would be done in part by co-opting African chiefs to enforce colonial forest laws, an experiment in local governmentality that appeared to be working in India.[116] In Tanganyika these policies failed. The problem was not with the reconstituted authority—wanyemzi (executive officers) instead of mapazi (ax wielders)—but in the policies they enforced. Once presiding over forest rites that venerated ancestors, once granting access to forests for subsistence and trade, chiefs now did the opposite, their main function being to keep peasants out of the forests except under tightly controlled circumstances. Colonial forestry also intruded onto peasant lands in the form of protected trees and mandatory planting of exotic trees. Peasants came to distinguish between government trees, *miti ya serekali,* such as mvule and mninga, that were protected by law, and traditional trees, *miti ya asili,* that people protected because of their spiritual or ancestral value.[117] Many chiefs understood that colonial forestry undermined their authority, and they did what they could to mitigate its burdens. They often did this with the compliance of administrative officials who prized taxes and revenues, against the will of foresters, whose authority stemmed from an ideology of scientific forestry.

While foresters and chiefs struggled over the meaning of forestry, peasants took matters into their own hands. Many invaded the unprotected forests to tap copal or collect wax that could be traded along the coast to pay taxes and buy cloth. Thousands earned cash by stripping mangrove bark, probably at the expense of working for a wage on a mangrove plantation or building a firebreak around a forest reserve. Peasants bargained with forest officials for access to land in forests as taungya—licensed cultivators. A new class of forest entrepreneurs emerged—pitsawyers, who wielded the handsaw alongside the lumberman's ax—opening up the woodlands that capitalists found unprofitable. A new colonial generation of African peasants and workers had little reverence for forests that were once seen as owned by ancestors and controlled by chiefs. A district officer observed in 1933, "The European impact has destroyed the respect of the younger generation for the old faiths and with it the protection they afforded to the forest."[118] World War II would build on these transformations, moving forestry from a peripheral sector of the colonial economy to a central player in development. In so doing, it gave the Forest Department far more influence in shaping African land use and patterns of forest exploitation.

Chapter 5

Forestry and Forced Resettlement in Colonial Tanzania, 1920–50

A CENTRAL aim of British policy in Tanganyika was to resettle peasants who farmed in forests and woodlands into concentrated "closer settlements." Colonial officials believed that dispersed peasant settlements undermined agricultural modernization and deprived the state of labor. Once resettled in villages under colonial oversight, peasants would plant cash crops, do corvée and wage labor, and pay taxes—in short, act as colonial subjects. Officials furthermore came to see closer settlement as a panacea for other colonial problems, including population loss through sleeping sickness, the protection of wildlife, and the prevention of an American-style dust bowl said to be caused by peasant and pastoral misuse of the land.

Although political officers and foresters disagreed on many conservation priorities, they found common cause in forced resettlement. Colonial foresters saw resettlement as a prerequisite to effective forest management, since scientific forestry was premised on separating people from forests. Foresters could periodically tap the labor of resettled peasants to cut firebreaks, fight forest fires, build roads, and replant harvested trees, while protecting forests from field fires and overcutting of trees. By the 1930s forestry's antagonism to peasants who lived and farmed in the forests extended to the woodlands, whose hardwood trees began to have an export value. The valuing of the woodlands was given impetus by ecological theories of forest succession, which asserted that, if separated from people, woodlands would reach a natural climax as closed forests, with positive effects on soils and the climate. Moreover, the dust bowl fears of the 1930s implied that Forest Department oversight was needed on the woodlands, a "great area of dry forest" that made up almost half the territory. By the late 1930s closer settlement therefore justified a new wave of forest reservation that targeted the vast, unreserved woodlands.

Yet in advocating depopulation of the woodlands through closer settlement, the Forest Department allied itself with wildlife and sleeping sickness policies that were antithetical to sound forestry. Wildlife proponents believed that game animals should be protected from people through game reserves, which would ease animal depredations on peasant fields. Sleeping sickness officers argued that peasants should be moved from the woodlands into concentrated settlements where intensive agriculture would beat back the tsetse-infested woodlands that endangered people and cattle. These methods in effect surrendered the woodlands to wildlife and tsetse, making them into no-man's-lands that were the opposite of the managed, cultivated forest landscape that scientific forestry strived for. Moreover, surrendering the landscape to wildlife unleashed animal destruction on the forests, while methods of combating sleeping sickness included the wholesale denuding of the woodlands. Despite these contradictions, foresters embraced sleeping sickness and wildlife controls as tools for the greater priority of forced resettlement, unleashing massive population removals in the 1930s and 1940s that disrupted the lives of tens of thousands of peasants.

From the 1920s peasants continuously resisted closer settlement. They did this despite the wildlife and tsetse threats that came with living in the forests, seeing little benefit to participating in the colonial system. By the 1930s colonialists targeted whole villages, even whole societies, for forced resettlement, leading many people to organize politically against relocation, a prelude to the nationalism of the 1950s, which expedited the end of colonial rule in Tanganyika. Chiefs who assented to forced relocations lost their legitimacy, while some saw the opportunity to improve their local standing by leading protests against the colonial regime. Forced resettlement fed an insurgent peasant consciousness that viewed forestry, wildlife reserves, and sleeping sickness controls alike as pretexts to deprive people of their land and control their labor.

Agricultural Development and Closer Settlement in the Rufiji Region

African farmers of the greater Rufiji region had a history of living in dispersed settlements in forests and woodlands. Although environmental limitations that prevented intensive agriculture accounts for some of this dispersion, even people living in the fertile Matumbi hills and the Rufiji floodplain avoided concentration. The Ngindo of the southeast coastal hinterland were representative of dispersed settlement patterns, occupying a woodlands landscape that thwarted concentration owing to river seasonality and soil infertility. Agricultural security meant using multiple fields and staggered planting to grow a mix of crops.[1] Peasants farmed fertile river valleys in the dry seasons while relying on rain-fed dry-land fields for the bulk of their crops.[2] People relocated to more fertile fields every few years, which was also a check on soil erosion. In the nineteenth century frequent movement of homesteads allowed some defense from Ngoni raids from the west or slave raiders from the coast. In the twentieth century it insulated communities from colonial exactions. Ngindo supplemented farming with forest activities that included beeswax and rubber collection and ivory trading, which helped people survive bad times. Dispersed settlement kept population densities low, which prevented epidemic exposure to the trypanosomes that caused sleeping sickness.

Though there was no centralized Ngindo chiefship, the title of *mwenye* common to headmen implied clan ownership of resources and ancestral control of forests. Historically many Ngindo subgroups occupied dense dry forests—vichaka, or misitu—surrounded by woodlands and bush. These misitu included names such as Chobo, Lioto, Kingwichiro, and Nangora, all of which were sacred forests. The most famous was the Mbweho msitu, located in the midst of a river complex northwest of Liwale town.[3] These misitu provided a sense of residence, land ownership, and cultural grounding. Clans valued specific trees as sites of spirits and ancestors, which local customs prohibited people from felling, even in their own fields. People offered beer and grain at such trees so that spirits would provide rain, approve new clan heads, bless new fields, or accept new immigrants.[4] Neither the German nor the British forest departments declared these misitu as reserves, focusing on coastal forests much further east.

Although colonial officials castigated the dispersed Ngindo settlement patterns, they also decried the land use of the Matumbi and Rufiji peoples in the fertile regions to the northeast. Matumbi settlements followed hill contours, tracing rivulets that emanated from forested hill tops.[5] Hamlets also dotted the length of the Rufiji River, often moving because of floods and complete shifting of the river channel. Between the Luhoi and Rufiji floodplain, settlement was more concentrated in a deltalike environment that demanded flood-season field huts to be built on stilts, which were accessible only by dugout canoes. Yet even here settlements were far too dispersed to accommodate the colonial development agenda.

Early colonial warfare accompanied by famine, disease, and mortality depleted the already low population densities of the coastal hinterland. The Kilwa district officer summarized the consequences of World War I: "owing to the number of troops scattered about on lines of communication, who continually harassed natives making demands on them for food and porterage, natives hid themselves in inaccessible places in the bush, living in small hovels."[6] By the 1920s there were an estimated 1.6 people per square kilometer in Kilwa District and only one person for every two and a half square kilometers in Liwale Subdistrict.[7] The smaller Rufiji District, with a population of about eighty thousand according to the 1931 census, had six people per square kilometer.

Dispersed settlements first became a colonial problem when British officials promoted cotton as a peasant cash crop in the 1920s as the cornerstone of the region's development policy. During the Depression colonial officials mandated that all peasants "in the cotton producing areas" intercrop their rows of maize with cotton, warning that those who refused would be conscripted as corvée laborers on public works.[8] Peasants resisted nonetheless, some by refusing to grow cotton when prices were low, others by moving out of the district or into the forests for refuge.[9] Colonialists turned to closer settlement to remedy this resistance.

The relationship between closer settlement and the colonial development agenda was especially palpable in Kilwa District. In 1924 district officer Bell reported, "A real attempt is being made to induce the natives to abandon the retrogressive habit of living away from their neighbors in badly-built hovels, hidden in the bush, a custom which is a relic of the war, and to build good huts in suitably situated settlements."[10] Bell selected suitable sites along district roads where land and water was available to encourage people to move.[11] The expected benefits of closer settlement included more labor for road clearing and other corvée labor. It would enable officials to instruct peasants in new methods of cotton cultivation. Game scouts would be able to protect peasant fields from elephants and other crop predators.[12] Closer settlement would also enable the British to reconstitute African chiefship through indirect rule, which was predicated on constructing cohesive African "tribes" on designated lands. By 1925 Kilwa District had some hundred closer settlements in the making, although officials admitted that people did not move willingly.[13] Early efforts to attract settlers through rural betterment gave way to compulsion by 1925. In the face of ongoing African resistance, colonial officials sought creative ways to force peasants to retreat from the forests.

Closer Settlement and the Wildlife Threat

The British administration in Tanganyika used the wildlife threat against peasant agriculture to enforce closer settlement. Peasants who resisted resettlement received no protection from crop predators, while hunting ordinances prohibited villagers from protecting their own fields effectively. By sheltering wildlife, forest reserves helped make the countryside away from colonial settlements uninhabitable. Moreover, colonial policy in the interwar period was to expand German-era wildlife reserves on a grand scale. Forest and wildlife conservation therefore greatly increased the animal danger to peasants living isolated in the countryside, yet failed to protect those living in colonial villages adequately.

Forests and woodlands that had been depopulated during World War I became wildlife havens after the war. Africans lacked adequate weapons to hunt or to protect their fields, a legacy of German firearms controls. The Kilwa district officer guessed that there were only five muskets in the district, compared to thousands at the outset of German rule.[14] Although the British allowed musket ownership, they required licenses to hunt and regulated powder sales.[15] Officials attributed baboon proliferations in Kilwa District during the 1920s to the firearms shortage. Some local bylaws, such as in Liwale Subdistrict, even banned spears and bows except when people had permits to tap rubber in forests, where leopard and lion attacks were frequent, or when there was explicit permission to hunt vermin.[16]

With the freedom to hunt vastly curtailed, elephants emerged as the "arch-enemy of the native gardens" in the interwar period.[17] Elephant numbers reached levels that had not been seen since the early nineteenth century, an outcome of German-era hunting ordinances, firearms controls, and wildlife reserves. Wartime violence scattered rural communities, forcing peasants to abandon fields and fruit trees and move deeper into the forests and woodlands for refuge. Elephants learned that they could raid abandoned fields and orchards with impunity. Elephant numbers also increased as herds migrated to Tanganyika from war zones in Mozambique and Nyasaland, making their first appearance in generations.[18] The Kilwa district officer compared elephants to lions: "once having tasted succulent native foodstuffs, they, like the man-eater after once tasting blood, cannot relinquish their new passion until they have been destroyed."[19] He believed that the only way to prevent crop damage was to cull the herds and drive the survivors into game reserves, where they would be protected. Throughout southeast Tanganyika elephant damage was a major cause of crop loss and famine. A 1923 Swahili newspaper reported, "All residents will be happy if the government permits a lot of elephants to be killed. The work [of killing elephants] that was just completed is good, but people are afraid that afterwards the problems and cruelty of the elephants will increase again."[20] It was said that "if elephants are killed, food will increase."[21] From Tunduru it was reported that for a third consecutive year lion and elephant attacks were causing famine and ravishing the countryside.[22]

British officials first addressed the elephant problem by licensing European trophy hunters in problem areas. But trophy hunters, each limited to twenty-five animals per year, favored bulls for their large tusks, leaving young males and females to raid fields with impunity. Game wardens culled herds throughout the 1920s and 1930s, yet elephants remained "an unmitigated nuisance . . . responsible for damage to native crops to the annual value of some thousands of pounds."[23] Elephants attacked European cotton plantations near Kilwa, which the government hoped would act as models for economic development.[24] Elephants were a problem along the Rufiji River because they found refuge in the Selous Game Reserve and the many forest reserves that dotted the river. In 1925, 134 families fled the Rufiji "closer settlement" of Tawi to regions free of elephants.[25] Elephant crop destruction was still rife along the Rufiji in the 1950s.[26] The Rufiji region was also plagued by monkeys, baboons, wild pigs, hippos, eland, and buffalo, some sheltered by the Matandu River Game Reserve, which bisected the region, others by the Selous Reserve or the forest reserves that checkered the landscape.[27]

Colonial officials saw closer settlement as a solution to the wildlife problem, while they used wildlife control as a means to enforce closer settlement. Game scouts protected only peasants who lived in villages, leaving those who remained in the forests to the mercies of animals.[28] Yet the elephant eradication campaign in the Matumbi hills in the 1920s had the unintended consequence of driving herds down to the Rufiji flood-plain, where they raided rice and cotton fields adjacent to closer settlements. Thereafter district officials surrendered the Kichi and Matumbi hills to elephants, making them into a no-man's-land in order to secure the Rufiji floodplain, where cotton production was a higher priority.[29]

The Selous Reserve undermined all efforts to protect peasant fields throughout Rufiji region. In 1928 colonial officials created the Selous Reserve by amalgamating the German-era Mohoro and Mahenge wildlife reserves.[30] Although an increasingly powerful international wildlife protection movement lobbied for this expansion, Tanganyikan officials agreed to the reserve because it aided the greater goal of closer settlement.[31] The enlarged Selous forced peasants living in and around its vast miombo woodlands to relocate owing to wildlife depredations.[32] During the 1930s the Selous was expanded continuously in an unbroken chain from the upper Rufiji southward to the headwaters of the Liwale River, closing off the western frontier of the coastal hinterland completely. To make room for the people who were forced to relocate, colonial officials eliminated the Mtetesi Reserve, south of the Mbwemkuru River, in 1935, although they expanded the Matandu Reserve, which bisected Kilwa District.[33] People settled in lands that for a generation had harbored animals whose crop-raiding habits were not easily eradicated. In the 1940s a report described the problem of the Selous Reserve: "It is a long narrow corridor—while game has abundant space to move north and south it is constantly overflowing to the east and west, much complicating the problem of cultivation protection."[34] European sport hunters invaded the Selous seasonally, worsening the animal problem for peasants east of the reserve. A villager at Barikiwa recalled that during the hunting season animals in the reserve fled from gun shots, moving eastward using access roads that brought them directly into villages.[35] Wildlife and forest reserves that sheltered animals thus threatened dispersed peasant households and closer settlements alike. Despite these threats to agriculture, colonial foresters noted approvingly that wildlife reserves aided forestry by driving peasants out and putting the woodlands on "cold storage" until a forestry infrastructure could be established.[36]

Sleeping Sickness Controls and the Attack on the "Forest Native"

The detection of human sleeping sickness in 1922 at Maswa, in north-central Tanganyika set in motion a campaign of landscape and social engineering that preoccupied British officials to the end of colonial rule.[37] The colonial obsession with sleeping sickness was at root a labor question, since mass outbreaks, such as that which had killed some two hundred thousand people around Lake Victoria at the turn of the century, undermined cash crop agriculture and other colonial development goals.[38] Sleeping sickness was spread by tsetse flies that carried trypanosomes from infected hosts—cattle, game, or people—to other hosts. Because tsetse inhabited foliage—riverine brush or miombo woodlands—disease transmission could be stopped in several ways: by separating people from woodlands; by eradicating the tsetse habitat; by killing wildlife reservoirs of trypanosomes; or, least likely, by exterminating the flies.[39] Europeans developed medical treatments for sleeping sickness in the first decade of the twentieth century, which included painful arsenic injections and a more effective drug called Bayer 205.[40] Although Africans had long adapted to tsetse environments, colonial rulers viewed sleeping sickness as a brake on development that had to be mastered.[41] In interwar Tanganyika the British viewed closer settlement as the best method to combat sleeping sickness, which had the added advantage of bringing the rural population under control. In addition, the sleeping sickness campaign aided forestry by evicting thousands of peasants from woodlands, preserving them until the Forest Department had the financing and manpower to map out new forest reserves.[42]

Figure 5.1. *Miombo* woodlands in Tanzania. Photograph by Michael Tuck. Reprinted by permission.

Figure 5.2. Sleeping sickness in Tanganyika, 1937. Map by Thaddeus Sunseri.

In 1922 the game warden Charles Swynnerton, who oversaw sleeping sickness measures in Tanganyika, resettled five thousand people from tsetse-infested bush at Maswa to closer settlements dense enough to keep back the bush by creating "open" (deforested) land, where tsetse could not survive.[43] The campaign eliminated "forest villages" in woodlands, surrendering the evacuated landscape to bush, woodlands, tsetse, and wildlife. The Maswa case inaugurated many others. By 1934 there were sixty closer settlements southwest of Lake Victoria, encompassing over 40 percent of the population of some districts and as many as one hundred ten thousand people in northwestern Tanganyika.[44] Sleeping sickness settlements expanded to the end of World War II, with an additional sixty-five thousand people moved by 1942.[45] In 1924 officials detected sleeping sickness in the Rufiji region, setting in motion population removals that bolstered the preexisting policy of closer settlement.

Sleeping sickness was endemic to the Rufiji basin before German rule. Ngindo people called it *uvimbe*—the swelling disease.[46] In 1899 Germans reported tsetse along the rubber trade route from Kilwa to Barikiwa that in 1903 became the Matandu Game Reserve.[47] Reports at the time worried that the flies would infect small cattle herds along the coast. Germans detected sleeping sickness in Lindi and Songea districts in 1913 and curtailed caravan traffic and labor recruitment in an effort to stem the outbreak.[48] A German medical officer set up camps for infected people on the upper Rovuma at Nyangwere and another lower down the river at Sassawara, with fifty and forty-three cases respectively. During World War I military horses north of the Rufiji died from *nagana* (bovine sleeping sickness). The German medical officer M. A. Taute believed that human sleeping sickness was spread in the region by combatants.[49] Hundreds of thousands of troops and porters occupied the area between the Rufiji and Mbwemkuru rivers, requisitioning food and labor and causing famine. Africans who had had endemic exposure to the disease before the war were weakened, making epidemic outbreaks more likely.

The presence of tsetse and sleeping sickness alone do not create an epidemic. Physical condition, immune status, and degree of stress affect one's ability to resist infection and illness.[50] Infected victims could develop a premunity, whereby the immune system produces antibodies to new variations of antigen. Limited exposure to disease vectors—wild animals, cattle, tsetse—helped develop premunity, although it did not provide unlimited resistance to severe stress from other illnesses, fatigue, or hunger.[51] This seems to have been the case among the Ngindo, whose contact with tsetse was ongoing, as huts located in the bush and near watercourses were close to wild animal reservoirs of trypanosomiasis, such as wild pigs and buffalo.[52] Frequent entry into woodlands to extract copal, rubber, beeswax, and honey, and to hunt and fish, provided endemic exposure to the disease that perhaps created premunity. Ngindo dispersed settlements may have kept population densities too low for epidemic outbreaks of sleeping sickness (and perhaps malaria).[53] The population density of Kilwa

District in the 1920s was estimated at 1.6 persons per sq. km., and it was about a quarter of that in Liwale Subdistrict.[54] The sleeping sickness officer Maclean noted, "When the population is as low as one person to the square mile, the people are too dispersed to be able to sustain an epidemic."[55] His successor, H. Fairbairn, translated Maclean's use of the term *person* to mean an individual taxpayer and his family, on average 3.3 persons, so that the population of Kilwa District in general, and Liwale in particular, were too low to sustain a sleeping sickness epidemic.

Even before the British detection of sleeping sickness in 1924 along the Mbwemkuru River in Kilwa District, local officials aimed to force people into closer settlements.[56] By then they could draw on the Maswa template of forced relocation, as well as Game Department guidelines, to justify moving people. In December 1924 officials found further sleeping sickness cases in the village of Namabao, on the western periphery of the Matandu Game Reserve.[57] They attributed three deaths to sleeping sickness and confirmed two additional cases after testing "practically the whole population." By March 1925 they reported forty-two sleeping sickness deaths at Namabao and a total of eighty-two deaths by the end of the year.[58] By that time officials had labeled a large swath of territory along the upper Matandu River as fly infested and in need of evacuation. They placed the area under "strict quarantine" and sent all the people of Namabao to a "segregation camp" at Lukiliro to the north, where they were treated with Bayer 205 and other drugs.[59]

Kilwa district officials cited African settlement in forests as the chief cause of sleeping sickness outbreaks, even though some villages were in forests too dense for tsetse to survive.[60] Characterizing forests as places unfit for human settlement, medical officers reported that sleeping sickness was spread when a person passed through a "tse-tse forest," followed by an incubation period of between eighteen and twenty-seven days.[61] Unacknowledged was the role of forest and wildlife policy in making forests and woodlands into reservoirs for animal vectors of sleeping sickness. It is questionable whether less than one hundred sleeping sickness deaths in Kilwa District, and a total of 11,500 deaths in Tanganyika from 1922 and 1946, constituted "epidemics of apocalyptic proportions," which warranted the radical landscape and social engineering that came with sleeping sickness settlements.[62] Incidences of the disease in Kilwa District amounted to only 0.1 percent, compared to the 1 percent incidence level considered tolerable in Nigeria.[63] The conclusion is that combating disease was an excuse for closer settlement and population removals. As a 1926 report stated, "The object of making these settlements is not merely to remove the people's homes from contact with tse-tse; it is the first step in an attempt to re-organise the mode of life of forest communities."[64] The medical officer Fairbairn argued for resettlement even in cases where sleeping sickness had not been detected, listing the same benefits that closer settlement was meant to achieve: protection from wildlife; more efficient administration; and better social and economic development.[65] In the Rufiji region, the Namabao sleeping sickness removals were a dress rehearsal for closer settlement on a huge scale in the coming decades.

Eliminating Liwale Subdistrict

The prior discussion helps make intelligible the massive social engineering that beset Liwale Subdistrict after 1942 under the guise of sleeping sickness control. The plan was to evacuate entirely the dispersed homesteads and villages of this large region and relocate them into closer settlements, making room for an enlarged Selous Reserve and more forest reserves. The Liwale scheme occurred when one would least expect such social disruption, when the colonial state opened up the Tanganyikan forests and woodlands to meet a World War II demand for wild rubber, copal, timber, and beeswax. Indeed, one of the advantages that the sleeping sickness surveyor listed in relocating the entire population of Liwale Subdistrict was "reducing the risk of their going into infected bush looking for wax and rubber."[66] Yet other considerations seem to have been far more important—some intersected with wartime production, others had more to do with issues of social control and perceptions of ecological breakdown. During this period, colonial priorities moved from sleeping sickness control to wartime production, then to a postwar development mania that included the Groundnut Scheme, revived forest reservation, and the continued expansion of the Selous Reserve. Policymakers were hard pressed to sort out the contradictions of these changing agendas.

The acting district officer, Rooke Johnston, first advocated evacuating Liwale Subdistrict in 1931, but central government officials viewed the proposal as disrupting agriculture and other economic activities during the Depression.[67] By 1942, as deputy provincial commissioner of Eastern Province, Johnston revived his plan, which was, he wrote, to better the people and their district in the only way possible, by "eliminating Liwale District" and extending the Selous Game Reserve into the vacuum created. The pretext for the plan was the detection in 1941 of sleeping sickness north of Liwale, which launched the removal of 190 families to a closer settlement at Madaba. In 1943 Governor Wilfrid Jackson assented to moving the people "to more favorable areas free of the dangers of fly and Sleeping Sickness and bringing them in close touch with civilization," while joining the emptied regions to the Selous Reserve "for which it appears decidedly more suited." In 1944, as Eastern Province commissioner, Johnston set in motion the removal of the remaining population of the district, some ninety-three hundred families, comprising about forty thousand people.

Social engineering on this scale, and at great expense, was justified by several concerns that characterized the interwar colonial psyche. By the 1930s British policymakers believed that drought and the expansion of human and cattle populations onto farm and pasture lands had caused massive soil erosion, bringing an American-style dust bowl to Africa.[68] Arguments for the Liwale removals repeatedly mentioned the fear of erosion.[69] Two years after Madaba became a closer settlement, officials advocated that its people be moved again because "agriculturally the area is deteriorating at an appalling rate . . . unless very costly anti-erosion measures are to be undertaken, the erosion will be progressive." It is notable that two key dust bowl elements—dense populations and cattle—were missing in Liwale Subdistrict. Instead, officials attributed erosion to torrential rains and shifting cultivation by peasants, the latter of which historically had allowed peasants to escape the effects of erosion by moving their fields frequently. Even though erosion was not an impending problem, the sleeping sickness officer argued that Liwale Subdistrict would become increasingly unproductive and its people would risk starvation if they were not moved.

Officials also used a contradictory argument to justify the evacuation of Liwale—that the region's population was not dense enough to master the environment by eliminating the habitat of tsetse. Relocation officers were obsessed not just with creating new settlements but also with filling them with enough people. They scoured the countryside for small settlements to remove, whether or not sleeping sickness was present. Yet closer settlements often did not have enough fertile land and reliable water to sustain the four thousand people each needed to be viable. Indeed, this was one of the reasons that people of Liwale Subdistrict preferred to live in dispersed settlements.

Besides fears of erosion and the need to make closer settlements viable with numbers, relocation would facilitate social control over a remote people who officials considered to be refractory and secluded from "civilizing influences." Officials frequently noted that the Ngindo and their neighbors had initiated the Maji Maji rebellion and that they were "mischief-makers and devotees of witchcraft and black magic."[70] Officials suspected villagers in the north district of being in "illicit possession of Rifles, Ivory and Rhino horn" and of harboring poachers active in the Selous Reserve.[71] It is perhaps in this vein that Mzee Kiputi recalled the Madaba removal as punishment for the theft of a government rifle.[72] Fearing that western Rufiji District was becoming a refuge for people escaping closer settlement, officials incorporated the far west into the enlarged Selous Reserve, reinforcing an infrastructure of colonial control. Addressing the great cost in evacuating all of Liwale Subdistrict, the sleeping sickness officer wrote that "the resulting saving in added ease of administration will far exceed the cost. If this district is to become of any use Government will eventually be *compelled* to concentrate these people."[73]

Although the government provided financial incentives to get people to move, exempting them from taxes in the first year as compensation for the loss of crop land, resettlement near the coast increased the tax base in subsequent years.[74] Kilwa District had twice the hut and poll taxes as the interior (eight shillings versus four), and proximity to the coast made taxes easier to collect.[75] Relocating people would make them into "productive useful citizens" and "increased control [would] increase production."[76] The state would no longer have to maintain roads in Liwale Subdistrict at the same level as before and could eliminate salaries for administrators, clerks, and police once Liwale town was converted into a simple game ranger's post. The need to protect scattered settlements from wildlife, especially elephants, would also cease. Once people were moved, "all marauding game [will] be outlawed and subject to be destroyed" in a twenty-five-kilometer zone around concentrated settlements. The Selous Reserve would be immediately expanded to prevent the emptied Liwale Subdistrict from becoming "a refuge for rogues, vagabonds and bandits."[77]

The main destination for evicted Liwale residents was Njinjo, about thirty kilometers from Kilwa on the coast. Njinjo lay on the eastern border of the Matandu River Game Reserve, which was abolished in 1945 to make way for the closer settlement and the expansion of the Selous. Many of the Njinjo people were in turn relocated to the coast so that they would not be governed by the transplanted Liwale chief.[78] As settlers filled

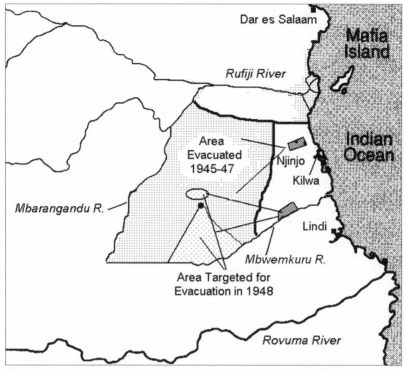

Figure 5.3. Liwale Closer Settlement Scheme. Map adapted by Thaddeus Sunseri.

all available land at Njinjo, officials added a second closer settlement to the east at Kikole. Officials forced some twenty thousand people, about half of those in Liwale Subdistrict, into these settlements, making them among the biggest population concentrations in Tanganyika.[79]

The people resettled at Njinjo and Kikole formed a labor pool for the mangroves near Kilwa, which had great priority for wartime and postwar military needs. During World War II, mangrove concessionaires supplied railway ties and beams to the East African War Supplies Board. Mangrove timber output rose from zero railway ties in 1940 to 58,305 in 1943.[80] The military demand for railway ties and other timber continued through the 1940s. The Njinjo-Kikole closer settlements furthermore provided labor for the Kiswere sisal estates south of Kilwa, where low wages, no rations, and "poor conditions" had impaired labor recruitment.[81]

The evacuation of some nineteen hundred families 282 kilometers to Njinjo caused great hardship.[82] Sleeping sickness officers cleared 377 kilometers of road and requisitioned nine two-ton trucks to move harvested food, elderly people, pregnant and nursing women, and children. They built camps every twenty-five to thirty-five kilometers en route to accommodate the evacuees. Herds of elephant that obstructed the lorries and endangered people had to be shot.[83] During the move some seven hundred family heads disappeared, reportedly returning to "their old districts, mostly N. and W. of Liwale."[84] People also migrated to other districts rather than be forced to live in the closer settlements. One-quarter of the people in central Liwale fled before they could be moved. Some filtered into the forests to hide, just as they had done for generations in the face of outside threats.[85] Drought delayed the evacuation two years after it had begun, so that in 1947 twenty-five to thirty thousand people remained in Liwale Subdistrict.[86]

The move was complicated by the inability to make Njinjo and Kikole into viable settlements. Five hundred to seven hundred fifty crop-raiding hippos lived in nearby Lake Maliwe. Fearing that the hippos would drive people away, the administration sought ways to eradicate them. The Kilwa game ranger rejected calls to kill the hippos with "bombs, depth charges, machine guns, etc." because it would "result in numbers of rogues being scattered all over the country attacking people on sight."[87] The provincial commissioner proposed to drain the lake and use tear gas to force the animals to the sea or into Rufiji District to become somebody else's problem. Finally, officials hired professional hunters to eradicate the hippos. One was "Dynamite Dan" Eldridge, another was a South African named von Schmarsow, who in 1947 shot sixty-five hippos out of Lake Maliwe for a profit of £12.50 each. Despite this slaughter, hippos continued to damage Njinjo crop lands.

Poor rains late in 1945 and at the outset of 1946 created "semi-starvation conditions" along the Matandu River, delaying the relocation of two thousand families to Njinjo. By that time people had begun to resist relocation, and officials described the district as being in "a marked state of tension and unrest" and on the brink of "Political Fitina [revolution]."[88] People turned against native authorities who acquiesced in the move. Two men who stated that they were the *wakili* (representatives) of Makata and Liwale regions made the long trip to Dar es Salaam in August 1947 to protest the evacuation of their districts. One was the native authority of Makata, seventy-year-old mwenye Mohammed Saidi Lupembe, who had first been appointed under German rule in 1905.[89] Lupembe asked the government, "Why have the people been moved? Is this not oppression?"[90] He objected both to the need to move at all and to the

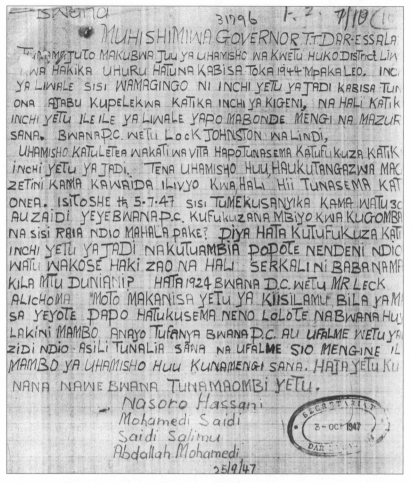

Figure 5.4. Letter of protest against Liwale forced resettlement. Tanzania National Archives, 31796, Nasoro Hassani, Mohamedi Saidi, Saidi Salimu, Abdallah Mohamedi to Governor, 25 September 1947.

lack of lorries to transport people and their food on the long trip, which forced people to leave food and property behind.[91] A month later, the representatives sent a petition to the governor expressing great remorse at being forced out (*kutufukuza*) of their ancestral lands around Liwale, "where there were numerous fertile valleys," to be moved to "foreign countries."[92] More than three hundred people traveled to the Southern Province capital at Lindi to confront the architect of the Liwale closer settlement, Rooke Johnston. "We have had no freedom at all from 1944 to the present day," their petition read. A month later the petitioners sent a letter to the chief secretary expressing their opposition to the evacuation. The government dismissed their objections and the evacuation moved into its third phase.

With north Liwale emptied, in early 1947 officials began to move people from about ten southern Liwale villages, altogether 5,100 families. Here they met organized resistance, as villagers refused to follow their chiefs coastward, preferring to settle southward along the Mbwemkuru River, to which the administration assented. Even before the final stage of relocation, in 1948, people abandoned the Njinjo closer settlement. The official report concluded, "At no time has the Scheme for the evacuation of Liwale gone smoothly, and the old files tell the same story for each move; opposition from the people, lack of transport, failure of rains, hunger and hardship."[93]

By 1947 colonial development priorities shifted. The British government embraced a massive scheme to produce vegetable fats for the metropole called the Groundnut Scheme, whose center of gravity would be at Nachingwea, across the Mbwemkuru River, but which initially targeted almost all evacuated Liwale regions for the cultivation of groundnuts. A tsetse officer extolled the emptied Liwale Subdistrict as ideal for groundnuts, especially since no compensation would have to be paid to people already evicted, "which might hold up the work."[94] Yet the labor needs of the Groundnut Scheme, coupled with resistance from the last Ngindo diehards, halted the "elimination of Liwale" in 1948. Suddenly the colonial state wanted to repopulate Liwale Subdistrict as a labor reservoir for the Groundnut Scheme. The Liwale chief, Mwenye Lipupu, telegrammed his people in Njinjo to return, and "a mass exodus followed."[95] By September 75 percent of the Njinjo people had returned to Liwale. A government report summarized the mood of Ngindo villagers: "At no time have the people of Liwale wanted to move. Their chiefs however took the line of least resistance and when they saw that the Government was serious, meekly acquiesced without consulting their people." Despite the truth of this assessment, a handful of lower-level headmen, like Saidi Lupembe, took considerable risk in protesting population removals. The fiasco of the Liwale Closer Settlement Scheme would have major repercussions for development policy in the 1950s. It fed the bitterness of Liwale peasants toward those leaders who went along with the removals and hardened attitudes against other relocation schemes on the horizon, including the Groundnut Scheme, the continuous expansion of Selous Game Reserve, and the proliferation of forest reserves, all of which characterized the final decade of British rule.

Under British rule, Tanganyikan officials considered closer settlement to be a prerequisite for economic and social development. They therefore used wildlife, sleeping sickness, and forest policies as tools to justify the mass eviction of rural people from forests and woodlands in order to amalgamate them into colonial villages. Sometimes these evacuations served their intended purpose: separating people from animals allowed game to proliferate, while evicting peasants from forests and woodlands protected trees from "fire and the ax." However, as the Liwale Closer Settlement Scheme demonstrated, massive landscape and social engineering had countless unforeseen consequences that confounded colonial expertise. Evicting people from the vast miombo woodlands of Liwale and expanding the Selous Reserve created an animal hazard that made other colonial projects, such as productive cash crop agriculture, untenable and risky. Moving people into closer settlements in order to combat sleeping sickness had the opposite effect, expanding the habitat of tsetse flies.[96] Finally, far from transforming Africans into quiescent colonial subjects, the extreme dislocation that came with closer settlement incubated a deep-seated antagonism to colonial development and conservationism of all sorts.

On the face of it forestry benefited from closer settlement as a means of putting the unreserved forests and woodlands in cold storage until the Forest Department had the financial wherewithal to manage the estate effectively. Yet surrendering the countryside to wildlife and tsetse flies was antithetical to the basic premise of scientific forestry, namely the sustainable economic management of trees. The ideal landscape for tsetse control was a bare corridor completely devoid of trees, brush, and people.[97] Forestry, on the other hand, depended on labor that was generally lost after people were relocated to closer settlements. As the conservator of forests put it in the 1950s, "We want local sources of labor, inhabited camp sites, local water supplies etc in and about these areas, not uninhabited wastes."[98] The compatibility between tsetse eradication and forestry was thus more imaginary than real. By identifying miombo woodlands as a landscape that threatened civilization and progress, the interwar development agenda excluded about 50 percent of Tanganyika Territory from the managed forest estate. Colonial foresters would redress this omission in the postwar years when they emerged as central players in development.

The Liwale Closer Settlement Scheme, and similar mass relocations in other parts of colonial Tanganyika, set the precedent for further attempts at relocation under the guise of social and economic betterment that would come in the 1950s and beyond. Indeed, mass relocation would become the leitmotif of twentieth-century Tanzania. Although the Liwale scheme taught colonial officials and an emergent generation of African bureaucrats how to evict tens of thousands of people in order to advance state goals, it also taught Africans how to protest in innovative ways, such as rallies, petitions, and deputations, and through desertion and noncompliance. In so doing it prepared the way for the mass nationalism of the 1950s.

CHAPTER 6

Forestry Unbound

Reservation and Resistance from World War II to Independence, 1946–61

IN 1951 the Ruponda district officer informed the chief of Liwale that the Forest Department had marked out a twenty-three-hundred-square-kilometer forest reserve, called Angai, on woodlands south of Liwale town.[1] The proposal mandated the expulsion of farmers from some twenty villages, ending their access to woodlands that they used for beekeeping and famine food. Coming just three years after the cancellation of the Liwale Closer Settlement Scheme, which had focibly resettled the entire district, the reaction of villagers was immediate and vocal. Hundreds of people voiced "bitter opposition" at local assemblies, convinced that the new reserve would mean their wholesale expulsion from farm lands. The chief of Liwale told district officials repeatedly and forcefully that neither he nor other elders could agree to new reserves in the current atmosphere. Fearing that local peasant leaders would use the occasion to "agitate politically" for the elimination of forest and game reserves throughout Tanganyika, district and forest officials scrapped the Angai proposal.

The cancellation of the Angai proposal did not deter colonial officials from expanding the total extent of forest reserves in Tanganyika by over ten times during the 1950s, focusing on the miombo woodlands that they had previously neglected. World War II and the Cold War changed perceptions of Tanganyika's forest resources, convincing British officials that hardwood timbers once considered marginal were now crucial for imperial economic stability.[2] "All forest in Tanganyika is regarded as exploitable," wrote the conservator of forests in 1951, reversing an attitude that had dominated the first fifty years of colonial forestry in Tanganyika.[3] With financing from the Colonial Development and Welfare Corporation, the Tanganyika Forest Department doubled its European foresters and African forest guards, empowering it to expand and police forest reserves throughout the territory. At the same time, private timber millers took a new interest in Tanganyika in light of the political independence of Britain's Asian possessions, which ruptured world supplies of teak and other hardwoods. As a result, the Tanganyika Forest Department, which had formerly "existed in little more than name," became a central player in colonial development.[4]

Africans immediately opposed the ambitions of the newly empowered Forest Department and the development agenda that accompanied it. Throughout Tanganyika the expansion of forest reserves and tree plantations, coupled with loss of land, fed peasant and pastoralist anger. Other forest workers joined the protests, including sawmill workers, pitsawyers, and taungya (licensed) cultivators, some threatened by reserve expansion or mechanized tree cutting, others seeking better working conditions. Increasingly they identified with the nationalist movement led by the Tanganyika African National Union (TANU), which targeted racial discrimination and land struggles to mobilize a mass following. As independence approached, in 1961, the forests were literally and metaphorically on fire, as farmers battled forest reserve expansion and other colonial interventions that threatened access to land and resources.

World War II and the Tanganyikan Forests

Initially World War II forced the Tanganyika Forest Department to retrench, as funds allocated to it before the war were redirected to wartime food production.[5] Fewer foresters were available to survey forests, police forest borders, plant new trees, or inspect timber. The war severed the main German export market for mvule hardwood timber and mpingo.[6]

Tanganyikan timber could not compete with Indian timber supplied to the Middle East theater of war owing to its distance from markets, unfamiliar uses, and high prices.[7]

This state of limbo ended abruptly after Italy's declaration of war in June 1940, inaugurating British military operations in Libya, Ethiopia, Sudan, and Somalia in tandem with ongoing war preparations in the Middle East.[8] The war monopolized overseas timber supplies, forcing Tanganyika to rely on its own forests for construction. In 1940 British war planners informed the East African Governor's Conference that military operations in East Africa and the Middle East required the "greatest possible quantity of timber."[9] By 1942 the Japanese takeover of southeastern Asia took hardwoods from Burma, Malaya, Borneo, and the Philippines from world markets, making formerly unmarketable Tanganyikan hardwoods suddenly of high value.[10] The British Timber Control Department, in tandem with the East African War Supplies Board in Nairobi, mandated timber prices and output.[11] In 1941 military orders doubled Tanganyikan timber exports over the previous year, and sawmills and pitsawyers worked feverishly to meet the demand. Although the Italian capitulation in Ethiopia, in May 1941, slowed military orders, the Middle East theater maintained a standing order for 2,270 tonnes of East African timber per month, while the Tanganyikan domestic market demanded another 1,360 tonnes per month.[12] Forestry committed itself to supplying fifteen thousand railway ties per month to the war effort and additional timber for military huts, barracks, portable bridges, vehicles, and tools.

In order to meet this wartime demand, the Tanganyikan government financed new sawmills, leased machinery to contractors at low prices, and subsidized food in order to attract Africans to work. Nine new mills opened in 1942, and the government reduced royalty rates on railway ties by 75 percent as an incentive for private contractors to increase output of otherwise marginal timbers.[13] Even with an imposed price reduction of 10 percent for military and government orders, Forest Department revenue increased by almost 50 percent in 1942, exceeding expenditure by £13,648 and by £26,168 the following year. Most timber came from "the more readily accessible forests" near railway and road lines.[14] Demand for railway ties in the war years rose from zero in 1940 to 1,188 cubic tons in 1941 and reached 20,000 cubic tons in 1942 before dropping to 11,292 cubic tons in 1943, still almost two hundred thousand ties annually. By 1944 fifteen different Tanganyikan tree species were used for ties, obtained increasingly from miombo woodlands, which the Forest Department suddenly prioritized for exploitation after fifty years of virtual neglect.[15] In Eastern Province eleven Indian and Greek timber contractors operated along the tracks of the Central Railway as far as Dodoma and south of Dar es Salaam to the Rufiji River, supplying timber from forest reserves and unreserved woodlands alike.

The newfound demand for Tanganyikan timbers launched a chronic labor shortage in forest industries that outlasted the war. Timber contractors hired African pitsawyers to supply railway ties, paying two shillings for each tie. A sawing team could supply about twenty ties per month.[16] This was profitable enough to attract some sisal plantation workers, threatening another wartime production priority owing to the wartime cutoff of Philippine Manila hemp (abaca).[17] Yet forest labor was irregular and inadequate, so railway tie output was far below demand at a time when the state required "the maximum possible turnout of labor for the production of ties."[18] Foresters complained that pitsawyers were "independent and sporadic" and difficult to supervise because they worked in small gangs isolated in the forests. The work required sawyers to penetrate the forests deeply, locating and felling species with an established demand. They dug pits and sawed logs on the spot to railway-tie size (about 12.5 centimeters by 25 centimeters by 2.5 meters), and carried the hundred-kilogram timbers to roadways. Contractors picked up the ties, transporting loads of twenty to twenty-five ties to the railway line or to Dar es Salaam. When not delayed by rains, contractors could supply about five thousand ties per month from coastal forests and woodlands, compared to ten thousand ties per month from the denser forests of the northeast highlands. By 1944 contractors struggled to supply eleven thousand ties per month, about 35 percent below production estimates, owing to labor bottlenecks and ever-greater difficulty locating exploitable trees near railways and roads.

Besides timber, the war in Asia curtailed plantation rubber supplies, leading war planners in London to prioritize rubber as a strategic commodity.[19] In response, the Tanganyika government declassified wild rubber as a protected forest product, waiving all royalties and fees, so Africans had incentive to tap rubber freely, even in forest reserves. Forest officials were skeptical that the obtainable quantities of rubber were worth the damage to the forests caused by rubber tappers, while a representative from Firestone Rubber in South Africa doubted that the rubber was of suitable quality for tire production.[20] Yet foresters proceeded to survey the forests and woodlands for rubber trees. In 1942 the Kisarawe district officer issued permits for twenty-five Africans to collect wild rubber in the Pugu and Vikindu coastal forest reserves.[21] The Ministry of Supply acted as the sole buyer of collected rubber, paying as much as two and a quarter shillings per kilogram, or "whatever sum was found necessary to get the native gatherer interested; . . . what had to be paid would be paid." By 1945 Tanganyika exported 158 tonnes of wild rubber, which paled in comparison to the twenty-seven hundred tonnes of rubber from derelict German-era plantations.[22]

Wartime demand for forest products led to a complete reassessment of Tanganyikan forests and woodlands. The chief secretary wrote in 1942, "The forest resources of the Territory, which were at no time extensive, are being seriously depleted and impaired by the present increased calls which military needs make upon them, and their rehabilitation after the war will be a charge which this Government will be compelled to meet."[23] In 1944 the Colonial Office allocated Colonial Development and Welfare funds to reorganize Tanganyikan forestry in anticipation of a postwar expansion of forest reserves.

Charcoal and Taungya Forest Cultivation

Wartime economic activity fueled urban growth in Tanganyika, which increased the consumer demand for food, construction timber, and fuelwood. Between 1943 and 1952 Dar es Salaam's population more than doubled, from 45,100 to about 100,000.[24] The war inaugurated a dependency on charcoal as the primary urban domestic fuel in Tanzania. Postwar development, especially the Groundnut Scheme, maintained this demand through the 1950s and beyond. In 1950 the Forest Department recorded over 368,000 cubic meters of firewood sold in Tanganyikan markets, which was dwarfed by the estimated 20 million cubic meters of fuelwood used for rural subsistence.[25] In order to fuel economic development, the Forest Department increased the extent of forest reserves so that more timber and fuel could be brought onto the market through rotational planting and harvesting. The forestry adviser to the colonial secretary underscored this newfound urgency after visiting Tanganyika in 1947, writing that previously there had been "undue concentration and expense on protection" of forests and that "the time has come to develop our forests economically instead."[26]

During World War II colonial officials opened up the forest reserves near Dar es Salaam to exploitation to meet the urban demand for charcoal.

The Vikindu market, south of Dar es Salaam, sold 480 tonnes of charcoal in 1943 and about twice that in 1944.[27] In Kisarawe District 15,700
tonnes of firewood and a further 4,200 tonnes of charcoal were sold in
1943.[28] About 28,300 cubic meters of timber were cut per year in Dar es
Salaam–area forests for commercial fuelwood alone, which foresters estimated to be four hundred hectares annually. Yet the senior forester of
Dar es Salaam District considered these quantities to be the minimum
needed for the city. He therefore opposed government controls on charcoal production (beyond forcing charcoal and wood to be sold in official markets) that might create a "serious shortfall."[29] Besides an acute
urban fuel scarcity from the late 1930s, there was insufficient timber and
poles for the houses needed for thousands of new urban workers.[30]
Fearing that the wood shortage would cause African unrest and urban
disorder, the government called on forest officials to facilitate the wood
markets.

Wood merchants, often Indians or Greeks, bought licenses and hired
pitsawyers to cut trees and saw them into planks or burn charcoal to be
sold in the official markets at Vikindu, Soga, and Pugu, where the Forest
Department collected an additional duty.[31] Many Africans entered the
wood business on their own, paying two shillings per month for licenses.
Yet a widespread illegal practice was for commercial contractors to simply buy fuelwood or charcoal from villagers, who cut trees as a free-issue
subsistence right.[32] In this way merchants did not have to hire pitsawyers,
while farmers could earn some cash without buying licenses. Women
predominated in Dar es Salaam's formal and informal wood markets, an
important supplement to their meager incomes. As many as 20 percent of
African households in Dar es Salaam sold charcoal and firewood in the
informal economy.[33]

Because the urban wood and charcoal markets were erratic and un-
reliable, the Forest Department created its own pole and fuel plantations
in forest reserves near Dar es Salaam. From the early 1920s the department
had experimented with tree plantations at Mogo and Pugu forest reserves,
on the city's periphery, where it planted some indigenous hardwoods
alongside exotic softwoods, especially the fast-growing *Cassia siamea* (ironwood). By World War II foresters planted few indigenous hardwoods because they grew too slowly and were susceptible to pests. Exploitable trees
were too sparse in natural forests, so it was hard to entice fuel contractors
to "take on the job of clearing it, even free of royalty."[34] The Forest Department therefore aimed to completely replace the natural trees of the

coastal forests near Dar es Salaam with fast-growing exotics that could be used for poles and fuel.

This push to expand fuelwood plantations conflicted with agricultural goals, since political and forestry officials alike believed that deforestation increased soil infertility and threatened long-term food production.[35] The challenge was to balance urban fuel requirements with food needs. At the same time, African farmers lost land as the growth of the city displaced them to make way for public works, water controls, and road and airport construction. As a result, peasants demanded greater access to the forests. In 1944 the chief of Vikindu and some of his people repeatedly asked the senior forester of Dar es Salaam District for permission to farm in Vikindu Forest Reserve.[36] The Kisarawe chief also requested that two of his people, whose lands were exhausted, be allowed to farm in the adjacent Pori la Serkali (Pugu Forest Reserve).[37] Officials agreed to these requests because they came at a time of grain shortfalls in local markets.[38]

The solution to the multiple concerns about urban fuel and food scarcity, soil infertility, and peasant landlessness was to increase taungya cultivation in coastal forest reserves. The conservator of forests insisted that taungya peasants live and farm in forest reserves so that foresters could control land allocation, tree planting timetables, and duration of peasant occupancy. In 1944 colonial officials selected the sixteen-hundred-hectare Vikindu Forest Reserve south of Dar es Salaam as the prototype for the new campaign. Vikindu was characterized by a secondary regeneration bush, some high canopy trees, and open grasslands called *viwara,* showing that forty years as a colonial forest reserve had depleted its forest cover.[39] British foresters viewed Vikindu solely in terms of fuel quantity, estimating that the remnant natural forest would produce less than thirty-five cubic meters per hectare, compared to 140 cubic meters per hectare once it was replanted with *Cassia siamea* and eucalyptus. Owing to the pressing needs for wood in the cities, the assistant conservator wrote, "Ecological considerations are of relatively minor importance."[40] The working plan aimed to completely clear all the natural vegetation within fifteen years, at which time the ironwood crop would be ready for rotational harvesting.

The Forest Department enlisted fuel contractors to cut Vikindu's trees before it brought in taungya peasants to clear the remaining bush for planting. The contractors paid royalties for the wood, and each year they agreed to clear a new parcel ahead of peasants until all the indigenous trees had been cut, which would take fifteen years. Thereafter they were to cut the annual rotations of exotic trees as they grew to sizes suitable for charcoal or poles. The Forest Department licensed some two hundred peasant householders to clear bush from designated plots and tend exotic trees interplanted with their own food crops.[41] They were not allowed to plant root crops or to build permanent houses, and every twelve to eighteen months, as planted trees conflicted with food crops, they were allocated new half-hectare plots in another sector of the reserve. In the early stages of the scheme the fuel contractor, Morogoro Garden Stores, failed to muster the wage labor needed to clear the tree cover in time for the peasants to plant their crops.[42] In order that the peasants not become frustrated and leave, the Forest Department offered monthly payments as an inducement to stay, which became a permanent feature of taungya schemes.[43] The Vikindu Scheme and subsequent tree plantations assumed that taungya peasants would reside in the forests "in perpetuity" at a time of general labor shortage.[44]

By the mid-1950s the Forest Department considered Vikindu to be a "model plantation," the template for additional fuel plantations in forest reserves west of Dar es Salaam, beginning with Pugu Forest.[45] Pugu had been heavily cut for fuel since becoming a forest reserve under German rule. By the 1950s African peasants and some commercial planters farmed the best lands in the reserve, making it difficult for the department to find land blocks large enough for tree plantations without "interfering considerably with native prescriptive rights."[46] In 1949 leaders of the adjacent Sungwi chiefdom requested that its people be allowed to farm in southern Pugu Forest under the same terms as the Vikindu settlers. District political and forest officers agreed, owing to "the need for the increased planting of fuel trees" to supply Dar es Salaam.[47] In addition, the Forest Department created two new forest reserves nearby, Hundogo in 1953 and Kazimzumbwi in 1954, "in order to extend the area of managed forest land supplying the Territory's capital with firewood and poles."[48] Foresters struggled to find fuel contractors willing to cut in Pugu Forest because it was poor in "firewood species," but by 1954 a parcel of forty-seven hectares had been sown with *Cassia siamea*.[49] In 1955 the department managed all five forest reserves of Kisarawe District as taungya schemes. By then Vikindu was in its ninth year, and 80 percent of its relic forest had been cleared and replanted.[50] Although some wage laborers and prisoners worked in the Kisarawe reserves, the Forest Department considered taungya cultivators to be cheaper and more efficient.[51]

Written contracts led taungya farmers to believe that they had permanent rights to forest lands.[52] Contracts referred to farmers as permit holders (*mwenye hati*), as landowners (*mwenye kiwanja cha kulima*), and as farmers (*wakulima*). The phrasing *kiwanja chake* (his or her land) suggested individual proprietorship, and references to farming by custom (*desturi*) evoked established Zaramo patterns of land use. While foresters often specified that forest farming was temporary, there was no time limit in the *taungya* contracts, and it was understood that farmers would rotate their lands within the forest plantation in ten-year cycles. In light of ongoing labor shortages in 1950s, the Forest Department worried more that peasants would vacate the forests if conditions were inadequate than that they would refuse to leave if ordered.

The Cold War, Groundnuts, and Timber Exploitation

After 1945 tensions in the Middle East and the advent of the Cold War boosted the demand for Tanganyikan timber, much of it directed to the Palestine Railway, which the British had extended from Tripoli to Beirut.[53] The Middle East was "the hub of [British] strategic defense planning," owing to oil and the Suez Canal, and a bulwark against Russian influence in Africa in the early stages of the Cold War.[54] In 1947 Palestine Railways ordered fifty thousand pitsawed railway ties from Tanganyika, most from woodland trees such as mninga.[55] Although orders for the railway ceased when the British quit Palestine in 1948, the Middle East continued to take as much as 80 percent of Tanganyikan timber in the late 1940s. The South African market also revived after the war, and increasingly Uganda and Kenya emerged as important destinations for Tanganyikan timber.

Even as the external market expanded, the major demand for Tanganyikan timber came from its growing internal market that was stimulated by regional geopolitics and development schemes. World coal and steel shortages after the war boosted local consumption of Tanganyikan wood for railway fuel and ties, especially after the Colonial Office directed that all imports be rationed. Tanganyikan Power and Lighting used only wood fuel along the Central Railway. Gold and diamond mining expanded after the war, consuming wood for fuel and mine shoring.

In light of this demand, the Forest Department began the postwar era with an aggressive plan for forest reservation. The new Forest Development Plan targeted 14.6 percent of the territory, some 129,500 square kilometers of woodlands, as productive forest reserves. Compared to the

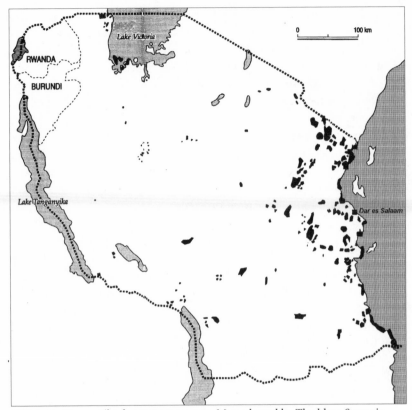

Figure 6.1. Tanganyika forest reserves, 1945. Map adapted by Thaddeus Sunseri.

1.4 percent of the territory (12,163 square kilometers) as forest reserves in 1944, this was a dramatic usurpation of land that would affect tens of thousands of rural dwellers throughout Tanganyika.

These plans for rapid forest reservation were possible because of the new earning capacity of the Forest Department coupled with aid from the Colonial Development and Welfare Corporation (CDW), which in 1947 doubled the department's budget and its European and African staff. Since 1940 the CDW had represented a new phase of imperial thinking and was a reaction to several wartime developments.[56] One was a defense of empire in light of American criticism implied by the Atlantic Charter of 1941, which had stressed a universal right of self determination. The CDW was also a reaction to a wave of African labor strikes in the 1940s that sought wage increases. The Colonial Office resisted wage increases during the war, hoping that raising productivity through investment

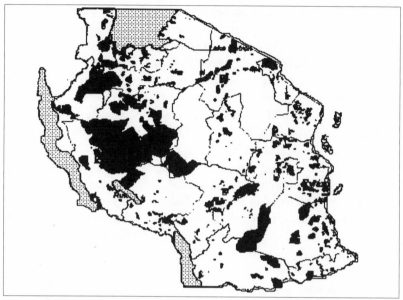

Figure 6.2. Tanganyika forest reserves, 1961. Map adapted by Thaddeus Sunseri.

would create higher living standards. Following the war, the Labour government saw the CDW as a way to improve African economic and social conditions in light of continued currency and market controls that created shortages of imported consumer goods. Labour hoped that economic development would ease the worst affects of capitalism and create the material improvement necessary for eventual African independence. Economic development would also enable the colonies to produce goods for British consumers and exports for the U.S. market, easing the UK's dollar shortage. Finally, the CDW was an investment in long-term economic links between the colonies and the metropole, which would hopefully ensure political allegiance during the Cold War and the long-term stability of the British Commonwealth.[57]

The Groundnut Scheme, which encapsulated this development thinking, would have a dramatic impact on forestry in southeastern Tanzania.[58] Following the war Britain depended on the United States for food imports, which created a drain on dollars. The "most serious and intractable part of the food position in Britain" was the shortage of fats and oils, estimated at about 4.5 million tonnes of groundnuts globally and 1.4 million tonnes for Britain alone.[59] Labour had promised to improve postwar living conditions in Britain. Easing the cooking oil shortage would lessen food rationing and win popular support for the government. The government expected the colonies to increase production of exportable goods while decreasing imports, especially from dollar zones, and therefore fixed dollar import ceilings for each colony in 1949.

The Groundnut Scheme began in 1946 when Unilever Corporation proposed that the Ministry of Food (through a new Overseas Food Corporation) grow 1.2 million hectares of groundnuts in Kenya, Northern Rhodesia, and Tanganyika.[60] This would be done by massive capital investment and mechanization that would raise African productivity. The *Times* reported, "In these broad considerations of public policy lies the modern justification of Empire. African communities could not of themselves devise or accomplish the revolution in their agricultural practice which must be effected if they are to survive. As little could the British people have any assurance of restoring their standards of nutritional efficiency if there were not under their control vast areas of unproductive land which only western science and technical skill can render fruitful."[61] Initially the scheme was organized into three huge swaths of land around Nachingwea, Tunduru, and Liwale, in the southern coastal hinterland. By 1947 twelve parcels had been cleared south of the Mbwemkuru River— expected to produce 12,970 tonnes of groundnuts annually—a fraction of the total area that was expected to be cleared in the next few years.[62] Half of all Groundnut Scheme land in Africa was to be on miombo lands at Nachingwea in the former Mtetesi Game Reserve, 113 kilometers southeast of Liwale. The scheme justified the abandonment of the Liwale Closer Settlement Scheme (see chapter 5) in order that labor and food reserves be available nearby.[63] Planners targeted the Liwale region for a second wave of groundnut production after 1950.

The British abandoned the Groundnut Scheme by 1950 after an expenditure of £36,000,000 succeeded in clearing only 18,600 hectares. Secondhand tractors, World War II materiel, and other machinery broke down. Workers conscripted for ground clearing and construction deserted or went on strike. Land had been improperly surveyed for groundnut suitability. However, because of the "blow for British prestige" that complete abandonment would signify, colonial planners continued a rump groundnut scheme into the 1950s on 60,750 hectares at Nachingwea, growing crops on parcels ranging from eight-hectare "peasant" farms to "production" farms of four to eight hundred hectares.[64] Shell Oil built a pipeline from Mtwara to Mtua to supply the project, using timber from surrounding woodlands.[65] Although scaled down from its original ambitions, this development agenda was nevertheless the largest financial input that southeast Tanganyika had ever seen.

The Groundnut Scheme set in motion frenzied railway construction in southern Tanganyika. It required a new port at Mtwara, which was the terminus for a railway to be built to Nachingwea to import heavy equipment and to export groundnuts. A parallel railway from Lindi intersected with the Mtwara line at Ruo until it was completely dismantled in 1954.[66] The Mtwara railway was justified on strategic as well as economic grounds. In the late 1940s British military planners viewed the British colonies in central and East Africa as support bases for the Middle East.[67] The Mtwara railway would provide an outlet for strategic raw materials—copper, coal, chrome, and mica—from the Rhodesias.[68] The European Recovery Program required that Britain supply the United States with "raw materials necessary for American rearmament," and the strategic aims of the Mtwara railway allowed its construction using European Recovery funds.[69] In 1953 the creation of the Central African Federation gave the railway an added justification as a means for Rhodesian minerals to bypass Portuguese and South African ports, as British relations with apartheid South Africa deteriorated.[70] By that time the Korean War demand for raw materials from central Africa choked feeder ports and railways, such as Beira, in Mozambique.[71] British colonial planners argued that the Mtwara railway would raise the welfare of the region's inhabitants while securing central and East Africa under British hegemony. A member of the East African High Commission wrote, "for about £10 million we could have a British controlled outlet from the hinterland of Africa, which is the only ace card we can hold to prevent economic domination of those British areas by foreign powers."[72] Sir Edward Twining, Tanganyika's governor, endorsed the extension of the railway to Lake Nyasa, and agreed to bring annual traffic to 170,000 tonnes by exporting groundnuts, coal from Ngaka, near Lake Nyasa, and timber.[73]

The impact of the Groundnut Scheme and the Mtwara railway on forestry was immediate and dramatic. The "virtual exclusion of the Forest Department from the Southern Province" came to an end as CDW funding enabled forestry to expand its operations.[74] Late in 1947, as the first bulldozers cleared groundnut land in Nachingwea, the Forest Department opened a new station in Lindi to meet a sudden demand for construction timber and railway ties from woodlands north and south of the Mbwemkuru River.[75] Private sawmillers arrived "all over the place," including two at Nachingwea that produced fifty thousand railway ties by

1949.[76] The heavy demand for ties left a shortfall in construction timber that African pitsawyers pushed to supply.

Contractors paid African pitsawyers high prices for timber of all sorts.[77] While some pitsawyers had licenses, the building frenzy induced widespread illegal cutting of timber and construction poles, leading the Forest Department to hire more African forest guards to patrol reserves and apprehend offenders. In 1949 the Southern Province forest officer banned pitsawing temporarily in an effort to rein in the black market and attempted to control sawyers through licensing and timber quotas. About ten pitsawing associations operated in the province, each restricted to ten mninga trees per month, and eventually only five.[78] Foresters directed pitsawyers to cut *Brachystegia* and *Isoberlina,* less valuable miombo trees, to supply African timber needs so that mvule and mninga would be reserved for the commercial market. They did this by mandating that mvule and mninga be exploited only with mechanized circular saws, which wasted less wood, created a more even cut, and made Tanganyikan timbers more competitive on the international market. This meant that African pitsawyers, for the most part able to afford only handsaws, were unable to profit from the most valuable tree species, which non-African commercial sawmillers were able to monopolize. As the nationalist movement unfolded, African pitsawyers complained about racial bias, and some court cases on the issue of racialized woodcutting received widespread attention.[79]

Besides construction timber and ties, the Mtwara railway took over twenty-eight thousand cubic meters of fuelwood annually for its locomotives, which the Forest Department hoped to salvage from cleared groundnut lands. The department required the Overseas Food Corporation (OFC) to pay a royalty on the scheduled trees that it cut for European and African housing and other infrastructure, as well as for ground clearing, calculating that it was due a royalty of £2 million from groundnut lands in 1947.[80] The OFC was not interested in salvaging trees on its lands, which grew too sparsely to be of much value and slowed groundnut planting. The Tanganyikan government therefore agreed that the OFC would pay royalties only on construction timber and not on trees destroyed to clear land. The global priority given to the Groundnut Scheme led the Forest Department to abandon sound forestry, prompting the Southern Province divisional forest officer to decry that there was no "scientific management" of the forests then under exploitation.[81]

Strained to adequately manage timber exploitation, given the scale of production under way, the Tanganyikan government courted private

Figure 6.3. Rondo Forest and Steel Brothers concession. Map adapted by Thaddeus Sunseri.

concessionaires to open up the forests and woodlands. The most important new player in Southern Province forestry was Steel Brothers Ltd., formerly one of the largest teak merchants in Burma. In 1948 Burma became independent, withdrew from the commonwealth, and nationalized its teak industry.[82] In response, Steel Brothers sought new investment arenas, and Tanganyika was a good prospect, in part because after 1948 many British forest officers formerly posted to India and Burma were reassigned to Tanganyika, one becoming an assistant conservator of forests.[83] The Forest Department with its new "Asian" blood hoped that Steel Brothers would solve the Southern Province timber bottleneck. Toward this end it granted Steels a twenty-year concession to exploit thirty-nine hundred square kilometers of the Rondo Plateau and its environs, with the government obtaining a 50 percent share of the operations, exempting Steels from timber royalties.[84] Located just north of the Mtwara railway and

Figure 6.4. *Mvule* trees on the Rondo Plateau, c. 1912. From Heinrich Schnee, ed., *Deutsches Kolonial-Lexikon,* 3 vols. (Leipzig: Quelle und Meyer, 1920), vol. 1, plate 24.

Figure 6.5. Working in the Rondo sawmill, 1953. Southern Province Development Plans, Public Record Office, CO 822/553.

twenty-five kilometers from Nachingwea, Rondo was a closed-canopy coastal forest with the largest remaining stands of mvule in Tanganyika, over 280 million cubic meters, in addition to mninga and secondary miombo species that now enjoyed market demand.[85] Steels' contract allowed a twenty-year planting-and-harvesting rotation, negotiated down from eighty-to-one-hundred-year rotations, which foresters considered necessary to replant Rondo's hardwoods. Although the conservator admitted that twenty years was too quick for sustainable forestry at Rondo, he bowed to the "very good profits" that the concession promised.[86] Once the original mvule had been cut out, Steels would grow teak and mvule on tree plantations that would yield "over five times as much timber as is standing on Rondo today." Steels' concession helped justify the extension of the Mtwara railway in 1950 by guaranteeing nearly twelve thousand tonnes of timber exports from the Rondo Plateau annually.[87] Yet in 1957 the Forest Department reported that the "special agreement" made with Steels "failed to provide the profits expected," in part because Steels paid no royalties.[88] Nevertheless, the Rondo concession accounted for almost one-fifth of all log timber cut in Tanganyika in 1954.[89]

Forest Reservation and Resistance in Liwale Subdistrict

The escalating demand for Tanganyikan timber led the Forest Department to launch a massive program of forest reservation on miombo woodlands, the only remaining unreserved forests left in the coastal hinterland. Until 1952 softwoods—especially *Podocarpus,* cedar, and sandalwood—dominated the export market, making the northern highlands the focus of Forest Department activity. By 1950 hardwoods made up about 50 percent of exports and thereafter far outdistanced softwoods, making up 90 percent of exports in 1957. Besides fine timbers such as mninga, mvule, and mahogany, many other hardwoods from coastal forests and woodlands had market value for furniture, railway ties, pit props, and charcoal.

Forest reservation proceeded at a fast pace after 1948. Already by 1956 the short-term goal of reserving 8 percent of the landscape was met, and by independence in 1961 the overall target of 14 percent had been exceeded.[90] Woodlands rose from 56 percent of all reserves in 1950 to 87 percent at independence. Woodlands reserves were virtually all classified as exploitable "productive" forest reserves, although even protective forests were not immune from exploitation. Late-colonial forestry aimed primarily to meet the colony's fuel, timber, and revenue needs rather than to protect water catchments.

With financing from the CDW and increased revenues from timber royalties, forest officials fanned out over the countryside surveying woodlands for reservation, sometimes aided by aerial surveys. In contrast to the often small, closed-canopy .German-era forest reserves, miombo reservation was on a huge scale, thus involved substantial dislocation of dispersed peasant populations. In order to coordinate forest management with new reservations, in 1955 the Forest Department's activities were organized into two circles.[91] The "reservation circle" surveyed and demarcated woodlands for reservation. The "intensive management circle" harvested and reforested forest reserves that had good concentrations of marketable timber.

Although the protection of water catchments had long been an important function of forestry, in the postwar years "forest protection" included treeless lands. The 1953 development plan for Southern Province specified that "For the conservation of water supplies a forest reserve may in fact have no forest in it at all since the term means an area in which cultivation and grazing are either under strict control or prohibited altogether. It may therefore have nothing more than grass or scrub cover."[92] As foresters were tasked with reserving land as rapidly as possible in the 1950s, forest definitions changed dramatically. The conservator of forests identified six types of land cover in Ruponda and Kilwa districts, including forest, woodland, intermediate woodland/bushland, bushland and thicket, wooded grassland, and "actively induced vegetation by Natives and Europeans."[93] Of these vegetation types he prioritized forest (only 0.4 percent of the total landscape), but excluded no land from potential reservation, including cultivated land. With no land free from the threat of appropriation, African chiefs and their people viewed forest reservation as a guise to take land and force people to move—another version of closer settlement. Although the Land Ordinance of 1923 prevented the wholesale expulsion of people before consulting chiefs, people could be ordered to cease cultivation in lands defined as forest reserves, thereby forcing their removal.[94]

Rapid forest reservation exacerbated peasant-state tensions, as seen in Liwale Subdistrict. Recently disrupted by the Liwale Closer Settlement Scheme, by the ongoing expansion of the Selous Game Reserve, and by the Groundnut Scheme, foresters returned to the district in 1951 in response to the call to reserve more forests. They first targeted twenty-three hundred square kilometers of woodlands along the Angai River, desirable because of its proximity to Steel Brothers' Rondo concession, the rump Groundnut Scheme at Nachingwea, and the Mtwara railway. Angai enclosed about ten rivers that flowed southeast to the Mbwemkuru River, the historical southern boundary of Liwale and Kilwa districts and the Ngindo homeland. The enclosed area was one of the last remaining open spaces of Liwale not enveloped by the Selous Reserve. When the Angai Reserve was first proposed to the Liwale chief in 1951, he reminded district officials of a government agreement from 1948, following the closer settlement fiasco, which promised the Ngindo a block of land impervious to encroachment by the Selous Game Reserve and further sleeping sickness removals.[95] The proposed Angai Forest broke the agreement just three years later.

In light of widespread peasant opposition to the Angai proposal, the Ruponda district officer reconnoitered the region, meeting with villagers in *barazas* (public meetings).[96] He found fourteen settlements in the area encompassing some three thousand people. They cultivated millet, rice, and maize in the river valleys and cassava in drier areas away from the river and used the woodlands as a famine reserve. Almost every household kept beehives in the woodlands, at a time when Tanganyika had emerged as one of the world's major beeswax exporters. The beeswax industry demanded a dispersed woodlands environment, since hives could not be concentrated too closely without diminishing production.[97] The villagers bristled at the talk of a forest reserve, regarding it as a pretext for yet another mass eviction.[98] The game ranger Constantine Ionides, whose department had encroached on Ngindo lands for two decades, affirmed that in 1948 it was agreed that "no land within the boundaries [was to be] used for other purposes since it was entirely for Ngindo use. . . . They feel very strongly on the subject."[99] In light of intense and vocal opposition, district officials scrapped the Angai proposal, concluding that "the local people should not be pushed around any more."[100]

Despite this retreat, the central government demanded that each district proceed with forest reservation, "the achievement of which aim the Government attaches the highest importance."[101] The secretary for agriculture and natural resources, who oversaw the Forest Department, complained about the slow pace of reservation due to popular resistance and demanded that local officials "start the ball rolling." In response, provincial forestry officials demarcated a new 950-square-kilometer Nyera-Kiperere Forest Reserve northeast of the Angai River, well within the "inviolable"

Ngindo territory confirmed in 1948. While foresters claimed that the new reserve protected a water catchment, its value as a fuel reserve for the Mtwara railway was the primary consideration. The chief of Liwale assented to the reserve, having won abandonment of the Angai proposal in which his ancestral lands lay. He was allocated seven hundred shillings to muster labor to cut the fire traces around the forest, which was gazetted in 1956.[102] The Forest Department concurrently demarcated the two-thousand-square-kilometer Lung'onya Forest Reserve, in northern Ungindo, by then part of the Selous Reserve, to which villagers had returned after being evicted a decade earlier, during the Liwale Closer Settlement Scheme.[103] As the Forest Department created new reserves of this scale throughout Tanganyika, forest encroachment became a major issue at a time of heightened nationalist consciousness.

Forest Encroachers, Arson, and Nationalism

Forest expansion intersected with nationalism in the 1950s by fueling widespread resentment against the colonial government. The backdrop was a British government that believed the East African territories would not be ready for self-government and independence for two decades or more.[104] The Colonial Office regarded Tanganyika as the least developed of these territories, thus the least prepared for self-government. The Tanganyika government sought to frustrate the nationalist movement by co-opting loyalist chiefs, by creating counterweights in the settler and Asian populations, and by allowing limited political reforms at the local and district levels, while denying most people meaningful enfranchisement. Yet these diversions generally failed, largely because African teachers, townsmen, and civil servants in the Tanganyika African National Union (TANU) used local grievances to demand an African voice in policy formation.[105] Events in neighboring colonies also influenced Tanganyikan nationalism. The Mau Mau War in Kenya, for example, fed official fears that popular disturbances in Tanganyika might blossom into rebellion in a territory with weak security forces. While the expansion of forest reserves aimed to foster economic development in order to stave off independence, it instead exacerbated local grievances. Recognizing this connection, TANU used forest struggles to expand its popular base.

The rapid creation of forest reserves led to clashes over land throughout Tanganyika. Following the indolent interwar years, when the Forest Department had largely turned a blind eye to peasant encroachment in forest reserves in much of the territory, the revived department of the 1950s was intent on firmly establishing forest boundaries "so that there should be no doubt in the minds of the public where these are situated."[106] With better financing to staff more forest guards, more encroachments were discovered in the often inaccessible reserves. In 1954, for example, "sizable intrusions" occurred in the Balangai, Mkusu, Jasini, and Mutai forests of Tanga Province. Almost immediately after Lung'onya Forest Reserve had been gazetted in 1957 in Liwale Subdistrict, "some hundreds of people entered . . . on the plea that the boundary river had changed its course."[107] In Tanga District in 1957 "two hundred invaders of Kihuwi and Kwamsambia reserves were evicted by police action." People sometimes destroyed the beacons marking forest boundaries before they encroached into the reserves.[108] In 1958 the Forest Department recorded forty-nine cases of encroachment, which it knew was an undercount because most cases were prosecuted in local courts and therefore not recorded.[109]

Taungya forest cultivation, although central to the Forest Department's efforts to muster labor for forest work, became a matter of contention whenever foresters decided that farmers were no longer needed, often violating people's understanding of the agreements. Since the 1895 Crown Land Act, under German rule, colonial officials had viewed peasant occupancy of land as subject to state dictates, and taungya was no exception. An elder in modern Tanzania recalled how taungya could be used to evict peasants from newly created forest reserves: "The way the Europeans evicted people was very shrewd. They divided the forest into sections and said, You can farm there. They permitted people to farm these sections but then they were told to plant trees wherever there were food crops. But then the trees in the farmland began to damage the food crops. So people gradually left, until eventually everyone was gone. In the end they announced a final date after which people could no longer live in the forest."[110] Many taungya cultivators resisted orders to move. In 1954 in Southern Province foresters repeatedly tried to evict one hundred taungya cultivators in Ruawa Reserve who refused to leave after the end of their three-year contract.[111] The Forest Department abandoned taungya as early as 1951 on the Rondo Plateau in favor of hiring labor directly because of such resistance.[112] Yet villagers repeatedly returned to Rondo Forest after being evicted. As the nationalist movement gained momentum in the late 1950s, the government made some concessions to taungya peasants to erode their support for TANU. In 1957 it amended the forest rules to allow peasants who were willing to do forest work for at least 120 days per year to reside in reserves.[113] Despite that concession, an uneasy relationship existed between taungya cultivators and foresters. Foresters generally referred to taungya peasants as forest squatters, implying impermanency, if not illegality, of occupation, while peasants resented doing forest work on land that they considered to be rightfully their own. Trees conflicted with peasant food crops and made work such as hoeing more difficult. Women, who appear to have done most taungya work, resented the added burden of tending trees alongside food crops, often without the aid of husbands, who worked for wages elsewhere in the colony.

From 1956 TANU and affiliated African political organizations aided taungya peasants near Dar es Salaam in negotiating forest contracts and also helped them resist eviction through court action. As with Vikindu and Pugu forests, in the 1950s the Forest Department and agricultural officers alike sought to increase food, timber, and charcoal production near the city. At the same time, the expansion of Dar es Salaam displaced peasants in the periurban farmlands. To make up for this loss of land, in 1954 the Forest Department issued taungya contracts for farmers in Mogo Forest Reserve, on the southwest periphery of the city.[114] In 1956 TANU representatives were present at Mogo when the taungya agreements were reissued. However, in 1959 the Forest Department decided to end taungya at Mogo, informing the farmers that they had "no right at all to farm in Mogo Government Forest." Encouraged by the overwhelming success of TANU in legislative council elections, the Mogo farmers refused to leave. The TANU-affiliated Tanganyika African Tenants' Association and Tanganyika African Traders' Union acted as advocates for the Mogo farmers, fighting their expulsion in the courts.[115] By mid-1960 the farmers remained in Mogo Forest and others had joined them.[116]

While many farmers resisted expulsion from forest reserves through determination and political maneuvering, others attacked reserves and tree plantations through arson.[117] From 1945 to 1959 the number of fires in forest reserves and tree plantations averaged 155 prosecutions annually, but the Forest Department specified that there were "many more."[118] Not all fires were arson. The eviction of peasants and pastoralists deprived the forests of regular, seasonal burning, allowing a buildup of explosive ground matter.[119] While preventive burning was part of forest management in the 1950s, sufficient labor was not available for forest burning in the entire territory as reserves expanded exponentially, far faster than available forest labor. This made forests vulnerable to natural, negligent, and intentional fires. Arson allowed peasants to attack symbols of colonial authority passively and anonymously. On the Rondo Plateau, for example, peasants ignored orders that they surround their farms with firebreaks, causing annual field fires to jump into the forest. Yet some fires that beset Rondo Forest were deliberate.[120] Sometimes peasants "attacked" forest reserves simply by refusing to fight forest fires, violating local bylaws.[121] In Tanganyika recorded cases of forest arson fluctuated from a high of 368 in 1949 to a low of sixty-four in 1959, perhaps curtailed by an expanded system of forest guards.

Politicizing Labor in the Sawmills

The 1950s was a decade of intense labor organizing in Tanganyika, as elsewhere in Africa. Unionization also came to the sawmills, which expanded tremendously after World War II, in tandem with the expansion of the forest estate. By 1955 some sixty-eight sawmills and many more carpentry shops operated in Tanganyika to supply domestic and export timber.[122] The TANU-affiliated Tanganyika Federation of Labor (TFL) tapped into labor struggles in order to increase its popular base, thereby pressuring the British government to expedite political reform.[123] This was seen in a series of strikes that beset the Steel Brothers sawmills on the Rondo Plateau over wage levels, working conditions, racial job preference, and even access to land. The Steel Brothers operation was a microcosm of colonial labor relations, bringing together taungya farmers, illegal squatters, labor migrants, waged sawmill workers, and pitsawyers against a private corporation and its partner in timber exploitation, the colonial state.

In 1949 Steel Brothers shipped a prefabricated sawmill from England and quickly employed a labor force of 640, which almost doubled by 1954.[124] The workforce included skilled Burmese and Chinese workers from Steels' Burma operations, as well as sixteen Europeans in supervisory roles, replicating a racial division of labor common in East Africa. Steels contracted independent loggers to cut mvule and mninga at Rondo, who were forced into a vassal relationship owing to racial preferences that prevented them for cutting first-schedule trees on their own. The Forest Department expanded Rondo Forest Reserve to make way for Steels' concession, taking land from villagers living on the forest periphery, some of whom remained as taungya cultivators until the Forest Department sought to evict them after 1951. Other peasants moved into the forest as illegal squatters, growing food to sell to sawmill workers.

Working in the Steel Brothers sawmill was intense and dangerous. Begun as a steam-driven operation, Steels' rapid timber output and large labor force of six to seven hundred workers per shift, some working multiple shifts owing to labor shortages, created a chaotic atmosphere.[125] Exposed circular saws posed a hazard to workers, and the government labor inspector cited dangerous conditions on several occasions. In 1959 a worker was electrocuted as he passed by a winch. The sawmill processed what was effectively a nonrenewable resource, since Steels did not reforest adequately to maintain production after the original mvule and mninga had been cut out. Workers therefore had no long-term security. Moreover, the timber market was erratic, so layoffs and production slumps alternated with labor shortages and production bottlenecks. The mill operated around the clock, and by 1954 the average employee work week was fifty-five hours.

Beginning in 1956 Steels' workers organized, seeking higher wages and food rations. They enlisted as their spokesman a local farmer, Juma Saidi, who resented Steels' concession for expanding onto his land. Saidi is a good example of what Steven Feierman has termed peasant intellectuals, leaders who emerged from local societies to articulate popular grievances, often filling vacuums created by the colonial co-option of chiefs.[126] In September 1957 Saidi led a strike after Steels dismissed five workers for presenting grievances to the sawmill manager. The labor inspector concluded that Saidi was the moving force behind the strike and that "his motives for entering into these discussions were tinged with political considerations. There is a history of political trouble on the Rondo Plateau connected with the cutting of logs by Steel Brothers, and it is known that Juma Saidi has been active in opposing any extension of the cutting rights of Steel Brothers, and has objected to the cutting of logs by Steel Brothers."[127] Steel Brothers flew in the district commissioner from Lindi on one of its own airplanes when it appeared that the strike, although peaceful, was taking on a political tinge. During the strike most of the workers joined the Building and Construction Workers' Union in Lindi, a union led by carpenters and masons who had a reputation for radicalism, and began negotiating through the union.[128] The workers refused to return to work by the 10 October deadline set by the mill manager. Eventually, Rashidi Kawawa, general secretary of the TFL and a member of TANU's central committee, arrived and convinced the workers to return to work after the mill manager guaranteed a raise in wage levels. Kawawa used the Steels strike to increase the influence of the TFL and TANU. Some fifteen hundred people responded to a union meeting called by TANU at nearby Nachingwea "to demonstrate their strength and to present a petition."[129] There is little doubt that most workers saw the union movement as operating in sync with the nationalist movement.

Although Steels' workers won better wages and rations, farmers such as Juma Saidi watched as the Rondo concession ate up their land. Peasant anger at the timber concession and colonial forestry's usurpation of land was seen in attacks against stands of mvule, Steels favored timber. Farmers ignored district foresters' orders to surround their farms with firebreaks, although it is possible that adequate household labor was simply unavailable for this arduous work, with many men absent as labor migrants, some at Steels' sawmill. Field fires and intentional arson alike destroyed mvule in Rondo Reserve. Farmers also ignored forest rules and cut down mvule growing in their fields. The conservator lamented, "The [Rondo] inhabitants are indifferent to the fate of the mvule and are in complete ignorance of the Native Authority regulations covering shamba [field] burning."[130] He summarized, "The view is commonly held that they [mvule] are preserved for the sole purpose of supplying timber for European houses."

Rapid forest reservation after World War II was part of what has been called the "second colonial occupation," a period when British colonial officials sought to develop their African territories along semi-industrial lines in order to raise living standards, integrate the colonies more fully into the empire, and allow greater political participation. This agenda aimed to solidify colonial control for at least another generation. Its counterpart was the new valuing of Tanganyikan hardwoods that came with the timber shortages created by World War II and the Cold War. The Forest Department became a key player in the 1950s development agenda, providing railway ties, mine shoring, timber, and fuel that would help maintain British power. The tenfold increase in forest reserves from the end of the war to independence in 1961 created a forest estate in Tanganyika that was more than half the size of Britain itself.

Such a large-scale expansion of forestry created profound social tensions. Many communities, just recovering from sleeping sickness and game park evictions, were confronted with a new state agenda of forced relocation. The Forest Department eased some rural anger with taungya forest cultivation, which allowed farmers to do forest work in exchange for land. However, taungya was a relationship fraught with tension, since the state tolerated forest farmers only as long as they fulfilled its needs.

Pitsawyers were aggrieved at colonial racial preferences that favored Asians in the exploitation of the most valuable hardwoods. They faced competition from technology and capital, as better transport and mechanization enabled sawmill entrepreneurs such as Steel Brothers to far outpace manual labor in the scale of production. Indeed, sawmillers employed Africans not as pitsawyers who put a finished product onto the market, but as loggers who used the ax only to fell trees. Finally, sawmill workers resented low wages, dangerous working conditions, and a labor structure that reserved skilled positions for foreign workers.

In seeking to develop Tanganyika rapidly so as to undermine nationalism and stave off independence, late-colonial forestry did the opposite. The bureaucratic elite of the main nationalist political party, TANU, used local grievances to rally common people to the cause of self-government and eventual independence. Taungya farmers and other peasants facing eviction from forests read into TANU's actions a promise of future access to land in forest reserves, while pitsawyers and other forest workers saw TANU as ending racial preferences that deprived them of equal access to resources. In 1958 TANU won 68 percent of the seats in the legislative council and, despite continued British obstruction, called for responsible self-government by Africans by 1959.[131] With further electoral successes in 1960, Julius Nyerere of TANU formed his first ministry in October and called for independence in 1961, years ahead of the British timetable. TANU's successes encouraged peasants to reclaim the forests. The Forest Department reported in 1960 that encroachments were on the rise as "political changes gave rise in some quarters to a misguided notion that forest reserves were there for the taking." District officials reported a "criminal attitude towards land" to be prevalent at Nachingwea. In Chilungula village a headman organized an invasion of an estate belonging to the Tanganyika Agricultural Corporation (successor to the OFC), while other people were said to be "living a wild life in the woods."[132] Meanwhile, Steel Brothers cut the last remaining stock of mvule on the Rondo Plateau and prepared to vacate Tanganyika as independence approached, making its entire workforce redundant.[133] As a harbinger of battles to come after independence, the Forest Department's 1960 annual report noted, "It is gratifying that the Minister [Nyerere] has affirmed that Government will punish those who break the law in this respect as in any other, and will not condone the attrition of the forest estate."[134] Farmers aggrieved by forest reserve expansion helped bring TANU into government, but once there TANU would set a different agenda.

CHAPTER 7

Creating Modern Tanzanians

State Forestry from Uhuru through Ujamaa, 1961–80

AFTER 1960 the African elite who came to control Tanzania set a modernization agenda that was a mixture of late-colonial developmentalism and African nationalism. TANU quickly disempowered the class of chiefs that had served as colonial functionaries and created an ideology of secular nationalism that aimed to modernize Tanzanians.[1] In relegating chiefs to the sidelines, the new state devalued symbols of chiefly authority, such as ancestral charters associated with forest shrines. If there was to be an "ax wielder" with authority over forest access, it would be the central state itself. Despite TANU's critique of colonialism, it shared late-colonial economic goals that aimed to increase export revenues, mechanize the countryside, transform subsistence peasants into surplus-producing farmers, and begin to industrialize. Tanzania's forests would serve this agenda by providing timber, poles, and fuel for economic growth. The major departure from colonial forestry was that the state initially opened the forests up to greater peasant access. Pitsawyers, taungya forest cultivators, and charcoal burners alike worked, farmed, and exploited the forests in the heady early years of African nationalism.

While British foresters remained for much of the 1960s, Tanzanians took over the Forest Division by the middle of the decade, combining Western scientific forestry with African nationalism.[2] Although some were initially uneasy with greater peasant access to the forests, Tanzanian foresters participated enthusiastically in the nationalist goal of increasing timber production. The nationalist agenda assumed a high rate of development that would convert backward peasants into modern farmers and workers. Tanzanians would become modern consumers, no longer reliant on poles, saplings, and thatch for their dwellings, but on timber, concrete, and corrugated iron for modern houses that reflected the sedentary lifestyle of the urban worker and intensive farmer. This vision denigrated the dispersed miombo woodlands' environment that covered half of Tanzania, readily accepting that it would be replaced with cultivated land, tree plantations, and exploitable natural forests interspersed with closed forest reserves that would preserve water catchments and guard against soil erosion. In many respects this agenda was torn from the colonial blueprint, except that now the resources and collective national will seemed to be available to bring it to fruition.

Even before the end of the 1960s the development agenda seemed to go awry. Capital-intensive agricultural projects failed, while most peasants resisted becoming the modern farmers that the state envisioned. Although brought to power in large part by a wave of peasant nationalism, the state viewed peasant-initiated projects as a usurpation of its authority, a sign that it was losing control at the local level. The result was an assertion of statism with the Arusha Declaration of 1967, whereby Julius Nyerere mandated the transformation of the countryside through ujamaa villagization, reminiscent of colonial closer settlement, but on a much larger scale. It called on forestry to participate in a campaign that was called socialism and self-reliance through rural restructuring and continued revenue generation. This was seen in vast state-sponsored industrial projects to manufacture charcoal for an export market. Villagization, coinciding with economic crisis, called for cash crop production at any cost, including opening up new land in forest reserves. By the 1970s ujamaa rural restructuring weakened Forest Division oversight, threatening the fundamentals of scientific forestry and forests alike.

Restructuring Forest Reserves in Independent Tanzania, 1961–70

Although the late-colonial goal of reserving 14 percent of the landscape as forest reserves had been achieved by 1961, the forest estate did not remain static after independence. Many peasants saw the independence struggle as bringing access to land that was often located in recently declared forest reserves. In this they were sometimes supported by newly elected Tanzanian local officials who sympathized with the peasant need for land, often to the chagrin of British foresters. District officials often granted access to forest lands to villagers who made the case that they could increase cash crops, and they excised some reserves or readjusted their boundaries to make way for peasants. A 1964 administrative order informed forest officers, "Some reserves are definitely of no value, either because their original purpose has vanished or because they were acquired during the reservation drive without detailed consideration of their value. These reserves should either be formally revoked or left unattended pending more detailed examination in the future. Pressure on these reserves will not be resisted and encroachment will be dealt with by revocation or excision if and when action becomes necessary but not before."[3]

This lax attitude encouraged peasants living adjacent to forest reserves to stake a claim to forest land. In January 1961, for example, the African district officer of Mzizima (formerly Kisarawe), J. Kimicha, asked the Forest Division whether land was available in Hundogo and Pande forest reserves for licensed cultivation.[4] While there were no openings in these forests, Kimicha learned that a forest parcel called Majohe was available for settlement. He wrote to the leader of one the prospective settlers, Shabani Pazi, that "there is no obstacle whatsoever if you and your 55 people want to farm in this forest."[5] In other cases district officers were unable to stop illegal occupation of forests. Some fifty householders who had organized themselves as the Mzizima African Farmers' Cooperative Society encroached into Hundogo Reserve, while other peasants exerted continuous pressure for forest lands. In the early 1960s the Forest Division excised several small German-era forest reserves close to Dar es Salaam because "they served no important forest value, present and future."[6] One of these was Mogo Forest, on the outskirts of Dar es Salaam, excised in 1966.[7] The high state priority given to cash crop production made forest reserves vulnerable to peasant pressure.[8] Many local officials tolerated de facto peasant occupancy of forest reserves, even though many peasants, especially those lacking taungya contracts, had no security of tenure.[9]

Although pressure for land near Dar es Salaam and in the northern highlands was extraordinary, illegal encroachment into forest reserves was countrywide. Foresters reported extensive settlement in nearly all forest reserves in Rufiji District. Luhoi River Forest Reserve, gazetted only in 1962, was repeatedly violated with little resistance from district authorities.[10] In 1968 the Forest Division reported sarcastically, "The Rufiji District Council continued its interest in depleting their famous Ruhoi Forest Reserve. A hundred and one encroachers are the current pioneers in the reserve."[11] Foresters claimed that most encroachment was in areas where land was not in short supply, thus reflecting "deliberate sabotage by the local people" with complicity from local authorities.[12]

Because of such local indifference and lack of cooperation, the Forest Division ignored local and district authority reserves by the mid-1960s, viewing their oversight as a waste of scarce department resources. Instead it focused on remarking the borders of the major catchment forests so that their jurisdiction could be "upheld in a court of law."[13] Often bypassing district authorities completely, foresters breached the centralization of power that TANU sought during the 1960s, in effect creating a parallel administrative structure. Yet the Forest Division demonstrated its commitment to TANU's development agenda by increasing forest revenues.

Concentrating its oversight on forest reserves, the Forest Division opened up unreserved woodlands to greater exploitation in what became known as the Dar es Salaam system. At the end of colonial rule the Forest Division allowed "the salvage exploitation of unalienated lands which will sooner or later be cleared for cultivation."[14] After purchasing a two-month license for one hundred shillings (raised to a hundred shillings per month by 1964), anyone could cut down any tree of any size on unreserved lands as long as a royalty payment was assessed. Potentially 212,245 square kilometers (24 percent of the landscape) was opened for exploitation, bringing revenue to the state from what was otherwise considered a "wasting asset," and benefiting African pitsawyers directly.[15] Lauding the revenues generated by the "marked increase of trees cut in the Dar es Salaam area, amounting to thirteen times the 1959 quantity in the case of muninga," the Forest Division extended the system to Rufiji and Morogoro districts in 1960 and to Tabora in 1965. The Dar es Salaam system valued unreserved woodlands only for their marketable trees, concluding that "sustained yield management is not practiced on public lands as these areas will ultimately succumb to agriculture."[16]

Pitsawyers also benefited from the departure after independence of expatriate timber industrialists. For example Steel Brothers, the largest late-colonial timber industrialist, left for British Guiana after having cut out most of the Rondo Plateau, and mvule exports immediately dropped by half. Other sawmillers left Tanzania after independence, creating a demand for pitsawyers. In 1961 hand-sawed timber accounted for 22 percent of Tanzania's total timber output, including more than half of all mvule and mninga, which African loggers had been prevented from cutting before independence.[17] Peasants and pitsawyers alike benefited from greater access to forest lands and resources in the first decade of independence.

Forestry and Development after Independence

The Tanzanian government gave great priority to achieving a high rate of economic growth in both agriculture and industry. Forestry's contribution, as laid out in the government's three-year development plan (1961–64), was to expedite the managed exploitation of natural forests while expanding tree plantations of mostly exotic softwoods to supply domestic and export wood needs. The Forest Division expected both "productive" forests and "protective" forests to be "highly productive of timber."[18] The division concentrated on replacing slow-growing indigenous trees with fast-growing softwoods, although some forests were allowed to regenerate naturally. The division granted private concessions to harvest natural forests, sometimes for specific hardwoods, with a clear attempt to Africanize exploitation. In this way a major part of the labor question was taken out of Forest Division oversight. In Kisarawe, Rufiji, and Nachingwea districts the division granted concessionaires exclusive cutting rights for mpingo and in Kilwa District an African cooperative was its sole harvester.[19] Pitsawyers worked in forests that concessionaires were unable or disinclined to harvest.[20]

The Forest Division expected that tree plantations would provide the bulk of the nation's consumer and development wood needs. A 1961 FAO study estimated that the country's demand for poles would increase by 2.3 times between 1960 and 2000, while the demand for sawn timber would quadruple in the same period (from about 150,000 cubic meters to 566,000 cubic meters).[21] Urban residents would increase the demand for paper and fuelwood. Natural forest reserves, overwhelmingly composed of scattered woodlands, could not supply the country's needs, thus rapid tree planting took center stage. Of the £465,000 allocated for forestry in the 1961 three-year plan, 65 percent went to softwood plantations.[22] The five-year plan that began in 1964 allocated £53,000 for protective forests and £770,000 (94 percent) for silviculture and reforestation.[23] Colonial rule ended with only 6,000 hectares of softwood plantations.[24] By 1968 the Forest Division expanded softwood plantations to 22,000 hectares on fifteen sites and aimed for 71,500 hectares by 2000 to meet projected national needs.[25] In the coastal hinterland the Forest Division expanded softwood plantations in Kisarawe, Pugu, and Bana forest reserves during the 1960s.[26]

Although colonial forest policy in the 1950s had always expected intensive management to follow forest reservation, independent Tanzania aimed for faster economic development to overcome the inequities of colonialism, backed by the World Bank, the UN/FAO, and other multilateral lenders. The government prioritized "economic projects which would yield the quickest and the highest returns in the near future."[27] These included highly capitalized agricultural settlement projects to accelerate cash crop output. Among these were tobacco schemes that demanded tens of thousands of hectares of fuelwood for curing. Every hectare of tobacco required 8.1 hectares of eucalyptus for curing, assuming rapid (five-year) planting and harvesting rotations.[28] Natural forests could not meet that demand because their trees were not concentrated enough for efficient exploitation, they were far from communications lines, and their hardwoods regenerated too slowly to be used sustainably. The Forest Division therefore planned for 2,400 hectares of new softwood plantations annually during the first five-year plan. In the Rovuma region householders were expected to grow a little less than one-half hectare of tobacco in the 1960s, which would require about two-thirds of a hectare of fuel trees per year.[29] This demand sent women into the woodlands to collect the needed fuelwood rather than add a little over three-quarters of a hectare of trees to household cropping regimes.

Policymakers hoped that economic development would transform Tanzanians into modern consumers of wood. Multilateral and bilateral donors and Tanzanian officials alike believed that peasants were conservative, backward, and in need of Western-style guidance in order to participate fully in economic modernization.[30] The first five-year plan attempted to modernize Tanzanians by moving from subsistence production to intensive farming of monocropped fields using machinery and fertilizers.[31] Echoing colonial attempts to modernize the countryside, the goal was for peasants to cease "the impermanent shifting life that is the root cause of poverty in the midst of plenty."[32] Modern Tanzanians would be sedentary farmers who lived in permanent houses constructed from sawed timber and plywood. Modernity assumed decreased consumption of poles, saplings, and fuelwood and increased use of sawed timber and electricity, hallmarks of industrial consumer society. A forest official pointed out that industrial nations consumed half a cubic meter of wood per capita per year, fifty times more than Tanzanians.[33] Increased timber consumption thus signified industrial modernity. Woodlands alone could not create modern Tanzanians because their trees were difficult to work with hand tools and were too scattered to be profitable for commercial sawyers. The modernization ideal therefore devalued woodlands as "uneconomic to harvest," inviting their neglect or replacement with softwood plantations.[34] The urban sector also demanded timber for construction, industry, and import substitution. One of the Forest Division's mandates was to create a forest estate that would attract the capital needed to develop industry. Forest policymakers therefore concluded that "to encourage the capital inflow needed, Tanzania must sell itself as a good potential investment area. . . . we must make potential investors aware that we have a resource that can be tapped profitably."[35] Rural and urban development demanded tree plantations, which in turn demanded labor.

Because forest exploitation was divided between state, private, and subsistence activities, sources are unclear about the numbers of forest workers or their origins. Every peasant family obtained poles and firewood from forests and woodlands, providing the bulk of the nation's wood needs at a subsistence level. The Forest Division itself employed modest numbers of wage laborers to clean forest boundaries, to plant and weed trees, and to cut and transport timber and poles.[36] In 1969 over five thousand people worked in the forests for wages, although the number fluctuated seasonally.[37] It was important that forest boundaries be cleaned before peasant field burning caused fires to jump into reserves or tree plantations. In stark contrast to the labor shortage of the colonial period, by 1970 there was "an enormous reserve of labor" willing to do forest work.[38] Because state forests were distributed throughout the country, often in inaccessible rural areas, it offered peasants one of the only means to earn cash to supplement household incomes. It also meshed with the government's goal of devolving wage labor from urban to rural areas.[39]

The work of clearing forest boundaries was immense given the size of forest reserves. In 1963, for example, foresters cleared 275 kilometers of reserve boundaries in the Morogoro, Coast, and Dodoma regions alone, although most reserves went unprotected. Inadequate funding in the 1960s meant that the ideal firebreak width of five to seven meters cleared annually was scaled down to two meters.[40]

On tree plantations, wage workers as well as prison labor planted, weeded, pruned, and thinned the tree crop at least once a year. Yet taungya cultivators did most work on tree plantations. During the first five-year plan some twenty thousand people made their living as taungya cultivators, altogether some four thousand households on ten of the division's twenty-one tree plantations.[41] The Forest Division lauded taungya as forestry's contribution to national agricultural development in light of state efforts to promote village settlement schemes and agricultural co-operatives. Taungya was a means for the Forest Division to articulate a nationalist vision of development based on peasant production at a time when there was pressure to release forest reserves for cultivation.[42] It allowed foresters to control the extent and location of peasant residence in forest reserves. In contrast to the piecemeal colonial-era taungya settlements, cultivators lived in forest villages that, at their most developed, included piped water, dispensaries, and recreation and welfare buildings. Taungya was an early form of villagization and helped stem urbanization and encourage rural industry and employment. It taught farmers forest skills, including tree planting, pruning, thinning, road construction, and equipment operation, for which they received a modest wage. The forest conservator R.G. Sangster saw taungya as necessary because the "failure of the forestry program will either deprive these people of their livelihood or will result in them remaining in the forest without tree-planting obligations and the consequent loss of forest land."[43]

It was not a foregone conclusion that peasants would accept taungya licenses, which forbade them to plant root crops, such as cassava, and mandated a tree-planting schedule that sometimes competed with food crop regimes. In Uzaramo, with its stark division between fertile and marginal land, the ability to grow cassava was a key factor in rural prosperity. In the 1950s a chief of Kariakoo, Saidi Chaurembo, asserted unequivocally that where cassava could not be grown, "no settlement can flourish."[44] For all its nutritional disadvantages, cassava was a labor-saving plant that could be grown in poor soils.[45] Thus, taungya rules were a severe hardship in the coastal hinterland. Taungya overburdened women in particular, who did most of the work tending trees alongside food crops. Tree plantations also sheltered crop predators. Taungya was most successful where land was scarce, as in the periurban environs of Dar es Salaam, where there was incentive for peasants to assume the added burdens of taungya while having no security of tenure. After the Arusha Declaration, taungya fell into disfavor because impermanent landholding contravened the goal of creating a sedentary peasantry.[46] Yet taungya continued out of necessity. On the Rondo Plateau, for example, foresters worried that taungya farmers would leave because land was available elsewhere with no obligation to tend trees.[47] In the 1970s many taungya villages recast themselves as ujamaa villages in order to stake a claim to forest land.

Charcoal and National Development

The Arusha Declaration called on the Forest Division to aggressively contribute to national development.[48] The division responded by using the forests near Dar es Salaam to produce charcoal on an industrial scale. While these forests had long been important suppliers of urban fuel, from the late 1960s the division attempted to compete in the international charcoal market.[49] The potential to bring in foreign exchange from this market paved the way for the nationalization of most forest industries and provided incentive to expand silviculture and taungya forest settlements.

From 1963 the Forest Division promoted an export charcoal industry when it approved a concession to exploit Vikindu Forest Reserve, south of Dar es Salaam. An expatriate businessman from Arusha sought the Vikindu concession to produce 135 tonnes of charcoal per month, eventually to be expanded to 540 tonnes per month.[50] He planned to export the charcoal to Europe and the Middle East, pointing out that the UK had a demand for 45,000 tonnes of powdered charcoal per year for synthetic rubber, tires, chemical and electrical products, and steel manufacture, while the Persian Gulf imported lump charcoal for domestic cooking. Foresters saw the scheme as making the Vikindu fuelwood plantations of the 1950s economically viable while finding a use for the remaining natural forest. The division hoped that it would bring 1.4 million Tanzanian shillings in foreign exchange annually and another 100,000 shillings per year from wood royalties. Although the project apparently foundered when the businessman objected to the need to form a cooperative with African charcoal burners, it launched an ongoing Tanzanian interest in the export charcoal market.

Following the demise of the Vikindu concession the Forest Division contacted charcoal dealers in the UK, United States, and the Persian Gulf, requesting information about their charcoal preferences and price requirements.[51] The division also investigated methods to expand Tanzania's charcoal production, which had been geared solely to meet domestic urban fuel needs. In 1970 Tanzania produced nineteen to twenty-one thousand tonnes of marketed charcoal per year.[52] Dar es Salaam consumers alone took more than half that amount, and their demand was expected to increase steadily as the urban population grew. Peasants produced most of this charcoal in earth kilns, which had low yields, uneven quality, and seasonal output. The rainy season delayed charcoal production substantially. The Forest Division resented its inability to monitor peasant charcoal production, which was scattered and hidden in forests and woodlands, often skirting forest controls. Peasants built kilns or pits close to sources of preferred hardwood logs, piling brush and earth over mounds of logs to prevent complete consumption of the wood.[53] Assembling a kiln for a single smelt usually took about two weeks. By 1970 the division moved to rationalize this production and triple its output to sixty thousand tonnes per year, half of which would be exported.

The Forest Division hoped to expand charcoal production by increasing its number of steel kilns. In 1969 the division owned ten steel kilns that altogether could produce only 540 tonnes (about 20,400 bags) annually. One kiln required six to eight hectares of forest per year to produce to capacity.[54] The second five-year plan (1969–74) allocated funds to purchase more steel kilns, since the division concluded that "local casual charcoal burners" were insufficient for an export industry.[55] By 1970 the division owned twenty-five kilns that produced 1,350 tonnes annually, still only 7 percent of total production and far below national goals. The division intended to add fifty more steel kilns by 1971, while still encouraging peasant production by purchasing trucks to transport charcoal from the distant countryside.[56] As the industry matured, foresters expected five thousand people to be permanently employed producing charcoal in steel kilns. Although steel kilns could use waste wood from cleared forests, they required steady wood supplies in order to offset the price of the kilns (five thousand shillings each) and to keep labor gangs fully employed. This in turn demanded ever greater forest exploitation.

The incentive to expand the charcoal industry was a Middle East export market that could bring needed foreign exchange. Ironically, the more

Figure 7.1. Charcoal truck bound for Dar es Salaam. Photograph by Thaddeus Sunseri.

Figure 7.2. Charcoal awaiting transport to Dar es Salaam. Photograph by Thaddeus Sunseri.

dependent Tanzania became on Middle East petroleum, the more it sought to export charcoal to the region to offset petroleum costs. Tanzania exported on average 28 tonnes of charcoal per year between 1965 and 1968, compared to Kenya's annual exports of 4,806 tonnes.[57] Somalia was also an important charcoal exporter until 1968, when it restricted exports, creating a sudden vacuum that Tanzania hoped to fill. While Kenya doubled its charcoal exports to 9,213 tonnes in 1968, Persian Gulf states required about 80,000 tonnes per year, favoring charcoal made from East African hardwoods, whose lump qualities made it especially suitable for domestic cooking.[58]

In 1969 a Kuwaiti importer ordered 3,000 tonnes of charcoal from Tanzania, which the Ministry of Natural Resources could not supply immediately.[59] In early 1970 the ministry agreed to supply 500 tonnes from a new clearance scheme in Ruvu North and Ruvu South forest reserves and from charcoal burners around Dar es Salaam. Unable to produce this amount, the Forest Division called on peasants from newly constituted ujamaa villages to increase output from earth kilns.[60] The ministry organized a Tanzanian state charcoal industry to centralize and expand production to 10,000 tonnes per year within two years, ultimately hoping to export 100,000 tonnes per year while employing as many as seven thousand people permanently, including an assistant forester to organize charcoal production. By April 1970 the Dar es Salaam district forest officer worried that the 500-tonne Kuwaiti order could not be met, so he stepped up purchases from charcoal burners on the roads north and south of Dar es Salaam. Rains delayed the movement of steel kilns into the forests, so only half the Kuwaiti order was met by May. Meanwhile, Middle East orders kept coming. A Kuwaiti firm sought 2,000 tonnes, Iraqis requested 6,000 tonnes, and a Karachi firm ordered 30,000 tonnes.[61] In 1970 Middle East countries ordered 70,000 tonnes of Tanzanian charcoal, but virtually all those orders went unfilled, despite the Forest Division's best efforts.[62] Yet in 1970 the Forest Division increased its charcoal production to 2,081 tonnes, compared to 622 tonnes in 1969, and by 1972 its output had more than doubled, to 4,493 tonnes.[63]

Hoping to supply charcoal to the Middle East and Europe and fulfil its national obligations as called for in the Arusha Declaration, the Forest Division set out to industrialize charcoal production. The foundation of the industry was to be a factory at Kibaha, west of Dar es Salaam, that could produce twelve to fifteen thousand tonnes of charcoal per year and by-products that included methanol, tar, and acetic acid.[64] Forest officials

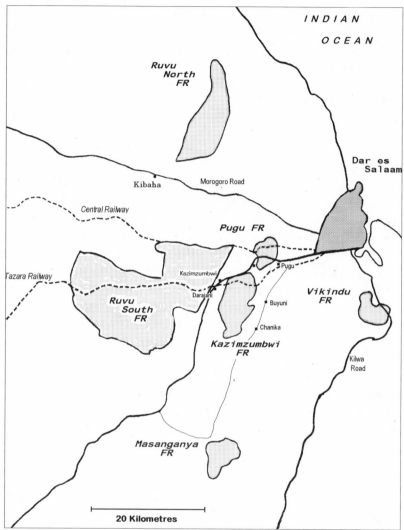

Figure 7.3. Dar es Salaam–area forest reserves, c. 1970. Map adapted by Thaddeus Sunseri.

expected the Kibaha factory to supply ten thousand tonnes of charcoal to the Middle East annually, and another ten thousand tonnes to Dar es Salaam consumers. The German chemical corporation Degussa requested a standing order of five hundred tonnes per month. The raw material would come from hardwoods cleared from Dar es Salaam–area forest reserves, especially Ruvu North and Ruvu South, which the division expanded in anticipation of the charcoal scheme. While it appears that the charcoal factory was never built, in the early 1970s the Forest Division began to clear forests in support of the proposal. As the natural forest was cleared, pines and eucalyptus replaced indigenous hardwoods, which grew fast although they were far less suitable for charcoal. In order to maintain "a constant flow of raw material after the Bana/Ruvu reserve gets exhausted," the division included Vikindu Reserve in the scheme.[65] In November 1971 the general manager of the Tanga Development Corporation requested six to ten steel kilns to produce charcoal for local and export needs from Tanga forests.[66]

The Kibaha charcoal project revived forest reserve expansion in the coastal hinterland west of Dar es Salaam, coinciding with ujamaa villagization. The focus was on two reserves that had colonial origins. The 1,250-hectare German-era Mtakuja Reserve (in Bagamoyo District), which had been expanded as the 11,142-hectare Bana Forest in 1957, became the 32,000-hectare Ruvu North Reserve in 1978.[67] Bana's initial purpose had been to supply fuel, timber, and poles to Bagamoyo town using taungya labor. Two other reserves, Banda and Kola, gazetted in Kisarawe District in 1958 on 15,028 hectares, grew into the 35,500-hectare Ruvu South Reserve in 1979.[68] While Ruvu North and South included some "natural forest," both were mainly "woodland and bushland" and cultivated land by 1967, with miombo tree species dominating.[69] Beginning in 1967 the Forest Division began pine trials in these forests and in nearby Pugu and Kazimzumbwi coastal forests to supply pulp and paper mills near Dar es Salaam.[70] The division planted 2,200 hectares of eucalyptus at Ruvu North beginning in 1972 in anticipation of the charcoal plant, whose first harvest was expected in 1978, by which time most of the natural forest would be converted into charcoal and long sold. The pine trials in particular were beset with problems, including plagues of giant rats, waterlogging, weed infestations, and drought in 1973–74 and 1979–80.[71] The success of Ruvu silviculture depended on the labor of peasants from nearby ujamaa villages, who combined food crops with "the weeding of fire wood and charcoal trees." Ujamaa villagization thus intersected with taungya methods of tending tree plantations, answering the question of where forest labor came from during this time of transition.

In the 1960s the Forest Division prepared to evict peasants from Ruvu North and South in order to convert the forests into monocrop tree plantations. It drew up a list of villagers to be expelled from Bana (Ruvu

North), along with a compensation schedule for the fruit trees and crops they would lose.[72] Men predominated among the 449 household heads in the reserve, with holdings that showed relative affluence. For example, Ramadhani Mwinyimkuu owned seven coconut trees, twenty-eight cashew trees, nine mango trees, ten banana trees, and one orange tree.[73] The roughly twenty female household heads included Fatuma Mbega, who owned forty-three cashew trees, eleven banana trees, one coconut tree, six mango trees, and eleven papaya trees. The division compensated immature trees at 50 percent of value and tree seedlings at 10 percent of value. There was no compensation for annual crops since villagers could harvest them before vacating the land. The evictions came at a time when the Tanzanian state discouraged individual farming and castigated prosperous rural farmers as kulaks.[74]

Opposition to the forest expansion came from over one hundred villagers living in a forest enclave called Mbuganyama, who refused to have their crops and abodes assessed for compensation.[75] Many of the men worked in Dar es Salaam, returning home seasonally to assist their wives with farming. The village chairman, S. J. Madebe, who claimed to be the father of all the villagers, led the resistance. When the Forest Division prepared to clear the forest for a tree plantation, the villagers announced their intent to form an ujamaa village, which was the cornerstone of post-Arusha development policy. In so doing, the villagers indicated their intent to farm communally, a means of avoiding the kulak taint. They furthermore offered to work as taungya forest cultivators, winning the endorsement of a regional forestry team and the approval of the Ministry of Natural Resources.[76] After this success, other farmers stepped forward. Rajabu Jusuf, claiming to be one of Madebe's children, demanded that his seventy-five-hectare farm be included in the village, but he was turned down. Some of his employees then threatened an assistant forester named Mziray, preventing him from felling trees in preparation of the tree plantation. The forest officer Sakaya believed that the claim of being an ujamaa village was simply a ruse, pointing out that all the householders continued to work on their own farms, creating "a class of landlords operating large estates" who also neglected to do forest work. He worried that other villagers who had agreed to leave the forest after receiving compensation would seek to reclaim their land. The case of Mbuganyama village shows that villagers learned quickly to exploit state priorities at a time of ujamaa nationalism in order to thwart the loss of land to the expansion of the forest reserve.

Ujamaa Villagization and Forest Encroachment

Following the Arusha Declaration, President Nyerere called on peasants living in dispersed settlements to concentrate into planned villages, where the state could provide services and direct development, a revival of colonial closer-settlement schemes.[77] Presidential circular no. 1 of 1969 ordered government departments to prioritize ujamaa villages in their spending and planning.[78] Encouragement to amalgamate before 1973 gave way to a TANU resolution that ordered all peasants to reside in planned villages. By the end of 1976 state officials had relocated 70 percent of peasants, some 11 million people, often by force.

Operation Planned Villages, as the directive was called, had contradictory, unplanned repercussions for forestry.[79] First, in some cases forestry became a tool of villagization when new or expanded forest reserves provided the legal basis for the removal of people from dispersed, hidden settlements—a pattern with clear colonial precedents. In some cases new forest reserves were created on land recently cleared of peasants, making it difficult for people to return once the villagization frenzy was over. Second, in 1972 management of many forests was devolved to the regional and district level, where oversight was weaker or where political agendas, such as villagization itself, took precedence. District officials often neglected forest boundaries and encouraged peasant encroachment into reserves. Third, concentrated into ujamaa villages, peasants increased pressure on nearby forests and woodlands, while lands that they were forced to leave regenerated.[80] Beyond the balance sheet of positive or negative effects on forests, villagization upset established norms of forest use and conflicted with the "ecological consciousness" of rural people, disrupting and devaluing their relationship to the environment.[81]

The expansion of Ruvu North and South forest reserves, coinciding with villagization in Dar es Salaam's hinterland, illustrates some of these points.[82] When British foresters created Kazimzumbwi Reserve in 1954, they expelled peasants, some of whom they relocated to the forest's western periphery on woodlands targeted to become Banda/Kola (Ruvu South) Reserve on the eve of independence. In the 1970s the state took over these lands, squeezing peasants between Kazimzumbwi and Ruvu South forests, creating the ujamaa village of Kazimzumbwi. One elder recalled the expansion of these forests since colonial times:

Indeed, those English also expelled us in order to mark the borders of the forest reserve. Thus people who were living inside the forest were all removed—some were brought to Kisarawe—those who had planted trees inside the reserve were compensated by the English government. This was phase one. Phase two was in the 1970s, and they did the same. They gathered together people who were scattered in this area and gathered them into the ujamaa village of Kazimzumbwi. Then it was forbidden to enter into the forest, and if you were caught there everything would be confiscated.[83]

In Ruvu North as well, villagization in effect defined the forest boundaries, as people evicted from forest settlements and relocated to ujamaa villages created a vacuum that became the de facto forest boundary.[84]

Although in cases such as these forest reserves expanded into areas once farmed, the opposite dynamic also took place, whereby local planners carved ujamaa villages out of forest reserves. A forester reported from Kasulu District in western Tanzania, for example, that "Zeze ujamaa village is completely in the interior of Mkuti forest reserve," and a piece of the reserve was distributed to *wajamaa* (citizens of ujamaa villages).[85] Some village planners hoped that closer access to forest resources would entice peasants to move, although in most cases the opposite was true, as relocated people, especially women, had to walk much longer distances to obtain daily cooking fuel.[86]

The relocation of millions of Tanzanians from scattered settlements to registered villages altered patterns of forest use. People built houses and other infrastructure from scratch, while scavenging fuelwood for domestic cooking and in some regions for tobacco curing.[87] This increased the pressure on forests near ujamaa villages. From the Mtwara region foresters reported that, as a result of ujamaa, areas that were once closed thicket and bush now came under "land malpractice," as regional officials allowed shifting cultivators to open up new land in forest reserves.[88] From 1975 to 1977 a national campaign to promote food production at a time of drought and dependency on food imports, dubbed Agriculture as a Matter of Life and Death (Kilimo cha Kufa na Kupona), gave local officials license to open forest reserves to agriculture. Policymakers abandoned conservation in response to Nyerere's call to "farm every place that can be farmed."[89] Officials took 145 hectares of Rondo Forest for maize cultivation under the slogan, Freedom Is Work, Freedom Is Planting Food.[90] The chief forester at Mtwara described the campaign as "another major blow to the Forestry Dept.

which witnessed the Forests' Massacre and burning on their own Crematorium."[91] Elsewhere, Natural Resources officers reported that the Kilimo campaign caused erosion by allowing peasants to cultivate on steep slopes inside forest reserves, creating mud slides in the rainy seasons.[92]

In contrast to clear cases of forest destruction caused by villagization, the relocation of millions of peasants protected many woodlands from annual field fires. Miombo were fire-adapted trees, thus relied on "cool burning" after the rainy season for seeds to germinate.[93] Too much pressure on the land, however, forced farmers to practice late, dry-season "hot burning," which destroyed saplings and decreased woodlands diversity. The removal of millions of peasants from scattered settlements allowed woodlands to regenerate into closed forests. In 1955 about 11 percent of the Tanzanian landscape was under (plantation and peasant) cultivation.[94] By 1991, as a result of three decades of pressure on peasants to amalgamate, agricultural land accounted for only 4.7 percent of the landscape.[95] Analyses of land cover changes in Kazimzumbwi and Pugu forest reserves and the surrounding areas show a range of forest modifications. "Natural" forest decreased by 25 percent as a result of agricultural encroachment, the expansion of tree plantations, and railway construction. Farmers encroached from the east as a result of periurban expansion of Dar es Salaam. However, depopulation in the west as a result of villagization increased the woodlands, bush lands, and thickets by 39 percent on former cultivated lands and grasslands. In regions of the country under less pressure by urban expansion, the regeneration of woodlands was likely to have been more pronounced.[96]

Villagization mandated that each community tend its own woodlots for domestic needs in order to decrease the pressure on forests.[97] Between 1975 and 1979 communities reportedly planted about twenty-five thousand hectares of tree plantations. However, tending village tree plantations was unpopular because it conflicted with agriculture, thus people neglected weeding, boundary maintenance, and protecting tree plantations from fires. Villagers were more concerned with immediate food needs than with a resource that took a long time to harvest, especially when wood was available from forests and woodlands. In some cases people intentionally set fire to tree plantations, viewing them as usurping their land and labor.[98] In 1977 the Forest Division noted, "Survival of these plantations is hampered by frequent annual fires, destruction by animals and shifting cultivation."[99] Village tree plantations failed to supply the country's needs, so pressure on forests continued.

By 1977 foresters were alarmed at the extent of peasant encroachment into forest reserves near ujamaa villages. The country's senior forest officer, M. C. P. Mtuy, asked regional foresters for information on the state of forestry and the extent of encroachment into reserves.[100] Mtuy had become concerned about what he perceived to be massive deforestation in Tanzania as a result of "the imprudent use of the axe and the hoe."[101] He decried that "the release of a forest reserve for agricultural purposes is applauded as a heroic step reflecting political independence," while foresters were portrayed as obstacles to development for doing their jobs.[102] From around the country foresters reported political and peasant pressure to release forests for agriculture. Political officers sometimes claimed that ujamaa ideology held that peasants should determine the path of development, even if that meant encroaching into forest reserves.

Reports from the southern coastal hinterland demonstrated many of these dynamics. The Agriculture as a Matter of Life and Death campaign there led village and district officials to open up new fields on public lands and in forest reserves. Foresters reported that the villages of Mtua and Nalengwe spilled into Lionja Forest Reserve in Nachingwea District and the village of Kimambi encroached into Nyera-Kiperere Forest Reserve.[103] In Liwale region villagers used the woodlands to poach meat and procure medicines, roots, forest foods, honey, and wood for construction and fuel. A forest officer condemned the use of fire to clear fields on public lands and forest reserves, to drive game from fields, to aid in hunting, to collect honey, and in some regions to destroy the habitat of tsetse flies in order to introduce a cattle industry. In Rufiji the district secretary of CCM (Chama cha Mapinduzi, TANU's successor) ordered that the forest reserves be divided up for citizens to clear and cultivate without Forest Division approval.[104] In several forests (Nyamuete, Mchungu, Utete, and Katundu) he encouraged people to plant cassava and cashews, which conflicted with tree growth. The CCM secretary told villagers to continue planting in Mchungu Forest Reserve, even after the regional natural resources officer directed them to cease. Some party officials ordered scheduled trees to be cut and burned in order to clear land for new fields. Officials allowed villagers to sell valuable timbers like mninga to the sawmill in Ikwiriri, without Forest Division licenses or approval. Such ujamaa-era disputes between political and forestry officials recalled interwar conflicts, when forestry was subordinated to agriculture (see chapter 4). Peasants exploited these ambiguities and policy conflicts, as they did in the 1930s, in order to protect their subsistence.

By the end of the 1970s the country's worsening financial situation (in the aftermath of drought and two oil price shocks) deprived the Forest Division of revenues needed to maintain forest boundaries. In 1979 the chief secretary of the Ministry of Natural Resources lamented the state of forest boundaries and firebreaks, which led peasants and pastoralists to encroach on reserves out of ignorance or, if intentional, to disregard legal repercussions.[105] Ambiguous boundaries made it difficult to prove whether or not encroachment was intentional. In 1976–77 in the Lindi region, funds were only adequate to clear the borders of eight of the region's twenty-two reserves. By 1979 many of the region's forest borders had disappeared, and the danger of fields and houses crossing into the forests was high.[106] The boundaries of Rufiji District's nineteen forest reserves had not been cleaned since 1972.[107] Peasants who entered the forests could justifiably claim that they didn't know that they were in a protected area. While the borders of Ruvu North and South forest reserves were cleaned in 1977, by 1979 they were already in need of repair. As a result, the forests were "invaded by charcoal burners," and it was difficult to prosecute them because there were no border markers.[108] The need to maintain borders at great cost year after year stretched the resources of the Ministry of Natural Resources at a time when national revenues were in a state of decay. Ujamaa was thus a time when peasants were able to reassert claims to lands taken from them when reserves were first created. While Tanzanian foresters had become embittered about their loss of influence by the late 1970s, the 1980s would see a complete reversal of the forest agenda, from managed exploitation to biodiversity preservation, which would in turn invigorate the national role of forestry.

The first twenty years of independence saw Tanzania's forests and woodlands opened to greater exploitation by taungya peasants, pitsawyers, charcoal burners, and ujamaa villagers as forestry was called on to help develop the new nation. Although foresters participated enthusiastically in the first phase of forest exploitation, even embracing industrial-scale charcoal production in order to supply domestic and export needs, they were far more cautious about the scale of encroachment that was unleashed with ujamaa villagization after 1973. Some foresters battled peasants living in forests in order to carve out new reserves, then watched as agricultural priorities and villagization reversed policy and made forestry a secondary concern. Despite their frustrations, foresters generally went along with ujamaa, adapting taungya forest cultivation to the needs of development and nationalism.

The coastal forest reserves west of Dar es Salaam illustrated this pattern. In 1981 the project manager of the Kibaha fuel scheme reported that the encroachment of surrounding villagers and other illegal exploitation threatened Ruvu North and South forest reserves. Yet his solution was not eviction, but the creation of a new forest village of six thousand workers who would plant trees and work for the "development, care, and harvest of this indigenous wealth."[109] The Ruvu planting schemes required, in the words of the project manager, more cooperation from citizens of the villages in combining food growing with tree planting.[110] This was essentially a reprise of taungya forest cultivation under the guise of ujamaa villagization.

Ujamaa-era forest encroachment showed peasant resilience at a time of extreme pressure from above and declining material circumstances. Yet it should not be forgotten that millions of peasants lost access to their lands, while the state's development goals disrupted their lives. At the same time, the haphazard exploitation of the forests at a time of economic dislocation and national crisis undermined sound forestry. Ujamaa planners completely bypassed local elders as decision makers.[111] The result was that forest exploitation neglected a local environmental awareness, such as where best to situate a plot of land, which trees to exploit, and when to use fire to clear fields. The bureaucratic elite in charge of the state wielded the ax in a much more heavyhanded way than chiefs of the past, ignoring local perceptions of land use and cultural grounding that stemmed from ancestral forests. By the 1980s the nationalist state would join with an international conservationist movement predicated on biodiversity preservation, which would challenge the colonial and postcolonial legacies of managed forestry and the historical rights of peasant communities.

CHAPTER 8

Biodiversity Preservation and Emergent Forest Conflicts, 1980–Present

THE 1980s began with a revolutionary departure from the colonial model of forest exploitation, one that viewed forests and woodlands as more than the sum of their wood mass. The emergent view valued forests as distinct biota that harbored unique plant and animal species.[1] From the late 1970s the global scientific community, concerned that forest loss causes species extinction, called for the protection of the world's remaining genetic resources.[2] The biodiversity perspective views forests as a global interest, whose use is best mediated by international conservationists rather than by states or local actors. Michael Goldman has referred to this as *ecogovernmentality*, whereby international conservationists backed by donor nations and world financial institutions determine the relationship between nature and surrounding communities.[3] These extrastate actors exert leverage on developing states to restructure their forest policies to accord with international biodiversity conventions. This leverage has been particularly clear since the mid-1980s, when economic decline sparked by the oil crises of the 1970s led Tanzania and other African states to accept economic restructuring programs that enshrine world financial institutions as key decision makers. The resulting neoliberal market reforms paved the way for greater commercialization of Tanzanian timbers and privatization of forest plantations. Conservationists hope that trade liberalization will lead to a decline in timber exploitation by making indigenous hardwoods too expensive for local use, although one of its consequences has been much higher rates of wood poaching, official corruption, and smuggling.[4] Because the biodiversity paradigm values forests primarily as living museums rather than as productive landscapes, it creates little demand for labor. The biodiversity shift thus undercuts the leverage that peasants once had, leaving them few alternatives except insurgent use of the forests.

In recent years conservationists have pronounced Tanzania's Eastern Arc and coastal forests to be habitats of exceptional biodiversity and call them "biodiversity hot spots" because they are under extreme threat of deforestation.[5] The biodiversity paradigm moves forest reserves in the direction of wildlife reserves, making them into spaces protected from the human hand. Moreover, the biodiversity paradigm does not stop at the boundaries of forest reserves; it views even unreserved forests, including miombo woodlands, as necessary for the survival of endangered fauna and flora. It seeks to move beyond the 14 percent of the landscape reserved as forests since independence to include remaining unreserved forests and woodlands, altogether half the landscape of Tanzania. The biodiversity paradigm threatens to unleash new struggles over access to land and resources, pitting peasants and pastoralists on one side against the state, conservationist organizations, and international donors on the other.

The intersection of neoliberal economics and biodiversity preservation, termed *green neoliberalism,* represents a new power dispensation over Tanzania's forests and woodlands.[6] Nongovernmental organizations (NGOs) with an agenda of biodiversity preservation and funding from international conservationist parents and bilateral and multilateral donors have emerged as key decision makers over whether and how Tanzanian forests will be exploited. The 2001 National Forest Program for Tanzania, which sets the forestry agenda in the new millennium, includes a formal role for bilateral development agencies and conservationist NGOs to manage forest reserves.[7] Over the past decade forest policy has included local communities as decision makers in forest management through participatory or community forest management programs. While these projects include local environmental committees selected from influential community members, NGOs typically coordinate and finance these projects with backing from Tanzanian forest officials and forest guards, whose salaries they pay.[8] Tanzanian forest policy enshrines "the international community" for the first time as a "stakeholder" in Tanzanian forest management.[9] The power shift over a little more than a century from the authority of local chiefs and elders, who once negotiated forest access with communities whose support they depended on, to the present, where non-Tanzanians with no local constituencies have a defining role in forest control, cannot be more jarring.

The Origins of the Biodiversity Paradigm

The idea of preserving forests for their own sake emerged in nineteenth-century Germany, where the concept of *Dauerwald* (permanent forest) or *Mischwald* (mixed forest) challenged scientific forestry. Whereas scientific forestry created an ordered landscape of tree plantations useful to industrial society, the Dauerwald concept recognized that "the forest is not merely an aggregation of individual trees, but is an integrated, organic entity, comprising all the innumerable living organisms that exist from the roots deep in the ground to the crowns that sway high in the sunlight."[10] Although this organic view had clear roots in German romanticism, it was bolstered in the twentieth century by the rise of ecological science, which viewed forests as an organic unity that included soils, flora, insects, and other fauna.[11] The longtime director of the Oxford Imperial Forestry Institute, R. S. Troup, articulated this view: "A forest is something more than a collection of trees. . . . The luxuriant forests of the tropics in particular contain a wealth of plant and animal life which thrives in the natural forest environment but disappears when the forest is destroyed. Over large areas of the tropics the destruction of the primeval forest has resulted in the disappearance of interesting plants, animals, birds, and other forms of life."[12] Early Tanzanian foresters recognized the intrinsic value of the forests. A Forest Division report from 1963 alluded to the benefits of preserving forests for their scientific interest, and foresters as a whole understood the value of protecting some forests as wildlife sanctuaries for tourism.[13] In 1977, when the biodiversity paradigm was emerging in the West, the senior forest officer M. C. P. Mtuy warned of the danger of the disappearance of wild animals, food plants, roots, medicines, fruits, and "aesthetic plants" owing to unbridled deforestation.[14] Yet these were always fleeting observations in the face of larger development and revenue priorities that privileged trees for their contribution to national economic growth.

From the 1960s a Western environmental movement emerged that feared that human misuse of the environment endangers plant and animal species.[15] Some of these concerns drew on neo-Malthusian fears that humans threaten the environment and use natural resources unsustainably. In the 1970s biologists based in Tanzania observed a decline in animal and vegetation communities, and proposed to the Ministry of Natural Resources the "conservation of the biological resource," particularly in the Eastern Arc rain forests.[16] Some called for the strict protection of montane and coastal canopy forests as their unique biota were becoming known.[17] A 1978 wildlife symposium at Arusha recommended that the governments of East Africa create "biosphere," or nature, reserves in areas where unique plant and animal species were at risk of extinction.[18] The Arusha symposium initiated increased protection of some forests, beginning with the Eastern Arc Mountain forests and the coastal forest of Pugu. Although the symposium recognized varied threats to these forests, including some legacies of state forestry—such as timber and pole extraction, mining, cash crops, and monoculture tree plantations—their main concern was population pressure.[19] The Arusha symposium offered a blueprint for forest preservation that included the protection of "critically important island ecosystems," an alliance between government, international donors, and conservationists, and a focus on peasants and pastoralists as the chief threat. The blueprint called on the Tanzanian government to protect some forests immediately as "inviolate reserves."[20] The recommendations had immediate effect. Following a 1979 visit by two Dar es Salaam university researchers to Magombera Forest, in the Uzungwa (Eastern Arc) Mountains, the government relocated villagers and their rice fields in order to adjust the forest boundary, squeezing the village closer to the Selous Game Reserve in an action reminiscent of colonial-era population relocations.[21] In 1992 the state created Uzungwa National Park out of the forest, "the first to be protected for biodiversity."[22]

Biodiversity concerns were seconded by studies sponsored by the Ministry of Natural Resources and the Swedish International Development Agency (SIDA), Forestry's biggest donor at the time, which concluded that Tanzanian forests were not exploited sustainably to meet the nation's commercial and domestic wood and fuel needs.[23] A handful of studies had projected contradictory assessments of Tanzania's forest cover, some suggesting that forests and woodlands had increased since the 1960s owing to 1970s rural relocation, while most warned of massive forest loss.[24] The minister of natural resources accepted the worst-case scenario, which estimated an annual loss of four hundred thousand hectares of forest and woodland as a result of fuelwood collection and the expansion of agriculture and pastoralism. Owing to the biodiversity threat and the perception of forest loss, in the early 1980s the Tanzanian government adopted a National Conservation Strategy that endorsed the sustainable use of natural resources, which the World Conservation Union (IUCN) and the United Nations Environmental Program (UNEP) had promoted in their 1980 World Conservation Strategy.[25] The new conservation movement aimed primarily to arrest peasant forest use, which was cited as the chief cause of deforestation.[26]

From the early 1980s biologists identified vichaka forests of the coastal hinterland as a distinct ecosystem, which they call coastal forest. Coastal forests differ from surrounding woodlands and the nearby Eastern Arc rain forests because of their extended annual dry season, their adaptation to water scarcity and poor soils, and their fragmentation and isolation, all of which engendered a large number of unique plant and animal species.[27] Biologists view the coastal forests as relics of "once extensive lowland forests" that became ecological islands owing to human encroachment and agriculture.[28] Some acknowledge the threat to these forests from colonial and postcolonial scientific forestry, especially its creation of "biologically sterile monocultures" of exotic tree plantations.[29] Despite this recognized human history, some conservationists pronounce these forests to be "pristine primary forest" that are under recent threat of human encroachment, putting their unique species at risk of extinction.[30]

Ecologists who define coastal forests as having distinct biota have advanced an agenda of forest protection that extends beyond existing forest reserves to include forest patches that have never been brought under state forestry, including some woodlands and forests that have no value as water catchments. The biodiversity agenda also redefines forest reserves as inviolate lands whose boundaries must be respected at all costs, bringing the police power of the state and the authority of international conventions to bear if necessary. Forest preservation thus draws a line in the sand with respect to peasant access, seeking to outlaw activities such as forest farming and charcoal burning that the state encouraged under ujamaa socialism in the name of national development. Moreover, it vilifies forest activities important for household survival, including hunting, stock grazing, harvesting of building poles, scavenging for cooking fuel, and collecting medicinal plants and famine foods.

Green Neoliberalism and the Fuelwood Trap

It was not a foregone conclusion that Tanzania would embrace the preservation of biodiversity as a cornerstone of forestry. Ujamaa ideology had prioritized rural development, which often meant opening up forest reserves to peasant crop production and resource extraction. Tanzanian timber and charcoal exports helped the country acquire needed foreign exchange revenues. However, the poor performance of the Tanzanian economy following the oil price shocks of the 1970s, several droughts, and war with Uganda ushered in neoliberal market reforms.[31] This path made Tanzania more dependent on multilateral and bilateral donors, who had begun to embrace the preservationist agenda under the rubric of "environmentally sustainable development." Donors were in a position to shape economic and conservation policy much more than in the past.[32]

The Tanzanian government accepted an International Monetary Fund accord to liberalize the economy in 1986, following the retirement of President Nyerere. His successor, Ali Hassan Mwinyi, admitted that Tanzania needed IMF aid because it lacked foreign exchange to purchase oil or food: "without oil, the country was coming to a standstill."[33] After the first oil crisis of 1973 a large share of foreign exchange went for oil imports, reaching 50 to 60 percent of Tanzania's export earnings by 1986. Yet oil provided only 7 percent of Tanzania's energy, and 87 percent went to industry and transport.[34] The oil dependency made Tanzania far more dependent on donor aid, enabling donors to direct how funds were used in the forest and other government sectors.

During the 1980s the World Bank emphasized that environmental sustainability must accompany economic development. By the 1990s the World Bank required client countries to devise environmental action plans in order to receive development aid.[35] Tanzania's accord with the IMF and its acceptance of structural adjustment programs (SAPs) initiated the privatization of the economy, allowing market forces to determine prices for goods and resource allocation. Structural adjustment forced the state to generate more revenue. One way to do this was to encourage tourism by expanding wildlife reserves and nature parks. At the same time, the state promoted Tanzania's valuable hardwood timbers on the international market. The sudden revaluing of the forests for tourism and timber revived a colonial-era dynamic for evicting peasants and pastoralists from protected spaces in order to strengthen state control.[36]

If structural adjustment sought to protect forests from peasants, it also pushed peasants into the forests as charcoal producers. Structural adjustment increased poverty by forcing the state to end food and kerosene subsidies, increasing their prices dramatically.[37] Kerosene prices rose ninefold from 1968 to 1982 as a result of world oil shocks, leading urban dwellers to rely increasingly on charcoal.[38] Prices rose further in the 1980s as the state decreased kerosene subsidies. In 1994 Dar es Salaam consumers spent 8.1 percent of the family budget on charcoal. Altogether some 325,000 Dar es Salaam families bought between 285,000 and 350,000 tonnes of charcoal annually.[39] Although the city's population had quadrupled since 1970, charcoal consumption grew at least thirtyfold in the same period.[40] The failure of industrial charcoal production, such as the Kibaha project of the 1970s, led cash-strapped peasants to fill the gap, as they had done since World War II. The country relied on wood for 92 percent of its energy needs—88 percent from fuelwood and 4 percent from charcoal. By the 1980s the inability of tree plantations to provide the country's fuel and timber needs had also become clear. Twenty-five thousand hectares of village tree plantations were inadequate for the rural demand for fuel and poles, while sixty-six thousand hectares of industrial softwood plantations and four thousand hectares of hardwood plantations were well below national needs.[41] Peasants used reserved and unreserved forests to make up the difference, especially since escalating prices made it economical to produce charcoal at distances ever further from Dar es Salaam and other cities. As the charcoal dependency boomed during the 1990s, conservationists stepped up their demands that forests be protected for their biodiversity value, increasingly calling for command-and-control approaches to solve the problem.[42]

Preserving Tanzania's Biodiversity Hot Spots

In the 1990s several conservationist NGOs emerged in Tanzania promoting a new forest policy that pressured the state, through donor funding, to conserve Tanzanian forests for their biodiversity and ecological values.[43] Most of their attention went to the Eastern Arc rain forests and secondarily to coastal forests, both of which they considered "hot spots," defined as "[t]he richest and most threatened reservoirs of plant and animal life on earth."[44] The most influential of these NGOs has been the Tanzania Forest Conservation Group (TFCG), founded in 1982 by expatriate biologists working in Tanzania. The TFCG summarizes its mission as "the conservation of the high biodiversity forests in Tanzania," especially "the Eastern Arc /Coastal forest biodiversity hot spot."[45] Second in influence is the Wildlife Conservation Society of Tanzania (WCST), founded in 1988 by ornithologists to "work towards the conservation of the flora, fauna, and environment of Tanzania for the benefit of mankind."[46] Former president Benjamin Mkapa is currently the patron of the WCST, and its executive committee includes Tanzanians in government and the private sector with connections to tourism, business, and the wildlife industry.[47] Its founders and supporters have included conservationists funded by UNEP, the Food and Agriculture Organization, CARE International, the World Bank, the IUCN, the World Wide Fund for Nature (WWF),[48] Conservation International, and the Swedish Society for Nature Conservation, to name just a few. These organizations find an outlet in the Tanzanian press, notably IPP Media (especially the *Guardian*), and through the Journalists' Environmental Association of Tanzania, all of which take a decidedly conservationist stance and disseminate their views on the state of Tanzanian forests and woodlands to other media outlets.[49] Indeed, some of IPP's journalists are members of conservationist NGOs, thus blurring the lines between journalism and advocacy.[50] Bilateral and multilateral donors and international and local NGOs provide 95 percent of forest sector expenditure at the end of the millennium, and in some regions they fund almost 90 percent of Forest Division staff.[51] Working in concert, these groups have formed a powerful bloc to orient Tanzanian forest policy toward biodiversity preservation.

The success of conservationist NGO pressure is seen in Tanzania's National Forest Program (NFP) for 2001–10, which enshrines biodiversity preservation as an operating framework for forestry. The NFP encapsulates "green neoliberalism," which Goldman defines as "*neocolonial* conservationist ideas of enclosure and preservation and *neoliberal* notions of market value and optimal resource allocation."[52] The NFP expands state oversight over the forest estate, the first major push in this direction since the high tide of forest reservation during the 1950s. This expansion is seen in the targeting of public lands for forest reservation, the use of zonation theories and gap analysis to increase forest protection, and the call for all the country's forests and woodlands to be owned by a single entity, whether it be the state, villages, or the private sector, thereby ending their use as a commons. While couched in a language of community conservation, gender sensitivity, and devolution of central state authority, the new agenda opens a new era of conflict over forest resources by

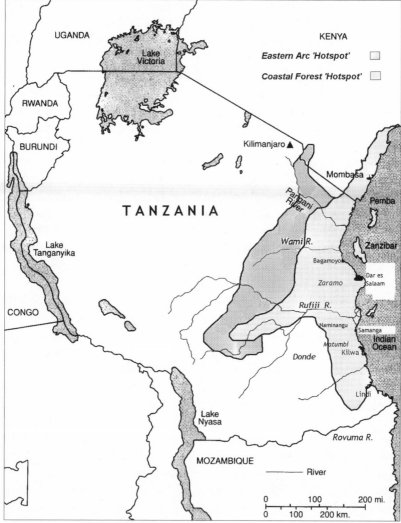

Figure 8.1. Conservation International's Eastern Arc and coastal forest biodiversity hotspot. Map adapted by Thaddeus Sunseri.

expanding state controls and making village governments accountable to donors rather than to their own residents.

The NFP's call for greater reservation of woodlands is a major departure from postcolonial patterns. After independence the Dar es Salaam system encouraged pitsawyers to scavenge valuable trees from these lands with the expectation that the land would then be brought under agriculture.

The woodlands had long been a peasant commons as the main source of cooking fuel, building poles, grazing land, and were important in some regions for the placing of beehives. The NFP considers that most of the country's deforestation has taken place on these lands as a result of peasant and pastoral misuse, and it aims forest policy for the first decade of the new millennium at bringing these vast, mostly unpopulated lands under central government control (even as game reserves) or under local community management as village forest reserves.[53] Conservationists recently define the woodlands as global ecoregions, calling for their biodiversity protection.[54]

The NFP includes community or participatory forest management (PFM) in its agenda. PFM has recently become the leitmotif of conservationist discourse, since conservationists have been accused of being more concerned about forests than people.[55] PFM aims to devolve ownership of some forests and woodlands to village communities, which will then be responsible for their management and protection.[56] The theory behind PFM is that if local communities have a vested interest in forest management, and benefit by obtaining fuelwood and building poles, they will aid in forest protection. PFM is ideally suited to forest management schemes by NGOs and donors, which target specific hot-spot forests for special attention. In seeking to balance peoples' wood needs with the need to stem forest degradation and the loss of biodiversity, PFM thus seeks to end the conflictual relationship that has developed between peasants, forestry officials, and NGOs. At its best, PFM facilitates democratization, political participation, and gender equity. From the perspective of long-term trends, however, PFM takes authority over forests from the local to the state and international levels. PFM privileges NGOs and the private sector in local forest management while increasing the overarching authority of the Tanzanian state. It thus creates several layers of power over local forests, where once there was a relationship between villagers and the state and, before that, villagers and chiefs. Although PFM is couched in a language of participation and negotiation, NGOs wield most power in local forest management, by distributing donor money and calling for state intervention if projects do not follow their blueprints. Conservationist NGOs use community forest management to extend controls over unreserved woodlands, since they believe that existing forest reserves are insufficient to stop biodiversity loss.[57]

The example of Hangai Forest, in southeastern Tanzania, illustrates the ambiguous nature of community forestry. After the Second World War the British colonial government attempted to make Hangai, a vast parcel of woodlands (then called Angai) in Liwale Subdistrict, into a state forest reserve (see chapter 6).[58] The government abandoned the effort after intense opposition from villagers. In 1996 the Liwale Subdistrict authority declared Hangai a district forest reserve, in response to the central government's policy of devolution of forest authority. Villagers protested what they feared was a move to exclude them from the forest.[59] After much negotiation, facilitated by a community conservation NGO, the interested parties agreed that Hangai would become a community forest reserve, owned by a trust of thirteen surrounding villages, who would share the forest's management with district authorities. Interviewed in 2004, villagers living adjacent to the forest expected that as a community forest reserve (*hifadhi ya jamii*) they would be allowed to harvest trees in the reserve and be better able to protect their communities from ongoing elephant, leopard, and lion attacks emanating from the forest.[60] Villagers hope the agreement will allow them to curtail tree cutting by "outsiders with money," which is perhaps a reference to the widespread illegal poaching of timber, often with complicity of district officials, that has characterized southern Tanzania since 2000.[61] "These [outsiders] are the ones that are destroying the forest," stated one elder. "People like me who have no money cannot get permission to cut down trees—these trees are not ours."[62] Independent reports of timber exploitation in southern Tanzania show that local communities benefit very little from timber exports. A general estimate is that for every cubic meter of hardwood cut, local communities accrue $3.50.[63] In contrast, the state takes $70 in harvest and export fees, exporters earn $330, and the finished product is sold for $1,500. While timber marketing benefits them little, some villagers underscore how important the forest remains as a source of famine food, especially for a wild yam called *ung'oko*, which is so popular that people sell it in markets.[64] Although most villagers hope that their control of and access to the forest will be improved as a community reserve, some wondered in 2004 why the forest still had not officially been handed over to them.[65] Villagers at Mihumo, adjacent to the forest, pointing out that they had not received a registration certificate for the forest, stated that it is too early to tell whether local access and control will be improved as a community forest.[66] Some complain that they are not allowed to keep beehives in the forest, which they rely on for 35 percent of village revenues. Forest policy requires them to concentrate their hives outside the forest rather than in the dispersed woodlands, leading to a decline in production. Moreover, community forestry shifts the burden of policing the forests to the village government, much like Native Authority forest reserves under colonial rule. Some villagers suspect that the central government remains in charge of the forest. A beekeeper in the village stated, "Although I have no evidence, I think that the central government is interfering here."[67] That peasants often view community forestry as a usurpation of local land rights was seen during the 2005 Tanzanian elections, when the World Wildlife Fund (as it was then called), a prominent organizer of community forestry, was told to stay away from some areas targeted to become forest reserves for the duration of the campaign because forest land issues had become "highly political."[68]

Although community forest management closes forests to peasant use, it attempts to redress the loss of forest income by developing new income-generating activities, such as ecotourism and butterfly breeding. It pressures people to cease growing annual crops, such as maize, that require clearing by fire in exchange for perennial tree crops like bananas.[69] However, NGO reports and independent studies alike conclude that not all villagers benefit equally from PFM.[70] Heini Vihemäki's research in the Eastern Arc forests shows that village environmental committees that oversee community forests are not necessarily neutral but are often biased against the poorer or less influential members of a community, who are often women.[71] Closing forests to free access hurts the poor most, especially households headed by females. It is easier for wealthy villagers to purchase food and fuel on the market, and to invest in long-term tree crops, than it is for poor peasants who cannot buy maize and charcoal on the market and have no money to buy alternate land. The need to tend village woodlots and clear forest reserve boundaries also falls on the poor as a corvée burden. In some cases villagers who break community conservation rules have been forced to tend village tree lots. Community forestry does not create meaningful employment to make up for the loss of forest resources. Many people participate in PFM as long as they receive compensation from the government or NGOs, rather than because they believe in biodiversity preservation. Liz Wily, an early advocate of PFM, summarizes some of its problems: "Communities serve less as decision-makers than those consulted, less as regulators than rule-followers, less as licensing authorities than as licensees and less as enforcers than as reporters of offences to still-dominant Government actors. . . . even so-called joint forest management approaches have tended to allocate community partners high operational responsibilities but minor powers to determine, for example, who may use and not use the forest, under what conditions, and to licence and enforce accordingly."[72] Community forestry thus uses a discourse that is overtly inclusive but that disguises differential power relations, in which NGOs and the government are often pitted against peasants.[73]

The biodiversity agenda seeks to increase the extent of protected forests and woodlands in Tanzania, moving from established forest reserves onto village and general lands.[74] This is done through zonation theory, which calls for the creation of buffer zones around forests that link them to other forests.[75] W. A. Rodgers writes, "Conservation oriented forest management cannot stop at the edge of the Forest Reserve; indeed, the most pressing and difficult task ahead is to take management actions and benefits to the people outside the core conservation areas."[76] Conservationists seek to connect coastal forest reserves and the "intervening habitats between the coastal forest patches" through buffer zones or corridors.[77] They expect peasants to plant and tend trees on village woodlots in buffer zones as an alternative to using wood from forests, in effect extending forest reserve boundaries and state authority onto peasant lands.[78]

One of the strategic aims of conservation policy is to increase wildlife populations, including crop destroyers such as elephants, both as an end unto itself and to promote tourism to generate incomes that will lessen pressure on forests.[79] Buffer zones aid this policy by allowing wildlife to migrate from one forest to another, using peasant lands as transit corridors.[80] Some conservationists write of an extinction debt—a past misuse of the forests that has created conditions that will lead to species extinction. This path of extinction cannot be arrested by retaining existing forests alone, in this view, but requires that gaps between forests be filled.[81] Indeed, "filling the gaps" is the primary management goal for the Eastern Arc and coastal forest hot spots for the next twenty years.[82] Although conservationist writings recognize that coastal forest isolation is an outcome of tens of thousands of years of history, they often suggest that forest fragmentation is recent, making a new phase of reserve expansion urgent.[83]

Creating wildlife corridors and filling in forest gaps has exacerbated the wildlife threat to peasants. In recent years lion attacks in Tanzania have increased as a result of corridor creation and nature park expansion; some 815 attacks have been recorded between 1990 and 2005—a 300 percent increase since 1990.[84] Although some of the conservationist literature warns that too many elephants might destroy "important coastal habitat," not much concern is voiced about the elephant threat to humans or their crops, which appears to be an acceptable risk.[85] Some conservationists justify the wildlife threat by asserting, wrongly, that Tanzania's forest re-serves had always been intended to protect wildlife.[86] Although forest re-serves harbor animals that endanger people and crops, this was never be-fore a stated goal of forest reservation.

Biodiversity Preservation and the Insurgent Response: The Kazimzumbwi Case

Beginning in the 1990s some conservationist NGOs pressured the state to expel peasants forcibly from forest reserves, some of which the WWF designated "priority areas" for conservation action.[87] This authoritarian approach was seen most dramatically in Kazimzumbwi Forest, south-west of Dar es Salaam. The Kazimzumbwi case illustrates that the bio-diversity agenda is fraught with conflict, as it seeks to separate people from forests and extend forest boundaries into surrounding lands occu-pied by peasants.

British foresters first designated Kazimzumbwi as a forest reserve in 1954, when it was included in the Dar es Salaam region's taungya forest cultivation schemes, meant to supply fuel and poles to urban consumers.[88] A Kazimzumbwi elder referred to this period as phase one, when the colonial state compensated some villagers for the loss of fruit trees in the forest, while others remained in the reserve as taungya cultivators. He re-called that "during the colonial period at least there was work inside the reserve and each person received his daily needs."[89] After 1970 the state mandated that people form an ujamaa village at Kazimzumbwi, which en-tailed a partial retreat from the forest as people concentrated in the village. Yet forest officials urged people to manufacture charcoal from forests and woodlands to supply urban and export demands. From the 1970s the ex-pansion of Dar es Salaam increased population pressure on Kazimzumbwi Forest and nearby Pugu Forest from the east, while the expansion of Ruvu South Forest Reserve drove villagers toward Kazimzumbwi from the west. Despite these disruptions, area peasants believed that they had legitimate rights to the forest reserve based on ancestral and taungya precedents.

In the 1970s expatriate biologists noted the unique endemism of many plant and animal species in the coastal forests around Dar es Salaam.[90] In the 1980s some founded the Wildlife Conservation Society of Tanzania as an advocacy NGO for Eastern Arc and coastal forest species preservation.[91] From the 1990s the WCST, the WWF, and forest officials held monthly planning meetings aimed at "sustainable conservation initiatives" in

Kazimzumbwi and Pugu forests. Because of population pressure from Dar es Salaam and the city's escalating demand for charcoal, the WCST came to view these forests as "the most important areas for protection in east Africa."[92] Conservation International, a funder of many Tanzanian biodiversity projects, has dubbed Kazimzumbwi and Pugu "hyperhot" forests, owing to their "high endemicity and a severe degree of threat" from surrounding communities.[93]

During the 1990s the WCST complained to the government of peasant "invasions" of Kazimzumbwi Forest in order to farm, extract timber and poles, and produce charcoal, even though some people had licenses.[94] The WCST paid for forest guards to patrol the reserve and arrest encroachers, while district police pressured villagers to leave the reserve. With WCST urging, the district administration "took culprits to court" and some had to pay small fines. The WCST funded forest boundary demarcations in the next few years. A local farmer named Mohammed Mtimkavu led peasant resistance, which included obstructing survey crews and continuing to occupy forest lands. Villagers in Nzasa petitioned the Forest Division to release reserve land for farming, and challenged the accuracy of redrawn forest borders. Some peasants threatened workers who were hired to mark forest borders, and uprooted newly planted boundary trees. As tensions escalated, police, forest officials, the WCST, and journalists monitored boundary clearing, and a peasant army veteran was shot in the leg in a scuffle with police. Officials confiscated the bicycles of charcoal

Figure 8.2. Bicycle taking charcoal to Dar es Salaam. Photograph by Thaddeus Sunseri.

burners and arrested scores of peasants, who were fined but allowed to harvest their forest crops. The WCST became increasingly frustrated as overlapping jurisdictions slowed prosecutions, while peasants continued to farm and take charcoal from the forest.

In 1995 the WCST enlisted support from newly elected president Benjamin Mkapa (future patron of the WCST) and the minister of natural resources and tourism, Zakia Meghji. In 1996 the vice president, Omary Ali Juma, visited Kazimzumbwi and "dictated that villagers stop encroachment."[95] Matters came to a head in October 1998, when the MNRT deployed riot police to evict 750 to 1,000 people from Nzasa village, adjacent to Kazimzumbwi Forest.[96] For two weeks the police burned the houses, crops, granaries, and belongings of the villagers. Meghji claimed that the police burned only the shacks of urban charcoal merchants but admitted that local villagers made charcoal in the reserve.[97] She emphasized that police would continue to evict people from the reserve and that the state would not compensate villagers for the loss of property or land, since occupation of the forest was illegal.

Kazimzumbwi peasants disputed their characterization as illegal squatters and charcoal burners. Some stated that they had lived in the area before it was a forest reserve and that the government had violated the original reserve boundaries demarcated in the 1950s.[98] An elderly woman related that her father had lived in Nzasa village and was buried there and that from colonial times through ujamaa they were never told that they lived inside a reserve, adding that they had no other place to live. Villager Said Abdallah, pointing to the graves of his ancestors, said that his family had lived in the area since the beginning of the century. The historical record shows Nzasa village on maps since at least German colonial times.[99] The Kazimzumbwi conflict continued beyond 1998. Press reports in 2004 described a state of war (*ni kama vita*) between charcoal burners and guards in the forest.[100] In recent years officials have evicted villagers to the west of the reserve, even as the boundary of Ruvu South Forest has pushed closer to the east, squeezing them between two forests. The Tanzania Forest Conservation Group has financed a team of forest guards for Ruvu South Reserve in light of ongoing charcoal and pole extraction.[101] Ruvu South, Kazimzumbwi, and Pugu forests are part of a TFCG-sponsored project called Misitu Yetu (Our Forests), which aims in part to unite the forests into one large reserve.[102]

The Kazimzumbwi case resembles other instances of conflict over land and resources in Tanzania and elsewhere in the world. Worldwide,

Figure 8.3. Kazimzumbwi villagers showing new forest reserve border. Photograph by Thaddeus Sunseri.

protected areas have increased in number from about thirty-five hundred in 1985 to over one hundred thousand in 2002, covering 17.1 million square kilometers, or 11.5 percent of the earth's land surface.[103] The extent of protected forests in Tanzania has increased from 1 percent of the landscape in 1914 to about 16 percent in 2000.[104] Another 13 percent of Tanzanian land was protected as national parks or wildlife reserves by 1995. Forest policy for the new millennium calls for the increase of forest reserves, while the twenty-year conservation strategy of the WWF and its allies calls for "restoring and increasing connectivity among fragmented forest patches in the Eastern Arc Mountains and coastal forests hotspot."[105] There is also a strong push to enhance forest protection by classifying the Eastern Arc and coastal forests according to the World Conservation Union's protected area codes, which specify that they be protected for biodiversity value rather than just as watersheds and for sustainable resource extraction.[106] In the past, protected-area codes have been applied mainly to game reserves and nature parks in order to strictly regulate local use. According to Neil Burgess and Rodgers, "Through such a process an important protected area "gap" in the conservation of African biodiversity, especially those within the Eastern Arc and coastal forests, could be closed without the need to create many additional reserves in a region of intense competition for natural resources."[107] The WWF also calls for the protection of miombo woodlands, despite their "modest biodiversity importance" and low levels of encroachment.[108]

Each stage of forest and wildlife reserve expansion has been marked by social conflict. Yet conservationists, guided by the biodiversity paradigm, see the extent of reserved forests as insufficient. A statement issued by the Tanzanian NGO Research on Poverty Alleviation decries that "of the 2.5 million hectares of forest in Coast and Dar es Salaam regions, only 369,523 hectares have been declared as reserved. The remaining 85.3 percent is left to the mercy of the public."[109] The conservationist press

Figure 8.4. Hardwood logs awaiting export, Kilwa-Masoko. Photograph by Thaddeus Sunseri.

lambastes the "unscrupulous clearing of the natural vegetation for pasture and tillage" that converts the country into semidesert.[110] Although illegal logging of valuable hardwoods—typically an activity of local and international businesses and corrupt government officials—is a major cause of forest degradation in the southern coastal hinterland, government and conservationist reports nonetheless cite the African practice of shifting agriculture as the main cause of deforestation.[111]

In calling for the strict protection of coastal forests, conservation NGOs assert that these ecosystems have an extraordinary value for humankind that supersedes local peasant interests and ancestral claims. In this view, these are global properties that require international protections. Conservationists therefore depict peasants and pastoralists adjacent to forests and woodlands harshly, as recent encroachers in pristine forests. According to WCST/BirdLife International's description of the "repeated illegal invasions of Kazimzumbwi," "As the city of Dar es Salaam engulfs the villages around Chanika unscrupulous villagers sell their land to city money and then invade the forest reserve to plant their crops. . . . High profits, low fines and poorly policed forests will always encourage attempts at exploitation. These people do not care about flood prevention or conservation of biodiversity which must remain the responsibility of central and regional Government."[112] Against this peasant threat, BirdLife International proposes a national park that links Pugu, Kazimzumbwi, and Ruvu South forests, expelling people who live in the corridors between. The proposal includes golf courses and hotels on nearby defunct sisal estates and encourages large mammals—elephants, giraffes, and impala—to repopulate the forests. Proposals like this correspond to Tanzanian policy to increase tourism and expand game reserves.[113] Yet this plan would dramatically increase crop destruction by animal predators, already rife in the lands surrounding the forests, while providing few employment opportunities for evicted peasants.

The identification of biodiversity ecoregions since the 1980s has launched a revolutionary conception of Tanzanian forests that depicts these lands as hot spots whose expansion as inviolate nature reserves is a global priority. Where forest-adjacent peasants once struggled with colonial and postcolonial states to maintain access to forests and their resources, they now contend with a global lobby funded by people who have never visited these forests. Despite a century of state-led forest exploitation under the rubric of scientific forestry, the conservationist lobby vilifies Tanzanian peasants and pastoralists as unscrupulous threats to the forests. Although conservationists often couch their agenda in a discourse of inclusion and participation, they dictate forest use. As a prominent biologist in this movement admits, "Forces for conservation do not as yet come from within the coastal residents themselves. It [conservation] is largely driven from outside these communities."[114]

Biodiversity preservation has revived colonial-era efforts to protect the Tanzanian landscape from its people. This is done by connecting existing forest reserves through wildlife corridors, by categorizing forest reserves according to strict new criteria, and by expanding reserves to include woodlands that are redefined as global ecoregions. The expansion of reserves subordinates peasants and pastoralists to management schemes designed by a global lobby and often confines them to inadequate lands squeezed between forests. The Kazimzumbwi case demonstrates this agenda's potential for violence. Besides physical violence through confrontation with police and forest guards, there is the violence of loss of forest land to grow food, for household needs, medicine, and famine food.[115] The transformation of forests into nature parks and game reserves exacerbates human-animal conflict, which conservationists view as an acceptable price to pay for the greater good of biodiversity and wildlife preservation.[116] Finally, redefining the forests as areas protected for their biodiversity makes them unworked landscapes, which deprives peasants of leverage that they once had as forest workers and taungya peasants. As one Kazimzumbwi elder stated, defending ongoing use of the forest for charcoal, "we are surrounded here by a forest reserve that we are completely prohibited from using. Anyone using it is considered to be nothing but a thief. We do this because there is no alternative, there is no employment."[117]

Conclusion: Power over the Forests

The biodiversity turn has dramatically reversed state conceptions of forests and woodlands, recasting them as spaces to be protected on behalf of their plant and animal species, but not their human populations. Under the biodiversity paradigm, forest reserves are viewed much the same as game reserves, meant more for tourists than for local people. It at best tolerates peasants living adjacent to their forests and at worst would eliminate them from the landscape. As one elder put it, "They [the state] have begun again to expand their forest and, as a result, the area we have to farm is too small. They are increasingly squeezing us." One result is the increasing threat that wildlife poses for people and their crops. Even outside Dar es Salaam, in Kazimzumbwi Forest, the threat of crop destruction by animals continues to be rife. Asked whether there are animals in the nearby forest reserve that cause damage to their crops, an elder replied with gallows humor, "They are listening to us now." There is very little need to work forests that are little more than natural history museums and genetic reservoirs, depriving surrounding communities of a crucial means of negotiating forest access and control that they had managed to maintain in the first century of scientific forestry. One young man outside Kazimzumbwi Forest underscored this lack of opportunity: "We are tired, because there is no means of earning an income. Our income in the area is trees—and we are prohibited completely from touching the trees. There are no industries anymore because they have been sold, yet we still have children [to feed]. We don't know what our future is." Because the extent of forest hot spots is regarded as inadequate for species survival, the biodiversity turn actively seeks to increase the extent of reserved forests and woodlands over the next twenty years and reclassify many of them as nature parks. Although current forest management in theory empowers rural communities to manage their forests, in practice it places international conservationists and local allies in charge of the conservationist agenda. Part of this process is the ongoing castigation and criminalization of peasant use of the forests, which, by depicting forest loss as recent and abrupt, erases the history of these forests as peopled spaces with a distinct human past. This is profoundly attested by the disappearance of ax wielders from many regions, even in the form of spirit mediums who once negotiated with wenembago forest spirits over forest access and social health. As one elder put it, "They have taken them [sacred sites] from us. There are no more traditions here."[118]

Notes

Unless otherwise noted, all translations are mine. I also conducted all interviews with the assistance of Edward Kileo.

Abbreviations

Annual Report	*Annual Reports of the Forest Department* (1923–78), Tanganyika/Tanzania
BAB	Bundesarchiv-Berlin
Beilage	*Beilage zum deutschen Kolonial-Blatt*
BLF	*Berichte über Land- und Forstwirtschaft*
CO	Colonial Office
COS	Chiefs of Staff
DEFE	Ministry of Defense
DKB	*Deutsches Kolonial-Blatt*
DOAZ	*Deutsch-Ostafrikanische Zeitung*
FO	Foreign Office
GSA	Geheimes Staatsarchiv-Preußischer Kulturbesitz
IJAHS	*International Journal of African Historical Studies*
IUCN	World Conservation Union
JAH	*Journal of African History*
MDS	*Mitteilungen aus den deutschen Schutzgebieten*
NFP	*National Forest Program*
PRO	Public Record Office/British National Archives
RKA	Reichskolonialamt (German Colonial Office)
TDB	Tanganyika District Books
TNA	Tanzania National Archives
TNR	*Tanganyika Notes and Records*
UNDP	United Nations Development Plan

Preface

1. Deodatus Mfugale, "Logging Scam: Forestry Officials under Fire," *Guardian* (Dar es Salaam), 12 July 2004.

2. "Women Celebrate Yesterday after the Ministry of Natural Resources and Tourism Ordered the Release of Their Timber," *Guardian,* 2 August 2004, 3.

3. Bilal Abdul-Aziz, "Log Containers Laden with Banned Trees," *Guardian,* 29 July 2004; Benjamin Thompson, "RC Admits Wanton Logging Rampant," *Guardian,* 6 August 2004; Pastory Nguvu, ". . . as Inspection at Dar Port Aborts," *Guardian,* 14 July 2004.

4. Simon Milledge, Ised K. Gelvas, and Antje Ahrends, *Forestry, Governance and National Development: Lessons Learned from a Logging Boom in Southern Tanzania* (Dar es Salaam: TRAFFIC East/Southern Africa, 2007); Murl Baker, Robert Clausen, Ramzy Kanaan, Michel N'Goma, Trifin Roule, and Jamie Thomson, *Conflict Timber: Dimensions of the Problem in Asia and Africa,* vol. 3, *African Cases* (Burlington, Vt.: ARD, 2003).

5. Secelela Balisidya, "Hifadhi ya Kazimzumbwi hatarini," *Nipashe,* 29 September 2004; Amri Lugungulo, "Mufindi Councillors Decry Wanton Forest Harvesting," *Guardian,* 26 July 2004, http://www.ippmedia.com.

6. Per Nilsson, "Wood—the Other Energy Crisis," in *Tanzania: Crisis and Struggle for Survival,* ed. Jannik Boesen, Kjell J. Havnevik, Juhani Koponen, and Rie Odgaard (Uppsala: Scandinavian Institute of African Studies, 1986), 159.

7. Amri Lugungulo, "Kisarawe Forest 'Thieves' Flee, Abandon Cycles," *Sunday Observer,* 18 July 2004.

8. W. A. Rodgers and N. D. Burgess, "Taking Conservation Action," in *Coastal Forests of Eastern Africa,* ed. Neil D. Burgess and G. Philip Clarke (Gland, Switzerland: IUCN, 2000), 317–34.

9. "Tanzania: Kikwete's Babes," *BBC Focus on Africa* 17, no.2 (April–June 2006): 6.

10. Marja-Liisa Swantz, *Ritual and Symbol in Transitional Zaramo Society* (New York: Africana Publishing, 1970), 121.

11. Carl Gösta Widstrand, *African Axes,* Studia Ethnographica Upsaliensia 15 (Uppsala: Almqvist and Wiksells, 1958), 87; Jan Vansina, *How Societies Are Born: Governance in West Central Africa before 1600* (Charlottesville: University of Virginia Press, 2004), 65–66; Henrietta L. Moore and Megan Vaughan, *Cutting Down Trees: Gender, Nutrition, and Agricultural Change in the Northern Province of Zambia, 1890–1990* (Portsmouth, N.H.: Heinemann, 1994), 3.

12. Bundesarchiv-Berlin (hereafter BAB), R1001/776, 1 September 1891.

13. James C. Scott, *Weapons of the Weak: Everyday Forms of Peasant Resistance* (New Haven: Yale University Press, 1985).

14. Kisserawe Political Officer to Scantling, 28 June 1946, Tanzania National Archives (hereafter TNA), ACC57.9.1.

15. Roderick Neumann, *Imposing Wilderness: Struggles over Livelihood and Nature Preservation in Africa* (Berkeley: University of California Press, 1998), 118.

16. For a case study of the politicizing of a sacred forest, see James L. Giblin, *A History of the Excluded: Making Family a Refuge from State in Twentieth-Century Tanzania* (Athens: Ohio University Press, 2005), 227–31.

17. Christopher Conte, *Highland Sanctuary: Environmental History in Tanzania's Usambara Mountains* (Athens: Ohio University Press, 2004); Neumann, *Imposing Wilderness;* Steven Feierman, *Peasant Intellectuals: Anthropology and History in Tanzania* (Madison: University of Wisconsin, 1990); Thomas Spear, *Mountain Farmers: Moral Economies of Land and Agricultural Development in Arusha and Meru* (Berkeley: University of California, 1997); Michael J. Sheridan, "The Sacred Forests of North Pare, Tanzania: Indigenous Conservation, Local Politics, and Land Tenure," Working Paper 224, African Studies Center, Boston University, 2000.

18. Carl Zimmer, "A Biological Hot Spot in Africa, With New Species Still to Discover," *New York Times,* 6 March 2007, D3.

19. On the biological history of the coastal forests, see Burgess and Clarke, *Coastal Forests.*

20. W. A. Rodgers, "The Miombo Woodlands," in *East African Ecosystems and Their Conservation,* ed. T. R. McClanahan and T. P. Young (New York: Oxford University Press, 1996), 299–325.

21. H. S. H. Watson, "The Ndola Miombo Conference," *Empire Forestry Review* 39, no. 1 (1960): 68–88.

22. Stephen J. Rockel, *Carriers of Culture: Labor on the Road in Nineteenth-Century East Africa* (Portsmouth, N.H.: Heinemann, 2006); Abdul Sheriff, *Slaves, Spices, and Ivory in Zanzibar: Integration of an East African Commercial Empire into the World Economy, 1770–1873.* (London: James Currey, 1987); Jonathon Glassman, *Feasts and Riot: Revelry, Rebellion, and Popular Consciousness on the Swahili Coast, 1856–1888* (Portsmouth, N.H.: Heinemann, 1994); Felicitas Becker, "Traders, 'Big Men' and Prophets: Political Continuity and Crisis in the Maji Maji Rebellion in Southeast Tanzania," *Journal of African History* 45, no. 1 (2004): 1–22.

23. Timothy Mitchell, *Rule of Experts: Egypt, Techno-Politics, Modernity* (Berkeley: University of California, 2002); James Scott, *Seeing Like a State: How Certain Schemes to Improve the Human Condition Have Failed* (New

Haven: Yale University Press, 1998); Joseph Morgan Hodge, *Triumph of the Expert: Agrarian Doctrines of Development and the Legacies of British Colonialism* (Athens: Ohio University Press, 2007).

24. K. Sivaramakrishnan, "Histories of Colonialism and Forestry in India," in *Natures Past: The Environment and Human History,* ed. Paolo Squatriti (Ann Arbor: University of Michigan Press, 2007), 103–44. Sivaramakrishnan draws here on a paradigm advanced in Paul Greenough, "*Naturae Ferae:* Wild Animals in South Asia and the Standard Environmental Narrative," in *Agrarian Studies: Synthetic Work at the Cutting Edge,* ed. James Scott and Nina Bhatt (New Haven: Yale University Press, 2001), 141–85.

25. Ramachandra Guha, *The Unquiet Woods: Ecological Change and Peasant Resistance in the Himalaya* (Oxford: Oxford University Press, 1989), 6.

26. Richard P. Tucker, "The Depletion of India's Forests under British Imperialism: Planters, Foresters, and Peasants in Assam and Kerala," in *The Ends of the Earth: Perspectives on Modern Environmental History,* ed. Donald Worster (Cambridge: Cambridge University Press, 1991), 118–40.

27. Michael Williams, *Deforesting the Earth: From Prehistory to Global Crisis* (Chicago: University of Chicago, 2003), 301–24.

28. Karl Jacoby, *Crimes against Nature: Squatters, Poachers, Thieves, and the Hidden History of American Conservation* (Berkeley: University of California, 2001), 11–15.

29. Williams, *Deforesting the Earth,* 307.

30. David A. Clary, *Timber and the Forest Service* (Lawrence: University Press of Kansas, 1986); A. Joshua West. "Forests and National Security: British and American Forest Policy in the Wake of World War I," *Environmental History* 8, no. 2 (2003): 279–81; Brian Balough, "Scientific Forestry and the Roots of the Modern American State: Gifford Pinchot's Path to Progressive Reform," *Environmental History* 7, no. 2 (2002): 198–225.

31. Forest history and other dimensions of environmental history have received increased attention from historians of Africa in recent years. See, for example, Conte, *Highland Sanctuary;* Neumann, *Imposing Wilderness;* Brad Weiss, *Sacred Trees, Bitter Harvests: Globalizing Coffee in Northwest Tanzania* (Portsmouth, N.H.: Heinemann, 2003); David Anderson, *Eroding the Commons: The Politics of Ecology in Baringo, Kenya, 1890–1963* (Oxford: James Currey, 2002); William Beinart, *The Rise of Conservation in South Africa: Settlers, Livestock, and the Environment, 1770–1950* (Oxford: Oxford University Press, 2003); Emmanuel Kreike, *Re-Creating Eden: Land Use, Environment, and Society in Southern Angola and Northern Namibia* (Portsmouth, N.H.: Heinemann, 2004); Stephen Dovers, Ruth Edgecombe, and Bill Guest, eds., *South Africa's Environmental History: Cases and Comparisons* (Athens: Ohio

University Press, 2002); William Beinart and JoAnn McGregor, eds., *Social History and African Environments* (Oxford: James Currey, 2003); Reginald Cline-Cole and Clare Madge, eds., *Contesting Forestry in West Africa* (Aldershot: Ashgate, 2000); Richard H. Grove, *Ecology, Climate, and Empire: Colonialism and Global Environmental History, 1400–1940* (Cambridge: White Horse Press, 1997); Tamara Giles-Vernick, *Cutting the Vines of the Past: Environmental Histories of the Central African Rain Forest* (Charlottesville: University Press of Virginia, 2002); David Anderson and Richard Grove, eds., *Conservation in Africa: People, Policies, and Practice* (Cambridge: Cambridge University Press, 1993); Nancy Jacobs, *Environment, Power, and Injustice: A South African History* (Cambridge: Cambridge University Press, 2003); Gregory Maddox, James Giblin, and Isaria Kimambo, eds., *Custodians of the Land: Ecology and Culture in the History of Tanzania* (London: James Currey, 1996); Jacob A. Tropp, *Natures of Colonial Change: Environmental Relations in the Making of the Transkei* (Athens: Ohio University, 2006).

32. Guha, *Unquiet Woods*, 5.

33. For an overview of such degradation narratives, see James C. McCann, *Green Land, Brown Land, Black Land: An Environmental History of Africa, 1800–1990* (Portsmouth, N.H.: Heinemann, 1999), 55–78; James Fairhead and Melissa Leach, *Misreading the African Landscape: Society and Forestry in a Forest-Savanna Mosaic* (Cambridge: Cambridge University Press, 1996); Gregory Maddox, "'Degradation Narratives' and 'Population Time Bombs': Myths and Realities about African Environments," in Dovers, Edgecombe, and Guest, *Environmental History*, 250–58.

34. William H. Rollins, "Imperial Shades of Green: Conservation and Environmental Chauvinism in the German Colonial Project," *German Studies Review* 22, no. 2 (1999): 192. For a critique, see Thaddeus Sunseri, "Forestry and the German Imperial Imagination: Conflict over Forest Use in German East Africa," in *Germany's Nature: Cultural Landscapes and Environmental History*, ed. Thomas Lekan and Thomas Zeller (New Brunswick, N.J.: Rutgers University Press, 2005), 81–107.

35. Hans G. Schabel, "Tanganyika Forestry under German Colonial Administration, 1891–1919," *Forest and Conservation History* 34, no. 3 (July 1990): 138. In addition to Schabel's work, Georg Hügel's dissertation provides an overview of forest policy in German East Africa. Hügel, however, was unable to use the German colonial archives in East Germany or the Tanzania National Archives. Georg Hügel, "Der Aufbau und die Entwicklung einer geregelten Forstwirtschaft in Deutsch-Ostafrika unter deutscher Kolonialverwaltung" (PhD diss., Göttingen University, 1988).

36. Schabel, "Tananyika Forestry," 139.

37. Gregory Barton, "Empire Forestry and the Origins of Environmentalism," *Journal of Historical Geography* 27, no. 4 (2001): 544; Barton, *Empire Forestry and the Origins of Environmentalism* (Cambridge: Cambridge University Press, 2002).

38. Raymond Bryant and Sinéad Bailey, *Third World Political Ecology* (London: Routledge, 1997), 2–3.

39. Laurence Becker, "Seeing Green in Mali's Woods: Colonial Legacy, Forest Use, and Local Control," *Annals of the Association of American Geographers* 91, no. 3 (2001): 505.

40. Nancy Lee Peluso and Michael Watts, "Violent Environments," in *Violent Environments,* ed. Nancy Lee Peluso and Michael Watts (Ithaca: Cornell University Press, 2001), 5; Michael Watts, "Political Ecology," in *A Companion to Economic Geography,* ed. Eric Sheppard and Trevor J. Barnes (Oxford: Blackwell, 2000), 257–74.

41. Bina Agarwal, "The Gender and Environment Debate: Lessons from India," *Feminist Studies* 18, no. 1 (1992): 119–58; Watts, "Political Ecology," 266; Melissa Leach, *Rainforest Relations: Gender and Resource Use among the Mende of Gola, Sierra Leone* (Washington, D.C.: Smithsonian Institution Press, 1994); Giles-Vernick, *Cutting the Vines.* Nancy Hunt makes clear the gendered role of forests along the Congo River in *A Colonial Lexicon of Birth Ritual, Medicalization, and Mobility in the Congo* (Durham: Duke University Press, 1999); Richard A. Schroeder, *Shady Practices: Agroforestry and Gender Politics in The Gambia* (Berkeley: University of California Press, 1999).

42. Swantz, *Ritual and Symbol.*

43. Aylward Shorter, *Chiefship in Western Tanzania: A Political History of the Kimbu* (Oxford: Oxford University Press, 1972). See also Tropp, *Colonial Change,* 79–88.

44. Swantz, *Ritual and Symbol,* 177. David Livingstone observed such a dance of women ax wielders in Zambia. Livingstone, *The Last Journals of David Livingstone,* ed. Horace Waller, 2 vols. (New York: Harper and Bros., 1875), 1:142.

45. James Scott, *The Moral Economy of the Peasant: Rebellion and Subsistence in Southeast Asia* (New Haven: Yale University Press, 1976); E. P. Thompson, *Whigs and Hunters: The Origin of the Black Act* (New York: Pantheon, 1975). For overviews of peasants studies see Allen Isaacman, "Peasants and Rural Social Protest in Africa," in *Confronting Historical Paradigms: Peasants, Labor, and the Capitalist World System in Africa and Latin America,* ed. Frederick Cooper (Madison: University of Wisconsin, 1993), 205–317; Henry Bernstein and Terence J. Byres, "From Peasant Studies to Agrarian Change," *Journal of Agrarian Change* 1, no. 1 (2001): 1–56.

46. An important early exception is Elias Mandala, *Work and Control in a Peasant Economy: A History of the Lower Tchiri (Shire) Valley of Malawi, 1850–1960* (Madison: University of Wisconsin Press, 1990).

47. Examples of how Thompson's use of moral economy has informed environmental studies include Guha, *Unquiet Woods;* Madhav Gadgil and Ramachandra Guha, *This Fissured Land: An Ecological History of India* (Berkeley: University of California, 1993); Neumann, *Imposing Wilderness;* Karl Jacoby, *Crimes against Nature: Squatters, Poachers, Thieves, and the Hidden History of American Conservation* (Berkeley: University of California Press, 2001). See also the introduction to *Nature and the Orient: The Environmental History of South and Southeast Asia,* ed. Richard Grove, Vinita Damodaran, and Satpal Sangwan (Delhi: Oxford University Press, 1998), 5. Although she does not explicitly use the concept of moral ecology, Giles-Vernick's explication of *doli,* a historical and ecological thought system, in the Sangha River basin of Central Africa has many parallels. Giles-Vernick, *Cutting the Vines,* 1–5.

48. Jean Birrell, "Common Rights in the Medieval Forest: Disputes and Conflicts in the Thirteenth Century," *Past and Present,* no. 117 (1987): 22–49.

49. Indra Munshi Saldanha, "Colonial Forest Regulations and Collective Resistance: Nineteenth-Century Thana District," in Grove, Damodaran, and Sangwan, *Nature and the Orient,* 708–33; Atluri Murali, "Whose Trees? Forest Practices and Local Communities in Andhra, 1600–1922," in *Nature, Culture and Imperialism: Essays on the Environmental History of South Asia,* ed. David Arnold and Ramachandra Guha (Delhi: Oxford University Press, 1996), 86–122; Arun Agrawal, *Environmentality: Technologies of Government and the Making of Subjects* (Durham: Duke University, 2005); Raymond L. Bryant, *The Political Ecology of Forestry in Burma, 1824–1994* (Honolulu: University of Hawai'i Press, 1996); Nancy Lee Peluso, "A History of State Forest Management in Java," in *Keepers of the Forest: Land Management Alternatives in Southeast Asia,* ed. Mark Poffenberger (West Hartford, Conn.: Kumarian Press, 1990), 27–55.

50. Scott, *Seeing Like a State,* 3–5.

Chapter 1: The Ax and the Copal Tree

1. C. S. Nicholls, *The Swahili Coast: Politics, Diplomacy and Trade on the East African Littoral, 1798–1856* (New York: African Publishing, 1971), 315–17; Richard F. Burton, *The Lake Regions of Central Africa* (New York: Harper and Brothers, 1860; repr. New York: Dover, 1995), 66–70; Norman Bennett, "France

and Zanzibar: 1844 to the 1860s," *International Journal of African Historical Studies* 6, no. 4 (1973): 602–32.

2. J. F. Elton, "On the Coast Country of East Africa, South of Zanzibar," *Journal of the Royal Geographical Society of London* 44 (1874): 229.

3. Martin Klamroth, "Beiträge zum Verständnis der religiösen Vorstellungen der Saramo im Bezirk Daressalam (Deutsch-Ostafrika)," *Zeitschrift für Kolonialsprachen* 1 (1910): 44; 3 (1912–13): 210.

4. Marja-Liisa Swantz, *Ritual and Symbol in Transitional Zaramo Society* (New York: Africana Publishing, 1970), 121; Fritz Bley, *Deutsche Pionierarbeit in Ostafrika* (Berlin: Paul Parey, 1891), 64; Carl Gösta Widstrand, *African Axes*, Studia Ethnographica Upsaliensia 15 (Uppsala: Almqvist and Wiksells, 1958), 144–45.

5. On the ax as a symbol of chiefs' power over tree cutting and men's role in agriculture, see Henrietta L. Moore and Megan Vaughan, *Cutting Down Trees: Gender, Nutrition, and Agricultural Change in the Northern Province of Zambia, 1890–1990* (Portsmouth, N.H.: Heinemann, 1994), 3–11.

6. The Zaramo ceremonial ax stemmed from the Luguru *mambaza*, an ornamental ceremonial ax. Roland Young and Henry A. Fosbrooke, *Smoke in the Hills: Political Tension in the Morogoro District of Tanganyika* (Evanston, Ill.: Northwestern University Press, 1960), 56. For other examples, see Aylward Shorter, *Chiefship in Western Tanzania: A Political History of the Kimbu* (Oxford: Oxford University Press, 1972), 136; Marcia Wright and Peter Lary, "Swahili Settlements in Northern Zambia and Malawi," *African Historical Studies* 4, no. 3 (1971): 566; Colleen Kriger, *Pride of Men: Ironworking in Nineteenth-Century West Central Africa* (Portsmouth, N.H.: Heinemann, 1999), 97–98, 146–49; Widstrand, *African Axes*, 32, 159–60.

7. Franz Stuhlmann, "Forschungsreise in Usaramo," *Mitteilungen aus den deutschen Schutzgebieten* (hereafter *MDS*) 7 (1894): 229.

8. Neil Burgess, Clare FitzGibbon and Phillip Clarke, "Coastal Forests," in *East African Ecosystems and Their Conservation*, ed. T. R. McClanahan and T. P. Young (New York: Oxford University Press, 1996), 329–59; G. P. Clarke, "Defining the Eastern African Coastal Forests," in *Coastal Forests of Eastern Africa*, ed. Neil D. Burgess and G. Philip Clarke (Gland, Switzerland: IUCN, 2000), 9–26.

9. Michael Williams, *Deforesting the Earth: From Prehistory to Global Crisis* (Chicago: University of Chicago Press, 2003), 10–11.

10. W. D. Hawthorne, "East African Coastal Forest Botany," in *Biogeography and Ecology of the Rain Forests of Eastern Africa*, ed. Jon C. Lovett and Samuel K. Wasser (Cambridge: Cambridge University Press, 1993), 58, 64.

11. Felix A. Chami, "Limbo: Early Iron-Working in South-Eastern Tanzania," *Azania* 27 (1992): 45–50; Felix A. Chami and Paul J. Msemwa, "A New Look at Culture and Trade on the Azanian Coast," *Current Anthropology* 38, no. 4 (1997): 675; Felix A. Chami, "The Archaeology of the Rufiji Region since 1987 to 2000," in *People, Contacts, and the Environment in the African Past,* ed. Felix Chami, Gilbert Pwiti, and Chantal Radimilahy (Dar es Salaam: Dar es Salaam University Press, 1996), 7–20; Peter R. Schmidt, "The Agricultural Hinterland and Settlement Trends in Tanzania," *Azania* 29–30 (1994–95): 261–62.

12. N. D. Burgess, L. K. Stubblefield, and C. Kwenyunga, "Soils," in Burgess and Clarke, *Coastal Forests,* 41.

13. A. V. Hartnoll and N. R. Fuggles Couchman, "The 'Mashokora' Cultivations of the Coast," *Tanganyika Notes and Records* (hereafter *TNR*) no. 3 (1937): 34–39.

14. Emmanuel Kreike, *Re-creating Eden: Land Use, Environment, and Society in Southern Angola and Northern Namibia* (Portsmouth, N.H.: Heinemann, 2004).

15. Rochus Schmidt, *Meine Reise in Usaramo und den Deutschen Schutzgebieten Central-Ostafrikas* (Berlin: Engelhardt'schen Landkartenhandlung, 1886), 14. Kurt Pfund, *Kreuz und quer durch Deutschostafrika* (Dresden, n.d. [1899?]), 8, 15; Bley, *Deutsche Pionierarbeit,* 7.

16. John Speke, *Journal of the Discovery of the Source of the Nile* (London: J. M. Dent and Co., 1906), 38.

17. Swantz, *Ritual and Symbol,* 149.

18. Thomas Spear, *The Kaya Complex: A History of the Mijikenda Peoples of the Kenya Coast to 1900* (Nairobi: Kenya Literature Bureau, 1978), 1–3; Hawthorne, "Forest Botany," 63; Michael J. Sheridan, "The Sacred Forests of North Pare, Tanzania: Indigenous Conservation, Local Politics, and Land Tenure," Working Paper 224, African Studies Center, Boston University, 2000. For West Africa, see James Fairhead and Melissa Leach, *Misreading the African Landscape: Society and Forestry in a Forest-Savanna Mosaic* (Cambridge: Cambridge University Press, 1996).

19. T. O. Beidelman, *The Matrilineal Peoples of Eastern Tanzania* (London: International African Institute, 1967), 17; Tanganyika District Books (hereafter TDB), Dar es Salaam Extra Province District Book, vol. 1, "Early Forms of Government." The word *pongo* is from *m'hongono,* an enclosure surrounded by dense bush. Sigvard von Sicard, *The Lutheran Church of the Coast of Tanzania, 1887–1914* (Lund: Gleerup, 1970), 107.

20. Selemani bin Mwenye Chande, "My Journey Up-Country in Africa," in *Swahili Prose Texts,* ed. Lyndon Harries (London: Oxford University Press, 1965), 258.

21. Klamroth, "Beiträge," 192–93; Swantz, *Ritual and Symbol,* 261–69; Swantz, *Blood, Milk, and Death: Body Symbols and the Power of Regeneration among the Zaramo of Tanzania* (Westport, Conn.: Bergin and Garvey, 1995), 41–48.

22. Klamroth, "Beiträge"; Beidelman, *Matrilineal Peoples,* 18–19.

23. *Mbago* was a common coastal hinterland word for chiefship. *Libago* meant ax in both KiMatumbi and KiNgindo. Edward Steere, *Short Specimens of the Vocabularies of Three Unpublished Languages* (London: Charles Cull: 1869), 5; Bernhard Krumm, "Kimatumbi-Wörterverzeichnis," *Sonderabdruck aus den Mitteilungen des Seminars für Orientalische Sprachen zu Berlin* 16 (Berlin: Reichsdrückerei, 1912): 5.

24. Klamroth, "Beiträge," 49, 52–54; Swantz, *Ritual and Symbol,* 218–19.

25. Klamroth, "Beiträge," 52–54.

26. Ibid., 59, 197.

27. Ibid., 60–61.

28. Ibid., 66–68.

29. Swantz, *Ritual and Symbol,* 206, 432.

30. Klamroth, "Beiträge," 118–20, 200–201.

31. Swantz, *Ritual and Symbol,* 173.

32. For a similar tradition see Edward Alpers, "Kingalu Mwana Shaha and Political Leadership in Nineteenth-Century Eastern Tanzania," in *In Search of a Nation: Histories of Authority and Dissidence in Tanzania,* ed. Gregory H. Maddox and James L. Giblin (Oxford: James Currey, 2005), 33–54.

33. TDB, Dar es Salaam Extra Province, vol. 1, "Wazaramo"; Klamroth, "Beiträge," 44; John Gray, "Dar es Salaam under the Sultans of Zanzibar," *TNR,* no. 33 (1952): 2.

34. TDB, Eastern Province, vol. 2, "Kibasira Family."

35. Abdul Sheriff, *Slaves, Spices, and Ivory in Zanzibar: Integration of an East African Commercial Empire into the World Economy, 1770–1873* (London: James Currey, 1987), 26–30.

36. Jan-Georg Deutsch, *Emancipation without Abolition in German East Africa, c. 1884–1914* (Athens: Ohio University Press, 2006), 17–43.

37. Sheriff, *Slaves, Spices,* 119.

38. Saidi Chaurembo in TDB, Dar es Salaam Extra-province, vol. 1, "Notes on the History of Dar es Salaam."

39. Gray, "Dar es Salaam," 10; Walter T. Brown, "The Politics of Business: Relations between Zanzibar and Bagamoyo in the Late Nineteenth Century," *African Historical Studies* 4, no. 3 (1971): 631–43.

40. George Houghton, "Gum Copal," *Hub,* November 1871, http://www .carriagemuseumlibrary.org/copal_zanzibar.htm (accessed 5 Sept. 2008). This

report is based on Burton, *Lake Regions,* 535–38. Other African tree resins, with different properties, were also called copal. Louis Edgar Andés, *Die Fabrikation der Kopal-, Terpentinöl-, und Spirituslacke* (Vienna: A. Hartleben, 1909); F. B. Patterson, ed., *The Story of Gum-Copal* (Newark: Murphy and Co., 1878).

41. Sheriff, *Slaves, Spices,* 125; Burgess, Stubblefield, and Kwenyunga, "Soils," in Burgess and Clarke, *Coastal Forests,* 42–43.

42. Thaddeus Sunseri, "The Political Ecology of the Copal Trade in the Tanzanian Coastal Hinterland, c. 1820–1905," *Journal of African History* 48, no. 1 (2007): 201–20.

43. Alys Trotter, "On Varnishes as Vehicles and as Protections," *Burlington Magazine for Connoisseurs* 21, no. 110 (1912): 91–95; 21, no. 113 (1912): 272–78.

44. Amin Jaffer, *Furniture from British India and Ceylon* (Salem: Peabody Essex Museum, 2001).

45. Sheriff, *Slaves, Spices,* 249–52.

46. Hatim Amiji, "The Bohras of East Africa," *Journal of Religion in Africa* 7, no. 1 (1975): 34.

47. In 1849, 1,822 firms manufactured wagons and carriages, compared to about six thousand firms at the end of the century. Thomas A. Kinney, *The Carriage Trade: Making Horse-Drawn Vehicles in America* (Baltimore: Johns Hopkins University Press, 2004), 34, 125; Susan Green, "Varnish Making, Part 4," *Carriage Driving World Magazine* (2003): 47–52.

48. "Copal of Zanzibar," *New York Coach-Maker's Magazine,* August 1870, 48; "Stimson, Valentine & Co.," *New York Coach-Maker's Magazine,* May 1863, 230–32, http://www.carriagemuseumlibrary.org/copal_zanzibar.htm; "Kopale," *Deutsches Kolonial-Lexikon,* ed. Heinrich Schnee, 3 vols. (Leipzig: Quelle und Meyer, 1920), 2:361–62.

49. A. Foelsing, "Ostafrikanische Kopal," BAB/R1001/516, 29 April 1907.

50. George W.W. Houghton, "Gum Copal," part 6, *Hub,* March 1872, 249.

51. Nicholls, *Swahili Coast,* 326–35; Norman Bennett, "Americans in Zanzibar: 1825–1845," *Essex Institute Historical Collections* 95 (1959): 239–62; Norman Bennett, "Americans in Zanzibar: 1845–1865," *TNR,* no. 51 (1961): 121–38.

52. Brady, *Commerce and Conquest,* 89.

53. Ibid., 98.

54. Nicholls, *Swahili Coast,* 359. A frasila is equivalent to approximately 16 kilograms.

55. Ibid., 346, 350.

56. Norman Bennett and George Brooks, eds., *New England Merchants in Africa: A History through Documents, 1802 to 1865* (Boston: Boston University Press, 1965), 554.

57. Norman Bennett, "Americans in Zanzibar: 1865–1915," *TNR*, 60 (1963): 49–66.

58. Sidney Perley, "Commercial History of Salem," *Essex Antiquarian* 1, no. 1 (1897): 5.

59. Bruno Kurtze, *Die Deutsch-Ostafrikanische Gesellschaft* (Jena: Gustav Fischer, 1913), 99; Brady, *Commerce and Conquest*, 117.

60. Jonathon Glassman, *Feasts and Riot: Revelry, Rebellion, and Popular Consciousness on the Swahili Coast, 1856–1888* (Portsmouth, N.H.: Heinemann, 1994), 146–53.

61. Gray, "Dar es Salaam," 3–4; Sheriff, *Slaves, Spices*, 121. Estimated copal exports from specific Swahili towns is found in Nicholls, *Swahili Coast*, opposite 374.

62. Sheriff, *Slaves, Spices and Ivory*, 124–33; James MacQueen, "Journey of Galvao da Silva to Manica Gold Fields," *Journal of the Royal Geographical Society of London* 30 (1860): 60.

63. Burton, *Lake Regions*, 61; Frederick Holmwood, "The Kingani River, East Africa," *Journal of the Royal Geographical Society of London* 47 (1877): 261; Joseph Thomson, "Notes on the Route Taken by the Royal Geographical Society's East African Expedition from Dar-es-Salaam to Uhehe; May 19th to August 29th, 1879," *Proceedings of the Royal Geographical Society and Monthly Record of Geography* 2, no. 2 (February 1880): 106; G. L. Sulivan, "Survey of the Lower Course of the Rufiji River," *Journal of the Royal Geographical Society of London* 45 (1875): 365; Henry M. Stanley, "Explorations in Central Africa," *Journal of the American Geographical Society of New York* 7 (1875): 182; J. Kirk, "On Recent Surveys of the East Coast of Africa," *Proceedings of the Royal Geographical Society of London* 22, no. 6 (1877–78): 454; William Beardall, "Exploration of the Rufiji River under the Orders of the Sultan of Zanzibar," *Proceedings of the Royal Geographical Society and Monthly Record of Geography* 3, no. 11 (November 1881): 647, 649.

64. J. F. Elton, *The Lakes and Mountains of Eastern and Central Africa* (London: John Murray, 1879; repr. London: Frank Cass, 1968), 72–80.

65. Gray, "Dar es Salaam," 14–15.

66. Elton, *Lakes and Mountains*, 73; Elton, "On the Coast," 228.

67. Elton, *Lakes and Mountains*, 78.

68. Elton, "On the Coast," 228.

69. Burton, *Lake Regions*, 538.

70. Ibid.

71. William B. Bates, "Journal and Observations, 8th Voyage, Brig *Richmond* 1845," in Bennett and Brooks, *New England Merchants*, 267.

72. Burton, *Lake Regions,* 537; Elton, "On the Coast," 229.

73. Nicholls, *Swahili Coast,* 359–60; Sheriff, *Slaves, Spices,* 124–25; "Visit to Messrs. Stimson, Valentine, & Co.'s Varnish Establishment," *New York Coach-Maker's Magazine,* May 1863, 230–32, Carriage Museum of America, http://www .carriagemuseumlibrary.org/stimson (accessed 5 Sept. 2008).

74. Reginald Coupland, *The Exploitation of East Africa, 1856–1890* (Evanston, Ill.: Northwestern University Press, 1967), 56–57; Sheriff, *Slaves, Spices,* 234–35.

75. Gray, "Dar es Salaam," 10; Saidi Chaurembo, TDB, Dar es Salaam Extra-province, 4 July 1955; Glassman, *Feasts and Riot,* 149–51.

76. Elton, "On the Coast," 228–29.

77. Ibid., 233.

78. Coupland, *Exploitation,* 307–18.

79. L. K. Rankin, "The Elephant Experiment in Africa: A Brief Account of the Belgian Elephant Expedition on the March from Dar es Salaam to Mpwapwa," *Proceedings of the Royal Geographical Society and Monthly Record of Geography* 4, no. 5 (1882): 276.

80. Elton, "On the Coast," 235, 239.

81. Jeremy Prestholdt, "On the Global Repercussions of East African Consumerism," *American Historical Review* 109, no. 3 (2004): 755–81; Prestholdt, *Domesticating the World: African Consumerism and the Genealogies of Globalization* (Berkeley: University of California, 2008), 62–78; Sven Beckert, "Emancipation and Empire: Reconstructing the Worldwide Web of Cotton Production in the Age of the American Civil War," *American Historical Review* 109, no. 5 (2004): 1–64; Bennett, "Americans in Zanzibar: 1845–1865," 121–38.

82. Joshua L. Rosenbloom, "Path Dependence and the Origins of Cotton Textile Manufacturing in New England," in *The Fibre That Changed the World: The Cotton Industry in International Perspective, 1600–1990s,* ed. Douglas A. Farnie and David J. Jeremy (Oxford: Oxford University Press, 2004), 376.

83. Nicholls, *Swahili Coast,* 333, 371. Due to rounding, percentages do not total 100.

84. Kinney, *Carriage Trade,* 34, 125.

85. Karen Tranberg Hansen, *Salaula: The World of Secondhand Clothing and Zambia* (Chicago: University of Chicago, 2000), 4–5; Prestholdt, "Global Repercussions"; Marion Johnson, "Cloth as Money: The Cloth Strip Currencies of Africa," *Textile History,* no. 11 (1980): 193–202; Christopher B. Steiner, "Another Image of Africa: Toward an Ethnohistory of European Cloth Marketed in West Africa, 1873–1960," *Ethnohistory* 32, no. 2 (1985): 91–110; Judith A. Byfield, *The Bluest Hands: A Social and Economic History of Women Dyers in Abeokuta (Nigeria), 1890–1940* (Portsmouth, N.H.: Heinemann, 2002);

Laura Fair, "Dressing Up: Clothing, Class and Gender in Post-abolition Zanzibar," *Journal of African History* 39, no. 1 (1998): 63–94; Sheryl McCurdy, "Fashioning Sexuality: Desire, Manyema Ethnicity, and the Creation of the Kanga, ca. 1880–1900," *International Journal of African Historical Studies* 39, no. 3 (2006): 441–69.

86. Jane Schneider, "The Anthropology of Cloth," *Annual Review of Anthropology* 16 (1987): 411.

87. On patronage networks in Uzigua, see James L. Giblin, *The Politics of Environmental Control in Northeastern Tanzania, 1840–1940* (Philadelphia: University of Pennsylvania Press, 1992), 73–78.

88. Sicard, *Lutheran Church,* 117; Speke, *Journal,* 29–30.

89. Burton, *Lake Regions,* 114–15.

90. Ibid., 538.

91. George Gregg to Michael Shepard, 12 May 1849, in Bennett and Brooks, *New England Merchants,* 442.

92. Beardall, "Exploration," 647–49.

93. Joseph Thomson, "Notes on the Basin of the River Rovuma, East Africa," *Proceedings of the Royal Geographical Society and Monthly Record of Geography* 4, no. 2 (1882): 74.

94. On connections between cloth and prestige, see Glassman, *Feasts and Riot,* 135.

95. Elton, *Lakes and Mountains,* 99.

96. Bley, *Deutsche Pionierarbeit,* 63.

97. E. Eberstein, "Über die Rechtsanschauungen der Küstenbewohner des Bezirkes Kilwa," *MDS* 9 (1896): 181–83.

98. Elton, "On the Coast," 228.

99. Nicholls, *Swahili Coast,* 359; R. W. Beachey, "The Arms Trade in East Africa in the Late Nineteenth Century," *Journal of African History* 3, no. 3 (1962): 451.

100. John F. Webb to Michael Shepard, 27 January 1852; William Hines to William H. Seward, 4 January 1864; both in Bennett and Brooks, *New England Merchants,* 493, 524.

101. Gavin White, "Firearms in Africa: An Introduction," *Journal of African History* 12, no. 2 (1971): 181.

102. Ibid., 183.

103. Schmidt, *Meine Reise,* 12.

104. C. J. P. Ionides, "Pages from a Tanganyika Game Rangers Note Book: Part 2," *TNR,* no. 30 (1951): 48–52. For a discussion of the role of firearms (and cloth and beads) in the formation of Yao territorial chiefdoms, see

Edward Alpers, "Trade, State, and Society among the Yao in the Nineteenth Century," *Journal of African History* 10, no. 3 (1969): 414–15.

105. Pfund, *Kreuz und quer*, 39.

106. Ziegenhorn, "Das Rufiyi-Delta," *MDS* 9 (1896): 80.

107. On the power of coinage to transform society, see Pier Larson, *History and Memory in the Age of Enslavement: Becoming Merina in Highland Madagascar, 1770–1822* (Portsmouth, N.H.: Heinemann, 2000), 131–47.

108. Hines to Seward, 25 October 1864; Ropes to Seward, 1 July 1865; both in Bennett and Brooks, *New England Merchants*, 532–33, 536.

109. Beardall, "Exploration," 641–56.

110. William Woodruff, "Growth of the Rubber Industry of Great Britain and the United States," *Journal of Economic History* 15, no. 4 (1955): 376–77.

111. Extract from notes of a discussion on the possible exploitation of rubber with Mr. Mitchell of the Firestone Co., n.d. [1942?], TNA 30512.

112. Juhani Koponen, *Development for Exploitation: German Colonial Policies in Mainland Tanzania, 1884–1914* (Helsinki: Finnish Historical Society, 1995), 212; Patrick Krajewski, *Kautschuk, Quarantäne, Krieg: Dhauhandel in Ostafrika, 1880–1914* (Berlin: Klaus Schwarz, 2006), 25.

113. Bley, *Deutsche Pionierarbeit*, 19–21.

114. Jamie Monson, "From Commerce to Colonization: A History of the Rubber Trade in the Kilombero Valley of Tanzania, 1890–1914," *African Economic History* 21 (1993): 115; Rainer Tetzlaff, *Koloniale Entwicklung und Ausbeutung: Wirtschafts- und Sozialgeschichte Deutsch-Ostafrikas 1885–1914* (Berlin: Duncker und Humblot, 1970), 124; Koponen, *Development for Exploitation*, 432.

115. John Iliffe, *A Modern History of Tanganyika* (Cambridge: Cambridge University Press, 1979), 130–31. For West and Central Africa, see Robert Harms, "The End of Red Rubber: A Reassessment," *Journal of African History* 16, no. 1 (1975): 73–88; Emily Lynn Osborn, "'Rubber Fever,' Commerce and French Colonial Rule in Upper Guinée, 1890–1913," *Journal of African History* 45, no. 3 (2004): 445–65; Tamara Giles-Vernick, *Cutting the Vines of the Past: Environmental Histories of the Central African Rain Forest* (Charlottesville: University Press of Virginia, 2002), 163–64.

116. Harms, "Red Rubber."

117. Chauncy Maples, "Masasi and the Rovuma District in East Africa," *Proceedings of the Royal Geographical Society and Monthly Record of Geography* 2, no. 6 (1880): 339; Thomson, "Basin of the Rovuma River," 74; Thomson, "Dar-es-Salaam to Uhehe," 107.

118. Monson, "Commerce to Colonization," 114.

119. Karl Kucklentz, *Das Zollwesen der deutschen Schutzgebiete in Afrika und der Südsee* (Berlin: Puttkammer und Mühlbrecht, 1914), 78–79; "Das ostafrikanische Schutzgebiet," *Beilage zum deutschen Kolonial-Blatt* (Berlin: Mittler und Sohn, 1894), 52 (hereafter *Beilage*); Krajewski, *Kautschuk*, 151.

120. Monson, "Commerce to Colonization," 115; G. P. Clarke and S. A. Robertson, "Vegetation Communities," in Burgess and Clarke, *Coastal Forests*, 90.

121. Raymond Dumett, "The Rubber Trade of the Gold Coast and Asante in the Nineteenth Century: African Innovation and Market Responsiveness," *Journal of African History* 12, no. 1 (1971): 87.

122. Monson, "Commerce to Colonization," 116.

123. "Kautschuck," in Schnee, *Deutsches Kolonial-Lexikon*, 252; Monson, "Commerce to Colonization," 115.

124. Lorne Larson, "A History of the Mbunga Confederacy ca. 1860–1907," *TNR*, nos. 81–82 (1977): 35–42; Beardall, "Exploration," 644, 647, 649, 653.

125. Felicitas Becker, "Traders, 'Big Men' and Prophets: Political Continuity and Crisis in the Maji Maji Rebellion in Southeast Tanzania," *Journal of African History* 45, no. 1 (2004): 5; Iliffe, *Modern History*, 73; J. Kirk, "A Visit to the Mungao District, near Cape Delgado," *Proceedings of the Royal Geographical Society of London* 21, no. 6 (1876–77): 588–89; Robert D. Jackson, "Resistance to the German Invasion of the Tanganyikan Coast, 1888–1891," in *Protest and Power in Black Africa*, ed. Robert I. Rotberg and Ali Mazrui (New York: Oxford University Press, 1970), 73.

126. Maples, "Masasi and the Rovuma," 348–49.

127. Becker, "Traders," 5; Terence Ranger, "European Attitudes and African Realities: The Rise and Fall of the Matola Chiefs of South-East Tanzania, *Journal of African History* 20, no. 1 (1979): 63–82.

128. Kurtze, *Deutsch-Ostafrikanische Gesellschaft*, 54–55.

129. Ibid., 180.

130. This was the reason that a Luguru chief, known as Mbagho ("ax"?), claimed that the Germans were initially welcomed. Maji Maji Research Project 1968, University College, Dar es Salaam, 1/68/1/4/1/3. See also Schmidt, *Meine Reise*, 19; J. A. Kieran, "Abushiri and the Germans," in *Hadith 2*, ed. Bethwell Ogot (Nairobi: East Africa Publishing House, 1970), 163–64.

131. Harald Sippel, "Recht und Herrschaft in kolonialer Frühzeit: Die Rechtsverhältnisse in den Schutzgebieten der Deutsch-Ostafrikanischen Gesellschaft (1885–1890)," in *Studien zur Geschichte des deutschen Kolonialismus in Afrika*, ed. Peter Heine and Ulrich van der Heyden (Pfaffenweiler: Centaurus-Verlagsgesellschaft, 1995), 474–81.

132. Krajewski, *Kautschuk*, 111.

133. The German text of the treaty is found in Kurtze, *Deutsch-Ostafrikanische Gesellschaft*, 183–96. The English version, which was authoritative in cases of dispute over treaty provisions, is found in "English Text of German Concession," in Her Majesty's Stationary Office, *Accounts and Papers*, vol. 74, Colonies and British Possessions, 9 February 1888–24 December 1888, 272–75.

134. Kieran, "Abushiri," 171–72; August Leue, *Dar-es-Salaam: Bilder aus dem Kolonialleben* (Berlin: Wilhelm Süsserott, 1903), 12.

135. Kieran, "Abushiri," 161.

136. Fritz Ferdinand Müller, *Deutschland-Zanzibar-Ostafrika: Geschichte einer deutschen Kolonialeroberung 1884–1890* (Berlin: Rütten and Loening, 1959), 220–44.

137. Glassman, *Feasts and Riot;* Jackson, "Resistance"; Kieran, "Abushiri"; Iliffe, *Modern History,* 91–98; Rochus Schmidt, *Geschichte des Araberaufstandes in Ost-Afrika: Seine Entstehung, seine Niederwerfung und seine Folgen* (Frankfurt a. d. Oder: Trowitzsch und Sohn, 1892), 22–25.

138. Kieran, "Abushiri," 171–72; Leue, *Dar-es-Salaam,* 12.

139. Hall to Freemantle, 27 September 1888, *Accounts and Records,* 88; Kieran, "Abushiri," 177, 188; Jackson, "Tanganyikan Resistance," 73.

140. Euan-Smith to Salisbury, 22 October 1888, *Accounts and Records,* 94.

141. Jackson, "Tanganyikan Resistance," 66.

142. Kucklentz, *Zollwesen,* 82.

143. "Denkschrift betreffend das ostafrikanische Schutzgebiet," *Beilage* (1894): 6.

144. Krajewski, *Kautschuk,* 150.

145. "Jahresbericht über die Entwicklung von Deutsch-Ostafrika," *Beilage* (1897): 88.

146. Gouvernements-Befehl no. 31, 25 July 1893, BAB/R1001/639; Imperial Governor to Caprivi, 1 September 1893.

147. *Jahresbericht über die Entwicklung der deutschen Schutzgebiete im Jahre 1896/97* (Berlin: Mittler und Sohn, 1898), 86–88.

148. *Jahresbericht über die Entwicklung der deutschen Schutzgebiete im Jahre 1897/98* (Berlin: Mittler und Sohn, 1899), 78–80.

149. Calculated from Monson, "Commerce to Colonization," 114; "Die Entwicklung von Deutsch-Ostafrika während der letzten zehn Jahre," *Deutsches Kolonial-Blatt* (hereafter *DKB*) 11 (1900): 180–82.

150. J. Forbes Munro, "British Rubber Companies in East Africa before the First World War," *Journal of African History* 24, no. 3 (1983): 369–79.

151. Kucklentz, *Zollwesen,* 89.

152. Schmidt, *Meine Reise,* 18; Stuhlmann, "Forschungsreise," 231.

153. In 1883 the British consul at Mozambique reported the discovery of a three-hundred-kilometer tract of copal-bearing coastal forest at Inhambane. John R. Jackson, *Commercial Botany of the Nineteenth Century* (London: Cassell and Co., 1890), 116–17.

154. "Die Entwicklung," *DKB* 11 (1900): 181.

155. Alexander Bursian, *Die Häuser- und Hüttensteuer in Deutsch-Ostafrika* (Jena: Gustav Fischer, 1910), 64, 69.

156. "Zur Rückgang des Ackerbaues unter unserer schwarzen Bevölkerung," *Deutsch-Ostafrikanische Zeitung* 1, 36 (11 November 1899): 1.

157. T. Siebenlist, *Forstwirtschaft in Deutsch-Ostafrika* (Berlin: Paul Parey, 1914), 34.

158. Foelsing, "Ostafrikanische Kopal," BAB/R1001/516; Christian Pfrank, "Der ostafrikanische Kopalbaum und seine Nutzbarmachung," *Kolonie und Heimat* 2, no. 15 (11 April 1909): 6.

Chapter 2: Colonizing the Mangroves of German East Africa

1. Circular Instruction no. 20, 26 May 1891, BAB/R1001/776.

2. "Verordnung des kaiserlichen Gouvernements von Deutsch-Ostafrika, betreffend Aenderungen des deutsch-ostafrikanischen Zolltariffs," *Beilage* (1894): 52.

3. Her Majesty's Stationary Office, *Accounts and Papers,* vol. 74, Colonies and British Possessions, 9 February 1888–24 December 1888, "English Text of German Concession," 272–75; Karl Grass, "Forststatistik für die Waldungen des Rufiydeltas, angefangen im Jahre 1902," *Berichte über Land- und Forstwirtschaft* (hereafter *BLF*) 2 (1904–6), 167; Patrick Krajewski, *Kautschuk, Quarantäne, Krieg: Dhauhandel in Ostafrika, 1880–1914* (Berlin: Klaus Schwarz, 2006), 164–71.

4. Felix A. Chami and Paul J. Msemwa, "A New Look at Culture and Trade on the Azanian Coast," *Current Anthropology* 38, no. 4 (1997): 673–77; Felix Chami, "Roman Beads from the Rufiji Delta, Tanzania: Incontrovertible Archaeological Link with the Periplus," *Current Anthropology* 40, no. 2 (1999): 237–41.

5. William Kirk, "The N.E. Monsoon and Some Aspects of African History," *Journal of African History* 3, no. 2 (1962): 263–67. For recent overviews of the debates on Swahili origins see Thomas Spear, "Early Swahili History Reconsidered," *International Journal of African Historical Studies (IJAHS)* 33,

no. 2 (2000): 257–89; Randall Pouwels, "Eastern Africa and the Indian Ocean to 1800: Reviewing Relations in Historical Perspective," *IJAHS* 35, nos. 2–3 (2002): 385–425.

6. John Sutton, "Kilwa: A History of the Ancient Swahili Town," *Azania* 33 (1998): 113–69; Abdul Sheriff, *Slaves, Spices, and Ivory in Zanzibar* (London: James Currey, 1987).

7. Luiz Drude de Lacerda, ed., *Mangrove Ecosystems: Function and Management* (Berlin: Springer Verlag, 2002), 72–75. In 1939 the conservator of Tanganyikan forests believed there to be nearly fifty thousand hectares of mangroves in Tanganyika (487 sq. km.), whereas reports from the 1950s give a figure of 839 sq. km. D. K. S. Grant, "Mangrove Woods of Tanganyika Territory, Their Silviculture and Dependent Industries," *TNR*, no. 5 (1939): 5–16.

8. Alexander Wood, Pamela Stedman-Edwards, and Johanna Mang, eds., *The Root Causes of Biodiversity Loss* (London: Earthscan, 2000), 310–11; Kjell Havnevik, *Tanzania: The Limits to Development from Above* (Uppsala: Nordiska Afrikainstitutet, 1993), 76–79; R. de la B. Barker, "The Rufiji River," *TNR*, no. 4(1936): 10–16.

9. For taxonomic and Swahili names of mangrove species, see Grant, "Mangrove Woods," 5.

10. John Middleton, *The World of the Swahili: An African Mercantile Civilization* (New Haven: Yale University Press, 1992), 62. Sheriff points out that in the most urban part of the coast historically, Zanzibar Old Town, there are fifty mosques in just eighty hectares. Abdul Sheriff, "Mosques, Merchants and Landowners in Zanzibar Stone Town," in *The History and Conservation of Zanzibar Stone Town*, ed. Sheriff (London: James Currey, 1995), 46.

11. Garth Myers, "The Early History of the 'Other Side' of Zanzibar Stone Town," in Sheriff, *History and Conservation,* 30–45; District Office, Dar es Salaam, to Government, 21 September 1907, TNA G8/630.

12. Grass, "Forststatistik," 192; Boeder to Government, 21 September 1907, TNA G8/630.

13. C. S. Nicholls, *The Swahili Coast: Politics, Diplomacy and Trade on the East African Littoral, 1798–1856* (New York: African Publishing, 1971), 353, 370. Nicholls mistakenly cites twenty thousand pounds (9,091 kg.) rather than twenty thousand poles. Richard F. Burton, *Zanzibar: City, Island, and Coast,* 2 vols. (London: Tinsley Brothers, 1872), 2:413.

14. Richard F. Burton, *The Lake Regions of Central Africa* (New York: Harper and Brothers, 1860; repr. New York: Dover Publications, 1995), 542. Nicholls says that at about the same time Arab traders were paying about six dollars per score. Nicholls, *Swahili Coast,* 353.

15. J. Kirk, "On Recent Surveys of the East Coast of Africa," *Proceedings of the Royal Geographical Society of London* 22 (1877–78): 454.

16. Erik Gilbert, *Dhows and the Colonial Economy of Zanzibar, 1860–1970* (Athens: Ohio University Press, 2004).

17. P. H. Johnston, "Some Aspects of Dhow Building," *TNR*, no. 27 (1949): 47–51; Lieutenant Emery, "Short Account of Mombas and the Neighboring Coast of Africa," *Journal of the Royal Geographical Society of London* 3 (1833): 280–83.

18. Hassan Juma, interview, Mbwa Maji, 31 July 2004.

19. Felix Chami, "The Archaeology of the Rufiji Region since 1987 to 2000," in *People, Contacts and the Environment in the African Past*, ed. Felix Chami, Gilbert Pwiti, and Chantal Radimilahy (Dar es Salaam: Dar es Salaam University Press, 1996), 7–20; B. Matiyas, "Excavations at Mang'aru, an Early Iron Working Phase Site in the Rufiji Region," in Chami, Pwiti, and Radimilahy, *People, Contacts*, 21–29; Havnevik, *Tanzania*, 163.

20. "Matumbi, das Hinterland von Samanga und die Landschaft Mohoro," *DKB* (1893/94): 493–94; Eberstein to Imperial Government, 7 September 1893, TNA G8/19, 39–41.

21. Fritz Bley, *Deutsche Pionierarbeit in Ostafrika* (Berlin: Paul Parey, 1891), 97; Hassan Juma, interview, Mbwa Maji, 31 July 2004.

22. "Bumi" Forest Reserve, Crown Land Protocol no. 40, 12 October 1911, TNA G8/687; Prüssing, "Ueber das Rufiyi-Delta," *MDS* 14 (1901): 108.

23. G. L. Sulivan, "Survey of the Lower Course of the Rufiji River," *Journal of the Royal Geographical Society of London* 45 (1875): 364–67.

24. Henry M. Stanley, "Explorations in Central Africa," *Journal of the American Geographical Society of New York* 7 (1875): 181–83; Ziegenhorn, "Rufiyi-Delta," 80; Hassan Juma, interview, Mbwa Maji, 31 July 2004.

25. Forsteinrichtungswerk Kiswere, April 1913, TNA G8/536.

26. Henry E. Lowood, "The Calculating Forester: Quantification, Cameral Science, and the Emergence of Scientific Forest Management in Germany," in *The Quantifying Spirit in the Eighteenth Century*, ed. Tore Frängsmyr, J. L. Heilbron, and Robin E. Rider (Berkeley: University of California Press, 1990), 315–42; Ravi Rajan, "Imperial Environmentalism or Environmental Imperialism? European Forestry, Colonial Foresters and the Agendas of Forest Management in British India, 1800–1900," in *Nature and the Orient: The Environmental History of South and Southeast Asia*, ed. Richard H. Grove, Vinita Damodaran, and Satpal Sangwan (Delhi: Oxford University Press, 1998), 324–71; Rajan, *Modernizing Nature: Forestry and Imperial Eco-Development 1800–1950* (Oxford: Clarendon Press, 2006), 37–44; James Scott, *Seeing Like a*

State (New Haven: Yale University Press, 1998), 11–12; Joachim Radkau, "Wood and Forestry in German History," *Environment and History* 2, no. 1 (1996): 63–76.

27. Richard H. Grove, *Green Imperialism: Colonial Expansion, Tropical Island Edens and the Origins of Environmentalism, 1600–1860* (Cambridge: Cambridge University Press, 1995), 364–79; "Influence of Forests on Climate," *Indian Forester* 11, no. 3 (1885): 146.

28. William H. Rollins, *A Greener Vision of Home: Cultural Politics and Environmental Reform in the German Heimatschutz Movement, 1904–1918* (Ann Arbor: University of Michigan Press, 1997), 200; Indra Munshi Saldanha, "Colonialism and Professionalism: A German Forester in India," *Environment and History* 2, no. 2 (1996): 200; Michael Imort, "A Sylvan People: Wilhelmine Forestry and the Forest as a Symbol of Germandom," in *Germany's Nature: Cultural Landscapes and Environmental History,* ed. Thomas Lekan and Thomas Zeller (New Brunswick, N.J.: Rutgers University Press, 2005), 55–80.

29. Christoph Ernst, "An Ecological Revolution? The 'Schlagwaldwirtschaft' in Western Germany in the Eighteenth and Nineteenth Centuries," in *European Woods and Forests: Studies in Cultural History,* ed. Charles Watkins (Wallingford, Conn.: CAB International, 1998), 83–92; "The Revenue of the Prussian State Forests," *Indian Forester* 19, no. 8 (1893): 298.

30. M. Büsgen, "Forstwirtschaft in den Kolonien," *Verhandlungen des deutschen Kolonialkongresses* (Berlin: Dietrich Reimer, 1910), 811; "The Forest Lands of Germany," *Indian Forester* 31, no. 6 (1905): 729–30.

31. Joachim Radkau, "Das 'hölzerne Zeitalter' und der deutsche Sonderweg in der Forsttechnik," in *"Nützliche Künste": Kultur- und Sozialgeschichte der Technik im 18. Jahrhundert,* ed. Ulrich Troitzsch (Münster: Waxmann, 1999), 97–117; Radkau, "Wood and Forestry," 70–72.

32. Ernst, "Ecological Revolution?" 91.

33. Dietrich Brandis, "Remarks on the Administrative Forest Staff of Prussia and the Training of Its Officers," *Indian Forester* 11, no. 10 (1885): 449–63; Heger to Foreign Office, 2 January 1889, BAB/R1001/7659.

34. Rajan, "Imperial Environmentalism," 343–62; Saldanha, "Colonialism and Professionalism"; Gregory Barton, "Keepers of the Jungle: Environmental Management in British India, 1855–1900," *Historian* 62, no. 3 (2000): 558; Nancy Lee Peluso, *Rich Forests, Poor People: Resource Control and Resistance in Java* (Berkeley: University of California Press, 1994), 63, 65; Peter Boomgaard, "Forest Management and Exploitation in Colonial Java, 1677–1897," *Forest and Conservation History* 36, no. 1 (1992): 4–14; Raymond L. Bryant,

The Political Ecology of Forestry in Burma, 1824–1994 (Honolulu: University of Hawai'i Press, 1996); Ulrike Kirchberger, "German Scientists in the Indian Forest Service: A German Contribution to the Raj?" *Journal of Imperial and Commonwealth History* 29, no. 2 (2001): 1–26.

35. Quoted in Rajan, "Imperial Environmentalism," 344.

36. By the nineteenth century field burning in Germany was confined mainly to moorlands. David Blackbourn, *The Conquest of Nature: Water, Landscape, and the Making of Modern Germany* (New York: Norton, 2006), 156–59. For Asia see K. Sivaramakrishnan, "Histories of Colonialism and Forestry in India," in *Natures Past: The Environment and Human History*, ed. Paolo Squatriti (Ann Arbor: University of Michigan, 2007), 116–17; Guha, *Unquiet Woods*, 51; Chandran, "Shifting Cultivation," 674–707; Pouchepadass, "British Attitudes," 123–51.

37. Bryant, *Political Ecology*, 67–71.

38. Ramachandra Guha and Madhav Gadgil, "State Forestry and Social Conflict in British India," *Past and Present*, no. 123 (1989): 141–77.

39. Juhani Koponen, *Development for Exploitation: German Colonial Policies in Mainland Tanzania, 1884–1914* (Helsinki: Finnish Historical Society, 1995), 588–89; Thaddeus Sunseri, *Vilimani: Labor Migration and Rural Change in Early Colonial Tanzania* (Portsmouth, N.H.: Heinemann, 2002).

40. Paul Greenough, "*Naturae Ferae:* Wild Animals in South Asia and the Standard Environmental Narrative," in *Agrarian Studies: Synthetic Work at the Cutting Edge*, ed. James Scott and Nina Bhatt (New Haven: Yale University Press, 2001), 141–85; Anthony Reid, "Humans and Forests in Pre-colonial Southeast Asia," in Grove, Damodaran, and Sangwan, *Nature and the Orient*, 106–26.

41. Bruno Kurtze, *Die Deutsch-Ostafrikanische Gesellschaft* (Jena: Gustav Fischer, 1913), 193–96; Karl Kucklentz, *Das Zollwesen der deutschen Schutzgebiete in Afrika und der Südsee* (Berlin: Puttkammer und Mühlbrecht, 1914), 80–81.

42. Protokoll des Kaiserlichen Gouvernements, 25 September 1895, TNA G8/530,; T. Siebenlist, *Forstwirtschaft in Deutsch-Ostafrika* (Berlin: Paul Parey, 1914), 23.

43. Rechenberg to KG, 30 October 1897, TNA G8/530.

44. Rechenberg to KG, 3 January 1898, TNA G8/530.

45. German Consul Zanzibar to KG, 29 January 1903, TNA G8/530.

46. "Die Entwicklung von Deutsch-Ostafrika," *DKB* 11 (1900): 181.

47. Rundererlass an die Bezirks- und Bezirksnebenämter sowie die Zolldirektion, 5 December 1894, BAB/R1001/7680.

48. Die Wald- und Culturverhältnisse in Deutsch-Ost-Afrika, 3 October 1894, BAB/R1001/7680.

49. Mohoro Forstverwaltung, Eberstein to Governor, 6 May 1897, TNA G8/588.

50. Rundererlass an alle Bezirksämter, 30 September 1898, TNA G8/588; Grass, "Forststatistik," 165–96.

51. Von der Decken to Foreign Office, 18 November 1898, BAB/R1001/7680, 196–98.

52. Grass report, 13 April 1900, TNA G8/514.

53. Bennigsen to Hohenlohe-Schillingsfürst, 2 July 1897, BAB/R1001/489, 4–5; Hans G. Schabel, "Tanganyika Forestry under German Colonial Administration, 1891–1919," *Forest and Conservation History* 34, no. 3 (July 1990): 136.

54. Götzen to Foreign Office, 24 April 1902, BAB/R1001/490.

55. Forest Administration in Rufiji, 22 April 1901, BAB/R1001/7723, 167–70.

56. Grass to KG, 8 October 1901, BAB/R1001/490, 3.

57. Krajewski, *Kautschuk,* 170–71.

58. Grass, "Forststatistik," 186.

59. Krajewski, *Kautschuk,* 205–42; Myron Echenberg, "Pestis Redux: The Initial Years of the Third Bubonic Plague Pandemic, 1894–1901," *Journal of World History* 13, no. 2 (2002): 429–49.

60. German Consul, Johannesburg to von Schuckmann, General Consul, Cape Town, 29 April 1898, BAB/R1001/7722, 83–85.

61. "Zusammenstellung der Einnahmen und Ausgaben des Forstbezirks "Rufiyi" in den Jahren 1899/1903," *BLF* 2 (1904–6): 283.

62. Thaddeus Sunseri, "Fueling the City: Dar es Salaam and the Evolution of Colonial Forestry, 1892–1960," in *Dar es Salaam: Histories from an Emerging East African Metropolis,* ed. James R. Brennan, Andrew Burton, and Yusufu Lawi (Nairobi: British Institute for Eastern Africa, 2007), 79–96.

63. J. E. G. Sutton, "Dar es Salaam: A Sketch of a Hundred Years," *TNR,* no. 71 (1970): 19; August Leue, *Dar-es-Salaam: Bilder aus dem Kolonialleben* (Berlin: Süsserott, 1903), 5.

64. Explanation of the Decree of 12 December 1893, BAB/R1001/7680, 9–11.

65. Grass to Government, 7 January 1903, 11 March 1904, TNA G8/529.

66. Stuhlmann to BA Mohoro, 16 October 1902, TNA G8/530.

67. Mohoro Forest Station to Government, 13 July 1908, TNA G8/531, 23–24; Grass to Referat VIII, 10 March 1904.

68. Stracke report (1911), BAB/R1001/673; Minister of Public Works to Dernburg, 27 September 1908, BAB/R1001/672.

69. Eberstein to Governor, 6 May 1897, TNA G8/588.

70. Thaddeus Sunseri, "Working in the Mangroves and Beyond: Scientific Forestry and the Labour Question in Early Colonial Tanzania," *Environment and History* 11, no. 4 (2005): 365–94.

71. Forstverwaltung Rufiyi, 1902–3, TNA G8/514.

72. Grass to KG, 8 October 1901, BAB/R1001/490, 7b.

73. Liebert to Foreign Office, 5 September 1899, BAB/R1001/489, 106.

74. Grass, "Forststatistik," 189.

75. Forstverwaltung Rufiyi, 1902–3, TNA G8/514.

76. *Jahresbericht über die Entwicklung der deutschen Schutzgebiete, 1905/06,* 115; Bewersdorf to Government, 30 October 1906, TNA G8/888.

77. "Sonderberichte der Forstverwaltung," *BLF* 3, no. 5 (1911): 293–94; Verkaufsliste, Salale Waldreservat to OAEG, 23 December 1913, TNA G8/589, 37–40; Helmut Schroeter and Roel Ramaer, *German Colonial Railways* (Krefeld: Röhr Verlag, 1993), 32; "Daressalam-Morogoro Eisenbahn," *DKB* 17 (1906): 11.

78. Jahresbericht der Forstverwaltung Rufiyi, 1910–11, 30 April 1911, TNA 58/98.

79. Jahresbericht des Forstamtes Rufiyi, April 1912, TNA G8/516.

80. Grass to Government, 7 January 1903, TNA G8/529. In 1903 about six thousand was paid as wood cutting and hauling wages, out of a total cost of ten thousand rupees.

81. Dietrich Brandis, "Review of Forest Administration during 1876–77," *Indian Forester* 4, no. 1 (1878): 275–85; "Mangrove Barks for Tanning," *Indian Forester* 39, no. 11 (1913): 545–47; Michael Adas, "Colonization, Commercial Agriculture, and the Destruction of the Deltaic Rainforests of British Burma in the Late Nineteenth Century," in *Global Deforestation and the Nineteenth-Century World Economy,* ed. Richard P. Tucker and J. F. Richards (Durham: Duke University Press, 1983), 95. Cutch, derived from *catechu,* refers to various tree barks and timbers used for leather dye.

82. Stracke report (1911), BAB/R1001/673, 139. Cf. Grant, "Mangrove Woods," 11.

83. Director of Royal Botanical Garden and Museum to Colonial Office, 5 August 1904, BAB/R1001/7659.

84. Grass report, 22 April 1901, BAB/R1001/7723, 167.

85. "Prospekt," September 1908, BAB/R1001/526, 3. Fifteen thousand cubic meters of wood produced about two thousand tonnes of bark. Hauge report, 1908, BAB/R1001/7725, 92; Mangrove Bark in DOA, 1900–1901, BAB/R1001/7723.

86. Übersichtliche Zusammenstellung der an der Küste Deutschostafrikas vorhandenen Mangrovenbestände, n.d. [1906?], BAB/R1001/672.

87. Bewersdorf to Government, 3 February 1910, BAB/R1001/673.

88. This method was still practiced later in the century. Gilbert, *Dhows*, 125.

89. Bewersdorf to Government, 3 February 1910, BAB/R1001/673. "Closed" forest stands were those with unbroken canopy layers.

90. Rechenberg to Colonial Office, 2 September 1911, BAB/R1001/673, 135.

91. Rechenberg to Colonial Office, 8 October 1910, BAB/R1001/673, 93.

92. Gilbert, *Dhows*, 118–21.

93. Schnee to Colonial Office, 14 April 1914, BAB/R1001/673, 209–10.

94. Haug to Feuerlein, 1908, BAB/R1001/7725, 87–93; Deutsch-Koloniale Gerb- und Farbstoffgesellschaft, "Prospekt," 1908, BAB/R1001/526; "Die Verhältnisse im Pachtgebiet der Deutsch-Kolonialen Gerb- und Farbstoff-Gesellschaft" (1910), 60.

95. Eckert to District Officers, 26 June 1904, TNA G8/630.

96. Kronlandsprotokoll no. 40, 12 October 1911, TNA G8/687.

97. Crown Land Protocol no. 47, 5 February 1912, TNA G8/687; Crown Land Protocol no. 48, 7 February 1912, TNA G8/688.

98. GSA, Schnee Nachlass, file 66, "Mimi akida Hamisa bin Mshangamwe," n.d.; file 62, "Kawaida ya kukata miti kujengea nyumba."

99. Jahresbericht des Forstamtes Rufiyi, April 1912, TNA G8/516, vol. 3.

100. Forsteinrichtung Kilwa (Kiperele), Haberkorn report, April 1913, TNA G8/536.

101. Jahresbericht des Forstamtes Rufiyi, April 1912, TNA G8/516, vol. 3.

102. Hassan Juma, interview, Mbwa Maji, 31 July 2004.

103. Nicholas Dirks, "From Little King to Landlord: Property, Law, and the Gift under the Madras Permanent Settlement," in *Colonialism and Culture*, ed. Nicholas Dirks (Ann Arbor: University of Michigan, 1992), 175–208.

Chapter 3: Insurgency in the Coastal Forests, 1904–1914

1. I first explored some of the themes in this chapter in Thaddeus Sunseri, "Reinterpreting a Colonial Rebellion: Forestry and Social Control in German East Africa, 1874–1915," *Environmental History* 8, no. 3 (2003): 430–51.

2. Otto Stollowsky, "On the Background to the Rebellion in German East Africa in 1905–1906," *International Journal of African Historical Studies* 21, no. 4 (1988): 691.

3. Michael Imort, "A Sylvan People: Wilhelmine Forestry and the Forest as a Symbol of Germandom," in *Germany's Nature: Cultural Landscapes and Environmental History,* ed. Thomas Lekan and Thomas Zeller (New Brunswick, N.J.: Rutgers University Press, 2005), 55–80.

4. Heger to Foreign Office, 2 January 1889, BAB/R1001/7659.

5. Eugen Krüger, "Die Wald- und Kulturverhältnisse in Deutsch-Ostafrika," *DKB* 5 (1894–95): 628–29.

6. Denkschrift über die Forstwirtschaft in Deutsch-Ostafrika, 25 June 1905, TNA G8/508, 33–34.

7. Krüger, "Wald- und Kulterverhältnisse," 626; Erläuterung zu der Verfügung vom 12. Dezember 1893, BAB/R1001/7680, 10.

8. Forstwesen in Deutsch-Ostafrika, BAB/R1001/7680, 3–5; "Der Kopalbaum auf der Station Nyangao," *Missions-Blätter von St. Ottilien* 19 (October 1904–September 1905): 135–36.

9. The Swahili version of the 1893 forest ordinance as applied to Rufiji District is found in untitled document 1581/94 (1894), TNA G8/19, 60–61.

10. Wissmann Memorandum, Forest Ordinance for Usambara, 20 October 1895, BAB/R1001/7680.

11. Liebert to Foreign Office, 19 April 1898, BAB/R1001/7680, 153.

12. "Waldschutz-Verordnung für Deutsch-Ost-Afrika," *Amtlicher Anzeiger für Deutsch-Ost-Afrika* 5, no. 24 (10 September 1904): 1–2.

13. Foreign Office to Imperial Government DOA, 31 May 1903, TNA G8/609.

14. Eckert report, 16 January 1904, TNA G8/609; Götzen to Foreign Office, 8 March 1904, BAB/R1001/7681, 111; Götzen report, 27 July 1904, BAB/R1001/7681 125.

15. "Kaiserliche Verordnung über die Schaffung von Kronland," in *Landesgesetzgebung des Deutsch-Ostafrikanischen Schutzgebietes* (Tanga/Dar es Salaam: Kaiserliches Gouvernement von Deutsch-Ostafrika, 1911), 212–14. While preventing the state from declaring as crown land property held privately, by chiefs or by native communities, all other land could be declared ownerless (*herrenlos*), thus the property of the German Reich. See Harald Sippel, "Aspects of Colonial Land Law in German East Africa: German East Africa Company, Crown Land Ordinance, European Plantations and Reserved Areas for Africans," in *Land Law and Land Ownership in Africa*, ed. R. Debusmann and S. Arnold (Bayreuth: Breitinger, 1996), 3–38.

16. "Forstwirtschaft," *Jahresbericht über die Entwicklung der deutschen Schutzgebiete* (Berlin: Ernst Siegfried Mittler und Sohn, 1904), 30–31.

17. Götzen to Foreign Office, 8 March 1904, BAB/R1001/7681, 111–12.

18. Vincenti and Haber report, 17 January 1906, 110–14; Booth report, 16 January 1906, 126–33; both in BAB/R1001/726.

19. Booth report, 16 January 1906, BAB/R1001/726, 126–33.

20. On this usage, see Jonathon Glassman, *Feasts and Riot: Revelry, Rebellion, and Popular Consciousness on the Swahili Coast, 1856–1888* (Portsmouth,

N.H.: Heinemann, 1994), 6; Juhani Koponen, *Development for Exploitation: German Colonial Policies in Mainland Tanzania, 1884–1914* (Helsinki: Finnish Historical Society, 1995), 125.

21. Forest reserves under German rule are listed in Tanzania National Archives, *Guide to the German Records*, 2 vols. (Dar-es-Salaam: National Archives of Tanzania, 1984), 1:332–39.

22. Forstwirtschaft Bezirk Dar es Salaam, 1898–1915, TNA G8/581, 40.

23. Landprotokoll no. 4, 15 April 1904, TNA G58/43.

24. Waldreservat Pugu, 4 August 1902, TNA G58/44; Michels report, 4 August 1902, TNA G8/631.

25. TNA G8/633, TNA G58/46, Massangania Forest Reserve; TNA G8/632, TNA G58/45, Vikindu Forest Reserve.

26. Waldreservate Mohoro "Mchungu," 5 February 1912, TNA G8/688.

27. Koponen, *Development*, 536–42; Roderick Neumann, *Imposing Wilderness: Struggles over Livelihood and Nature Preservation in Africa* (Berkeley: University of California Press, 1998); John M. MacKenzie, *The Empire of Nature: Hunting, Conservation, and British Imperialism* (Manchester: Manchester University Press, 1988); Bernhard Gißibl, "German Colonialism and the Beginnings of International Wildlife Preservation in Africa," *German Historical Institute Bulletin*, suppl. 3 (2006): 121–43.

28. Bericht der zur Erforschung der Ursachen des Aufstandes eingesetzten Kommission, BAB/R1001/726, 99a.

29. Thaddeus Sunseri, "Famine and Wild Pigs: Gender Struggles and the Outbreak of the Maji Maji War in Uzaramo (Tanzania)," *Journal of African History* 38, no. 2 (1997): 235–59.

30. John Iliffe, *A Modern History of Tanganyika* (Cambridge: Cambridge University Press, 1979), ch. 6; G. C. K. Gwassa, *The Outbreak and Development of the Maji Maji War* (Cologne: Rüdiger Köppe, 2005); "Kinjikitile and the Ideology of Maji Maji," in *The Historical Study of African Religion*, ed. T. O. Ranger and I. N. Kimambo (Berkeley: University of California Press, 1972), 202–17; Felicitas Becker, "Traders, 'Big Men' and Prophets: Political Continuity and Crisis in the Maji Maji Rebellion in Southeast Tanzania," *JAH* 45, no. 1 (2004): 1–22.

31. For revisionist views, see Marcia Wright, "Maji Maji: Prophecy and Historiography," in *Revealing Prophets: Prophecy in Eastern African History*, ed. David Anderson and Douglas H. Johnson (London: James Currey, 1995), 124–42; Sunseri, "Famine and Wild Pigs"; Thaddeus Sunseri, "Statist Narratives and Maji Maji Ellipses," *IJAHS* 33, no. 3 (2000): 567–84; Jamie Monson, "Relocating Maji Maji: The Politics of Alliance and Authority in the Southern Highlands of Tanzania, 1870–1918," *JAH* 39, no.1 (1998): 95–120.

32. Booth report, 16 January 1906, BAB/R1001/726, 129.

33. Götzen to Foreign Office, 10 November 1905, TNA G8/723, 149; Boeder report, 21 December 1905, 119; Schultz report, 23 December 1905, 121a–b; Causes of the Uprising in Dar es Salaam District, 11 December 1905, 111b.

34. Waldreservate Bezirk Kilwa, 8 September 1904, TNA G8/652.

35. Interview at Kinjumbi village, 24 July 2004.

36. Back telegram, 10 August 1905, BAB/R1001/721, 29; Stollowsky, "Background to the Rebellion," 689.

37. "Die Unruhen in Deutsch-Ostafrika," *Deutsche Kolonialzeitung* 22, no. 33 (19 August 1905): 353; Götzen to Foreign Office, 20 August, 27 August 1905, BAB/R1001/722; Back to Berlin admiralty, 6 August 1905, BAB/R1001/721, 11.

38. "Landwirtschaftliche und Kulturbestrebungen des Gouvernements," *Beilage* (1906): 27. On Maji Maji and the decline of the rubber trade, see Koponen, *Development*, 237–40; Wright, "Maji Maji," 137.

39. Waldreservate Bezirk Kilwa "Liwale," 1899–1909, TNA G8/653.

40. "Bekanntmachung," *Amtlicher Anzeiger* 2, no. 34 (14 November 1901).

41. R. M. Bell, "The Maji Maji Rebellion in the Liwale District," *TNR*, no. 28 (1950): 38–57.

42. Waldreservat Liwale, 9 April 1905, TNA G8/653; Bell, "Maji-Maji," 47–48.

43. Lott to Government, 20 December 1906, TNA G8/653; Kilwa Entschädigung, TNA G3/101, 95.

44. Berg report, 12 June 1895, BAB/R1001/214, 12.

45. Verhandlung der Landkommission no. 2, Rufiji District, 6 October 1904, TNA G8/671; Keudel to Imperial Government, 1 April 1905, TNA G8/671.

46. Hans Paasche, *Im Morgenlicht: Kriegs-, Jagd- und Reise-Erlebnisse in Ostafrika* (Berlin: C. A. Schwetschke und Sohn, 1907), 98–108.

47. Booth report, 16 January 1906, BAB/R1001/726, 126.

48. Waldkarte des Bezirks Dar es Salaam, 1904, TNA G8/581, 40; Booth report, BAB/R1001/ 726, 128b.

49. Testimony of Pazi Kitoweo of Msanga, recorded by John Booth, 22 December 1905, TNA 726.

50. Booth report, BAB/R1001/726, 127–28.

51. Maji Maji Research Project, Collected Papers (Department of History, University College, Dar es Salaam 1968), 7/68/2/3/1, Mzee Abdala Undi, 24 May 1968, 2.

52. "Bericht über die Tätigkeit des Detachements des Majors Johannes vom 11. März bis 3. August 1906," *DKB* 18 (1907): 336–44.

53. "Waldschutz-Verordnung" (1904), 1–2.

54. "Ein Teufelsbaum," *Missions-Blätter von St. Ottilien* 4 (1900): 57–58.

55. Bericht von der Zerstörung der Nyangao-Mission, 9 September 1905, BAB/R1001/723, 49.

56. Sunseri, "Famine and Wild Pigs."

57. Haber report, 9 September 1906, BAB/R1001/726, 88a.

58. Ibid., 89a.

59. Rechenberg to Colonial Department, 17 May 1907, BAB/R1001/7682, 22–23; "Sonderbare Finanzpolitik," *Deutsch-Ostafrikanische Zeitung* 9, no. 4 (26 January 1907): 1–2.

60. Haber to Foreign Office, 16 July 1906, BAB/R1001/724, 116–17.

61. "Waldschutz-Verordnung" (1904), 1–2; Waldschutz-Verordnung, 27 February 1909, *Landes-Gesetzgebung*, 588–91.

62. Verordnung, betreffend die Erhaltung von Privatwaldungen, 17 August 1908, *Landes-Gesetzgebung*, 587–88; T. Siebenlist, *Forstwirtschaft in Deutsch-Ostafrika* (Berlin: Paul Parey, 1914), 54–56; M. Büsgen, "Forstwirtschaft in den Kolonien," in *Verhandlungen des Deutschen Kolonialkongresses* (Berlin: Dietrich Reimer, 1910), 803.

63. Koponen, *Development*, 290–93; Sippel, "Colonial Land Law," 21.

64. Gouvernementsrat, Wald- und Jagdreservate und gesunde Eingeborenenpolitik, June 1913, TNA G8/589.

65. Otto to Colonial Office, 22 February 1908; Dernburg to Otto, 29 February 1908, TNA G8/894, 6.

66. In 1906 the forest administration was made a separate office. Siebenlist, *Forstwirtschaft*, 1–3; "Zur Frage der Abänderung des Arbeits- und Organisationsplans der Forstverwaltung," 25 October 1907, TNA G8/850.

67. Büsgen, "Forstwirtschaft," 809.

68. Engler, Direktor der Botanischen Zentralstelle für die Kolonien und Königlichen Botanischen Garten und Museum to RKA, 16 November 1907, BAB/R1001/7659, 221–24; von Arnim to von Bülow, 19 February 1909, 280–82.

69. Wirtschaftliche Erschliessung der Waldungen der deutschen Schutzgebiete, May 1909, 174–75, BAB/R1001/668.

70. Siebenlist, *Forstwirtschaft*, 35–37.

71. Verwerthung von Hölzern aus den Kolonien, 1912–13, BAB/R1001/7666.

72. Renner to von Humboldt, 15 August 1913, BAB/R1001/668, 224–25.

73. H. Schroeter and R. Ramaer, *German Colonial Railways* (Krefeld: Röhr Verlag, 1993), 32.

74. "Daressalam-Morogoro Eisenbahn," *DKB* 17 (1906): 11; M. F. Hill, *Permanent Way*, vol. 2, *The Story of the Tanganyika Railways* (Nairobi: East African Railways and Harbors, 1957), 95; Baltzer to OAEG, BAB/R1001/7666, 42.

75. Auszug aus der Bau- und Betriebskoncession der OAEDS, 1904, TNA G8/850.

76. Dar es Salaam Forest District, Eckert report, n.d. [1906?], TNA G8/514.

77. TNA G8/634, Mkonore Forest Reserve; TNA G8/635, Tongoro Forest Reserve; TNA G8/637, Kisserawe Forest Reserve; TNA G8/638, Mpigi Forest Reserve.

78. Forstwirtschaft Bezirk, Dar es Salaam, 1913–15, TNA G8/582.

79. I borrow this usage from Ranajit Guha, "The Prose of Counter-Insurgency," in *Subaltern Studies II: Writings on South Asian History and Society*, ed. Ranajit Guha (Delhi: Oxford University Press, 1983), 1–42; Andrew Zimmerman, "'What Do You Really Want in German East Africa, Herr Professor?' Counterinsurgency and the Science Effect in Colonial Tanzania," *Comparative Studies in Society and History* 48, no. 2 (2006): 419–61.

80. Siebenlist, *Forstwirtschaft*, 7.

81. Waldreservat Mpanga, 26 August 1910, TNA G8/677; Winterfeld report, 4 December 1905, BAB/R1001/726, 91b–92a.

82. Methner to RKA, 2 March 1914, BAB/R1001/6229/1, 93. On the creation of Victoria Falls, see JoAnn McGregor, "The Victoria Falls, 1900–1940: Landscape, Tourism, and the Geographical Imagination," *Journal of Southern African Studies* 29, no. 3 (2003): 717–37.

83. Stollowsky, "Background to the Rebellion," 684–86; Waldreservate Bezirk Rufiji "Rondondo," 8 April 1911, TNA G8/680.

84. Haber report, 9 September 1905, BAB/R1001/726, 82b; "Entdeckung einer grossen Höhle in den Matumbi-Bergen," *DKB* 21 (1910): 654–56; Crosse-Upcott, "Origin," 71–73.

85. Humann to Kilwa District Office, 7 February 1912, TNA G55/59.

86. Grass to Imperial Government, 23 July 1906, TNA G1/97.

87. "Kipo," 31 October 1908, TNA G8/674; "Mtanza," 12 November 1910, TNA G8/676. See also Paasche, *Im Morgenlicht*, 111–15, 282, 290–92.

88. The files on these declarations include TNA G8/683, Namuete; TNA G8/684, Nerumba; TNA G8/685, Kumbi; TNA G8/686, Nandunda.

89. Adolf Graf von Götzen, *Deutsch-Ostafrika im Aufstand* (Berlin: Dietrich Reimer, 1909), 231.

90. TNA G8/655, Tongomba; G8/656, Kisangi; G8/609, Waldreservate Allgemein.

91. Bericht der zur Erforschung der Ursachen des Aufstandes eingesetzten Kommission, BAB/R1001/726, 99a.

92. "Zu den Unruhen im Rufiji-Bezirk," *Deutsch-Ostafrikanische Zeitung* (*DOAZ*) 15, no. 75 (17 September 1913): 2.

93. Waldreservat Tamburu, Crown Land Protocol no. 32, 9 June 1911, TNA G8/681.

94. Waldreservat Namakutwa, Haberkorn to Government, 15 March 1912, TNA G8/682.

95. TNA G8/675, Katundu; TNA G8/676, Mtanza; TNA G8/673, Mohoro.

96. TNA G8/584, Forstwirtschaft Bezirk Kilwa; TNA G8/657, Pindiro Forest Reserve.

97. "Videant Consules," *DOAZ* 14, no. 3 (8 January 1913): 1–2.

98. Büsgen, "Forstwirtschaft," 811.

99. Christopher Conte, *Highland Sanctuary: Environmental History in Tanzania's Usambara Mountains* (Athens: Ohio University Press, 2004), 74–75.

100. Jahresbericht des Forstamtes Rufiyi, April 1912, TNA G8/516.

101. Siebenlist, *Fortswirtschaft*, 3.

102. Jahresbericht des Forstamtes Rufiyi, April 1912, TNA G8/516, 15–17.

103. Mohoro Forest Office to Government, 9 July 1914, TNA G8/589, 71–72.

104. Kurasini Forest Reserve, 30 July 1910, TNA G8/629.

105. Mohoro Forest Office to Government, 20 February 1913, TNA G8/589.

106. Thaddeus Sunseri, "Fueling the City: Dar es Salaam and the Evolution of Colonial Forestry, 1892–1960," in *Dar es Salaam: Histories from an Emerging East African Metropolis,* ed. James R. Brennan, Andrew Burton, and Yusufu Lawi (Nairobi: British Institute for Eastern Africa, 2007), 79–96.

107. Lademann to Government, 14 July 1913, TNA G8/589.

108. Götzen Runderlass, 30 August 1905, BAB/R1001/700, 135.

109. The medicinal use of trees is outlined in R. E. S. Tanner, "Some Southern Province Trees with their African Names and Uses," *TNR,* no. 31 (1951): 61–70.

110. Tongomba Forest Reserve, 20 May 1924, TNA AB875; Waechter to Rechenberg, 25 February 1907, TNA G8/581.

111. Utete District Officer to Government, 14 July 1913, TNA G8/589, 29–30.

112. Kilwa Strafbuch 1908–09, TNA G11/1, 24, 102, 113, 194, 195, 232.

113. Waldreservat Kipo, 1908–10, TNA G8/674; "Sonderberichte der Forstverwaltung," *BLF* 3, no. 5 (1911): 294.

114. "Jahresberichte der Lokalforstbehörden," *Der Pflanzer,* Beiheft 1(1910–11), 6.

115. Holtz to District Office, 21 February 1910, TNA G8/882.

116. Waldreservat Bunduki, October 1910, TNA G58/4.

117. Siebenlist, *Forstwirtschaft,* 26–27.

118. *Jahresbericht* (1907), 115; Bewersdorf to Government, 30 October 1906, TNA G8/888; Eckert to Mogo Forest Station, 30 August 1905, TNA G35/1, 56; Rufiyi Fortsverwaltung, 30 April 1910, Jahresbericht 1909/10, TNA G8/515.

119. Jahresbericht der Rufiyi Forstverwaltung, 30 April 1911, TNA G8/515.

120. Michels report, 26 June 1906, TNA G35/1.

121. Siebenlist, *Forstwirtschaft*, 41.

122. Hans G. Schabel, "Tanganyika Forestry under German Colonial Administration, 1891–1919," *Forest and Conservation History* 34 (July 1990): 130–41.

123. Interview, Mlamleni village, 17 July 2004.

124. Interviews, Kinjumbi village, Naminangu forest, 24 July 2004; Mambisi settlement, Pugu forest, 17 July 2004; Mwita, "Mbwamaji," 8.

Chapter 4: State Forestry in a Colonial Backwater, 1920–1940

1. Baldwin to DO Utete, 20 January 1933, TNA ACC61/118/I.

2. Hartnoll to Asst. Conservator of Forests, 25 January 1933, TNA ACC61/118/I.

3. D. K. S. Grant, "Forestry in Tanganyika," *Empire Forestry Journal* 3, no. 1 (1924): 33.

4. Ray Bourne, "Some Ecological Conceptions," *Empire Forestry Journal* 13, no. 1 (1934): 15–30; Peder Anker, *Imperial Ecology: Environmental Order in the British Empire, 1895–1945* (Cambridge, Mass.: Harvard University Press, 2001); Helen Tilley, "African Environments and Environmental Sciences: The African Research Survey, Ecological Paradigms, and British Colonial Development, 1920–1940," in *Social History and African Environments,* ed. William Beinart and JoAnn McGregor (Oxford: James Currey, 2003), 109–30.

5. Peter Clutterbuck, "Forestry and the Empire," *Empire Forestry Journal* 6, no. 1 (1927): 184.

6. Charles Miller, *Battle for the Bundu: The First World War in East Africa* (New York: Macmillan, 1974), ch. 17; Angus Buchanan, *Three Years of War in East Africa* (New York: Negro Universities Press, 1969).

7. W. J. McMillan report (n.d.—1920s), TDB–Rufiji District Book.

8. Bell to Chief Secretary, 31 January 1925, Kilwa Annual Report 1924, TNA AB58.

9. Altmann to D.O. Dar es Salaam, 6 September 1915; Dietz to Schnee, 15 November 1915; both in TNA G8/882.

10. Buchanan, *Three Years of War,* 150, 162.

11. West, "Forests and National Security," 272–78.

12. R. S. Troup, *Colonial Forest Administration* (Oxford: Oxford University Press, 1940), 5; "A Scheme to Provide Home-Grown Timber," *International Review of Agricultural Economics* 9, no. 4 (1918): 348–50.

13. Clutterbuck, "Forestry."

14. John Sheail, *An Environmental History of Twentieth-Century Britain* (New York: Palgrave, 2002), 83.

15. Ravi Rajan, *Modernizing Nature: Forestry and Imperial Eco-Development, 1800–1950* (Oxford: Clarendon Press, 2006), 125–29.

16. Clutterbuck, "Forestry," 192. Softwoods are from coniferous trees while hardwoods are from broadleaf trees. Troup wrote that the terms referred "less to the degree of hardness than to the origin of the timber and the use to which it is put." Ninety percent of softwoods came from forests of the Northern Hemisphere, while 65 percent of hardwood forests were in tropical regions. Troup, *Colonial Forest Administration,* 13–14.

17. Hugh Watson, "Statistics of Imports of Timber to the United Kingdom," *Empire Forestry Journal* 14, no. 1 (1935): 60–63.

18. Grant, "Forestry," 33–38.

19. Ibid., 35–36.

20. Christopher Conte, *Highland Sanctuary: Environmental History in Tanzania's Usambara Mountains* (Athens: Ohio University Press, 2004); Roderick Neumann, *Imposing Wilderness: Struggles over Livelihood and Nature Preservation in Africa* (Berkeley: University of California Press, 1998).

21. *Annual Reports of the Forest Department* (1923–31) (hereafter *Annual Report*).

22. Chief Secretary to Forest Conservator, 23 May 1925, Rufiji Annual Reports, TNA AB94.

23. "Forests: Protection," TDB–Rufiji District Book, Utete District.

24. "Miscellaneous Forestry," n.d. [1927?], TDB–Rufiji District Books.

25. Tongomba Forest Reserve, 20 May 1924, TNA AB875.

26. *Annual Report* (1924), 2.

27. John Iliffe, *A Modern History of Tanganyika* (Cambridge: Cambridge University Press, 1979), 318–21; Thomas Spear, "Indirect Rule, the Politics of Neo-Traditionalism, and the Limits of Invention in Tanzania," in *In Search of a Nation: Histories of Authority and Dissidence in Tanzania,* ed. Gregory H. Maddox and James L. Giblin (Oxford: James Currey, 2005), 70–85.

28. TDB–Kisarawe District, "Native Administration"; Rufiji District, "Native Administration."

29. TDB–Rufiji District, "Provincial Administration."

30. District Officer, Liwale, to Provincial Commissioner, Southern Province, 11 March 1936, Forest Reserves and Forestry Conservation, TNA 16/25/3, 275.

31. Waldreservat Bezirk Kilwa "Liwale," 1899–1909, TNA G8/653.

32. TDB–Nachingwea District, vol. 2, "Miscellaneous—Forestry," n.d. [1929?]; Conservator of Forests to Provincial Commissioner, 17 April 1936, TNA 16/25/3, 279–81.

33. *Annual Reports* (1931), 2, and (1934), 2.

34. *Annual Report* (1939), 1.

35. James L. Giblin, "Some Complexities of Family and State in Colonial Njombe," in Maddox and Giblin, *In Search of a Nation*, 141–43; Roland Young and Henry A. Fosbrooke, *Smoke in the Hills: Political Tension in the Morogoro District of Tanganyika* (Evanston, Ill.: Northwestern University Press, 1960), 148.

36. "Tanganyika Territory," *Empire Forestry Journal* 17, no. 2 (1938): 325–26; TDB–Morogoro District, "Native Authority Clan Reserves," (1931).

37. *Annual Report* (1932), 4.

38. Shabani Kiputi, interview, Barikiwa, 22 July 2004. Maps of clan forest reserves for Morogoro District are found in TDB–Morogoro District, "Forest Reserves."

39. *Annual Report* (1937), 8.

40. Public Lands included nonprivate and other ownerless land outside forest reserves.

41. *Annual Report* (1928), 2.

42. Tanganyika Forest Division, *Tanganyika's Timber Resources* (Dar es Salaam: Ministry of Lands, Forests, and Wildlife, n.d. [1962]), 7–8, 10–11.

43. DO Kilwa to Asst. Conservator of Forests, Lindi, 17 June 1949, TNA 16/25/3, 372.

44. *Annual Report* (1939), 6.

45. TNA 270/IR/8, Dar es Salaam Forest Station, Kimboga Division, 1930.

46. W. A. Rodgers, "The Miombo Woodlands," in *East African Ecosystems and Their Conservation*, ed. T. R. McClanahan and T. P. Young (New York: Oxford University Press, 1996), 299–325; Troup, *Colonial Forest Administration*, 110–12.

47. Rodgers, "Miombo Woodlands," 302.

48. Charisius to Government, 16 January 1907, BAB/R1001/227, 4–6.

49. Grant, "Forestry," 36.

50. Bourne, "Ecological Conceptions," 16–17; Troup, *Colonial Forest Administration*, 110–11.

51. An early Swahili mention of the use of the saw (ca. 1903), is GSA, Schnee Nachlass, file 66, "Mimi Akida Hamisi bin Mshangamwe."

52. *Annual Report* (1929), 8.

53. *Annual Report* (1936), 12–13.

54. Neumann argues that free issue enabled employers to lower men's wages, as wives subsidized households by collecting firewood and construction poles. Neumann, "Forest Rights," 60–61.

55. R. S. Troup, *Report on Forestry in Tanganyika Territory* (Dar es Salaam: Government Printer, 1936), 22; Roland E. Richter, "Land Law in Tanganyika since the British Military Occupation and under the British Mandate of the League of Nations, 1916–1946," in *Land Law and Land Ownership in Africa,* Bayreuth African Studies 41, ed. R. Debusmann and S. Arnold (Bayreuth: Breitinger, 1996), 39–80.

56. TDB–Rufiji District, "Miscellaneous—Forestry," 12 August 1934; Brett to Chief Secretary, 14 November 1933, TNA 21120, vol. 1.

57. *Annual Report* (1934), 11.

58. TDB–Rufiji District, "Forestry." On the end of free-issue timber for canoe construction after 1936, see Jamie Monson, "Canoe-Building under Colonialism: Forestry and Food Policies in the Inner Kilombero Valley, 1920–40," in *Custodians of the Land: Ecology and Culture in the History of Tanzania,* ed. Gregory Maddox, James Giblin, and Isaria Kimambo (Athens: Ohio University Press, 1996), 210–12.

59. Michael W. Tuck, "Woodland Commodities, Global Trade, and Local Struggle: The Beeswax Trade in British Tanzania," *Journal of Eastern African Studies,* 3, no. 1 (2009) (forthcoming).

60. *Annual Report* (1928), 8.

61. A. R. W. Crosse-Upcott, "Social Aspects of Ngindo Bee-Keeping," *Journal of the Royal Anthropological Institute of Great Britain and Ireland* 86, no. 2 (1956): 81–108.

62. DO Ruponda, Report on Proposed Forest Reserve, 27 August 1951, TNA 16/25/3, 376.

63. Issa Pilipili, interview, Mkundi, 21 July 2004.

64. Issue of Forest Produce to Natives, 1931, TNA 270/K/1/D.

65. Msham Abdalla Mbondo, interview, Barikiwa, 22 July 2004.

66. Asst. Conservator of Forests to Conservator of Forests, 12 February 1930, TNA 270/K/1/D.

67. Andrew Burton, *African Underclass: Urbanization, Crime, and Colonial Order in Dar es Salaam* (Athens: Ohio University, 2005), 56; TDB–Dar es Salaam Extra-province, "What Is a House?"

68. Grant to Chief Secretary, 20 October 1927, TNA 270/K/1/D.

69. Troup, *Forestry in Tanganyika,* 22.

70. *Annual Report* (1925), 7–8. In 1928 all unscheduled trees on public lands could be cut free of charge for domestic use, including "for pit-props and other mining material." *Annual Report* (1928), 2–3.

71. *Annual Report* (1936), 13–14.

72. *Annual Report* (1928), 10.

73. Conservator of Forests to Chief Secretary, 28 September 1934, TNA 22455; Imperial Economic Committee, *An Index of the Minor Forest Products of the British Empire* (London: HMSO, 1936), 44; letter from R.G. Shaw, Gibson and Co., 4 July 1933; Acting Provincial Commissioner, Lindi, to Chief Secretary, 19 August 1933; both in TNA 13809.

74. Grant to Chief Secretary, 29 November 1932, TNA 13809.

75. Conservator of Forests to Chief Secretary, 5 October 1933; Conservator of Forests to Chief Secretary, 3 May 1934, TNA 13809.

76. Kitching to Chief Secretary, 29 March 1934, TNA 13809.

77. Abdalla Kapunga, interview, Mambisi, 17 July 2004.

78. Ali Abdalla, interview, Kinjumbi, 24 July 2004.

79. Mohammed Abdalla and Ali Saidi, interview, Kitope, 24 July 2004.

80. Kitching, Provincial Commissioner Southern to Chief Secretary, 29 March 1934, TNA 13809.

81. TDB–Nachingwea District, vol. 1, "Forestry"—"Kitope Gum Copal Forest."

82. District Office Kilwa to Provincial Commissioner, Lindi, 2 August 1933, TNA 16/25/3, 170; District Office Liwale to District Office Kilwa, 21 August 1933, 172.

83. TDB–Lindi District Book, "Kitope Gum Copal."

84. Acting Provincial Commissioner, Lindi, to Chief Secretary, 29 August 1933, TNA 13809.

85. TDB–Rufiji District, "Coastwise Exports of Produce from Mbwera, Salale, Mohoro," 1921–1936; *Annual Report* (1936), 11.

86. Secretary, East African Supplies Board, to Chief Secretary, 20 May 1942, TNA 13809, vol. 2.

87. Member for Agricultural and Natural Resources, 15 June 1951, TNA 13809/II.

88. Interview, Mkundi Village, 21 July 2004.

89. TNA AB162, Forest Concession-Rufiji Delta.

90. Erik Gilbert, *Dhows and the Colonial Economy of Zanzibar, 1860–1970* (Athens: Ohio University Press, 2004), 121–24.

91. *Annual Report* (1923), 3.

92. TDB–Rufiji District, "Forestry," 12 August 1934. Figures for mangrove pole exports are listed in D. K. S. Grant, "Mangrove Woods of Tanganyika Territory, Their Silviculture and Dependent Industries," *TNR*, no. 5 (1939): 5–16.

93. Figures on bark exports derive from *Annual Reports*. See also Gilbert, *Dhows*, 124–29.

94. Hassan Juma, interview, Mbwa Maji, 31 July 2004.

95. Kilwa District Officer to Provincial Commissioner, Lindi, 2 December 1932, TNA 16/25/2.

96. Conservator of Forests to Provincial Commissioner, Southern Province, 10 February 1933, TNA 16/25/2.

97. Kilwa District Officer to Provincial Commissioner, 12 February 1934, TNA 16/25/2, vol. 2.

98. Kitching to Chief Secretary, 5 June 1934, TNA 16/25/2, vol. 2.

99. Grant to Chief Secretary, 30 June 1934, TNA 16/25/2, vol. 2.

100. Surridge to Grant, 10 August 1934, TNA 16/25/2, vol. 2.

101. Grant to Chief Secretary, 17 December 1934, TNA 16/25/2, vol. 2; *Annual Report* (1934), 3.

102. Grant, "Mangrove Woods," 13.

103. Grant, "Mangrove Woods"; *Annual Report* (1926), 4–5; TDB–Rufiji District, "Silviculture."

104. Grant, "Mangrove Woods," 15.

105. Grant, "Mangrove Woods."

106. Troup, *Colonial Forest Administration*, 174–76, 237; Christopher Conte, "Nature Reorganized: Ecological History in the Plateau Forests of the West Usambara Mountains, 1850–1935," in Maddox, Giblin, and Kimambo, *Custodians*, 112; Raymond Bryant, *The Political Ecology of Forestry in Burma, 1824–1994* (Honolulu: University of Hawai'i, 1996), 70–71.

107. Third Annual Report of the Forest Department (1923), TNA AB.32.

108. *Annual Report* (1925), 10; Twining to Lyttelton, 5 February 1954, PRO, CO 822/806, 52–57.

109. Forestry, Annual Report 1928, TNA 270/JA/8; TDB–Rufiji District, "Utete District: Forests."

110. *Annual Report* (1929), 9. Photographs in the following sources show taungya peasants as women in Kenya and Uganda. H. M. Glover, "Soil Conservation in Parts of Africa and the Middle East," *Empire Forestry Review* 33, no. 1 (1954): 39–44, plates 2, 3; G. J. Leggat, "A Uganda Softwood Scheme," *Empire Forestry Review* 33, no. 4 (1954): 345–51.

111. *Annual Report* (1939), 6.

112. Marja-Liisa Swantz, *Ritual and Symbol in Transitional Zaramo Society* (New York: Africana Publishing, 1970).

113. TDB–Kilwa District, "Land Tenure in Matumbi Tribal Area."

114. Mzee Issa Pilipili, interview, Mkundi, 21 July 2004.

115. Swantz, *Ritual and Symbol*, 218–19.

116. Arun Agrawal, *Environmentality: Technologies of Government and the Making of Subjects* (Durham: Duke University, 2005), 112–26.

117. Interview, Mkundi Village, 21 July 2004.

118. District Office Songea to Provincial Commissioner, Lindi, 21 April 1933, TNA 16/25/3.

Chapter 5: Forestry and Forced Resettlement in Colonial Tanzania

1. Cf. Roderick Neumann, "Africa's 'Last Wilderness': Reordering Space for Political and Economic Control in Colonial Tanzania," *Africa* 71, no. 4 (2001): 653–55. Examples of precolonial intensive agriculture are rare in East Africa, but see Mats Widgren and John Sutton, eds., *Islands of Intensive Agriculture in Eastern Africa* (Athens: Ohio University Press, 2004).

2. TDB–Kilwa District Books, "Laws, Manners and Customs," sheet 26.

3. TDB–Nachingwea, vol. 1, "Tribal History and Legends," sheets 1, 25, 31 (1928).

4. Ibid., sheet 6. Two such traditional trees were *msoro* (*mhoro*) and *kimandembe*. Interview, Mkundi Village, 21 July 2004.

5. On Matumbi settlement patterns, see Ambrosius Maier, "Aus den Matumbibergen," *Missions-Blätter von St. Ottilien* 14 (October 1909–September 1910): 115–18.

6. Bell to Chief Secretary, 31 January 1925, TNA AB.58.

7. Kilwa Annual Report, 1924, TNA AB.58.

8. TDB–Rufiji District Books, "Half Yearly Baraza of All Native Authorities Held at Utete on 28.8.30."

9. Eastern Province Annual Report, 18 August 1927, TNA AB.41.

10. Henniker-Gotley to Chief Secretary, 12 January 1924, TNA AB.15.

11. Bell to Chief Secretary, 31 January 1925, TNA AB.58.

12. Ibid.

13. Melville to Chief Secretary, 29 August 1921, TNA AB.3; Bell to Chief Secretary, 10 February 1926, TNA AB.60.

14. Annual Report 1925, Kibata Subdistrict, TNA AB.60, 49–62.

15. W. A. Rodgers and J. D. Lobo, "Elephant Control and Legal Ivory Exploitation: 1920–1976," *TNR*, nos. 84–85 (1980): 30.

16. Liwale report, 1 April 1922, TNA AB.60, 46–48.

17. Henniker-Gotley to Chief Secretary, 12 January 1924, TNA AG.15.

18. Game Warden to Chief Secretary, 6 August 1923, TNA AB.1132; W. A. Rodgers, "Past Wangindo Settlement in the Eastern Selous Game Reserve," *TNR,* nos. 77–78 (1976): 23.

19. Henniker-Gotley to Chief Secretary, 12 January 1924, TNA AB.15.

20. "Habari ya Miji: Lindi," *Mambo Leo* 4 (1923): 11.

21. Ibid.

22. Ibid.

23. Henniker-Gotley to Chief Secretary, 12 January 1924, TNA AB.15; TDB–Rufiji District Books, "Ivory Registered at Utete Boma, 1924–33." In contrast to hunted tusks, which averaged twenty-one kilograms, "found" tusks from elephants that died naturally weighed on average eight kilograms. Rodgers and Lobo, "Elephant Control," 32.

24. Annual Report 1925, Kibata Subdistrict, TNA AB.60.

25. Rufiji Annual Report for 1925, TNA AB.97.

26. Mwenyezi Kikale to DC Utete, 26 December 1946, 278; Mwenyezi Kikale to DC Utete, 7 January 1947, 283; Mwenyezi Kikale Rufiji to DC Utete, 23 May 1947, 303; Mattheson report, 4 April 1952; all in TNA 274/G1.1. Compare Rodgers and Lobo, "Elephant Control," 35; interviews, Mtanza, Mloka villages, 3–4 June 2001.

27. Annual Report 1925, Kibata Subdistrict, TNA AB.60; Bell to Chief Secretary, 31 January 1925, TNA AB.58; Chief Secretary to Forest Conservator, 23 May 1925, TNA AB.94; Neumann, "Africa's 'Last Wilderness,'" 648–55.

28. Annual Report, Kibata Subdistrict, 1925, TNA AB.60.

29. TDB–Eastern Province, Rufiji District, "Natural History."

30. For maps showing the growth of the Selous see Gordon Matzke, "The Development of the Selous Game Reserve," *TNR,* nos. 79–80 (1976): 42–48.

31. Helge Kjekshus, *Ecology Control and Economic Development in East African History* (Berkeley: University of California, 1977); Gordon Matzke, *Wildlife in Tanzanian Settlement Policy: The Case of the Selous* (Maxwell School, Syracuse University: Syracuse, 1977); idem, "Development of the Selous"; Roderick Neumann, *Imposing Wilderness: Struggles over Livelihood and Nature Preservation in Africa* (Berkeley: University of California, 1998); John M. MacKenzie, *The Empire of Nature: Hunting, Conservation and British Imperialism* (Manchester: Manchester University Press, 1988).

32. Acting Chief Secretary to Commissioners and Administrative Officers, 1 September 1923, TNA AB.1132.

33. Gordon Matzke, "Large Mammals, Small Settlements, and Big Problems: A Study of Overlapping Space Preferences in Southern Tanzania" (PhD diss., Syracuse University, 1975), 62–64.

34. Proposed Amendments of the Selous Game Reserve, n.d. [1944?], TNA 31796.

35. Interview, Barikiwa Village, 22 July 2004.

36. Divisional Forest Officer to Conservator of Forests, Morogoro, 10 October 1951, TNA 16/25/3.

37. Kjekshus, *Ecology Control*, 166; Kirk Hoppe, *Lords of the Fly: Sleeping Sickness Control in British East Africa, 1900–1960* (Westport, Conn.: Praeger, 2003), 90.

38. Juhani Koponen, *Development for Exploitation: German Colonial Policies in Mainland Tanzania, 1884–1914* (Helsinki: Finnish Historical Society, 1995), 475–84; Michael Worboys, "The Comparative History of Sleeping Sickness in East and Central Africa, 1900–1914," *History of Science* 32 (1994): 89–102.

39. John M. MacKenzie, "Experts and Amateurs: Tsetse, Nagana, and Sleeping Sickness in East and Central Africa," in *Imperialism and the Natural World*, ed. John M. MacKenzie (Manchester: Manchester University Press, 1990), 197.

40. Wolfgang U. Eckart, *Medizin und Kolonialimperialismus: Deutschland 1884–1945* (Paderborn: Friedrich Schöningh, 1997), 340–49, 509–13.

41. Kjekshus, *Ecology Control;* James Giblin, "Trypanosomiasis Control in African History: An Evaded Issue?" *Journal of African History* 31, no.1 (1990): 59–80.

42. R. S. Troup, *Colonial Forest Administration* (Oxford: Oxford University Press, 1940), 49–50.

43. Hoppe, *Lords of the Fly,* 92–93; Kjekshus, *Ecology Control,* 165–76.

44. Kjekshus, *Ecology Control,* 171.

45. H. Fairbairn, "The Agricultural Problems Posed by Sleeping Sickness Settlements," *East African Agricultural Journal* 9 (July 1943): 20.

46. Gordon Matzke, "Settlement and Sleeping Sickness Control—A Dual Threshold Model of Colonial and Traditional Methods in East Africa," *Social Science and Medicine* 13D (1979): 212.

47. "Zum Vorkommen der Tsetse-Fliege," *Deutsch-Ostafrikanische Zeitung* 1, no. 43 (23 December 1899): 1.

48. *Amtlicher Anzeiger für Deutsch-Ostafrika* 14:9 (8 February 1913): 1; 14:30 (4 June 1913): 1; David F. Clyde, *History of the Medical Services of Tanganyika* (Dar es Salaam: Government Printer, 1962), 31–32; Luise White, "Tsetse Visions:

Narratives of Blood and Bugs in Colonial Northern Rhodesia," *Journal of African History* 36, no. 2 (1995): 219–45.

49. M. Taute, "A German Account of the Medical Side of the War in East Africa, 1914–1918," *TNR*, no. 8 (1939): 1–20; George Maclean, "The Relationship between Economic Development and Rhodesian Sleeping Sickness in Tanganyika Territory," *Annals of Tropical Medicine and Parasitology* 23, no. 1 (26 April 1929): 42, 45.

50. Maryinez Lyons, *The Colonial Disease: A Social History of Sleeping Sickness in Northern Zaire, 1900–1940* (Cambridge: Cambridge University Press, 1992), 46–47.

51. Matzke, "Settlement," 209–14; Giblin, "Trypanosomiasis Control"; John Ford, *The Role of Trypanosomiases in African Ecology: A Study of the Tsetse Fly Problem* (Oxford: Clarendon Press, 1971), 477–80.

52. Matzke, "Settlement," 212.

53. Randall M. Packard, *The Making of a Tropical Disease: A Short History of Malaria* (Baltimore: Johns Hopkins University, 2007), 24.

54. Matzke "Settlement," 210.

55. Quoted in Fairbairn, "Agricultural Problems," 17.

56. Bell to Chief Secretary, 31 January 1925, TNA AB.58.

57. William H. Dye, "The Relative Importance of Man and Beast in Human Trypanosomiasis," *Transactions of the Royal Society of Tropical Medicine and Hygiene* 21, no. 3 (1927): 189.

58. Bell to Chief Secretary, 10 February 1926, TNA AB.60; Dye, "Relative Importance," 189.

59. G. Maclean, "A Report on Human Trypanosomiasis in Tanganyika Territory for the Year Ending 31st December 1926," PRO, CO 691/90/11, 1–20.

60. On "densification," see Charles Swynnerton, "How Forestry May Assist towards the Control of the Tsetse Flies," in Troup, *Colonial Forest Administration*, app. 2; Hoppe, *Lords of the Fly*, 97. Dye's map of fly zones around Namabao village includes "Fly Free Hills and Jungle" northwest of the Matandu reserve. Dye, "Relative Importance," 188.

61. Maclean, "Human Trypanosomiasis."

62. Ann Beck, *Medicine and Society in Tanganyika, 1890–1930: A Historical Inquiry* (Philadelphia: American Philosophical Society, 1977), 45; White, "Tsetse Visions," 223.

63. Ford, *Role of Trypanosomiases,* 479.

64. Maclean, "Human Trypanosomiasis," 4.

65. Dean E. McHenry, *Tanzania's Ujamaa Villages: The Implementation of a Rural Development Strategy* (Berkeley: University of California Press, 1979), 17.

66. J. Sidley Scott to Sleeping Sickness Officer, Tabora, 1 March 1944, TNA 31796.

67. TDB–Kilwa District Book, vol. 2, "Liwale Closer Settlement Scheme"; Kitching to CS DSM, 5 June 1934, TNA 16/25/2, vol. 2.

68. David Anderson, "Depression, Dust Bowl, Demography and Drought: The Colonial State and Soil Conservation in East Africa during the 1930s," *African Affairs* 83, no. 332 (1984): 321–43; John McCracken, "Conservation and Resistance in Colonial Malawi: The 'Dead North' Revisited," in *Social History and African Environments,* ed. William Beinart and JoAnn McGregor (Oxford: James Currey, 2003), 155–74; William Beinart, "Soil Erosion, Conservation and Ideas about Development: A Southern African Exploration, 1900–1960," *Journal of Southern African Studies* 11, no. 1 (1984): 52–83; S. Ravi Rajan, *Modernizing Nature: Forestry and Imperial Eco-Development, 1800–1950* (Oxford: Clarendon Press, 2006), 179–90.

69. J. Sidley Scott to Sleeping Sickness Officer, Tabora, 1 March 1944, TNA 31796.

70. To the Secretary of State, n.d. [1948?], 87, TNA 31796.

71. Provincial Office Lindi to Administrative Secretary, 9 January 1945, TNA 31796; "Note of discussion," TNA 31796.

72. Shabani Kiputi, interview, Barikiwa, 22 July 2004.

73. Sleeping Sickness Officer to Administrative Secretary, Dar es Salaam, 22 October 1943, TNA 31796; emphasis in original.

74. Ibid.

75. Rooke Johnston to Chief Secretary, 26 August 1947, TNA 31796.

76. J. Sidley Scott to Sleeping Sickness Officer, Tabora, 1 March 1944, TNA 31796.

77. Provincial Office, Lindi, to Secretariat, DSM, 18 November 1947, TNA 31796. Neumann discusses the Liwale Closer Settlement Scheme in "Africa's 'Last Wilderness,'" 641–65.

78. Rooke Johnston to Chief Secretary, 13 September 1944; Sleeping Sickness Officer to Administrative Secretary, Dar es Salaam, 22 October 1943; both in TNA 31796.

79. Tanganyika PC's Reports 1944–45: Southern Province, PRO, CO 1018/72.

80. Divisional Annual Reports 1943, Central Division Report, TNA 270/JA/23.

81. Tanganyika PC's Reports 1944–45: Southern Province, PRO, CO 1018/72, 2.

82. TDB–Kilwa District Book, vol. 2, "Liwale Closer Settlement Scheme" (1948).

83. Kilwa DC to PC Southern, 28 October 1947, TNA 31796.

84. Tanganyika Provincial Commissioner's Reports 1944–45: Southern Province, PRO, CO 1018/72, 4.

85. Interview, Barikiwa, 22 July 2004.

86. Rooke Johnston to Chief Secretary, 26 August 1947, TNA 31796; DC Kilwa to PC Southern, 28 October 1947, TNA 31796.

87. TDB-Kilwa District Book, vol. 2, "Liwale Closer Settlement Scheme," 1948, sheet 21.

88. Rooke Johnston to Secretariat, 9 January 1945; Sidley Scott to Sleeping Sickness Officer, Tabora, 1 March 1944; both in TNA 31796.

89. TDB–Nachingwea District Book, vol. 1, "The Native Authorities of Liwale District."

90. Shabani Kiputi, interview, Barikiwa, 22 July 2004.

91. Acting Chief Secretary to PC Southern, 15 August 1947, TNA 31976.

92. Nasoro Hassani, Mohamedi Saidi, Saidi Salimu, Abdallah Mohamedi to Governor, 25 September 1947, TNA 31796.

93. TDB–Kilwa District, vol. 2, "Liwale Closer Settlement Scheme," 1948, sheet 8.

94. Memorandum for Territorial Tsetse Committee, 9 December 1947, TNA 31976, vol. 2.

95. TDB–Kilwa District Book, vol. 2, "Liwale Closer Settlement Scheme," 1948.

96. Kjekshus, *Ecology Control*, 161–68.

97. S. Napier-Bax, *Notes on Anti-Tsetse Clearings* (Dar es Salaam: Government Printer, 1932), 9.

98. Conservator of Forests to Divisional Forest Officer, Lindi, 24 October 1951, TNA 16/25/3, 400.

Chapter 6: Forestry Unbound

1. District Commissioner Ruponda to Provincial Commissioner Lindi, 7 August 1951, TNA 16/25/3, 369.

2. Reginald A. Cline-Cole, "Wartime Forest Energy Policy and Practice in British West Africa: Social and Economic Impact on the Labouring Classes, 1939–45," *Africa* 63, no. 1 (1993): 56–79.

3. W. J. Eggeling, *Forestry in Tanganyika, 1946–50* (Dar es Salaam: Government Printer, 1951), 1.

4. Ibid., 11.

5. *Annual Report* (1939), 1–3.

6. Artur Korn, "Die Holzwirtschaft unserer unter Mandat stehenden Kolonie Deutsch-Ostafrika während der vergangenen zehn Jahre," *Tropenpflanzer* 35 (1932): 465.

7. *Annual Report* (1940), 3; "Importance of Timber in War," *Indian Forester* 67, no. 2 (1942): 112–14.

8. David Killingray and Richard Rathbone, introduction to *Africa and the Second World War,* ed. Killingray and Rathbone (New York: St. Martin's, 1986), 9.

9. Secretary to the Governor's Conference to Chief Secretary, 17 December 1940, TNA 29184.

10. Timber Control under Defense Regulations, HQ. E.A., 10/7/44, TNA 28993; A. Rule, "East African Timber Production," *Empire Forestry Review* 24, no. 1 (1945): 47; Michael Cowen and Nicholas Westcott, "British Imperial Economic Policy during the War," in Killingray and Rathbone, *Africa and the Second World War,* 20–67.

11. N. D. G. James, *A History of English Forestry* (Oxford: Blackwell, 1981), 226.

12. Timber Control Meeting of Secretariat, 15 March 1941, TNA 29184; *Annual Report* (1941), 4; (1945), 3.

13. Chief Secretary Montague to Government, 10 October 1942, TNA 29184.

14. *Annual Report* (1943), 2.

15. *Annual Report* (1944), 17.

16. Forest Department to Pike, 27 January 1942, TNA ACC57.

17. Nicholas Westcott, "The Impact of the Second World War on Tanganyika, 1939–49," in Killingray and Rathbone, *Africa and the Second World War,* 146; John Iliffe, *A Modern History of Tanganyika* (Cambridge: Cambridge University Press, 1979), 343–44.

18. Provincial Commissioner Dar es Salaam to District Chiefs, 17 October 1944, TNA ACC57.

19. Letter to Chief Secretary to Governor's Conference Nairobi, 4 April 1942, TNA 30512; extracts from S/S Telegram 210, 16 April 1942; Westcott, "Impact," 146.

20. Collection of Wild Rubber in Forest Reserves, 1942, TNA 30511; extract from notes of a discussion on the possible exploitation of rubber with Mr. Mitchell of the Firestone Co. (South Africa), n.d. [1942?], TNA 30512.

21. Political [Officer], Kisarawe, to Forester, DSM, 15 December 1942, TNA ACC57, 9/1 Ilala, vol. 1.

22. Rubber production is difficult to gauge for 1942–43. *Annual Reports* for the war years list wild rubber quantities as "unquotable."

23. Chief Secretary Montague to Government, 10 October 1942, TNA 29184.

24. Thaddeus Sunseri, "'Something Else to Burn': Forest Squatters, Conservationists and the State in Modern Tanzania," *Journal of Modern African Studies* 43, no. 4 (2005): 609–40; J. E. G. Sutton, "Dar es Salaam: A Sketch of a Hundred Years," *TNR*, no. 71 (1970): 19; Andrew Burton, *African Underclass: Urbanisation, Crime, and Colonial Order in Dar es Salaam* (Athens: Ohio University Press, 2005).

25. Eggeling, *Forestry in Tanganyika*, 3. The latter figure was based on an estimated 1.6 million households, each consuming about 12 cubic meters of fuel wood annually.

26. W. M. Robertson, "The Forest Adviser's Visit to Tanganyika," *East African Agricultural Journal* 13 (1947): 197–99.

27. Political, Kisarawe, to Forester, DSM, 12 July 1944; Political, Kisarawe to Political, DSM, 4 April 1945; both in TNA ACC57/9/1.

28. District Commissioner, Kisarawe, to Provincial Commissioner, Eastern, 25 May 1945, TNA ACC57/9/1.

29. Scantling, Senior Forester to District Commissioner Dar es Salaam, 17 April 1945, TNA ACC57/9/1.

30. Burton, *African Underclass*, 90, 110.

31. Political, Kisarawe, to Political, DSM, 20 July 1944, TNA ACC57/9/1.

32. Such a case was recorded in Political, Kisarawe, to Senior Forester, DSM, 10 March 1945, TNA ACC57/9/1.

33. Burton, *African Underclass*, 67.

34. Conservator of Forests to Senior Forester DSM, "DSM Fuel Supply: Reafforestation," 28 November 1946, TNA ACC57/9/1.

35. Senior Forester DSM to District Commissioner DSM, 13 April 1945, TNA ACC57/9/1.

36. Senior Forester DSM to Conservator of Forests Morogoro, 15 November 1944, TNA ACC57/9/1.

37. Wakili Kisarawe to District Commissioner Kisarawe, 12 August 1945, TNA ACC57/9/1.

38. Political, Kisarawe, to Political, DSM, 4 April 1945, TNA ACC57/9/1.

39. J. D. Farquhar, *Working Plan for the Vikindu Plantations, Kisarawe District, Eastern Province, 1952–1967* (Dar es Salaam: Government Printer, 1954), 3.

40. Ibid., 4–12.

41. Ibid., 5; Senior Forester DSM to Conservator of Forests, 15 November 1944, TNA ACC57/9/1.

42. W. A. Brooks for District Commissioner Kisarawe, Notes on Forest Safari with Bwana Miti, 22 October 1956, TNA ACC540/F2/2.

43. Farquhar, *Working Plan,* 6.

44. Oxford Forestry Institute, Plant Sciences Library, "Forest Adviser's Note on a Visit to Tanganyika, October-November 1951," 5.

45. *Annual Report* (1954), 24.

46. M. S. Parry to Acting Conservator of Forests, Morogoro, October 1945; Proposal for Squatter Scheme, 1 March 1949; Acting Conservator of Forests to Political Kisarawe, 5 March 1949; all in, TNA ACC57/9/1.

47. Morogoro Forest Dept. to Regional Mines Officer, Dept. of Land and Mines, 21 December 1951, TNA 18982, vol. 2.

48. *Annual Reports* (1954), 6, 13, 22; (1955), 12, 23.

49. *Annual Report* (1954), 24.

50. *Annual Report* (1955), 26.

51. Ibid., 19.

52. W. A. Brooks for District Commissioner Kisarawe, Notes on Forest Safari with Bwana Miti, 22 October 1956, TNA ACC540/F.2/2. For a copy of the contract that specifies Mogo forest, see Hati ya Ruhusa ya Kulima Katika Pori Linalohifadhiwa na Serikali, TNA ACC540/F2/2.

53. Deborah Bernstein, *Constructing Boundaries: Jewish and Arab Workers in Mandatory Palestine* (Albany: SUNY Press, 2000), 168–69. For a map of the Palestine Railway see Paul Cotterell, *The Railways of Palestine and Israel* (Abingdon, UK: Tourret Publishing, 1984), 33, 68.

54. Ronald Hyam, introduction to *The Labour Government and the End of Empire, 1945–1951,* ed. Hyam (London: HMSO, 1992), lviii; CAB 128/11 "Palestine: Military Implications of Future Policy," 15 January 1947, in Hyam, *Labour Government,* 45; David D. Devereux, "Britain, the Commonwealth and the Defence of the Middle East, 1948–56," *Journal of Contemporary History* 24, no. 2 (1989): 327–45.

55. *Annual Report* (1946), 21.

56. Frederick Cooper, *Decolonization and African Society: The Labor Question in French and British Africa* (Cambridge: Cambridge University Press, 1996), 110–24; Joseph Morgan Hodge, *Triumph of the Expert: Agrarian Doctrines of Development and the Legacies of British Colonialism* (Athens: Ohio University Press, 2007), 178–79, 200–202.

57. Hyam, introduction, xliii–xliv.

58. A. J. Wakefield, "The Groundnut Scheme," *East African Agricultural Journal* 14 (January 1948): 131–34; Hyam, introduction, xliii–xliv; Allister E. Hinds, "Imperial Policy and Colonial Sterling Balances, 1943–56," *Journal of Imperial and Commonwealth History* 19, no. 1 (1991): 24–44; Matteo Rizzo, "What Was Left of the Groundnut Scheme? Development Disaster and Labour

Market in Southern Tanganyika, 1946–1952," *Journal of Agrarian Change* 6, no. 2 (2006): 205–38; Hodge, *Triumph of the Expert,* 209–13.

59. Wakefield, "Groundnut Scheme," 131; "Full Scale Groundnut Scheme Now Approved," *Tanganyika Standard,* 8 February 1947, 2.

60. Edith Tilton Penrose, "A Great African Project," *Scientific Monthly* 66, no. 4 (1948): 322–36; Iliffe, *Modern History,* 440–42.

61. "A Plan for East Africa," *Times,* 6 February 1947.

62. Map of groundnut lands, TNA 13809/I.

63. Sleeping Sickness Officer, Tabora, to Tsetse and Trypanosomiasis Committee, DSM, 22 January 1948; Acting Provincial Commissioner Southern to Member for Agriculture and Natural Resources, DSM, 19 February 1948; both in TNA 31796.

64. "A Review of Development Plans in the Southern Province of Tanganyika 1953," PRO, CO 822/553, 45–46; "Production of Groundnuts in East Africa: Cabinet Conclusions," 7 December 1950, PRO/CAB 128/18, CM 83 (50) 4, in Hyam, *Labour Government,* 293–94.

65. OFC to Hutt, Member for Development, 21 October 1950, TNA 35114, vol. 2.

66. Kathleen M. Stahl, *Tanganyika: Sail in the Wilderness* (The Hague: Mouton, 1961), 101.

67. H. C. Brookfield, "New Railroad and Port Developments in East and Central Africa," *Economic Geography* 31, no. 1 (1955): 69.

68. Ministry of Defense (hereafter DEFE) 4/2, COS 28(47)5, "African Development: Draft Report by the Chiefs of Staff on Transport in Africa," 19 February 1947; FO 800/435, "African Development: Beira Port and Railway," 23 October 1948; DEFE 4/19, COS 6 (49) 2, "The Strategic Aspect of the Proposed Railway Development in East and Central Africa," 10 January 1949; T 229/712, "Survey on East and Central Railway Link," 12 January 1950. In Hyam, *Labour Government,* document nos. 118, 128, 130, 135.

69. DEFE 4/19, COS 6 (49) 2, "Strategic Aspect," T 229/712 "Survey," in Hyam, *Labour Government,* 278, 293.

70. David Birmingham and Terence Ranger, "Settlers and Liberators in the South," in *History of Central Africa,* ed. Birmingham and Phyllis Martin (London: Longman, 1983), 2:363; Brookfield, "New Railroad," 65.

71. Brookfield, "New Railroad," 60–70.

72. Robius to Dawson, 25 September 1950, PRO, CO 822/154/2, 124.

73. East Africa Railways and Harbors Administration to Secretary of State for the Colonies, 17 October 1950, PRO, CO 822/154/2; Mtwara Port and Railway, Statement of Intentions, 11 October 1950.

74. *Annual Report* (1948), 5.

75. *Annual Report* (1947), 1.

76. Handing Over Notes, Southern Forest Division, July 1952, TNA ACC270/A/16/SD.

77. Annual Report Southern Division 1949, TNA ACC270/A/20/SD.

78. Handing Over Notes, Southern Forest Division, July 1952, TNA ACC270/A/16/SD.

79. Assistant Conservator of Forests to District Commissioner, Kisarawe, 18 November 1948, TNA ACC57/9/1; Eggeling, *Forestry in Tanganyika*, 13.

80. Groundnut Scheme Forestry Matters, vol. 1, Chief Secretary's Minutes, 29 February 1947, TNA 35114.

81. Handing Over Notes, Southern Forest Division, July 1952, TNA ACC270/A/16/SD.

82. *Annual Report* (1948), 1, 20.

83. Hyam, introduction, xxv; Raymond L. Bryant, *The Political Ecology of Forestry in Burma, 1824–1994* (Honolulu: University of Hawai'i Press, 1996), 168–70; H. E. W. Braund, *Calling to Mind: Being Some Account of the First Hundred Years (1870–1970) of Steel Brothers and Company Limited* (Oxford: Pergamon Press, 1975).

84. Conservator of Forests to Provincial Commissioner, Lindi, 17 August 1948, 18; Conservator of Forests to A. H. Pike, September 1948; both in TNA 16/25/15.

85. *Annual Report* (1948), 1. A map of the concession is found in "A Review of Development Plans in the Southern Province of Tanganyika 1953," PRO, CO 822/553.

86. Conservator of Forests to A. H. Pike, September 1948, TNA 16/25/15; Plant Sciences Library, Oxford Forest Institute, "Forest Adviser's Note on a Visit to Tanganyika," October–November 1951, 5.

87. Report of Working Party, 12/1950, PRO, CO 822/154/2, 107.

88. R. G. Sangster, *Forestry in Tanganyika, 1951–55* (Dar es Salaam: Government Printer, 1956), 12.

89. *Annual Report* (1954), 36.

90. Figures from *Annual Reports,* 1950–60.

91. *Annual Report* (1955), 11.

92. Review of Development Plans, 59, PRO, CO 822/553.

93. Forest Conservator to Provincial Commissioner Lindi, 17 July 1952, TNA 16/25/3, 435–39.

94. Fauz Twaib, "The Dilemma of the Customary Landholder: The Conflict between Customary and Statutory Rights of Occupancy in Tanzania," in

Land Law and Land Ownership in Africa, ed. R. Debusmann and S. Arnold (Bayreuth: Breitinger, 1996), 88.

95. District Commissioner, Ruponda, to Provincial Commissioner, Lindi, 7 August 1951, TNA 16/25/3, 369.

96. Ruponda District had recently been carved out of parts of Liwale subdistrict and Lindi District. DO Ruponda, Report on Proposed Forest Reserve, 27 August 1951, TNA 16/25/3, 376. On the use of barazas to elicit information see Peter Pels, "The Pidginization of Luguru Politics: Administrative Ethnography and the Paradoxes of Indirect Rule," *American Ethnologist* 23, no. 4 (1996): 749–53.

97. Michael Tuck, "Woodland Commodities, Global Trade and Local Struggles: The Beeswax Trade in the British Tanzania," *Journal of Eastern African Studies* 3, no. 1 (2009) (forthcoming).

98. District Officer Peace to District Commissioner, Ruponda, Report on Proposed Angai River Forest Reserve, TNA 16/25/3.

99. Ionides to District Commissioner, Ruponda, 6 November 1951, TNA 16/25/3, 405.

100. Trotman to all Provincial Commissioners and Conservator of Forests, 9 February 1952, TNA 16/25/3, 411.

101. Ibid.

102. District Commissioner Ruponda to Div. Forest Officer, 20 December 1952, 7 September 1953, TNA 16/25/3.

103. *Annual Report* (1957), 14.

104. John Iliffe, "Breaking the Chain at Its Weakest Link: TANU and the Colonial Office," in *In Search of a Nation: Histories of Authority and Dissidence in Tanzania,* ed. Gregory H. Maddox and James L. Giblin (Oxford: James Currey, 2005), 168–97.

105. Henry Bienen, *Tanzania: Party Transformation and Economic Development* (Princeton: Princeton University Press, 1970), 64–65.

106. *Annual Report* (1954), 17.

107. *Annual Report* (1957), 14.

108. *Annual Report* (1957), 7, 17; Roderick Neumann, *Imposing Wilderness: Struggles over Livelihood and Nature Preservation in Africa* (Berkeley: University of California Press, 1998), 118.

109. *Annual Report* (1958), 12.

110. Ali Abdala Kionga and Bakari Swalehe Mbonde, interview, Kinjumbi, 24 July 2004; Richard A. Schroeder, *Shady Practices* (Berkeley: University of California Press, 1999), 114-25.

111. *Annual Report* (1954), 18; R. Steele, Handing Over Notes, Southern Province, November 1955, TNA ACC270/A/16/SD.

112. Diary of Division Forest Officer Southern Division, 3 March 1951, TNA ACC270/A/15/SD.

113. *Annual Report* (1957), 3.

114. TNA ACC540/F2/2, Mogo Forest Reserve.

115. The affiliation between TATU and TANU is mentioned in "Ripoti ya Tume ya Rais ya Kuchunguza Matukio ya Tarehe 26 na 27 January 2001," par. 52. TATU was founded in 1956 by African businessmen seeking to compete with Asians.

116. Assistant Conservator of Forests, Kisarawe, to District Officer, Mzizima, 21 July 1960, TNA ACC540/DC23/3.

117. For examples of arson directed against forest reserves in other settings, see Karl Jacoby, *Crimes against Nature: Squatters, Poachers, Thieves, and the Hidden History of American Conservation* (Berkeley: University of California Press, 2001), 72–76; Ramachandra Guha, *The Unquiet Woods: Ecological Change and Peasant Resistance in the Himalaya* (Oxford: Oxford University Press, 1989), 123–25.

118. Data from *Annual Reports* (1945–59); *Annual Report* (1960), 12.

119. Annual Report of the Southern Forest Division, 31 December 1949, TNA ACC 270/A/20/SD.

120. Acting Conservator of Forests to Conservator of Forests, Rondo, 6 January 1951, TNA ACC 270/A/20/SD.

121. W. M. Robertson, "Fire and Forest," *East African Agricultural Journal* 13 (1947): 1–2.

122. *Annual Report* (1955), 38.

123. Andrew Coulson, *Tanzania: A Political Economy* (Oxford: Clarendon Press, 1982), 139.

124. Acting Conservator of Forests, Annual Report for 1950, 6 January 1951, TNA ACC270/A/20/SD; TNA ACC640/4/25/32/I, Ministry of Labor; Braund, *Calling to Mind*, 57.

125. TNA ACC460/4/25/21/I, Ministry of Labor.

126. Steven Feierman, *Peasant Intellectuals: Anthropology and History in Tanzania* (Madison: University of Wisconsin Press, 1990).

127. Strike Report—Steel Bros. Limited, Rondo, TNA ACC460/4/25/21/I.

128. Shivji describes the BCWU as among the most radical unions in Tanganyika because it tended to be more tenacious in its strikes and because it refused to affiliate with the much larger Transport and Government Workers' Union. Issa Shivji, *Law, State and the Working Class in Tanzania, c. 1920–1964* (London: James Currey, 1986), 187, 195.

129. Shivji, *Law, State,* 185–86; Tanganyika District Books, Nachingwea, vol. 2, Extracts from Annual Reports of the District Commissioners (1957).

130. Bryce, Acting Conservator of Forests, Annual Report for 1950, TNA ACC270/A/20/SD.

131. Iliffe, *Modern History,* 558–62.

132. TDB–Nachingwea District, vol. 2, Extracts from Annual Reports, 1960, "Land."

133. Information Officer, Southern Province, Press Release—Southern Province Industries, 1961, TNA ACC593 FO/1/4; Godfrey Stalin Mwafongo, "The Sky-Scraping Rondo Forest," *Nationalist,* no. 2141 (15 March 1971).

134. *Annual Report* (1960), 12.

Chapter 7: Creating Modern Tanzanians

1. Steven Feierman, *Peasant Intellectuals: Anthropology and History in Tanzania* (Madison: University of Wisconsin Press, 1990), 223–36; Henry Bienen, *Tanzania: Party Transformation and Economic Development* (Princeton: Princeton University Press, 1970), 67–70.

2. Andrew Hurst, "Not Yet Out of the Woods: A Political Ecology of State Forest Policy and Practice in Mainland Tanzania, 1961–1998" (PhD diss., Oxford University, 2004).

3. "The Organization of Protection Forestry," TNA 604/FD.32/01.

4. Mzizima to Asst. Conservator of Forests, Kisarawe, 6 January 1961, TNA ACC540/DC23/1.

5. Mzizima to Bwana Shabani Pazi, TNA ACC540/DC23/1.

6. These included Mpigi, Mkonore, and Tongoro forests. *Annual Report* (1966), 4.

7. Z. G. N. Maagi, M. J. Mkude, and E. J. Mlowe, *The Forest Area of Tanzania Mainland,* Forest Resource Study Series, no. 34 (Dar es Salaam: Tanzanian Ministry of Natural Resources and Tourism, 1979), app. 2.

8. Feierman, *Peasant Intellectuals,* 233–34.

9. This was seen in a court case from the early 1960s that acknowledged a peasant right to usufruct in government reserves. "Abdalla Chapila vs. Mohamedi Mwinyigoha and Five Others," *Journal of African Law* 13, no. 3 (1969): 179–81.

10. Local and district authority reserves succeeded Native Authority reserves after chiefship was abolished in Tanzania after independence. Andrew Coulson, *Tanzania: A Political Economy* (Oxford: Clarendon Press, 1982), 136; *Annual Report* (1967), 11.

11. *Annual Report* (1968), 10.

12. *Annual Report* (1964), 16; (1965), 16.

13. "The Organization of Protection Forestry," TNA ACC 604/FD.32/01.

14. *Annual Report* (1960), 10; Andrew Hurst, "State Forestry and Spatial Scale in the Development Discourses of Post-colonial Tanzania: 1961–1971," *Geographical Journal* 169, no. 4 (2003): 360; M. S. Parry, "Recent Progress in the Development of Miombo Woodland in Tanganyika," *East African Agricultural and Forestry Journal* 31(January 1966): 307–15.

15. *Annual Report* (1961), 3.

16. "Forestry in Tanzania," n.d. [1968?], TNA ACC604/FD/32/01/II.

17. *Annual Report* (1961), 19–20; R. P. Farrer, "The First Eight Years on the Rondo," *Empire Forestry Review* 39, no. 1 (1960): 89–93; Information Officer, Southern Province, Press Release—Southern Province Industries, 1961, TNA ACC593 FO/1/4.

18. *Annual Report* (1962), 10; (1963), 5.

19. Timber Concessions, TNA 16/25/15.

20. *Annual Report* (1963), 10–11.

21. R. G. Sangster, "Forestry in Tanganyika," in *The Natural Resources of East Africa,* ed. E. W. Russell (Nairobi: East African Literature Bureau, 1962), 122–125; G. J. Kileo, "Forestry in Tanzania," in *East Africa: Its People and Resources,* ed. W. T. W. Morgan (London: Oxford University Press, 1972), 215–20.

22. *Annual Report* (1961), ii.

23. Regional Forest Officer to Forests, DSM, 10 November 1964, TNA ACC604/FD.32/01/I.

24. *Annual Report* (1960), 15. Altogether there were about fifteen thousand hectares of state and local authority tree plantations in Tanganyika in 1960, only eight hundred of which grew hardwoods.

25. "Forestry in Tanzania," n.d. [1968?], TNA ACC604/FD/32/01/II. In 2001 there were eighty-three thousand hectares of state tree plantations in Tanzania. Ministry of Natural Resources and Tourism, *National Forest Program* (hereafter *NFP*), sec. 2.1, "Land Use in Tanzania."

26. *Annual Report* (1966), 18.

27. Government of Tanganyika, "The Three Year Development Plan, 1961–64," in *Readings on Economic Development and Administration in Tanzania,* ed. Hadley E. Smith (Dar es Salaam: Institute of Public Administration, 1966), 348–59.

28. Kileo memorandum, 21 November 1966, TNA ACC604/32/01/I.

29. Coulson, *Tanzania,* 156.

30. Ibid., 161.

31. Ibid., ch. 17; TNA ACC604/FD/31/02—Mpango wa Tatu wa Maendeleo ya Miaka Mitano (1976/77–1980/81).

32. Parry, "Recent Progress," 308.

33. "Forest Estate Planning," Procter to Director of Forestry, 28 February 1968; "Forestry in Tanzania," n.d. [1968?], TNA ACC604/FD/32/01/II.

34. "Forest Estate Planning," Director of Forestry to Silvicultural Section, 20 March 1968, TNA ACC604/FD/32/01/II.

35. "Proposed Forestry Public Relations Program Forestry Development Plan 1969–74," 22 April 1968, TNA ACC604/FD.32/02/I.

36. O. V. Garratt, Adviser on Prison Administration, to Secretary of State for the Colonies, "Tour of Tanganyika," 1960, 7, PRO, CO 822/2724.

37. Coulson, *Tanzania*, 279.

38. Sangster, *Forestry in Tanganyika*, 17; Per Sköld, *Report to the Government of Tanzania on Development of the Forest Sector in Tanzania* (Rome: FAO, 1969), 27.

39. On the importance of forestry wages to supplement subsistence incomes, see Elizabeth Daley, "Land and Social Change in a Tanzanian Village Part 1: Kinyanambo, 1920s–1990," *Journal of Agrarian Change* 5, no. 3 (2005): 390–91.

40. "The Organization of Protection Forestry": Draft Administrative Order to All Forest Officers, TNA 604/FD.32/01.

41. Sangster, "Forestry and Rural Development," TNA 604/FD.32/01.

42. Hurst, in contrast, asserts that "foresters had little basis to articulate a vision of peasant involvement in forests for development." Hurst, "Out of the Woods," 108.

43. Sangster, "Forestry and Rural Development," TNA 604/FD.32/01.

44. TDB–Kisarawe District Book, vol. 1, "The Physical Background and Its Influence on Settlement," 4.

45. The problems of overreliance on cassava are discussed in Marilyn Little, "Colonial Policy and Subsistence in Tanganyika, 1925–49," *Geographical Review* 81, no. 4 (1991): 375–88.

46. Hurst, "Out of the Woods," 87.

47. Regional Forest Officer, Mtwara, to Director of Natural Resources, Dar es Salaam, 16 January 1970, TNA ACC604/FD33/19.

48. *Annual Report* (1968), 1–2; Wizara ya Ardhi, Maliasili na Utalii-FD.32/01, Kileo to Senior Forest Officer (Planning), Forest Officer (Marketing), Forest Economist, Forest Officer (W.P.), Forester (General Duties) (1967), TNA ACC604.

49. Thaddeus Sunseri, "'Something Else to Burn': Forest Squatters, Conservationists and the State in Modern Tanzania," *Journal of Modern African Studies* 43, no. 4 (2005): 609–40.

50. Forest Industries Development: Charcoal, 1963, TNA ACC604/FD/39/20/14.

51. Principal Secretary, Forests and Wildlife, to various firms in England and United States, 18 March 1965, TNA ACC604/FD/39/20/14.

52. Industrial Studies and Development Centre, Report on Production and Exports of Charcoal, 9 May 1970, TNA ACC604/FD/39/20/14.

53. Saad S. Yahya, "Woodfuel and Change in Urban Tanzania," in *Fuelwood Revisited: What Has Changed in the Last Decade?*, CIFOR Occasional Paper 39 (2003), ed. Michael Arnold, Gunnar Köhlin, Reidar Persson, and Gillian Shepherd, 241–43.

54. Regional Director of Ag, Mwanza, to Director of Natural Resources, 24 September 1969, TNA ACC604/FD/39/20/14.

55. Director of Natural Resources to Secretary, Central Tender Board, 26 September 1969, TNA ACC604/FD/39/20/14.

56. Industrial Studies and Development Centre, Report on Production and Exports of Charcoal, 9 May 1970, TNA ACC604/FD/39/20/14.

57. "Report on Production and Exports of Charcoal," 9 May 1970, TNA ACC604/FD/39/20/4.

58. Halai and Sons, Karachi, to Chief Conservator of Forests, DSM, 25 October 1971, TNA ACC604/FD/39/20/14.

59. Tanganyika Industrial Corporation to Export Promotion Bureau, 16 September 1969, TNA ACC604/FD/39/20/14.

60. District Forest Officer, DSM, to Regional Director of Agriculture, Coast Region, 24 February 1970, TNA ACC604/FD/39/20/14.

61. Halai and Sons to Chief Conservator of Forests, 25 October 1971; Director of Forestry to Director General of the Board, Iraq, 19 November 1971; both in TNA ACC604/FD/39/20/14.

62. K. Openshaw, *Forest Industries Development Planning Tanzania—Present Consumption and Future Requirements of Wood in Tanzania* (Rome: UNDP/FAO, 1971), 14.

63. *Annual Report* (1970), 8; (1972), 9.

64. Industrial Studies and Development Centre, Report on Production and Exports of Charcoal, 9 May 1970, TNA ACC604/FD/39/20/14.

65. D. L. Mgeta, Assistant Promotion Officer, Tanganyika Development and Finance Company Ltd. to Principal Secretary, Ministry of National [Natural] Resources and Tourism, 28 January 1971, TNA ACC604/FD/39/20/14.

66. J. C. Kilembe, General Manager, Tanga Development Corporation Ltd. to Director, Forestry, 3 November 1971, TNA ACC604/FD/39/20/14.

67. Bagamoyo Forest Circulars, 14 March 1957, TNA ACC7/13/1; *Annual Report* (1957), 54; John Holmes, *Natural Forest Handbook for Tanzania,* 2 vols. (Morogoro: Sokoine University, 1995), 1:52.

68. *Annual Report* (1958), 42; Holmes, *Natural Forest Handbook,* 1:52.

69. J. E. G. Sutton, "Dar es Salaam: A Sketch of a Hundred Years," *TNR,* no. 71 (1970): 16.

70. "Employment in Forest Plantations," 12 March 1964, TNA ACC604/FD/32/01; Tanganyika Development Finance Co. Ltd. to Principal Secretary, Ministry of Natural Resources, 1 February 1972, TNA ACC604/FD/39/20/14; Ruvu North Forest Reserve Charcoal Inventory, May–June 1971, TNA ACC604/FD/33/15/II.

71. D. C. C. Magawa to Mwenyekiti, Kamati ya Maendeleo ya Mkoa, Kibaha, 31 March 1983, TNA ACC604/FD/33/15/II.

72. Safari Report—Ruvu North Forest Reserve, 15 September 1972, TNA ACC604/FD/33/15/I.

73. Bana Forest Project, 1967–74, Compensation List, August 1968, TNA ACC604/FD/33/15/II.

74. Coulson, *Tanzania,* 320.

75. Safari Report—Ruvu North Forest Reserve, 15 September 1972, TNA ACC604/FD/33/15/I.

76. Wakulima Wote to Wizara ya Maliasili, Madebe, 28 June 1972, TNA ACC604/FD/33/15/II.

77. Dean E. McHenry, *Tanzania's Ujamaa Villages: The Implementation of a Rural Development Strategy* (Berkeley: University of California Press, 1979); James Scott, *Seeing Like a State: How Certain Schemes to Improve the Human Condition Have Failed* (New Haven: Yale University Press, 1998), ch. 7; Leander Schneider, "Freedom and Unfreedom in Rural Development: Julius Nyerere, *Ujamaa Vijijini,* and Villagization," *Canadian Journal of African Studies* 38, no. 2 (2004): 344–92.

78. Coulson, *Tanzania,* 241–48.

79. Hurst, "Out of the Woods," ch. 5; John Shao, "The Villagization Program and the Disruption of the Ecological Balance in Tanzania," *Canadian Journal of African Studies* 20, no. 2 (1986): 232. Yusufu Lawi discusses how Ujamaa influenced ecological consciousness in Iraqw, in northern Tanzania, in "Tanzania's Operation *Vijiji* and Local Ecological Consciousness: The Case of Eastern Iraqwaland, 1974–1976," *Journal of African History* 48, no. 1 (2007): 69–93.

80. Neil Burgess, Jennifer D'Amico Hales, Emma Underwood, Eric Dinerstein, et al., *Terrestrial Ecoregions of Africa and Madagascar: A Conservation Assessment* (Washington, D.C.: Island Press, 2004), 311.

81. Lawi, "Operation *Vijiji*."

82. Daley, "Land and Social Change."

83. Interview, Kazimzumbwi-Darajani, 17 July 2004.

84. D. C. C. Magawa to Mwenyekiti, Kamati ya Maendeleo ya Mkoa, Kibaha, 31 March 1983, TNA ACC604/FD/33/15/II.

85. N. S. Mero, "An Outlook of Forestry in Tanzania—Kasulu District," 5 May 1977, TNA ACC604/FD/32/01/II, 4.

86. Lawi, "Operation *Vijiji*," 77.

87. A. S. M. Mgeni, "Fuelwood Crisis in Tanzania Is Women's Burden," *Quarterly Journal of Forestry* 78, no. 4 (October 1984): 247–49; Fred Håkon Johnsen, "Burning with Enthusiasm: Fuelwood Scarcity in Tanzania in Terms of Severity, Impacts and Remedies," *Forum for Development Studies*, no. 1 (1999): 110.

88. E. M. Temu to Mtuy, 7 May 1977, TNA ACC604/FD/32/01/II.

89. Michael J. Sheridan, "The Environmental Consequences of Independence and Socialism in North Pare, Tanzania, 1961–88," *Journal of African History* 45, no. 1 (2004): 97.

90. Afisa Mali Asili to Mradi wa Msitu Rondo, 1 October 1974, TNA ACC604/FD33/19.

91. E. M. Temu to Mtuy, 7 May 1977, TNA ACC604/FD/32/01/II.

92. G. P. Mashurano to Mtuy, 24 May 1977, TNA ACC604/FD/32/01/II; Sheridan, "Environmental Consequences," 98–99.

93. W. A. Rodgers, "The Miombo Woodlands," in *East African Ecosystems and Their Conservation*, ed. T. R. McClanahan and T. P. Young (New York: Oxford University Press, 1996), 308–9.

94. Sangster, *Forestry in Tanganyika*, 1.

95. *NFP*, sec. 2.1, "Land Use in Tanzania."

96. E. K. Shishira, P. Z. Yanda, and J. G. Lyimo, "Vegetation Dynamics and Management Implications in the Pugu and Kazimzumbwi Forest Reserves, Tanzania," *Coenoses* 13, no. 3 (1998): 149–58.

97. Mgeni, "Fuelwood Crisis," 248.

98. Johnsen, "Burning with Enthusiasm," 114.

99. *Annual Report* (1977), 9.

100. Mtuy, Forest Division Dar es Salaam, 28 March 1977, TNA ACC604/FD/32/01/II.

101. M. C. P. Mtuy, "An Outlook for Forestry in Tanzania" (Dar es Salaam: Forest Division, 1976), typescript, TNA ACC604/FD/32/01/II.

102. Ibid., 5.

103. B. T. Kimaryo to Mtuy, 13 April 1977., TNA ACC604/FD/32/01/II

104. D. M. Kombe to Mtuy, 20 April 1977, TNA ACC604/FD/32/01/II.

105. Mnzava to Regional Development Officers and Project Chiefs, 19 October 1979, TNA ACC604/FD/31/02.

106. Afisa Maliasili Mkoa, Lindi, to Mkurugenzi wa Misitu, Dar es Salaam, 16 January 1979, TNA ACC604/FD/31/02.

107. Afisa Maliasili, Utete/Rufiji, to Mkurugenzi wa Maendeleo, 9 April 1979, TNA ACC604/FD/31/02.

108. Meneja Mradi wa Misutu, Ruvu/Kibaha, to Mkurugenzi wa Misitu, Dar es Salaam, 23 November 1979, TNA ACC604/FD/31/02.

109. Magawa to F. P. O. Mafinga, 13 October 1981; Magawa to Chief Manager, RTC Coast, 21 October 1981; both in TNA/ACC604/FD/33/15/II.

110. Magawa to Kamati ya Maendeleo ya Mkoa, Kibaha, 31 March 1983, TNA/ACC604/FD/33/15/II.

111. Lawi, "Operation *Vijiji*," 75.

Chapter 8: Biodiversity Preservation and Emergent Forest Conflicts

1. Andrew Hurst, "Not Yet Out of the Woods: A Political Ecology of State Forest Policy and Practice in Mainland Tanzania, 1961–1998," (PhD diss., Oxford University, 2004), ch. 7.

2. Gareth Porter, Janet Welsh Brown, and Pamela S. Clark, *Global Environmental Politics*, 3rd ed. (Boulder: Westview, 2000), 124–25.

3. Michael Goldman, *Imperial Nature: The World Bank and Struggles for Social Justice in the Age of Globalization* (New Haven: Yale University Press, 2005), 184–85.

4. Simon Milledge, Ised K. Gelvas, and Antje Ahrends, *Forestry, Governance and National Development: Lessons Learned from a Logging Boom in Southern Tanzania* (Dar es Salaam: TRAFFIC East/Southern Africa, 2007).

5. Norman Myers, Russell A. Mittermeier, Cristina G. Mittermeier, Gustavo A. B. da Fonseca, and Jennifer Kent, "Biodiversity Hotspots for Conservation Priorities," *Nature* 403, no. 6772 (2000): 853–58.

6. Goldman, *Imperial Nature*, 93–97.

7. Tanzania Ministry of National Resources and Tourism, *National Forest Programme in Tanzania 2001–2010* (Dar es Salaam: Ministry of National Resources and Tourism, 2001), 108–10 (hereafter *NFP 2001*).

8. Kerry A. Woodcock, *Changing Roles in Natural Forest Management: Stakeholders' Roles in the Eastern Arc Mountains, Tanzania* (Aldershot: Ashgate, 2002), 48–49.

9. *NFP 2001*, i.

10. Franz Heske, *German Forestry* (New Haven: Yale University Press, 1938), 42.

11. Ibid., 180–85; Peder Anker, *Imperial Ecology: Environmental Order in the British Empire, 1895–1945* (Cambridge, Mass.: Harvard University Press, 2001), 81–82.

12. R. S. Troup, *Colonial Forest Administration* (Oxford: Oxford University Press, 1940), 47.

13. "The Organization of Protection Forestry," TNA 604/FD/32/01; *Annual Report* (1967).

14. M. C. P. Mtuy, "An Outlook for Forestry in Tanzania" (Dar es Salaam: Forest Division, 1976), TNA ACC604/FD/32/01/II, 2.

15. Ramachandra Guha, *Environmentalism: A Global History* (New York: Longman, 2000), 2–6.

16. Rodgers to Regional Natural Resources Officer, 8 November 1979, TNA ACC604/FD/31/02.

17. K. M. Howell, "Pugu Forest Reserve: Biological Values and Development," *African Journal of Ecology* 19, nos. 1–2 (1981): 73–81.

18. Christopher Conte, *Highland Sanctuary: Environmental History in Tanzania's Usambara Mountains* (Athens: Ohio University Press, 2004), 4; A. W. Diamond, "A Summary of Conservation Resolutions Adopted at This Symposium," *African Journal of Ecology* 19, nos. 1–2 (1981): 213; Hurst, "Out of the Woods," 155–61.

19. L. H. Brown, "The Conservation of Forest Islands in Areas of High Human Density," *African Journal of Ecology* 19, nos. 1–2 (1981): 27–32.

20. Ibid., 28; Diamond, "Conservation Resolutions," 213.

21. W. A. Rodgers and Katherine Homewood, "Biological Values and Conservation Prospects for the Forests and Primate Populations of the Uzungwa Mountains, Tanzania," *Biological Conservation* 24, no. 4 (1982): 285–304; Roderick Neumann, "Africa's 'Last Wilderness': Reordering Space for Political and Economic Control in Colonial Tanzania," *Africa* 71, no. 4 (2001): 641–65.

22. W. A. Rodgers, "The Conservation of the Forest Resources of Eastern Africa: Past Influences, Present Practices, and Future Needs," in *Biogeography and Ecology of the Rain Forests of Eastern Africa*, ed. Jon C. Lovett and Samuel K. Wasser (Cambridge: Cambridge University Press, 1993), 290.

23. A. B. Temu, B. K. Kaale, and J. A. Maghembe, *Wood-Based Energy for Development* (Dar es Salaam: Ministry of Natural Resources and Tourism, 1984), 1; Hurst, "Out of the Woods," 90.

24. W. A. Rodgers, W. Mziray, and E. K. Shishira, "The Extent of Forest Cover in Tanzania Using Satellite Imagery," Research Paper no. 12, Institute of Resource Assessment, University of Dar es Salaam, 1985; Rodgers, "Conservation of the Forest Resources."

25. Adolfo Mascarenhas, "The Relevance of the 'Miti' Project to Wood-Based Energy in Tanzania," in Temu, Kaale, and Maghembe, *Wood-Based Energy,* 26–46.

26. Ibid., 40.

27. G. P. Clarke, "Defining the Eastern African Coastal Forests," in *Coastal Forests of Eastern Africa,* ed. Neil Burgess and G. Philip Clarke (Gland, Switzerland: IUCN, 2000), 9–26; W. D. Hawthorne, "East African Coastal Forest Botany," in Lovett and Wasser, *Biogeography and Ecology,* 57–99.

28. L. H. Brown, "Conservation," 27.

29. D. M. Hall, S. Staddon, K. M. Hall, and E. Fanning, eds., *Kazimzumbwi Forest Reserve: A Biodiversity Survey,* Frontier Tanzania Technical Report no. 26 (Dar es Salaam: Society for Environmental Exploration, 2002), 32–33.

30. Norman Myers, Jon C. Lovett, and Neil Burgess, "Eastern Arc Mountains and Coastal Forests," in *Hotspots: Earth's Biologically Richest and Most Endangered Terrestrial Ecoregions,* ed. Russell A. Mittermeier, Norman Myers, and Cristina Goettsch Mittermeier (Mexico City: Conservation International, 1999), 210.

31. Aili Mari Tripp, *Changing the Rules: The Politics of Liberalization and the Urban Informal Economy in Tanzania* (Berkeley: University of California Press, 1997), 63–64.

32. Hurst, "Out of the Woods"; Goldman, *Imperial Nature.*

33. Dean M. McHenry Jr., *Limited Choices: The Political Struggle for Socialism in Tanzania* (Boulder: Lynne Rienner, 1994), 168.

34. Per Nilsson, "Wood—the Other Energy Crisis," in *Tanzania: Crisis and Struggle for Survival,* ed. Jannik Boesen, Kjell J. Havnevik, Juhani Koponen, and Rie Odgaard (Uppsala: Scandinavian Institute of African Studies, 1986), 159.

35. Goldman, *Imperial Nature,* 96–97.

36. Dan Brockington, *Fortress Conservation: The Preservation of the Mkomazi Game Reserve, Tanzania* (Oxford: James Currey, 2002).

37. Tripp, *Changing the Rules,* 76–77; Michael Watts, "Empire of Oil: Capitalist Dispossession and the Scramble for Africa," *Monthly Review* 58, no. 4 (2006): 1–17.

38. Fred Håkon Johnsen, "Burning with Enthusiasm: Fuelwood Scarcity in Tanzania in Terms of Severity, Impacts and Remedies," *Forum for Development Studies,* no. 1 (1999): 122; Barry Munslow, Yemi Katerere, Adriaan Ferf, and Phil O'Keefe, *The Fuelwood Trap: A Study of the SADCC Region* (London: Earthscan, 1988), 125.

39. Saad S. Yahya, "Woodfuel and Change in Urban Tanzania," in *Fuelwood Revisited: What Has Changed in the Last Decade?* CIFOR Occasional Paper 39 (2003), ed. Michael Arnold, Gunnar Köhlin, Reidar Persson, and Gillian Shepherd, 240; Ole Hofstad, "Woodland Deforestation by Charcoal Supply to Dar es Salaam," *Journal of Environmental Economics and Management* 33, no. 1 (1997): 23. A major discrepancy between these two authors is that the former estimates a bag of charcoal to weigh twenty-eight kilograms while the latter estimates forty-five kilograms.

40. I. D. Thomas, "Population Density around Dar es Salaam," *TNR,* no. 71 (1970): 165; Tripp, *Changing the Rules,* 30.

41. Dennis P. Dykstra, "Forestry in Tanzania," *World Forestry* 81, no. 11 (1983): 742–46.

42. Johnsen, "Burning," 117.

43. Woodcock, *Changing Roles,* 148.

44. "What Is a Biodiversity Hotspot?" *Arc Journal,* no. 20 (March 2007): 4.

45. "Brief History," *Arc Journal,* no. 18 (November 2005): 2; Tanzania Forest Conservation Group, http://www.tfcg.org/docs/about_us.htm.

46. Neil Baker and Liz Baker, "Coastal Forests Project Tanzania: Important Bird Areas," n.d., BirdLife International, http://home.no.net/stenih/coastalforest .htm; Wildlife Conservation Society of Tanzania, "Mission," http://www .wcstarusha.org (both accessed 5 Sept. 2008).

47. *Miombo: The Newsletter of the Wildlife Conservation Society of Tanzania* 28 (January 2006): 3.

48. The Worldwide Fund for Nature was formerly called the World Wildlife Fund, and still is in North America.

49. For example, Secelela Balisidya, "Hifadhi ya Kazimzumbwi hatarini," *IPP Media,* 29 September 2004, http://ippmedia.com.

50. Secelela Balisidya, cited above, is information officer for the TFCG. *Arc Journal,* no. 18 (November 2005): 11.

51. Rodgers, "Conservation of the Forest Resources," 292, 317; Hurst, "Out of the Woods"; "What Are the Eastern Arc Mountain Forests Worth to Tanzania?" *Arc Journal,* no. 19 (2005): 11.

52. Michael Goldman, "Constructing an Environmental State: Eco-governmentality and other Transnational Practices of a 'Green' World Bank," *Social Problems* 48, no. 4 (2001): 501; emphasis in original.

53. *NFP* 2001, xi–xii.

54. Adrian Kahemela, "TFCG Establishes New Community Forest Conservation Network," African Rainforest Conservancy, http://www.africarainforest .org/article_kahemela.html (accessed 5 Sept. 2008); WWF, "Central and Eastern Miombo Woodlands—A Global Ecoregion," Worldwide Fund for Nature, http://www.panda.org/about_wwf/where_we_work/ecoregions/central_eastern _miombo_woodlands.cfm (accessed 5 Sept. 2008).

55. Mac Chapin, "A Challenge to Conservationists," *World Watch* 17, no. 6 (2004): 17–32; Peter R. Wilshusen, Steven R. Brechin, Crystal L. Fortwangler, and Patrick C. West, "Reinventing a Square Wheel: Critique of a Resurgent 'Protection Paradigm' in International Biodiversity Conservation," *Society and Natural Resources* 15, no. 1 (2002): 17–40.

56. W. M. Adams and D. Hulme, "If Community Conservation Is the Answer in Africa, What Is the Question?" *Oryx* 35, no. 3 (2001): 193–200; Liz Alden Wily et al., "Community Management of Forests in Tanzania," *Forests, Trees and People Newsletter,* no. 42 (2000): 36–45; Hurst, "Out of the Woods."

57. W. A. Rodgers, "Forest Biodiversity Loss: A Global Perspective," n.d. [1997?], 74–75, Biodiversity Economics, http://biodiversityeconomics.org/ applications/library_documents/lib_document.rm?document_id=543 (accessed 5 Sept. 2008).

58. Ruponda District Commissioner to Provincial Commissioner, Lindi, 7 August 1951, TNA 16/25/3, 369.

59. Dominick de Waal, "Setting Precedents in the Hangai Forest," *Forests, Trees and People Newsletter,* no. 44 (2001): 42–46; Irmeli Mustahahti, "Msitu wa Angai: Haraka, haraka, haina baraka! Why Does Handing over the Angai Forest to Local Villages Proceed So Slowly?" in *Anomalies of Aid: A Festschrift for Juhani Koponen,* ed. Jeremy Gould and Lauri Siitonen (Helsinki: Interkont, 2007), 168–86.

60. Interview, Likombora village, 22 July 2004.

61. Timber poaching is discussed in Milledge, Gelvas, and Ahrends, *Forestry.*

62. Interview, Likombora village, 22 July 2004.

63. Milledge, Gelvas, and Ahrends, *Forestry,* 72.

64. Interview, Likombora village, 22 July 2004. Forest famine foods, including ung'oko, are discussed in H. Missano, C. W. Njebele, L. Kayombo, and B. Ogle, "Dependency on Forests and Trees for Food Security," Working Paper 261 (Uppsala: Swedish University of Agricultural Sciences, 1994), 22–24.

65. Interview, Likombora Village, 22 July 2004.

66. Interview, Mihumo Village, 22 July 2004.

67. Ibid.

68. Tanzania Ministry of Natural Resources and Tourism, *Resettlement Action Plan for Farm Plots Displaced for Biodiversity Conservation in the Derema*

Forest Corridor: Prepared for Consideration of Compensation Funding by the World Bank (September 2006), 11, Tanzania Ministry of Natural Resources and Tourism, http://nfp.co.tz/highlights.html (accessed 5 Sept. 2008).

69. Critical Ecosystem Partnership Fund, "CEFP Final Project Completion Report," http://www.cefp.net; "Brief History," *Arc Journal,* no. 18 (November, 2005): 2–3.

70. Charles Meshack, "Transaction Costs of Participatory Forest Management: Empirical Evidence from Tanzania," *Arc Journal,* no. 16 (2003): 6–9.

71. Heini Vihemäki, "Politics of Participatory Forest Conservation: Cases from the East Usambara Mountains, Tanzania," *Journal of Transdisciplinary Environmental Studies,* Special Issue on Power, Development and Environment 4, no. 2 (2005): 2, 8–9; G. L. K. Jambiya and H. Sosovele, "Poverty and the Environment: The Case of Amani Nature Reserve," REPOA (Research on Poverty Alleviation) Policy Brief 00.5 (n.d.), REPOA, http://www.repoa.or.tz/documents_storage/ (accessed 5 Sept. 2008).

72. Liz Alden Wily, "Can We Really Own the Forest? A Critical Examination of Tenure Development in Community Forestry in Africa," paper presented at the International Association for the Study of Common Property, Oaxaca, Mexico, 9–14 August 2004, 3.

73. Vihemäki, "Politics."

74. *NFP,* xiii.

75. Rodgers, "Conservation," 304, 310–13.

76. Ibid., 313.

77. Critical Ecosystem Partnership Fund, *Eastern Arc Mountains and Coastal Forests of Tanzania and Kenya Biodiversity Hotspot* (Washington, D.C.: Conservation International, 2004), 10, http://www.cepf.net (accessed 5 Sept. 2008).

78. Roderick Neumann, "Primitive Ideas: Protected Area Buffer Zones and the Politics of Land in Africa," *Development and Change* 28, no. 3 (1997): 564.

79. WWF, *Eastern Africa Coastal Forests,* 16.

80. Rodgers, "Conservation," 310.

81. Guy Cowlishaw, "Predicting the Pattern of Decline of African Primate Diversity: An Extinction Debt from Historical Deforestation," *Conservation Biology* 13, no. 5 (1999): 1183–93.

82. WWF, *Eastern Africa Coastal Forests,* 28–30; Critical Ecosystem Partnership Fund, "Proceedings of a Workshop," Amani Nature Reserve, Tanzania, 11–12 September 2006.

83. Neil Burgess, "New Conservation Investment into the Eastern Arc Mountains and Eastern African Coastal Forests Biodiversity 'Hotspot,'" *Arc Journal,* no. 16 (2003): 13–14.

84. Craig Packer, Dennis Ikanda, Bernard Kissui, and Hadas Kushnir, "Conservation Biology: Lion Attacks on Humans in Tanzania," *Nature* 436, no. 7053 (18 August 2005): 927–28.

85. WWF, *Eastern Africa Coastal Forests,* 16; Paul Nnyiti, "Tourist Hunting in Tanzania," *Miombo: The Newsletter of the Wildlife Conservation Society of Tanzania,* no. 28 (January 2006): 9, 12–13.

86. Neil Burgess and Alan Rodgers, "Protected Area Categories: Why They Matter for the Eastern Arc and Coastal Forests in Tanzania," Project Report 5, Conservation and Management of the Eastern Arc Mountain Forests Project, n.d. [2004], 1, Eastern Arc Mountains Conservation Endowment Fund, http://www.easternarc.org. tz/strategy/ (accessed 5 Sept. 2008).

87. WWF, *Eastern Africa Coastal Forests,* 43; W. A. Rodgers and N. D. Burgess, "Taking Conservation Action," in Burgess and Clarke, *Coastal Forests,* 317–34.

88. *Annual Report* (1954), 6; Hall et al., *Kazimzumbwi Forest Reserve,* 32–33.

89. Interview, Kazimzumbwi-Darajani, 17 July 2004.

90. Brown, "Conservation"; Howell, "Pugu Forest Reserve."

91. Rodgers and Burgess, "Taking Conservation Action"; W. A. Rodgers, "Institutions and Forest Policy Reform in Tanzania—A Case Study of the Role of NGOs," East African Biodiversity Project and Wildlife Conservation Society of Tanzania, Dar es Salaam, 1997, 4–6, 14–17, World Bank, http:// www .worldbank.org/afr/afr_for/fulltext/tnzna-2.doc (accessed 5 Sept. 2008).

92. Swedish Society for Nature Conservation, "SSNC's Partners in Africa—Wildlife Conservation Society of Tanzania," http://www.snf.se/snf/ english/international-partners-africa.htm.

93. CEFP, *Eastern Arc Mountains,* 5.

94. Rodgers, "Institutions," 14.

95. Rodgers and Burgess, "Taking Conservation Action," 331.

96. Michael Okema, "Tanzania's Squatters Hide in Plain Sight," *East African,* 19–25, http://www.nationaudio.com/News/EastAfrican/1910/Opinion/Opinion2.html, October 1998; Nicodemus Odhiambo, "Violent Eviction from Tanzanian Forest Ends in Court," *Environment News Service,* 29 June 1999, http://www.forests.org/archive/africa/tanzview.htm.

97. "Meghji ametoa Mpya!" *An-Nuur,* no. 172 (23–29 October 1998), http://www.igs.net/~kassim/an-nuur/172/barua172.htm.

98. "Wafadhili wana mchango gani?" *An-Nuur,* no. 171 (16–22 October 1998), http://igs.net/~kassim/an-nuur/171/171-12.htm#nsaza; Odhiambo, "Violent Evictions," 2.

99. Mkonore Forest Reserve, 2 September 1910, TNA G8/634; Tanganyika District Books, Kisarawe District Book, vol. 1, Dar es Salaam District Map B.

100. Balisidya, "Hifadhi ya Kazimzumbwi."

101. "TFCG's Participatory Forest Management Programme," *Arc Journal*, no. 18 (November 2005): 9.

102. Hall et al., *Kazimzumbwi Forest Reserve*, 33.

103. Charles Geisler, "Endangered Humans: How Global Land Conservation Efforts are Creating a Growing Class of Invisible Refugees," *Foreign Policy* (May–June 2002): 80–81; IUCN, "The Durban Action Plan: Revised Version," March 2004, p. 227, http://cmsdata.iucn.org/downloads/durbanactionen.pdf (accessed 13 Sept. 2008).

104. *NFP* 2001, 22.

105. WWF, *Eastern Africa Coastal Forests*, 43.

106. Ibid., 30.

107. Burgess and Rodgers, "Protected Area Categories."

108. WWF, *Eastern Africa Coastal Forests*, 6, 13, 46; WWF, "Central and Eastern Miombo," http://www.panda.org/about_wwf/where_we_work/ecoregions/central_eastern_miombo_woodlands.cfm (accessed 5 Sept. 2008).

109. "Illegal Logging Cuts a Swath Across Tanzania," *Panafrican News Agency*, 10 February 2000.

110. "Tanzania Pledges New Law to Govern Forests," *Panafrican News Agency*, 19 February 2002.

111. WWF, *Eastern Africa Coastal Forests*, 5; Milledge, Gelvas, and Ahrends, *Forestry*.

112. Baker and Baker, *IBA 50-Coastal Forests: Kisarawe District, Tanzania*, http://home.no.net/stenil1.

113. Judica Tarimo, "MPs Alarmed at Destruction of Forests, Trees," *Guardian*, 19 July 2005, http://www.ippmedia.com/ipp/guardian/2005/07/19/44796.html.

114. W. A. Rodgers, "Why a Book on Coastal Forests?" in Burgess and Clarke, *Coastal Forests*, 7.

115. Nancy Lee Peluso and Michael Watts, "Violent Environments," in Nancy Lee Peluso and Michael Watts, *Violent Environments* (Ithaca: Cornell University Press, 2001), 3–38.

116. See, for example, articles in *Miombo: The Newsletter of the Wildlife Conservation Society of Tanzania*, no. 28 (January 2006).

117. This and other quotes in this section are from interviews with the author, Kazimzumbwi-Darajani, 17 July 2004.

118. "*Hakuna mila ye yote tena hapa.*" Interview, Kazimzumbwi-Darajani, 17 July 2004.

Glossary

akida (pl., maakida). A non-European colonial subdistrict administrator.

askari. An African soldier or policeman.

baraza. A public meeting.

boriti (pl., maboriti). Most common name for a mangrove rafter.

Cassia siamea. Known as ironwood, an exotic species commonly grown on tree plantations.

ceara. *Manihot glaziovii,* a plantation rubber tree.

copal. An aromatic, often fossilized resin and the tree from which it comes (in East Africa *Hymenaea verrucosa*).

coria (korija). A unit of twenty.

frasila. A unit of weight equivalent to just over sixteen kg.

Hochwald. A system of long-term planting and harvesting rotations (German, high forest).

ironwood. *Cassia siamea,* a plantation tree not indigenous to East Africa.

jumbe (pl., majumbe). Under colonial rule, a generic term for an African headman.

kaniki. A blue Indian calico cloth.

kichaka (pl., vichaka). A dry lowland canopy forest (or coastal forest).

Landolphia. Genus of liana rubber vines and shrubs.

liana. Wild rubber.

maakida. German-appointed subdistrict administrators (See *akida*).

maboriti. Mangrove rafters (See *boriti*).

maji. Water.

majumbe. General term for village headmen, especially under colonial rule (See *jumbe*).

mapazi. Zaramo ancestral chiefs or lineage heads (See *pazi*).

mashokora. A Zaramo form of farming in the forests.

mchu. Mangrove of the genus *Avicennia*.

miombo. The most common woodland trees (*Brachystegia* spp. and *Isoberlinia* spp.), or the woodlands themselves.

misitu. Vichaka or coastal forests (See *msitu*).

mkaka. Mangrove of the genus *Rhizophora*.

mkandaa. Mangrove of the genus *Ceriops*.

mkole. *Grewia similis,* the most important tree for Zaramo women's rites.

mkomafi. Mangrove of the genus *Xylocarpus*.

mkongo. *Afzelia quanzensis* (pod mahogany), a coastal hardwood valued for dugout canoes.

mnangu. Common coastal Bantu word for the copal tree (*Hymenaea verrucosa*).

mndewa. Local lineage heads (See *wandewa*).

mninga. *Pterocarpus angolensis,* a valuable Tanzanian hardwood.

mninga-maji. *Pterocarpus holtzii,* a Tanzanian hardwood valued by commercial loggers.

mnyemzi (pl., wanyemzi). A Zaramo native authority.

mpingo. African blackwood (*Dalbergia melanoxylon*), often called ebony.

mpira. Liana rubber.

    —ya chini. Liana rubber extracted from the roots of the liana.

    —ya kuponda. Liana rubber extracted by crushing the vines.

msandarusi. East African copal tree (*Hymenaea verrucosa*) (Swahili).

mshinzi. Mangrove of the genus *Bruguiera*.

msikundazi. Mangrove of the genus *Heritiera*.

msitu (pl., misitu). A dense forest, coterminous with *kichaka*.

mvule. *Milicia excelsa,* the most valuable hardwood tree in colonial Tanzania.

mwenembago (pl., wenembago). Among the Zaramo, a potentially fearsome forest spirit or forest guardian (Zaramo, ax wielder).

mwenye. Common name for a chief in southeastern Tanzania.

mwenye mhaazi. Lit., ax wielder (Zaramo).

ngalawa. A coastal outrigger vessel.

pangapanga. *Millettia stuhlmanii,* a termite-resistant decorative hardwood used for furniture, flooring, and veneers.

pazi (pl., mapazi). A Zaramo and Ndengereko term for chief; from *mhaazi,* ceremonial ax.

Raubwirtschaft. The destructive use of forest resources (German, plunder economy).

Schlagwaldwirtschaft. Rotational forestry; scientific forestry in general (German, clear-cutting forestry).

taungya. Hill cultivation, a licensed forest cultivator (Burmese).

uhuru. Freedom.

ujamaa. Tanzanian socialism.

Urwald. Primeval forest (German).

vichaka. Coastal forests, coterminous with misitu (See *kichaka*).

wajamaa. Tanzanian residents of an *ujamaa* village.

wandewa. Local lineage heads (See *mndewa*).

wanyemzi. Native authorities (See *mnyemzi*).

wenembago. See *mwenembago.*

Wildbrennen. Disparaging term for shifting cultivation (German, wild burning).

Bibliography

Archives and Libraries

Bundesarchiv-Berlin (Federal Archives), Berlin-Lichterfelde
Geheimes Staatsarchiv, Preußischer Kulturbesitz, Berlin-Dahlem
Humboldt University Library, Berlin
Plant Sciences Library, Oxford University
Public Records Office (British National Archives), Kew, London
Staatsbibliothek, Berlin
Stadt- und Universitätsbibliothek, Frankfurt
Tanzania National Archives, Dar es Salaam
University of Dar es Salaam Library

Articles and Books

"Abdalla Chapila vs. Mohamedi Mwinyigoha and Five Others." *Journal of African Law* 13, no. 3 (1969): 179–81.

Adams, W. M., and D. Hulme. "If Community Conservation Is the Answer in Africa, What Is the Question?" *Oryx* 35, no. 3 (2001): 193–200.

Adas, Michael. "Colonization, Commercial Agriculture, and the Destruction of the Deltaic Rainforests of British Burma in the Late Nineteenth Century." In *Global Deforestation and the Nineteenth-Century World Economy,* ed. Richard P. Tucker and J. F. Richards, 95–110. Durham: Duke University Press, 1983.

Agarwal, Bina. "The Gender and Environment Debate: Lessons from India." *Feminist Studies* 18, no. 1 (1992): 119–58.

Agrawal, Arun. *Environmentality: Technologies of Government and the Making of Subjects.* Durham: Duke University Press, 2005.

Alpers, Edward. "Kingalu Mwana Shaha and Political Leadership in Nineteenth-Century Eastern Tanzania." In *In Search of a Nation: Histories of Authority and Dissidence in Tanzania,* ed. Gregory H. Maddox and James L. Giblin, 33–54. Oxford: James Currey, 2005.

———. "Trade, State, and Society among the Yao in the Nineteenth Century." *Journal of African History* 10, no. 3 (1969): 405–20.

Amiji, Hatim. "The Bohras of East Africa." *Journal of Religion in Africa* 7, no. 1 (1975): 27–61.

Anderson, David M. "Depression, Dust Bowl, Demography and Drought: The Colonial State and Soil Conservation in East Africa during the 1930s." *African Affairs* 83, no. 332 (1984): 321–43.

———. *Eroding the Commons: The Politics of Ecology in Baringo, Kenya, 1890–1963.* Oxford: James Currey, 2002.

Anderson, David M., and Richard Grove, eds. *Conservation in Africa: People, Policies, and Practice.* Cambridge: Cambridge University Press, 1993.

Andés, Louis Edgar. *Die Fabrikation der Kopal-, Terpentinöl-, und Spiritus-lacke.* Vienna: A. Hartleben, 1909.

Anker, Peder. *Imperial Ecology: Environmental Order in the British Empire, 1895–1945.* Cambridge, Mass.: Harvard University Press, 2001.

Baker, Murl, Robert Clausen, Ramzy Kanaan, Michel N'Goma, Trifin Roule, and Jamie Thomson. *Conflict Timber: Dimensions of the Problem in Asia and Africa.* Vol. 3, *African Cases.* Burlington, Vt.: ARD, 2003.

Baker, Neil, and Liz Baker. "Coastal Forests Project Tanzania: Important Bird Areas." BirdLife International, http://home.no.net/stenil1/coastalforest.htm (accessed 5 Sept. 2008).

Balough, Brian. "Scientific Forestry and the Roots of the Modern American State: Gifford Pinchot's Path to Progressive Reform." *Environmental History* 7, no. 2 (2002): 198–225.

Barker, Ronald de la B. "The Rufiji River." *Tanganyika Notes and Records,* no. 4 (1937): 10–16.

Barton, Gregory. "Empire Forestry and the Origins of Environmentalism." *Journal of Historical Geography* 27, no. 4 (2001): 529–52.

———. *Empire Forestry and the Origins of Environmentalism.* Cambridge: Cambridge University Press, 2002.

———. "Keepers of the Jungle: Environmental Management in British India, 1855–1900." *Historian* 62, no. 3 (2000): 557–74.

Baumann, Oskar. *Der Sansibar-Archipel.* Vol. 1, *Die Insel Mafia und ihre kleineren Nachbarinseln.* Leipzig: Duncker and Humblot, 1896.

Beachey, R. W. "The Arms Trade in East Africa in the Late Nineteenth Century." *Journal of African History* 3, no. 3 (1962): 451–67.

Beardall, William. "Exploration of the Rufiji River under the Orders of the Sultan of Zanzibar." *Proceedings of the Royal Geographical Society and Monthly Record of Geography* 3, no. 11 (November 1881): 641–56.

Beck, Ann. *Medicine and Society in Tanganyika, 1890–1930: A Historical Inquiry.* Philadelphia: American Philosophical Society, 1977.

Becker, Felicitas. "Traders, 'Big Men' and Prophets: Political Continuity and Crisis in the Maji Maji Rebellion in Southeast Tanzania." *Journal of African History* 45, no. 1 (2004): 1–22.

Becker, Laurence. "Seeing Green in Mali's Woods: Colonial Legacy, Forest Use, and Local Control." *Annals of the Association of American Geographers* 91, no. 3 (2001): 504–26.

Beckert, Sven. "Emancipation and Empire: Reconstructing the Worldwide Web of Cotton Production in the Age of the American Civil War." *American Historical Review* 109, no. 5 (2004): 1–64.

Behr, H. F. von. "Die Völker zwischen Rufiyi und Rovuma." *Mitteilungen aus den deutschen Schutzgebieten* 6 (1893): 69–87.

Beidelman, T. O. *The Matrilineal Peoples of Eastern Tanzania.* London: International African Institute, 1967.

Beinart, William. *The Rise of Conservation in South Africa: Settlers, Livestock, and the Environment, 1770–1950.* Oxford: Oxford University Press, 2003.

———. "Soil Erosion, Conservation and Ideas about Development: A Southern African Exploration, 1900–1960." *Journal of Southern African Studies* 11, no. 1 (1984): 52–83.

Beinart, William, and JoAnn McGregor, eds. *Social History and African Environments.* Oxford: James Currey, 2003.

Bell, R. M. "The Maji Maji Rebellion in the Liwale District." *Tanganyika Notes and Records,* no. 28 (1950): 38–57.

Bennett, Norman. "Americans in Zanzibar: 1825–1845." *Essex Institute Historical Collections* 95 (July 1959): 239–62.

———. "Americans in Zanzibar: 1845–1865." *Tanganyika Notes and Records,* no. 51 (1961): 121–38.

———. "Americans in Zanzibar: 1865–1915." *Tanganyika Notes and Records,* no. 60 (1963): 49–66.

———. "France and Zanzibar: 1844 to the 1860s." *International Journal of African Historical Studies* 6, no. 4 (1973): 602–32.

Bennett, Norman, and George Brooks, eds. *New England Merchants in Africa: A History through Documents, 1802 to 1865.* Boston: Boston University Press, 1965.

Bernstein, Deborah. *Constructing Boundaries: Jewish and Arab Workers in Mandatory Palestine.* Albany: SUNY Press, 2000.

Bernstein, Henry, and Terence J. Byres. "From Peasant Studies to Agrarian Change." *Journal of Agrarian Change* 1, no. 1 (2001): 1–56.

Bienen, Henry. *Tanzania: Party Transformation and Economic Development.* Princeton: Princeton University Press, 1970.

Birmingham, David, and Terence Ranger. "Settlers and Liberators in the South." In *History of Central Africa,* vol. 2, ed. David Birmingham and Phyllis Martin, 336–82. London: Longman, 1983.

Birrell, Jean. "Common Rights in the Medieval Forest: Disputes and Conflicts in the Thirteenth Century." *Past and Present,* no. 117 (November 1987): 22–49.

Blackbourn, David. *The Conquest of Nature: Water, Landscape, and the Making of Modern Germany.* New York: Norton, 2006.

Bley, Fritz. *Deutsche Pionierarbeit in Ostafrika.* Berlin: Paul Parey, 1891.

Boomgaard, Peter. "Forest Management and Exploitation in Colonial Java, 1677–1897." *Forest and Conservation History* 36, no. 1 (January 1992): 4–14.

Bourne, Ray. "Some Ecological Conceptions." *Empire Forestry Journal* 13, no. 1 (1934): 15–30.

Brady, Cyrus Townsend, Jr. *Commerce and Conquest in East Africa, with Particular Reference to the Salem Trade with Zanzibar.* Salem, Mass.: Essex Institute, 1950.

Brandis, Dietrich. "Remarks on the Administrative Forest Staff of Prussia and the Training of Its Officers." *Indian Forester* 11, no. 10 (1885): 449–63.

———. "Review of Forest Administration during 1876–77." *Indian Forester* 4, no. 1 (1878): 275–85.

Braund, H. E. W. *Calling to Mind: Being Some Account of the First Hundred Years (1870–1970) of Steel Brothers and Company Limited.* Oxford: Pergamon Press, 1975.

"A Brief History of the Tanzania Forest Conservation Group." *Arc Journal,* no. 18 (November 2005): 2.

Brockington. Dan. *Fortress Conservation: The Preservation of the Mkomazi Game Reserve, Tanzania.* Oxford: James Currey, 2002.

Brookfield, H. C. "New Railroad and Port Developments in East and Central Africa." *Economic Geography* 31, no. 1 (1955): 60–70.

Brown, L. H. "The Conservation of Forest Islands in Areas of High Human Density." *African Journal of Ecology* 19, nos. 1–2 (1981): 27–32.

Brown, Walter T. "The Politics of Business: Relations between Zanzibar and Bagamoyo in the Late Nineteenth Century." *African Historical Studies* 4, no. 3 (1971): 631–43.

Bryant, Raymond L. *The Political Ecology of Forestry in Burma, 1824–1994.* Honolulu: University of Hawai'i Press, 1996.

Bryant, Raymond L., and Sinéad Bailey. *Third World Political Ecology.* London: Routledge, 1997.

Buchanan, Angus. *Three Years of War in East Africa.* New York: Negro Universities Press, 1969.

Burgess, Neil. "New Conservation Investment into the Eastern Arc Mountains and Eastern African Coastal Forests Biodiversity 'Hotspot.'" *Arc Journal,* no. 16 (March 2004): 13–14.

Burgess, Neil, Clare FitzGibbon, and Phillip Clarke. "Coastal Forests." In *East African Ecosystems and Their Conservation,* ed. T. R. McClanahan and T. P. Young, 329–59. New York: Oxford University Press, 1996.

Burgess, Neil, and Alan Rodgers. "Protected Area Categories: Why They Matter for the Eastern Arc and Coastal Forests in Tanzania." Project Report no. 5, Conservation and Management of the Eastern Arc Mountain Forests Project, [2004]. Eastern Arc Mountains Conservation Endowment Fund, http://www.easternarc.or.tz/strategy (accessed 5 Sept. 2008).

Burgess, Neil, L. K. Stubblefield, and C. Kwenyunga. "Soils." In *Coastal Forests of Eastern Africa,* ed. Neil D. Burgess and G. Philip Clarke, 41–46. Gland, Switzerland: IUCN, 2000.

Burgess, Neil, Jennifer D'Amico Hales, Emma Underwood, Eric Dinerstein, et al. *Terrestrial Ecosystems of Africa and Madagascar: A Conservation Assessment.* Washington, D.C.: Island Press, 2004.

Bursian, Alexander. *Die Häuser- und Hüttensteuer in Deutsch-Ostafrika.* Jena: Gustav Fischer, 1910.

Burton, Andrew. *African Underclass: Urbanization, Crime, and Colonial Order in Dar es Salaam.* Athens: Ohio University Press, 2005.

Burton, Richard F. *The Lake Regions of Central Africa.* New York: Harper and Brothers, 1860; repr. New York: Dover, 1995.

———. *Zanzibar: City, Island, and Coast.* 2 vols. London: Tinsley Brothers, 1872.

Büsgen, M. "Forstwirtschaft in den Kolonien." *Verhandlungen des deutschen Kolonialkongresses.* Berlin: Dietrich Reimer, 1910: 801–17.

Byfield, Judith A. *The Bluest Hands: A Social and Economic History of Women Dyers in Abeokuta (Nigeria), 1890–1940.* Portsmouth, N.H.: Heinemann, 2002.

Chami, Felix. "The Archaeology of the Rufiji Region since 1987 to 2000." In *People, Contacts and the Environment in the African Past,* ed. Felix Chami, Gilbert Pwiti, and Chantal Radimilahy, 7–20. Dar es Salaam: Dar es Salaam University Press, 1996.

———. "Limbo: Early Iron-Working in South-Eastern Tanzania." *Azania* 27 (1992): 45–50.

———. "Roman Beads from the Rufiji Delta, Tanzania: Incontrovertible Archaeological Link with the Periplus." *Current Anthropology* 40, no. 2 (1999): 237–41.

Chami, Felix, and Paul J. Msemwa. "A New Look at Culture and Trade on the Azanian Coast." *Current Anthropology* 38, no. 4 (1997): 673–77.

Chande, Selemani bin Mwenye. "My Journey Up-Country in Africa." In *Swahili Prose Texts,* comp. Carl Velten, ed. Lyndon Harries, 234–59. London: Oxford University Press, 1965.

Chandran, M. D. Subash. "Shifting Cultivation, Sacred Groves and Conflicts in Colonial Forest Policy in the Western Ghats." In *Nature and the Orient: The Environmental History of South and Southeast Asia,* ed. Richard Grove, Vinita Damodaran, and Satpal Sangwan, 674–707. Delhi: Oxford University Press, 1998.

Chapin, Mac. "A Challenge to Conservationists." *World Watch* 17, no. 6 (2004): 17–32.

Clarke, G. P. "Defining the Eastern African Coastal Forests." In *Coastal Forests of Eastern Africa,* ed. Neil D. Burgess and G. Philip Clarke, 9–26. Gland, Switzerland: IUCN, 2000.

Clarke, G. P., and S. A. Robertson. "Vegetation Communities." In *Coastal Forests of Eastern Africa,* ed. Neil D. Burgess and G. Philip Clarke, 83–102. Gland, Switzerland: IUCN, 2000.

Clary, David A. *Timber and the Forest Service.* Lawrence: University Press of Kansas, 1986.

Cline-Cole, Reginald A. "Wartime Forest Energy Policy and Practice in British West Africa: Social and Economic Impact on the Labouring Classes, 1939–45." *Africa* 63, no. 1 (1993): 56–79.

Cline-Cole, Reginald, and Clare Madge, eds. *Contesting Forestry in West Africa.* Aldershot: Ashgate, 2000.

Clutterbuck, Peter. "Forestry and the Empire." *Empire Forestry Journal* 6, no. 1 (1927): 184–92.

Clyde, David F. *History of the Medical Services of Tanganyika.* Dar es Salaam: Government Printer, 1962.

Conte, Christopher. *Highland Sanctuary: Environmental History in Tanzania's Usambara Mountains.* Athens: Ohio University Press, 2004.

———. "Nature Reorganized: Ecological History in the Plateau Forests of the West Usambara Mountains, 1850–1935." In *Custodians of the Land: Ecology and Culture in the History of Tanzania,* ed. Gregory Maddox,

James Giblin, and Isaria Kimambo, 96–121. Athens: Ohio University Press, 1996.

Cooper, Frederick. *Decolonization and African Society: The Labor Question in French and British Africa.* Cambridge: Cambridge University Press, 1996.

———. *Plantation Slavery on the East Coast of Africa.* Portsmouth, N.H.: Heinemann, 1997.

"Copal of Zanzibar." *New York Coach-Maker's Magazine* 12, no. 3 (August 1870): 48.

Cotterell, Paul. *The Railways of Palestine and Israel.* Abingdon, UK: Tourret Publishing, 1984.

Coulson, Andrew. *Tanzania: A Political Economy.* Oxford: Clarendon Press, 1982.

Coupland, Reginald. *The Exploitation of East Africa, 1856–1890.* Evanston: Northwestern University Press, 1967.

Cowen, Michael, and Nicholas Westcott. "British Imperial Economic Policy during the War." In *Africa and the Second World War,* ed. David Killingray and Richard Rathbone, 20–67. New York: St. Martin's, 1986.

Cowlishaw, Guy. "Predicting the Pattern of Decline of African Primate Diversity: An Extinction Debt from Historical Deforestation." *Conservation Biology* 13, no. 5 (1999): 1183–93.

Critical Ecosystem Partnership Fund. "CEPF Final Project Completion Report." 2006. http://www.cepf.net/xp/cepf/ (accessed 5 Sept. 2008).

———. *Eastern Arc Mountains and Coastal Forests of Tanzania and Kenya Biodiversity Hotspot.* Washington, D.C.: Conservation International, 2004. http://www.cepf.net/xp/cepf/ (accessed 5 Sept. 2008).

———. "Proceedings of a Workshop to Document Lessons Learnt from the Critical Ecosystem Partnership Fund's Investment in the Restoration of Forest Connectivity in the Eastern Arc Mountains and Coastal Forests of Kenya and Tanzania." Amani Nature Reserve, Tanzania, 11–12 September 2006. http://www.cepf.net/xp/cepf/static/pdfs/CEPF_SFD2 _WorkshopReportFINAL.pdf (accessed 5 Sept. 2008).

Crosse-Upcott, A. R. W. "The Origin of the Majimaji Revolt." *Man* 60 (1960): 71–73.

———. "Social Aspects of Ngindo Bee-keeping." *Journal of the Royal Anthropological Institute of Great Britain and Ireland* 86, no. 2 (1956): 81–108.

Daley, Elizabeth. "Land and Social Change in a Tanzanian Village 1: Kinyanambo, 1920s–1990." *Journal of Agrarian Change* 5, no. 3 (2005): 363–404.

Deutsch, Jan-Georg. *Emancipation without Abolition in German East Africa, c. 1884–1914.* Athens: Ohio University Press, 2006.

Devereux, David D. "Britain, the Commonwealth and the Defence of the Middle East, 1948–56." *Journal of Contemporary History* 24, no. 2 (1989): 327–45.

Diamond, A. W. "A Summary of Conservation Resolutions Adopted at This Symposium." *African Journal of Ecology* 19, nos. 1–2 (1981): 213.

Dirks, Nicholas. "From Little King to Landlord: Property, Law, and the Gift under the Madras Permanent Settlement." In *Colonialism and Culture*, ed. Nicholas Dirks, 175–208. Ann Arbor: University of Michigan Press, 1992.

Dovers, Stephen, Ruth Edgecombe, and Bill Guest, eds. *South Africa's Environmental History: Cases and Comparisons.* Athens: Ohio University Press, 2002.

Dumett, Raymond. "The Rubber Trade of the Gold Coast and Asante in the Nineteenth Century: African Innovation and Market Responsiveness." *Journal of African History* 12, no. 1 (1971): 79–101.

Dye, William H. "The Relative Importance of Man and Beast in Human Trypanosomiasis." *Transactions of the Royal Society of Tropical Medicine and Hygiene* 21, no. 3 (1927): 187–98.

Dykstra, Dennis P. "Forestry in Tanzania." *World Forestry* 81, no. 11 (1983): 742–46.

Eberstein, E. "Über die Rechtsanschauungen der Küstenbewohner des Bezirkes Kilwa." *Mitteilungen aus den deutschen Schutzgebieten* 9 (1896): 170–183.

Echenberg, Myron. "Pestis Redux: The Initial Years of the Third Bubonic Plague Pandemic, 1894–1901." *Journal of World History* 13, no. 2 (2002): 429–49.

Eckart, Wolfgang U. *Medizin und Kolonialimperialismus: Deutschland 1884–1945.* Paderborn: Friedrich Schöningh, 1997.

Eggeling, William J. *Forestry in Tanganyika, 1946–50.* Dar es Salaam: Government Printer, 1951.

Elton, J. F. "The African Gum Copal Tree." *Indian Forester* 1, no. 1 (July 1875): 36–40.

———. *The Lakes and Mountains of Eastern and Central Africa.* London: Frank Cass, 1968.

———. "On the Coast Country of East Africa, South of Zanzibar." *Journal of the Royal Geographical Society of London* 44 (1874): 227–51.

Emery, Lieutenant. "Short Account of Mombas and the Neighboring Coast of Africa." *Journal of the Royal Geographical Society of London* 3 (1833): 280–83.

Ernst, Christoph. "An Ecological Revolution? The 'Schlagwaldwirtschaft' in Western Germany in the Eighteenth and Nineteenth Centuries." In *Euro-*

pean Woods and Forests: Studies in Cultural History, ed. Charles Watkins, 83–92. Wallingford, Conn.: CAB International, 1998.

Fair, Laura. "Dressing Up: Clothing, Class and Gender in Post-Abolition Zanzibar." *Journal of African History* 39, no. 1 (1998): 63–94.

Fairbairn, H. "The Agricultural Problems Posed by Sleeping Sickness Settlements." *East African Agricultural Journal* 9 (July 1943): 17–22.

Fairhead, James, and Melissa Leach. *Misreading the African Landscape: Society and Forestry in a Forest-Savanna Mosaic.* Cambridge: Cambridge University Press, 1996.

Farquhar, J. D. *Working Plan for the Vikindu Plantations, Kisarawe District, Eastern Province, 1952–1967.* Dar es Salaam: Government Printer, 1954.

Farrer, R. P. "The First Eight Years on the Rondo." *Empire Forestry Review* 39, no. 1 (1960): 89–93.

Feierman, Steven. *Peasant Intellectuals: Anthropology and History in Tanzania.* Madison: University of Wisconsin Press, 1990.

Ford, John. *The Role of the Trypanosomiases in African Ecology: A Study of the Tsetse Fly Problem.* Oxford: Clarendon Press, 1971.

"The Forest Lands of Germany." *Indian Forester* 31, no. 6 (1905): 729–30.

Gadgil, Madhav, and Ramachandra Guha. *This Fissured Land: An Ecological History of India.* Berkeley: University of California Press, 1993.

Geisler, Charles. "Endangered Humans: How Global Land Conservation Efforts Are Creating a Growing Class of Invisible Refugees." *Foreign Policy* (May/June 2002): 80–81.

Giblin, James L. *A History of the Excluded: Making Family a Refuge from State in Twentieth-Century Tanzania.* Athens: Ohio University Press, 2005.

———. *The Politics of Environmental Control in Northeastern Tanzania, 1840–1940.* Philadelphia: University of Pennsylvania Press, 1992.

———. "Some Complexities of Family and State in Colonial Njombe." In *In Search of a Nation: Histories of Authority and Dissidence in Tanzania,* ed. Gregory H. Maddox and James L. Giblin, 128–48. Athens: Ohio University Press, 2005.

———. "Trypanosomiasis Control in African History: An Evaded Issue?" *Journal of African History* 31, no. 1 (1990): 59–80.

Gilbert, Erik. *Dhows and the Colonial Economy of Zanzibar, 1860–1970.* Athens: Ohio University Press, 2004.

Giles-Vernick, Tamara. *Cutting the Vines of the Past: Environmental Histories of the Central African Rain Forest.* Charlottesville: University Press of Virginia, 2002.

Gißibl, Bernhard. "German Colonialism and the Beginnings of International Wildlife Preservation in Africa." *German Historical Institute Bulletin,* suppl. 3 (2006): 121–43.

Glassman, Jonathon. *Feasts and Riot: Revelry, Rebellion, and Popular Consciousness on the Swahili Coast, 1856–1888.* Portsmouth, N.H.: Heinemann, 1994.

Glover, H. M. "Soil Conservation in Parts of Africa and the Middle East." *Empire Forestry Review* 33, no. 1 (1954): 39–44.

Goldman, Michael. "Constructing an Environmental State: Eco-governmentality and Other Transnational Practices of a 'Green' World Bank." *Social Problems* 48, no. 4 (2001): 499–523.

———. *Imperial Nature: The World Bank and Struggles for Social Justice in the Age of Globalization.* New Haven: Yale University Press, 2005.

Götzen, Adolf Graf von. *Deutsch-Ostafrika im Aufstand.* Berlin: Dietrich Reimer, 1909.

Grant, D. K. S. "Forestry in Tanganyika." *Empire Forestry Journal* 3, no. 1 (1924): 33–38.

———. "Mangrove Woods of Tanganyika Territory, Their Silviculture and Dependent Industries." *Tanganyika Notes and Records* no. 5 (1939): 5–16.

Grass, Karl. "Forststatistik für die Waldungen des Rufiyideltas, angefangen im Jahre 1902." *Berichte über Land- und Forstwirtschaft* 2 (1904–6): 165–96.

Gray, John. "Dar es Salaam under the Sultans of Zanzibar." *Tanganyika Notes and Records,* no. 33 (1952): 1–21.

Green, Susan. "Varnish Making, Part 4." *Carriage Driving World Magazine* 17, no. 6 (2003): 47–52.

Greenough, Paul. "*Naturae Ferae:* Wild Animals in South Asia and the Standard Environmental Narrative." In *Agrarian Studies: Synthetic Work at the Cutting Edge,* ed. James Scott and Nina Bhatt, 141–85. New Haven: Yale University Press, 2001.

Grove, Richard H. *Ecology, Climate, and Empire: Colonialism and Global Environmental History, 1400–1940.* Cambridge: White Horse Press, 1997.

———. *Green Imperialism: Colonial Expansion, Tropical Island Edens, and the Origins of Environmentalism, 1600–1860.* Cambridge: Cambridge University Press, 1995.

Grove, Richard, Vinita Damodaran, and Satpal Sangwan, eds. *Nature and the Orient: The Environmental History of South and Southeast Asia.* Delhi: Oxford University Press, 1998.

Guha, Ramachandra. *Environmentalism: A Global History.* New York: Longman, 2000.

———. *The Unquiet Woods: Ecological Change and Peasant Resistance in the Himalaya.* Oxford: Oxford University Press, 1989.

Guha, Ramachandra, and Madhav Gadgil. "State Forestry and Social Conflict in British India." *Past and Present,* no. 123 (May 1989): 141–177.

Guha, Ranajit. "The Prose of Counter-insurgency." *Subaltern Studies: Writings on South Asian History and Society* 2 (Delhi: Oxford University Press, 1983), 1–42.

Gwassa, G. C. K. "Kinjikitile and the Ideology of Maji Maji." In *The Historical Study of African Religion,* ed. T. O. Ranger and I. N. Kimambo, 202–17. Berkeley: University of California Press, 1972.

———. *The Outbreak and Development of the Maji Maji War.* Cologne: Rüdiger Köppe, 2005.

Hall, D. M., S. Staddon, K. M. Howell, and E. Fanning, eds. *Kazimzumbwi Forest Reserve: A Biodiversity Survey.* Frontier Tanzania Technical Report no. 26. Dar es Salaam: Society for Environmental Exploration, 2002.

Hansen, Karen Tranberg. *Salaula: The World of Secondhand Clothing and Zambia.* Chicago: University of Chicago Press, 2000.

Harms, Robert. "The End of Red Rubber: A Reassessment." *Journal of African History* 16, no. 1 (1975): 73–88.

Hartnoll, A. V., and N. R. Fuggles Couchman. "The 'Mashokora' Cultivations of the Coast." *Tanganyika Notes and Records,* no. 3 (1937): 34–39.

Hatchell, G. W. "The Ngalawa and the Mtepe." *Tanganyika Notes and Records,* no. 57 (1961): 211–15.

Havnevik, Kjell. *Tanzania: The Limits to Development from Above.* Uppsala: Nordiska Afrikainstitutet, 1993.

Hawthorne, W. D. "East African Coastal Forest Botany." In *Biogeography and Ecology of the Rain Forests of Eastern Africa,* ed. Jon C. Lovett and Samuel K. Wasser, 57–99. Cambridge: Cambridge University Press, 1993.

Heske, Franz. *German Forestry.* New Haven: Yale University Press, 1938.

Hill, Mervyn F. *Permanent Way.* Vol. 2, *The Story of the Tanganyika Railways.* Nairobi: East African Railways and Harbours, 1957.

Hinds, Allister E. "Imperial Policy and Colonial Sterling Balances, 1943–56." *Journal of Imperial and Commonwealth History* 19, no. 1 (1991): 24–44.

Hodge, Joseph Morgan. *Triumph of the Expert: Agrarian Doctrines of Development and the Legacies of British Colonialism.* Athens: Ohio University Press, 2007.

Hofstad, Ole. "Woodland Deforestation by Charcoal Supply to Dar es Salaam." *Journal of Environmental Economics and Management* 33, no. 1 (1997): 17–32.

Holmes, John. *Natural Forest Handbook for Tanzania,* 2 vols. Morogoro: Sokoine University of Agriculture, 1995.

Holmwood, Frederick. "The Kingani River, East Africa." *Journal of the Royal Geographical Society of London* 47 (1877): 253–67.

Hoppe, Kirk. *Lords of the Fly: Sleeping Sickness Control in British East Africa, 1900–1960.* Westport, Conn.: Praeger, 2003.

Houghton, George. "Gum Copal." *Hub,* November 1871; October–December 1871; January–March 1872. Carriage Museum of America, http://www .carriagemuseumlibrary.org/copal_zanzibar.htm. (accessed 5 Sept. 2008).

Howell, K. M. "Pugu Forest Reserve: Biological Values and Development." *African Journal of Ecology* 19, nos. 1–2 (1981): 73–81.

Hügel, Georg. "Der Aufbau und die Entwicklung einer geregelten Forstwirtschaft in Deutsch-Ostafrika unter deutscher Kolonialverwaltung." PhD diss., Göttingen University, 1988.

Hunt, Nancy. *A Colonial Lexicon of Birth Ritual, Medicalization, and Mobility in the Congo.* Durham: Duke University Press, 1999.

Hurst, Andrew. "Not Yet Out of the Woods: A Political Ecology of State Forest Policy and Practice in Mainland Tanzania, 1961–1998." PhD diss., Oxford University, 2004.

———. "State Forestry and Spatial Scale in the Development Discourses of Post-colonial Tanzania: 1961–1971." *Geographical Journal* 169, no. 4 (2003): 358–69.

Hyam, Ronald, ed. *The Labour Government and the End of Empire, 1945–1951.* London: HMSO, 1992.

Iliffe, John. "Breaking the Chain at Its Weakest Link: TANU and the Colonial Office." In *In Search of a Nation: Histories of Authority and Dissidence in Tanzania,* ed. Gregory H. Maddox and James L. Giblin, 168–97. Oxford: James Currey, 2005.

———. *A Modern History of Tanganyika.* Cambridge: Cambridge University Press, 1979.

———. "The Organization of the Maji Maji Rebellion." *Journal of African History* 8, no. 3 (1967): 495–512.

Imort, Michael. "A Sylvan People: Wilhelmine Forestry and the Forest as a Symbol of Germandom." In *Germany's Nature: Cultural Landscapes and Environmental History,* ed. Thomas Lekan and Thomas Zeller, 55–80. New Brunswick, N.J.: Rutgers University Press, 2005.

Imperial Economic Committee. *An Index of the Minor Forest Products of the British Empire.* London: HMSO, 1936.

"Importance of Timber in War." *Indian Forester* 67, no. 2 (1942): 112–14.

"Influence of Forests on Climate." *Indian Forester* 11, no. 3 (1885): 146.

Ionides, C. J. P. "Pages from a Tanganyika Game Rangers Note Book II." *Tanganyika Notes and Records,* no. 30 (1951): 48–52.

Isaacman, Allen. "Peasants and Rural Social Protest in Africa." In *Confronting Historical Paradigms: Peasants, Labor, and the Capitalist World System in Africa and Latin America*, ed. Frederick Cooper, 205–317. Madison: University of Wisconsin Press, 1993.

IUCN. "The Durban Action Plan: Revised Version." March 2004, 227. http://cmsdata.iucn.org/downloads/durbanactionen.pdf (accessed 13 Sept. 2008).

Jackson, John R. *Commercial Botany of the Nineteenth Century.* London: Cassell and Co., 1890.

Jackson, Robert D. "Resistance to the German Invasion of the Tanganyikan Coast, 1888–1891." In *Protest and Power in Black Africa*, ed. Robert I. Rotberg and Ali Mazrui, 37–79. New York: Oxford University Press, 1970.

Jacobs, Nancy. *Environment, Power, and Injustice: A South African History.* Cambridge: Cambridge University Press, 2003.

Jacoby, Karl. *Crimes against Nature: Squatters, Poachers, Thieves, and the Hidden History of American Conservation.* Berkeley: University of California Press, 2001.

Jaffer, Amin. *Furniture from British India and Ceylon.* Salem, Mass.: Peabody Essex Museum, 2001.

Jambiya, G. L. K., and H. Sosovele. "Poverty and the Environment: The Case of Amani Nature Reserve." REPOA (Research on Poverty Alleviation) Policy Brief 00.5, n.d. REPOA, http://www.repoa.or.tz/ (accessed 5 Sept. 2008).

James, N. D. G. *A History of English Forestry.* Oxford: Blackwell, 1981.

Johnsen, Fred Håkon. "Burning with Enthusiasm: Fuelwood Scarcity in Tanzania in Terms of Severity, Impacts and Remedies." *Forum for Development Studies,* no. 1 (1999): 107–31.

Johnson, Marion. "Cloth as Money: The Cloth Strip Currencies of Africa." *Textile History* 11 (1980): 193–202.

Johnston, P. H. "Some Aspects of Dhow Building." *Tanganyika Notes and Records,* no. 27 (1949): 47–51.

Kahemela, Adrian. "TFCG Establishes New Community Forest Conservation Network." n.d., African Rainforest Conservancy, http://www.africarainforest.org/alt/article_kahemela.html (accessed 5 Sept. 2008).

Kieran, J. A. "Abushiri and the Germans." in *Hadith 2,* ed. Bethwell Ogot, 157–201. Nairobi: East Africa Publishing House, 1970.

Kileo, G. J. "Forestry in Tanzania." In *East Africa: Its People and Resources,* ed. W. T. W. Morgan, 215–20. London: Oxford University Press, 1972.

Killingray, David, and Richard Rathbone, eds. *Africa and the Second World War.* New York: St. Martin's, 1986.

Kinney, Thomas A. *The Carriage Trade: Making Horse-Drawn Vehicles in America.* Baltimore: Johns Hopkins University Press, 2004.

Kirchberger, Ulrike. "German Scientists in the Indian Forest Service: A German Contribution to the Raj?" *Journal of Imperial and Commonwealth History* 29, no. 2 (2001): 1–26.

Kirk, John. "On Recent Surveys of the East Coast of Africa." *Proceedings of the Royal Geographical Society of London* 22, no. 6 (1877–78): 453–55.

————. "A Visit to the Mungao District, near Cape Delgado." *Proceedings of the Royal Geographical Society of London* 21, no. 6 (1876–77): 588–89.

Kirk, William. "The N.E. Monsoon and Some Aspects of African History." *Journal of African History* 3, no. 2 (1962): 263–67.

Kjekshus, Helge. *Ecology Control and Economic Development in East African History.* Berkeley: University of California Press, 1977.

Klamroth, Martin. "Beiträge zum Verständnis der religiösen Vorstellungen der Saramo im Bezirk Daressalam (Deutsch-Ostafrika)." *Zeitschrift für Kolonialsprachen* (1910–13), 1:37–70, 2:118–53, 3:189–223.

Koponen, Juhani. *Development for Exploitation: German Colonial Policies in Mainland Tanzania, 1884–1914.* Helsinki: Finnish Historical Society, 1995.

Korn, Artur. "Die Holzwirtschaft unserer unter Mandat stehenden Kolonie Deutsch-Ostafrika während der vergangenen zehn Jahre." *Tropenpflanzer* 35 (1932): 465–77.

Krajewski, Patrick. *Kautschuk, Quarantäne, Krieg: Dhauhandel in Ostafrika, 1880–1914.* Berlin: Klaus Schwarz, 2006.

Kreike, Emmanuel. *Re-creating Eden: Land Use, Environment, and Society in Southern Angola and Northern Namibia.* Portsmouth, N.H.: Heinemann, 2004.

Kriger, Colleen. *Pride of Men: Ironworking in Nineteenth-Century West Central Africa.* Portsmouth, N.H.: Heinemann, 1999.

Krüger, Eugen. "Die Wald- und Kulturverhältnisse in Deutsch-Ostafrika." *Deutsches Kolonial-Blatt* 5 (1894): 623–29.

Krumm, Bernhard. "Kimatumbi-Wörterverzeichnis." *Sonderabdruck aus den Mitteilungen des Seminars für Orientalische Sprachen zu Berlin* 16. Berlin: Reichsdrückerei, 1912.

Kucklentz, Karl. *Das Zollwesen der deutschen Schutzgebiete in Afrika und der Südsee.* Berlin: Puttkammer und Mühlbrecht, 1914.

Kurtze, Bruno. *Die Deutsch-Ostafrikanische Gesellschaft.* Jena: Gustav Fischer, 1913.

Lacerda, Luiz Drude de, ed. *Mangrove Ecosystems: Function and Management.* Berlin: Springer Verlag, 2002.

Larson, Lorne. "A History of the Mbunga Confederacy ca. 1860–1907." *Tanzania Notes and Records,* nos. 81–82 (1977): 35–42.

Larson, Pier. *History and Memory in the Age of Enslavement: Becoming Merina in Highland Madagascar, 1770–1822.* Portsmouth, N.H.: Heinemann, 2000.

Lawi, Yusufu. "Tanzania's Operation Vijiji and Local Ecological Consciousness: The Case of Eastern Iraqwaland, 1974–1976." *Journal of African History* 48, no. 1 (2007): 69–93.

Leach, Melissa. *Rainforest Relations: Gender and Resource Use among the Mende of Gola, Sierra Leone.* Washington, D.C.: Smithsonian Institution Press, 1994.

Leggat, G. J. "A Uganda Softwood Scheme." *Empire Forestry Review* 33, no. 4 (1954): 345–51.

Lekan, Thomas, and Thomas Zeller, eds. *Germany's Nature: Cultural Landscapes and Environmental History.* New Brunswick, N.J.: Rutgers University Press, 2005.

Leue, August. *Dar-es-Salaam: Bilder aus dem Kolonialleben.* Berlin: Wilhelm Süsserott, 1903.

Little, Marilyn. "Colonial Policy and Subsistence in Tanganyika, 1925–49." *Geographical Review* 81, no. 4 (1991): 375–88.

Lowood, Henry E. "The Calculating Forester: Quantification, Cameral Science, and the Emergence of Scientific Forest Management in Germany." In *The Quantifying Spirit in the Eighteenth Century,* ed. Tore Frängsmyr, John L. Heilbron, and Robin E. Rider, 315–42. Berkeley: University of California Press, 1990.

Lyons, Maryinez. *The Colonial Disease: A Social History of Sleeping Sickness in Northern Zaire, 1900–1940.* Cambridge: Cambridge University Press, 1992.

Maagi, Z. G. N., M. J. Mkude, and E. J. Mlowe. *The Forest Area of Tanzania Mainland.* Forest Resource Study Series, no. 34. Dar es Salaam: Tanzanian Ministry of Natural Resources and Tourism, 1979.

MacKenzie, John M. *The Empire of Nature: Hunting, Conservation, and British Imperialism.* Manchester: Manchester University Press, 1988.

———. "Experts and Amateurs: Tsetse, Nagana, and Sleeping Sickness in East and Central Africa." In *Imperialism and the Natural World,* ed. John M. MacKenzie, 187–212. Manchester: Manchester University Press, 1990.

Maclean, George. "The Relationship between Economic Development and Rhodesian Sleeping Sickness in Tanganyika Territory." *Annals of Tropical Medicine and Parasitology* 23, no. 1 (26 April 1929): 37–46.

MacQueen, James. "Journey of Galvao da Silva to Manica Gold Fields." *Journal of the Royal Geographical Society of London* 30 (1860): 55–61.

Maddox, Gregory. "'Degradation Narratives' and 'Population Time Bombs': Myths and Realities about African Environments." In *South Africa's Environmental History: Cases and Comparisons,* ed. Stephen Dovers, Ruth Edgecombe, and Bill Guest, 250–58. Athens: Ohio University Press, 2002.

Maddox, Gregory, and James L. Giblin, eds. *In Search of a Nation: Histories of Authority and Dissidence in Tanzania.* Oxford: James Currey, 2005.

Maddox, Gregory, James Giblin, and Isaria Kimambo, eds. *Custodians of the Land: Ecology and Culture in the History of Tanzania.* London: James Currey, 1996.

Maier, Ambrosius. "Aus den Matumbibergen." *Missions-Blätter von St. Ottilien* 14 (October 1909–September 1910): 115–18.

Maji Maji Research Project. *Collected Papers.* Dar es Salaam: Department of History, University College, 1968.

Mandala, Elias. *Work and Control in a Peasant Economy: A History of the Lower Tchiri Valley of Malawi, 1850–1960.* Madison: University of Wisconsin Press, 1990.

"Mangrove Barks for Tanning." *Indian Forester* 39, no. 11 (1913): 545–47.

Maples, Chauncy. "Masasi and the Rovuma District in East Africa." *Proceedings of the Royal Geographical Society and Monthly Record of Geography* 2, no. 6 (1880): 337–53.

Mascarenhas, Adolfo. "The Relevance of the 'Miti' Project to Wood-Based Energy in Tanzania." In *Wood-Based Energy for Development,* ed. A. B. Temu, B. K. Kaale, and J. A. Maghembe, 26–46. Dar es Salaam: Ministry of Natural Resources and Tourism, 1984.

Matiyas, B. "Excavations at Mang'aru, an Early Iron Working Phase Site in the Rufiji Region." In *People, Contacts and the Environment in the African Past,* ed. Felix Chami, Gilbert Pwiti, and Chantal Radimilahy, 21–29. Dar es Salaam: Dar es Salaam University Press, 1996.

Matzke, Gordon. "The Development of the Selous Game Reserve." *Tanzania Notes and Records,* nos. 79–80 (1976): 37–48.

———. "Large Mammals, Small Settlements, and Big Problems: A Study of Overlapping Space Preferences in Southern Tanzania." PhD diss., Syracuse University, 1975.

———. "Settlement and Sleeping Sickness Control—A Dual Threshold Model of Colonial and Traditional Methods in East Africa." *Social Science and Medicine* 13D (1979): 209–14.

————. *Wildlife in Tanzanian Settlement Policy: The Case of the Selous.* Syracuse: Maxwell School of Citizenship and Public Affairs, Syracuse University, 1977.

McCann, James C. *Green Land, Brown Land, Black Land: An Environmental History of Africa, 1800–1990.* Portsmouth, N.H.: Heinemann, 1999.

McCracken, John. "Conservation and Resistance in Colonial Malawi: The 'Dead North' Revisited." In *Social History and African Environments,* ed. William Beinart and JoAnn McGregor, 155–74. Oxford: James Currey, 2003.

McCurdy, Sheryl. "Fashioning Sexuality: Desire, Manyema Ethnicity, and the Creation of the Kanga, ca. 1880–1900." *International Journal of African Historical Studies* 39, no. 3 (2006): 441–69.

McGregor, JoAnn. "The Victoria Falls, 1900–1940: Landscape, Tourism, and the Geographical Imagination." *Journal of Southern African Studies* 29, no. 3 (2003): 717–37.

McHenry, Dean. *Limited Choices: The Political Struggle for Socialism in Tanzania.* Boulder: Lynne Rienner, 1994.

————. *Tanzania's Ujamaa Villages: The Implementation of a Rural Development Strategy.* Berkeley: University of California Press, 1979.

Meshack, Charles. "Transaction Costs of Participatory Forest Management: Empirical Evidence from Tanzania." *Arc Journal,* no. 16 (2003): 6–9.

Mgeni, A. S. M. "Fuelwood Crisis in Tanzania Is Women's Burden." *Quarterly Journal of Forestry* 78, no. 4 (Oct. 1984): 247–49.

Middleton, John. *The World of the Swahili: An African Mercantile Civilization.* New Haven: Yale University Press, 1992.

Milledge, Simon, Ised K. Gelvas, and Antje Ahrends. *Forestry, Governance and National Development: Lessons Learned from a Logging Boom in Southern Tanzania.* Dar es Salaam: TRAFFIC East/Southern Africa, 2007.

Miller, Charles. *Battle for the Bundu: The First World War in East Africa.* New York: Macmillan, 1974.

Missano, H., C. W. Njebele, L. Kayombo, and B. Ogle. "Dependency on Forests and Trees for Food Security." Working Paper 261. Swedish University of Agricultural Sciences, Uppsala, 1994.

Mitchell, Timothy. *Rule of Experts: Egypt, Techno-politics, Modernity.* Berkeley: University of California Press, 2002.

Monson, Jamie. "Canoe-Building under Colonialism: Forestry and Food Policies in the Inner Kilombero Valley, 1920–40." In *Custodians of the Land: Ecology and Culture in the History of Tanzania,* ed. Gregory Maddox, James Giblin, and Isaria Kimambo, 200–212. Athens: Ohio University Press, 1996.

———. "From Commerce to Colonization: A History of the Rubber Trade in the Kilombero Valley of Tanzania, 1890–1914." *African Economic History* 21 (1993): 113–30.

———. "Relocating Maji Maji: The Politics of Alliance and Authority in the Southern Highlands of Tanzania, 1870–1918." *Journal of African History* 39, no. 1 (1998): 95–120.

Moore, Henrietta, and Megan Vaughan. *Cutting Down Trees: Gender, Nutrition, and Agricultural Change in the Northern Province of Zambia, 1890–1990.* Portsmouth, N.H.: Heinemann, 1994.

Mtuy, M. C. P. "An Outlook for Forestry in Tanzania." Dar es Salaam: Forest Division, 1976.

Müller, Fritz Ferdinand. *Deutschland-Zanzibar-Ostafrika: Geschichte einer deutschen Kolonialeroberung, 1884–1890.* Berlin: Rütten and Loening, 1959.

Munro, J. Forbes. "British Rubber Companies in East Africa before the First World War." *Journal of African History* 24, no. 3 (1983): 369–79.

Munslow, Barry, Yemi Katerere, Adriaan Ferf, and Phil O'Keefe. *The Fuelwood Trap: A Study of the SADCC Region.* London: Earthscan Publications, 1988.

Murali, Atluri. "Whose Trees? Forest Practices and Local Communities in Andhra, 1600–1922." In *Nature, Culture, Imperialism: Essays on the Environmental History of South Asia,* ed. David Arnold and Ramachandra Guha, 86–122. Delhi: Oxford University Press, 1996.

Mustahahti, Irmeli. "Msitu wa Angai: Haraka, haraka, haina baraka! Why Does Handing over the Angai Forest to Local Villages Proceed So Slowly?" In *Anomalies of Aid: A Festschrift for Juhani Koponen,* ed. Jeremy Gould and Lauri Siitonen, 168–86. Helsinki: Interkont Books, 2007.

Mwita, Sosthenes Paulo. "Mbwamaji: Where Villagers Enlist the Help of the Dead," *Daily News* (Dar es Salaam), 22 May 2001, 8.

Myers, Garth. "The Early History of the 'Other Side' of Zanzibar Stone Town." In *The History and Conservation of Zanzibar Stone Town,* ed. Abdul Sheriff, 30–45. London: James Currey, 1995.

Myers, Norman, Jon C. Lovett, and Neil Burgess. "Eastern Arc Mountains and Coastal Forests." In *Hotspots: Earth's Biologically Richest and Most Endangered Terrestrial Ecoregions,* ed. Russell A. Mittermeier, Norman Myers, and Cristina Goettsch Mittermeier, 205–13. Mexico City: Conservation International, 1999.

Myers, Norman, Russell A. Mittermeier, Cristina G. Mittermeier, Gustavo A. B. da Fonseca, and Jennifer Kent. "Biodiversity Hotspots for Conservation Priorities." *Nature* 403, no. 6772 (2000): 853–58.

Napier-Bax, S. *Notes on Anti-Tsetse Clearings*. Dar es Salaam: Government Printer, 1932.

Neumann, Roderick. "Africa's 'Last Wilderness': Reordering Space for Political and Economic Control in Colonial Tanzania." *Africa* 71, no. 4 (2001): 641–65.

———. "Forest Rights, Privileges and Prohibitions: Contextualising State Forestry Policy in Colonial Tanganyika." *Environment and History* 3, no. 1 (1997): 45–68.

———. *Imposing Wilderness: Struggles over Livelihood and Nature Preservation in Africa*. Berkeley: University of California Press, 1998.

———. "Primitive Ideas: Protected Area Buffer Zones and the Politics of Land in Africa." *Development and Change* 28, no. 3 (1997): 559–82.

Nicholls, C. S. *The Swahili Coast: Politics, Diplomacy and Trade on the East African Littoral, 1798–1856*. New York: African Publishing Corporation, 1971.

Nilsson, Per. "Wood—the Other Energy Crisis." In *Tanzania: Crisis and Struggle for Survival*, ed. Jannik Boesen, Kjell J. Havnevik, Juhani Koponen, and Rie Odgaard, 159–72. Uppsala: Scandinavian Institute of African Studies, 1986.

Nnyiti, Paul "Tourist Hunting in Tanzania." *Miombo: The Newsletter of the Wildlife Conservation Society of Tanzania*, no. 28 (January 2006): 9, 12–13.

Odhiambo, Nicodemus. "Violent Evictions from Tanzanian Forest Ends in Court." *Environment News Service*, 29 June 1999, http://www.forests.org/archive/africa/tanzview.htm.

Okema, Michael. "Tanzania's Squatters Hide in Plain Sight." *East African*, 19–25 October 1998, http://www.nationaudio.com/News/EastAfrican/1910/Opinion/Opinion2.html.

Openshaw, Keith. *Forest Industries Development Planning: Tanzania—Present Consumption and Future Requirements of Wood in Tanzania*. Rome: UNDP/FAO, 1971.

Osborn, Emily Lynn. "'Rubber Fever,' Commerce and French Colonial Rule in Upper Guinée, 1890–1913." *Journal of African History* 45, no. 3 (2004): 445–65.

Paasche, Hans. *Im Morgenlicht: Kriegs-, Jagd- und Reise-Erlebnisse in Ostafrika*. Berlin: C. A. Schwetschke und Sohn, 1907.

Packard, Randall M. *The Making of a Tropical Disease: A Short History of Malaria*. Baltimore: Johns Hopkins University, 2007.

Packer, Craig, Dennis Ikando, Bernard Kissui, and Hadas Kushnir. "Conservation Biology: Lion Attacks on Humans in Tanzania." *Nature* 436, no. 7053 (2005): 927–28.

Parry, M. S. "Recent Progress in the Development of Miombo Woodland in Tanganyika." *East African Agricultural and Forestry Journal* 31 (January 1966): 307–15.

Patterson, F. B. *The Story of Gum-Copal.* Newark: Murphy and Co., 1878.

Pels, Peter. "The Pidginization of Luguru Politics: Administrative Ethnography and the Paradoxes of Indirect Rule." *American Ethnologist* 23, no. 4 (1996): 749–53.

Peluso, Nancy Lee. "A History of State Forest Management in Java." In *Keepers of the Forest: Land Management Alternatives in Southeast Asia,* ed. Mark Poffenberger, 27–55. West Hartford, Conn.: Kumarian Press, 1990.

———. *Rich Forests, Poor People: Resource Control and Resistance in Java.* Berkeley: University of California Press, 1994.

Peluso, Nancy Lee, and Michael Watts. "Violent Environments." In *Violent Environments,* ed. Nancy Lee Peluso and Michael Watts, 3–38. Ithaca: Cornell University Press, 2001.

Penrose, Edith Tilton. "A Great African Project." *Scientific Monthly* 66, no. 4 (1948): 322–36.

Perley, Sidney. "Commercial History of Salem." *Essex Antiquarian* 1, no. 1 (1897): 5.

Pfrank, Christian. "Der ostafrikanische Kopalbaum und seine Nutzbarmachung." *Kolonie und Heimat* 2, no. 15 (11 April 1909): 6.

Pfund, Kurt. *Kreuz und quer durch Deutschostafrika.* Dresden, n.d. [1899?].

Porter, Gareth, Janet Welsh Brown, and Pamela S. Clark. *Global Environmental Politics.* 3rd ed. Boulder: Westview, 2000.

Pouchepadass, Jacques. "British Attitudes towards Shifting Cultivation in Colonial South India: A Case Study of South Canara District, 1800–1920." In *Nature, Culture, Imperialism: Essays on the Environmental History of South Asia,* ed. David Arnold and Ramachandra Guha, 123–51. Delhi: Oxford University Press, 1996.

Pouwels, Randall. "Eastern Africa and the Indian Ocean to 1800: Reviewing Relations in Historical Perspective." *International Journal of African Historical Studies* 35, nos. 2–3 (2002): 385–425.

Prestholdt, Jeremy. *Domesticating the World: African Consumerism and the Genealogies of Globalization.* Berkeley: University of California Press, 2008.

———. "On the Global Repercussions of East African Consumerism." *American Historical Review* 109, no. 3 (2004): 755–81.

Prüssing. "Ueber das Rufiyi-Delta." *Mitteilungen aus den deutschen Schutzgebieten* 14 (1901): 106–13.

Radkau, Joachim. "Das 'hölzerne Zeitalter' und der deutsche Sonderweg in der Forsttechnik." In *"Nützliche Künste": Kultur- und Sozialgeschichte der Technik im 18. Jahrhundert,* ed. Ulrich Troitzsch, 97–117. Münster: Waxmann, 1999.

———. "Wood and Forestry in German History." *Environment and History* 2, no. 1 (1996): 63–76.

Rajan, Ravi. "Imperial Environmentalism or Environmental Imperialism? European Forestry, Colonial Foresters, and the Agendas of Forest Management in British India, 1800–1900." In *Nature and the Orient: The Environmental History of South and Southeast Asia,* ed. Richard H. Grove, Vinita Damodaran, and Satpal Sangwan, 324–71. Delhi: Oxford University Press, 1998.

———. *Modernizing Nature: Forestry and Imperial Eco-development, 1800–1950.* Oxford: Clarendon Press, 2006.

Ranger, Terence. "European Attitudes and African Realities: The Rise and Fall of the Matola Chiefs of South-East Tanzania. *Journal of African History* 20, no. 1 (1979): 63–82.

———. *Voices from the Rocks: Nature, Culture and History in the Matopos Hills of Zimbabwe.* Oxford: James Currey, 1999.

Rankin, L. K. "The Elephant Experiment in Africa: A Brief Account of the Belgian Elephant Expedition on the March from Dar es Salaam to Mpwapwa." *Proceedings of the Royal Geographical Society and Monthly Record of Geography* 4, no. 5 (1882): 273–89.

Reid, Anthony. "Humans and Forests in Pre-colonial Southeast Asia." In *Nature and the Orient: The Environmental History of South and Southeast Asia,* ed. Richard H. Grove, Vinita Damodaran, and Satpal Sangwan, 106–26. Delhi: Oxford University Press, 1998.

"The Revenue of the Prussian State Forests." *Indian Forester* 19, no. 8 (1893): 298.

Richter, Roland E. "Land Law in Tanganyika since the British Military Occupation and under the British Mandate of the League of Nations, 1916–1946." In *Land Law and Land Ownership in Africa,* Bayreuth African Studies 41, ed. Robert Debusmann and Stefan Arnold, 39–80. Bayreuth: Breitinger, 1996.

Rizzo, Matteo. "What Was Left of the Groundnut Scheme? Development Disaster and Labour Market in Southern Tanganyika, 1946–1952." *Journal of Agrarian Change* 6, no. 2 (2006): 205–38.

Robertson, W. M. "Fire and Forest." *East African Agricultural Journal* 13 (1947): 1–2.

———. "The Forest Adviser's Visit to Tanganyika." *East African Agricultural Journal* 13 (1947): 197–99.

Rockel, Stephen J. *Carriers of Culture: Labor on the Road in Nineteenth-Century East Africa.* Portsmouth, N.H.: Heinemann, 2006.

Rodgers, W. A. "The Conservation of the Forest Resources of Eastern Africa: Past Influences, Present Practices, and Future Needs." In *Biogeography and Ecology of the Rain Forests of Eastern Africa,* ed. Jon C. Lovett and Samuel K. Wasser, 283–331. Cambridge: Cambridge University Press, 1993.

———. "Forest Biodiversity Loss: A Global Perspective." n.d. [1997?], Biodiversity Economics, http://biodiversityeconomics.org/applications/library _documents/lib_document.rm?document_id=543 (accessed 5 Sept. 2008).

———. "Institutions and Forest Policy Reform in Tanzania—A Case Study of the Role of NGOs." Dar es Salaam: East African Biodiversity Project, 1997, World Bank, http://www.worldbank.org/afr/afr_for/fulltext/tnzna-2 .doc (accessed 5 Sept. 2008).

———. "The Miombo Woodlands." In *East African Ecosystems and Their Conservation,* ed. T. R. McClanahan and T. P. Young, 299–325. New York: Oxford University Press, 1996.

———. "Past Wangindo Settlement in the Eastern Selous Game Reserve." *Tanzania Notes and Records,* nos. 77–78 (1976): 21–26.

———. "Why a Book on Coastal Forests?" In *Coastal Forests of Eastern Africa,* ed. Neil D. Burgess and G. Philip Clarke, 2–7. Gland, Switzerland: IUCN, 2000.

Rodgers, W. A., and N. D. Burgess. "Taking Conservation Action." In *Coastal Forests of Eastern Africa,* ed. Neil D. Burgess and G. Philip Clarke, 317–34. Gland, Switzerland: IUCN, 2000.

Rodgers, W. A., and Katherine Homewood. "Biological Values and Conservation Prospects for the Forests and Primate Populations of the Uzungwa Mountains, Tanzania." *Biological Conservation* 24, no. 4 (1982): 285–304.

Rodgers, W. A., and J. D. Lobo. "Elephant Control and Legal Ivory Exploitation: 1920–1976." *Tanzania Notes and Records,* nos. 84–85 (1980): 25–54.

Rodgers, W. A., W. Mziray, and E. K. Shishira. "The Extent of Forest Cover in Tanzania Using Satellite Imagery." Research Paper no. 12, University of Dar es Salaam, Institute of Resource Assessment, 1985.

Rollins, William H. *A Greener Vision of Home: Cultural Politics and Environmental Reform in the German Heimatschutz Movement, 1904–1918.* Ann Arbor: University of Michigan Press, 1997.

———. "Imperial Shades of Green: Conservation and Environmental Chauvinism in the German Colonial Project." *German Studies Review* 22, no. 2 (1999): 187–213.

Rosenbloom, Joshua L. "Path Dependence and the Origins of Cotton Textile Manufacturing in New England." In *The Fibre That Changed the World: The Cotton Industry in International Perspective, 1600–1990s,* ed. Douglas A. Farnie and David J. Jeremy, 365–91. Oxford: Oxford University Press, 2004.

Rule, A. "East African Timber Production." *Empire Forestry Review* 24, no. 1 (1945): 47–51.

Saldanha, Indra Munshi. "Colonial Forest Regulations and Collective Resistance: Nineteenth-Century Thana District." In *Nature and the Orient: The Environmental History of South and Southeast Asia,* ed. Richard H. Grove, Vinita Damodaran and Satpal Sangwan, 708–33. Delhi: Oxford University Press, 1998.

———. "Colonialism and Professionalism: A German Forester in India." *Environment and History* 2, no. 2 (1996): 195–219.

Sangster, R. G. "Forestry in Tanganyika." In *The Natural Resources of East Africa,* ed. E. W. Russell, 122–25. Nairobi: East African Literature Bureau, 1962.

———. *Forestry in Tanganyika, 1951–55.* Dar es Salaam: Government Printer, 1956.

Schabel, Hans G. "Tanganyika Forestry under German Colonial Administration, 1891–1919." *Forest and Conservation History* 34, no. 3 (July 1990): 130–41.

Schlich, W. "Remarks on the Sunderbuns." *Indian Forester* 1, no. 1 (1875): 6–11.

Schmidt, Peter R. "The Agricultural Hinterland and Settlement Trends in Tanzania." *Azania* 29–30 (1994–95): 261–62.

Schmidt, Rochus. *Geschichte des Araberaufstandes in Ost-Afrika: Seine Entstehung, seine Niederwerfung und seine Folgen.* Frankfurt a.d. Oder: Trowitzsch und Sohn, 1892.

———. *Meine Reise in Usaramo und den deutschen Schutzgebieten Central-Ostafrikas.* Berlin: Verlag der Engelhardt'schen Landkartenhandlung, 1886.

Schnee, Heinrich, ed. *Deutsches Kolonial-Lexikon.* 3 vols. Leipzig: Quelle und Meyer, 1920.

Schneider, Jane. "The Anthropology of Cloth." *Annual Review of Anthropology* 16 (October 1987): 409–48.

Schneider, Leander. "Freedom and Unfreedom in Rural Development: Julius Nyerere, *Ujamaa Vijijini,* and Villagization." *Canadian Journal of African Studies* 38, no. 2 (2004): 344–92.

Schroeder, Richard A. *Shady Practices: Agroforestry and Gender Politics in The Gambia.* Berkeley: University of California Press, 1999.

Schroeter, Helmut, and Roel Ramaer. *German Colonial Railways.* Krefeld: Röhr Verlag, 1993.

Scott, James. *The Moral Economy of the Peasant: Rebellion and Subsistence in Southeast Asia.* New Haven: Yale University Press, 1976.

———. *Seeing Like a State: How Certain Schemes to Improve the Human Condition Have Failed.* New Haven: Yale University Press, 1998.

———. *Weapons of the Weak: Everyday Forms of Peasant Resistance.* New Haven: Yale University Press, 1985.

Shao, John. "The Villagization Program and the Disruption of the Ecological Balance in Tanzania." *Canadian Journal of African Studies* 20, no. 2 (1986): 219–39.

Sheail, John. *An Environmental History of Twentieth-Century Britain.* New York: Palgrave, 2002.

Sheridan, Michael J. "The Environmental Consequences of Independence and Socialism in North Pare, Tanzania, 1961–88." *Journal of African History* 45, no. 1 (2004): 81–102.

———. "The Sacred Forests of North Pare, Tanzania: Indigenous Conservation, Local Politics, and Land Tenure." Working Paper 224, African Studies Center, Boston University, 2000.

Sheriff, Abdul. "Mosques, Merchants and Landowners in Zanzibar Stone Town." In *The History and Conservation of Zanzibar Stone Town,* ed. Abdul Sheriff, 46–66. London: James Currey, 1995.

———. *Slaves, Spices, and Ivory in Zanzibar: Integration of an East African Commercial Empire into the World Economy, 1770–1873.* London: James Currey, 1987.

Shishira, E. K., P. Z. Yanda, and J. G. Lyimo. "Vegetation Dynamics and Management Implications in the Pugu and Kazimzumbwi Forest Reserves, Tanzania." *Coenoses* 13, no. 3 (1998): 149–58.

Shivji, Issa. *Law, State and the Working Class in Tanzania, c. 1920–1964.* London: James Currey, 1986.

Shorter, Aylward. *Chiefship in Western Tanzania: A Political History of the Kimbu.* Oxford: Oxford University Press, 1972.

Sicard, Sigvard von. *The Lutheran Church of the Coast of Tanzania, 1887–1914.* Lund: Gleerup, 1970.

Siebenlist, Theodor. *Forstwirtschaft in Deutsch-Ostafrika.* Berlin: Paul Parey, 1914.

Sippel, Harald. "Aspects of Colonial Land Law in German East Africa: German East Africa Company, Crown Land Ordinance, European Plantations and Reserved Areas for Africans." In *Land Law and Land Ownership in Africa,* ed. Robert Debusmann and Stefan Arnold, 3–38. Bayreuth: Breitinger, 1996.

————. "Recht und Herrschaft in kolonialer Frühzeit: Die Rechtsverhältnisse in den Schutzgebieten der Deutsch-Ostafrikanischen Gesellschaft (1885–1890)." In *Studien zur Geschichte des deutschen Kolonialismus in Afrika*, ed. Peter Heine and Ulrich van der Heyden, 466–94. Pfaffenweiler: Centaurus-Verlagsgesellschaft, 1995.

Sivaramakrishnan, K. "Histories of Colonialism and Forestry in India." In *Natures Past: The Environment and Human History*, ed. Paolo Squatriti, 103–44. Ann Arbor: University of Michigan Press, 2007.

————. *Modern Forests: Statemaking and Environmental Change in Colonial Eastern India*. Stanford: Stanford University Press, 1999.

Sköld, Per. *Report to the Government of Tanzania on Development of the Forest Sector in Tanzania*. Rome: FAO, 1969.

Spear, Thomas. "Early Swahili History Reconsidered." *International Journal of African Historical Studies* 33, no. 2 (2000): 257–89.

————. "Indirect Rule, the Politics of Neo-Traditionalism, and the Limits of Invention in Tanzania." In *In Search of a Nation: Histories of Authority and Dissidence in Tanzania*, ed. Gregory H. Maddox and James L. Giblin, 70–85. Oxford: James Currey, 2005.

————. *The Kaya Complex: A History of the Mijikenda Peoples of the Kenya Coast to 1900*. Nairobi: Kenya Literature Bureau, 1978.

————. *Mountain Farmers: Moral Economies of Land and Agricultural Development in Arusha and Meru*. Berkeley: University of California, 1997.

Speke, John. *Journal of the Discovery of the Source of the Nile*. London: J. M. Dent, 1906.

Stahl, Kathleen M. *Tanganyika: Sail in the Wilderness*. The Hague: Mouton, 1961.

Stanley, Henry M. "Explorations in Central Africa." *Journal of the American Geographical Society of New York* 7 (1875): 174–282.

Steere, Edward. *Short Specimens of the Vocabularies of Three Unpublished Languages*. London: Charles Cull: 1869.

Steiner, Christopher B. "Another Image of Africa: Toward an Ethnohistory of European Cloth Marketed in West Africa, 1873–1960." *Ethnohistory* 32, no. 2 (1985): 91–110.

Stollowsky, Otto. "On the Background to the Rebellion in German East Africa in 1905–1906." *International Journal of African Historical Studies* 21, no. 4 (1988): 677–96.

Stuhlmann, Franz. "Dr. F. Stuhlmanns Forschungsreise in Usaramo." *Mitteilungen aus den deutschen Schutzgebieten* 7 (1894): 225–32.

Sulivan, G. L. "Survey of the Lower Course of the Rufiji River." *Journal of the Royal Geographical Society of London* 45 (1875): 364–67.

Sunseri, Thaddeus. "'Every African a Nationalist': Scientific Forestry and Forest Nationalism in Colonial Tanzania." *Comparative Studies in Society and History* 49, no. 4 (2007), 883–913.

———. "Famine and Wild Pigs: Gender Struggles and the Outbreak of the Maji Maji War in Uzaramo (Tanzania)." *Journal of African History* 38, no. 2 (1997): 235–59.

———. "Forestry and the German Imperial Imagination: Conflict over Forest Use in German East Africa." In *Germany's Nature: Cultural Landscapes and Environmental History,* ed. Thomas Lekan and Thomas Zeller, 81–107. New Brunswick, N.J.: Rutgers University Press, 2005.

———. "Fueling the City: Dar es Salaam and the Evolution of Colonial Forestry, 1892–1960." In *Dar es Salaam: Histories from an Emerging East African Metropolis,* ed. James R. Brennan, Andrew Burton, and Yusufu Lawi, 79–96. Nairobi: British Institute for Eastern Africa, 2007.

———. "The Political Ecology of the Copal Trade in the Tanzanian Coastal Hinterland, c. 1820–1905." *Journal of African History* 48, no. 1 (2007): 201–20.

———. "Reinterpreting a Colonial Rebellion: Forestry and Social Control in German East Africa, 1874–1915." *Environmental History* 8, no. 3 (2003): 430–51.

———. "'Something Else to Burn': Forest Squatters, Conservationists and the State in Modern Tanzania." *Journal of Modern African Studies* 43, no. 4 (2005): 609–40.

———. "Statist Narratives and Maji Maji Ellipses." *International Journal of African Historical Studies* 33, no. 3 (2000): 567–84.

———. *Vilimani: Labor Migration and Rural Change in Early Colonial Tanzania.* Portsmouth, N.H.: Heinemann, 2002.

———. "Working in the Mangroves and Beyond: Scientific Forestry and the Labour Question in early Colonial Tanzania." *Environment and History* 11, no. 4 (2005): 365–94.

Sutton, J. E. G. "Dar es Salaam: A Sketch of a Hundred Years." *Tanzania Notes and Records,* no. 71 (1970): 1–19.

———. "Kilwa: A History of the Ancient Swahili Town." *Azania* 33 (1998): 113–169.

Swantz, Marja-Liisa. *Blood, Milk, and Death: Body Symbols and the Power of Regeneration among the Zaramo of Tanzania.* Westport, Conn.: Bergin and Garvey, 1995.

———. *Ritual and Symbol in Transitional Zaramo Society.* New York: Africana Publishing, 1970.

Swynnerton, Charles. "How Forestry May Assist towards the Control of the Tsetse Flies." In R. S. Troup, *Colonial Forest Administration,* app. 2. Oxford: Oxford University Press, 1940.

Tanganyika Forest Division. *Tanganyika's Timber Resources.* Dar es Salaam: Ministry of Lands, Forests and Wildlife, n.d. [1962].

Tanganyika. Government. "The Three Year Development Plan 1961–64." In *Readings on Economic Development and Administration in Tanzania,* ed. Hadley E. Smith, 348–59. Dar es Salaam: Institute of Public Administration, 1966.

Tanganyika. Territory. *Annual Reports of the Forest Department.* Government Printer: Dar es Salaam, 1923–1961.

Tanner, R. E. S. "Some Southern Province Trees with their African Names and Uses." *Tanganyika Notes and Records,* no. 31 (1951): 61–70.

Tanzania. Government. *Annual Reports of the Forest Department.* Government Printer: Dar es Salaam, 1961–1978.

Tanzania. Ministry of National Resources and Tourism. *National Forest Programme in Tanzania, 2001–2010.* Dar es Salaam: Ministry of National Resources and Tourism, 2001.

———. *Resettlement Action Plan for Farm Plots Displaced for Biodiversity Conservation in the Derema Forest Corridor: Prepared for Consideration of Compensation Funding by the World Bank,* September 2006, Tanzania Ministry of Natural Resources and Tourism, http://nfp.co.tz/highlights.html (accessed 5 Sept. 2008).

Tanzania National Archives. *Guide to the German Records.* 2 vols. Dar es Salaam: National Archives of Tanzania, 1984.

Taute, M. "A German Account of the Medical Side of the War in East Africa, 1914–1918." *Tanganyika Notes and Records,* no. 8 (1939): 1–20.

Temu, A. B., B. K. Kaale, and J. A. Maghembe. *Wood-Based Energy for Development.* Dar es Salaam: Ministry of Natural Resources and Tourism, 1984.

Tetzlaff, Rainer. *Koloniale Entwicklung und Ausbeutung: Wirtschafts- und Sozialgeschichte Deutsch-Ostafrikas 1885–1914.* Berlin: Duncker und Humblot, 1970.

"TFCG's Participatory Forest Management Program." *Arc Journal,* no. 18 (November 2005): 9.

Thomas, I. D. "Population Density around Dar es Salaam." *Tanzania Notes and Records,* no. 71 (1970): 165.

Thompson, E. P. *Whigs and Hunters: The Origin of the Black Act.* New York: Pantheon, 1975.

Thomson, Joseph. "Notes on the Basin of the River Rovuma, East Africa." *Proceedings of the Royal Geographical Society and Monthly Record of Geography* 4, no. 2 (1882): 65–79.

———. "Notes on the Route Taken by the Royal Geographical Society's East African Expedition from Dar-es-Salaam to Uhehe; May 19th to August 29th, 1879." *Proceedings of the Royal Geographical Society and Monthly Record of Geography* 2, no. 2 (February 1880): 102–22.

Tilley, Helen. "African Environments and Environmental Sciences: The African Research Survey, Ecological Paradigms, and British Colonial Development, 1920–1940." In *Social History and African Environments,* ed. William Beinart and JoAnn McGregor, 109–30. Oxford: James Currey, 2003.

Tripp, Aili Mari. *Changing the Rules: The Politics of Liberalization and the Urban Informal Economy in Tanzania.* Berkeley: University of California Press, 1997.

Tropp, Jacob A. *Natures of Colonial Change: Environmental Relations in the Making of the Transkei.* Athens: Ohio University, 2006.

Trotter, Alys. "On Varnishes as Vehicles and as Protections." *Burlington Magazine for Connoisseurs* 21, no. 110 (1912): 91–95; 21, no. 113 (1912): 272–78.

Troup, R. S. *Colonial Forest Administration.* Oxford: Oxford University Press, 1940.

———. *Report on Forestry in Tanganyika Territory.* Dar es Salaam: Government Printer, 1936.

Tuck, Michael W. "Woodland Commodities, Global Trade, and Local Struggles: The Beeswax Trade in British Tanzania." *Journal of Eastern African Studies* 3, no. 1 (2009) (forthcoming).

Tucker, Richard P. "The Depletion of India's Forests under British Imperialism: Planters, Foresters, and Peasants in Assam and Kerala." In *The Ends of the Earth: Perspectives on Modern Environmental History,* ed. Donald Worster, 118–40. Cambridge: Cambridge University Press, 1991.

Twaib, Fauz. "The Dilemma of the Customary Landholder: The Conflict between Customary and Statutory Rights of Occupancy in Tanzania." In *Land Law and Land Ownership in Africa,* ed. Robert Debusmann and Stefan Arnold, 81–112. Bayreuth: Breitinger, 1996.

Vansina, Jan. *How Societies Are Born: Governance in West Central Africa before 1600.* Charlottesville: University of Virginia Press, 2004.

Vihemäki, Heini. "Politics of Participatory Forest Conservation: Cases from the East Usambara Mountains, Tanzania." *Journal of Transdisciplinary Environmental Studies* (special issue on Power, Development and Environment) 4, no. 2 (2005): 1–16.

"Visit to Messrs. Stimson, Valentine, and Co.'s Varnish Establishment." *New York Coach-Maker's Magazine* 5, no. 3 (May 1863): 230–32. Carriage Museum of America, http://www.carriagemuseumlibrary.org/stimson (accessed 5 Sept. 2008).

Waal, Dominick de. "Setting Precedents in the Hangai Forest." *Forests, Trees and People Newsletter,* no. 44 (2001): 42–46.

Wakefield, A. J. "The Groundnut Scheme." *East African Agricultural Journal* 14 (January 1948): 131–34.

Waller, Horace, ed. *The Last Journals of David Livingstone,* vol. 1. New York: Harper and Bros., 1875.

Waller, Richard D. "Tsetse Fly in Western Narok, Kenya," *Journal of African History* 31, no. 1 (1990): 81–101.

Watson, Hugh. "The Ndola Miombo Conference." *Empire Forestry Review* 39, no. 1 (1960): 68–88.

———. "Statistics of Imports of Timber to the United Kingdom," *Empire Forestry Journal* 14, no. 1 (1935): 60–63.

Watts, Michael. "Empire of Oil: Capitalist Dispossession and the Scramble for Africa." *Monthly Review* 58, no. 4 (September 2006): 1–17.

———. "Political Ecology." In *A Companion to Economic Geography,* ed. Eric Sheppard and Trevor J. Barnes, 257–74. Oxford: Blackwell, 2000.

Weiss, Brad. *Sacred Trees, Bitter Harvests: Globalizing Coffee in Northwest Tanzania.* Portsmouth, N.H.: Heinemann, 2003.

West, A. Joshua. "Forests and National Security: British and American Forest Policy in the Wake of World War I." *Environmental History* 8, no. 2 (2003): 270–93.

Westcott, Nicholas. "The Impact of the Second World War on Tanganyika, 1939–49." In *Africa and the Second World War,* ed. David Killingray and Richard Rathbone, 143–59. New York: St. Martin's, 1986.

"What Are the Eastern Arc Mountain Forests Worth to Tanzania?" *Arc Journal,* no. 19 (December 2005): 11–12.

"What Is a Biodiversity Hotspot?" *Arc Journal,* no. 20 (March 2007): 4.

White, Gavin. "Firearms in Africa: An Introduction." *Journal of African History* 12, no. 2 (1971): 173–84.

White, Luise. "Tsetse Visions: Narratives of Blood and Bugs in Colonial Northern Rhodesia." *Journal of African History* 36, no. 2 (1995): 219–45.

Widgren, Mats, and John Sutton, eds. *Islands of Intensive Agriculture in Eastern Africa.* Athens: Ohio University Press, 2004.

Widstrand, Carl Gösta. *African Axes.* Studia Ethnographica Upsaliensia 15. Uppsala: Almqvist and Wiksell, 1958.

Williams, Michael. *Deforesting the Earth: From Prehistory to Global Crisis.* Chicago: University of Chicago Press, 2003.

Wilshusen, Peter R., Steven R. Brechin, Crystal L. Fortwangler, and Patrick C. West. "Reinventing a Square Wheel: Critique of a Resurgent 'Protection

Paradigm' in International Biodiversity Conservation." *Society and Natural Resources* 15, no. 1 (2002): 17–40.

Wily, Liz Alden. "Can We Really Own the Forest? A Critical Examination of Tenure Development in Community Forestry in Africa." Paper presented at the International Association for the Study of Common Property, Oaxaca, Mexico, 9–14 August 2004.

Wily, Liz Alden, et al. "Community Management of Forests in Tanzania." *Forests, Trees and People Newsletter,* no. 42 (2000): 36–45.

Wood, Alexander, Pamela Stedman-Edwards, and Johanna Mang, eds. *The Root Causes of Biodiversity Loss.* London: Earthscan, 2000.

Woodcock, Kerry A. *Changing Roles in Natural Forest Management: Stakeholders' Roles in the Eastern Arc Mountains, Tanzania.* Aldershot: Ashgate, 2002.

Woodruff, William. "Growth of the Rubber Industry of Great Britain and the United States." *Journal of Economic History* 15, no. 4 (1955): 376–91.

Worboys, Michael. "The Comparative History of Sleeping Sickness in East and Central Africa, 1900–1914." *History of Science* 32 (1994): 89–102.

Worldwide Fund for Nature. "Central and Eastern Miombo Woodlands—A Global Ecoregion." n.d. http://www.panda.org/about_wwf/where_we _work/ecoregions/central_eastern_miombo_woodlands.cfm (accessed 5 Sept. 2008).

————. *The Eastern Africa Coastal Forests Ecoregion: Strategic Framework for Conservation, 2005–2025.* Nairobi: WWF, 2006.

Wright, Marcia. "Maji Maji: Prophecy and Historiography." In *Revealing Prophets: Prophecy in Eastern African History,* ed. David Anderson and Douglas H. Johnson, 124–42. London: James Currey, 1995.

Wright, Marcia, and Peter Lary. "Swahili Settlements in Northern Zambia and Malawi." *African Historical Studies* 4, no. 3 (1971): 547–73.

Yahya, Saad S. "Woodfuel and Change in Urban Tanzania," In *Fuelwood Revisited: What Has Changed in the Last Decade?* ed. Michael Arnold, Gunnar Köhlin, Reidar Persson, and Gillian Shepherd, 232–53. CIFOR Occasional Paper 39, 2003.

Young, Roland, and Henry A. Fosbrooke. *Smoke in the Hills: Political Tension in the Morogoro District of Tanganyika.* Evanston, Ill.: Northwestern University Press, 1960.

Ziegenhorn. "Das Rufiyi-Delta." *Mitteilungen aus den deutschen Schutzgebieten* 9 (1896): 78–85.

Zimmerman, Andrew. "'What Do You Really Want in German East Africa, Herr Professor?' Counterinsurgency and the Science Effect in Colonial Tanzania." *Comparative Studies in Society and History* 48, no. 2 (2006): 419–61.

Index